The Art and Science of REAL ESTATE INVESTMENT ANALYSIS

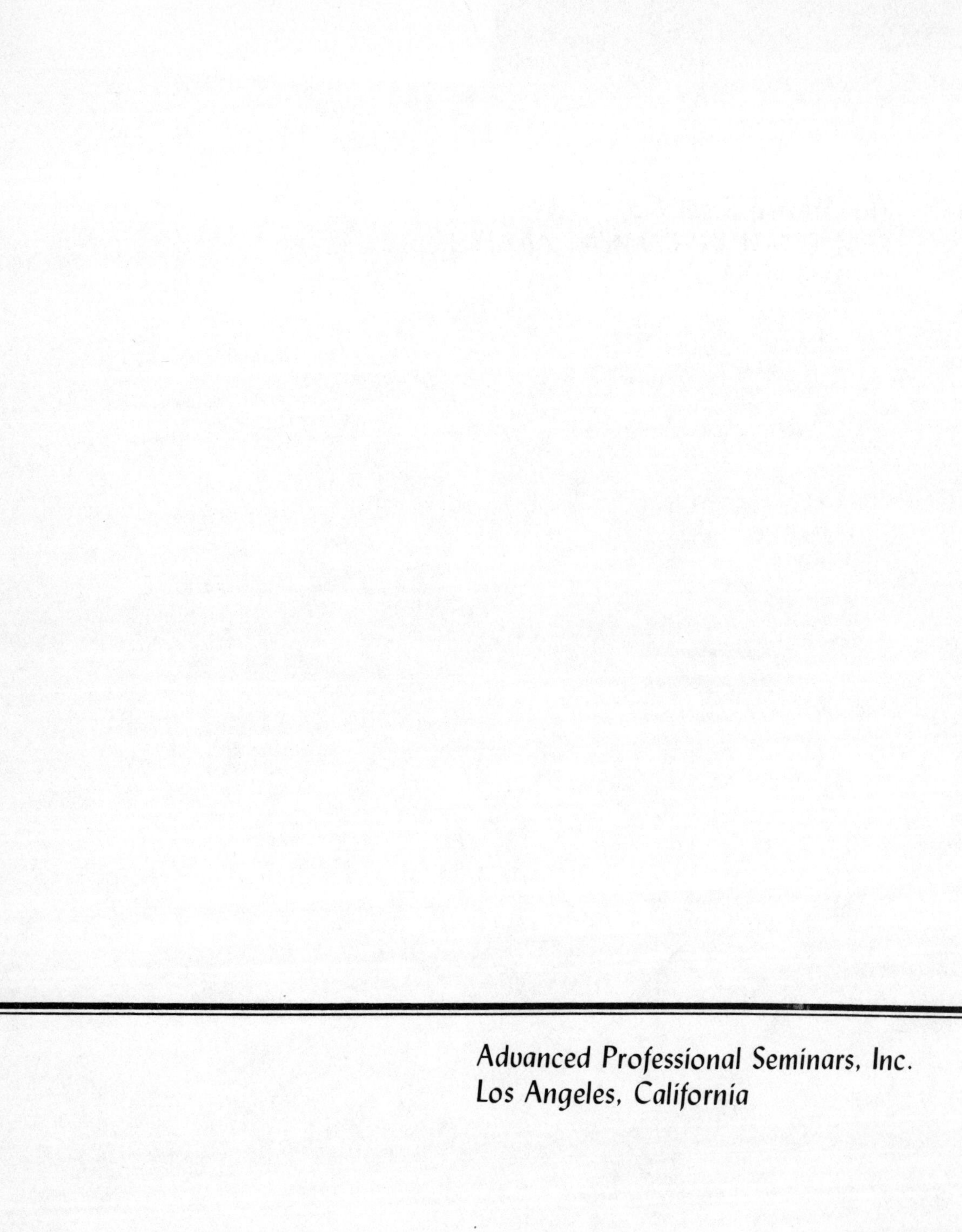

Advanced Professional Seminars, Inc.
Los Angeles, California

The Art and Science of

REAL ESTATE INVESTMENT ANALYSIS

BY EDWARD JOHN GOLDEN

ISBN 0-9604532-0-2
Printed in the United States of America
Address all inquiries to:
Advanced Professional Seminars, Inc.
P. O. Box 45791
Los Angeles, California 90045

Cover design by Ed Brookins

Dedicated to
my wife and partner
Marylee,
whose patience and talents in transforming
years of blackboard notes
into a manuscript
have been indispensable to the compilation
of this text.

I wish to express my deepest appreciation for the editorial talents of Martha Stuckey and George Palmer of Victoria House Publishers, Portland Oregon, who contributed substantially to the final shaping of this book.

I also want to thank my friends Alan S. "Scotty" Herd, real estate consultant and statewide coordinator for the University of California Extension, for his encouragement in this endeavor, and especially for introducing me to such outstanding editors; and Thomas A. Kenster, shopping center and mortgage finance expert, who gave me my first teaching opportunity.

Contents

I.
Foundation

I.

Introduction to Concepts

During my years of teaching real estate investment analysis and taxation, from basic principles to advanced levels, on the various statewide campuses of the University of California since 1965, I have focused on the practical rather than the theoretical, the straightforward rather than the abstruse. The essentially practical analytical techniques that I teach have been developed and refined in a career of banking and commercial finance, corporate comptrollership and investment management.

Selecting texts for my courses presented real problems. Most of the theories and formulas that apply to investment analysis are available only in college-level math books prepared for, and understandable by, only full-time math students or those especially gifted in penetrating the intricacies of abstract and actuarial mathematics. I found it difficult to assign such texts to extension students who work all day and take class in the evening, many of whom have no formal training or interest in higher mathematics. Instead, I concentrated on translating the complex and intricate formulas into simplified step-by-step procedures, using only the four basic arithmetic procedures of addition, subtraction, multiplication and division, which all of us can do, and explaining them in plain conversational language. The results of this approach have been so visibly effective, with achievement in class and in business application consistently rewarding, that I was encouraged to compile these same materials and methods into this book.

The "science" in the title describes the use of sound, classical mathematical formulas and accounting procedures in solving financial and business problems. The "art" lies in looking at numbers in creative and imaginative ways. It is an innovation of this book that real estate numbers are presented in such a way that related data form patterns and diagrams which enable visual, and sometimes spontaneous, analysis or structural projection. Further, the basic philosophy of numbers has been addressed to speed up and shortcut voluminous calculations using standard yield measurement formula, by an original recognition of the powers of *proportions,* all presented in plain English.

Traditional cash flow elements, in chronological order, with practical analysis techniques, are pulled together in a case study.

The material is organized into the normal flow elements of *income, expenses, loan payments* and *equity return,* both before and after taxation, presented in chronological order. Interwoven into this flow are detailed explanations of all the fundamental nuts and bolts techniques of capitalization, leverage, timing, band of investment, mortgage-equity technique, internal rate of return and net present value. Finally, all elements will be combined in a model case study, demonstrating practical applications.

A unique 3-column format is used, and demonstrated in a specially designed analysis form.

All material is presented from the beginning in visual-ease three-column *arrangement,* in logical *sequence,* with related elements placed in strategic *juxtaposition* to each other. This three-column format is the cornerstone of this book, and it is incorporated into the Standard Analysis Investment Form, which I designed especially for my classes and this text. To introduce you to the format, a blank one is included on page 24; it highlights the positioning of the necessary elements, without the confusion of actual numbers.

This positioning of related figures—a place for every figure, and every figure in its place—facilitates still another of this book's innovations. Instead of the investor's net cost return being the random effect of foregoing price and finance, the analytical and projecting approach is to start at the bottom line *first,* with the investor's cash and percent objectives programmed into the matrix as a cause, rather than effect. The procedure is then upward through the computation of required financing to achieve the price and terms as the effect.

With this format, you can do a sophisticated analysis in your head.

If I were to put the entire purpose of this book in a nutshell, it is this: using the methods explained here, you will be able to do an analysis in your head, and do it quickly—and that means money to you. If you protest that you can't do such complex math mentally, for the moment take my word for it: by the time we finish together, you will realize that you are doing far more than you ever thought you could. The human brain can register, store, retrieve and coordinate many things simultaneously (*e.g.* hearing every sound from a 100-piece orchestra).

You will note that I do not discuss computers—at least not as such. The computer is after all only a device to make quick calculations using the same basic arithmetic covered here. When you understand what the computer is doing, then it is a most valuable servant indeed, as a time and effort saver. As a matter of fact, though you might not recognize it as such, the Standard Analysis Form that I recommend is actually a computer printout of the conventional analysis steps. But the successful analyst will never become the servant of the computer by looking to it to do the control thinking.

While some of the more modern techniques are necessarily complex, most of the complexities in my approach are in sheer volume of computations, not in abstruseness of mystical formulae.

Why such a large number of computations? Think for a moment how you would go about explaining, in complete chronological detail, the process of tying shoelaces. The step-by-step instructions would fill several pages, yet—once mastered—you can complete all these steps very quickly and automatically, combining many of them into simultaneous operations. Think, too, of all the hundreds of physics principles you actuate when driving a car. But all you need to know, or wish to, is that when you do certain things, certain results follow.

So it is with the techniques in this book—the doing is considerably shorter and simpler than the many-step explanation. In mastering the step-by-step procedures outlined here, you will in reality be performing highly evolved abstract and actuarial formulas, but mercifully unaware.

Start your calculations with the bottom line (profit) first, not last.

To summarize, this book stresses the advantage of computing from the bottom to the top, and from the right-hand cash flow column to the left-hand capital structure column by intensive use of capitalization.

In this text, you will be introduced to the modern concept of yield, called the "time value of money" as distinct from the more commonplace concept of yield "in perpetuity." In simple terms, the time value concept recognizes that money received today has more value than that received in the future; and that the farther away the future date, the less it is worth. The future benefits are called *future worth* or *future value,* and the value now, reduced by discounting at a given interest rate, is called *present value.* When you buy a building, for example, the equity you invest is actually the discounted present value of the future benefits of the income stream and the final net proceeds realized when the property is sold.

Compound interest tables provide data on present and future values.

These values, future and present, were computed at various interest rates and for various time periods and compiled into six standard compound interest tables by mathematicians many years ago. The six tables greatly simplify the calculation of solutions to all problems involving money and interest in financial and appraisal analysis. The tables are explained in Chapter 18 and partially reproduced in the Appendix. They are referred to throughout this book as Table 1, Table 2, etc.

2.

Organization of Data

The first step in analysis of any kind is arrangement of information, particularly figures. I have developed a format which has been extremely helpful to students, for it enables them to visualize complex financial relationships which in turn facilitates speedy "negotiating" analysis—distinct from less critically timed "office" analysis. This analysis format, depicted on page 24, consists of three basic characteristics which I call *arrangement, sequence* and *juxtaposition;* even though these terms are my own device, the form itself is based on traditional methods used effectively by accountants.

Our arrangement of figures borrows from familiar accounting formats.

Most of us are familiar with the way accountants arrange figures into columns, with income listed in the far right-hand column, expenses in the next (second from right) and component parts of expenses next to that (third from right). In the accountant's world, this format is called "short extending." It is their style of *arrangement.* We see further that, quite logically, the largest amount (income) is at the top of the statement and all deductions are subtracted from it; in other words, smaller figures are below the larger. This we describe as *sequence.*

Now, continuing our accounting metaphor, there are two basic reports in any financial operation: the profit and loss statement and the balance sheet. The P&L, in terms of sequence, starts at the top with gross income, and then deducts operating expenses and all other charges, to arrive at the bottom of the column with what is left: profit, breakeven, or loss. The balance sheet, on the other hand, is a picture of the operation as it would appear if everything stopped and all assets and liabilities were counted up at that moment. In other words, the P&L figures are constantly moving, flowing from income out to expenses, whereas the balance sheet is a still picture of the existing financial structure. Among ourselves, let's redefine these two functions and say that the P&L is *dynamic* (moving) and the balance sheet is *static* (still).

But we call these formats by different names.

So much for the way in which accountants arrange their figures, into logical sequence. Enter now the analyst, who takes up where the accountant leaves off, drawing conclusions from the figures reported by the accountant, both the static (balance sheet) and the dynamic (P&L) figures.

In analyzing investment real estate, we use these concepts in slightly modified form. We call the customary P&L statement a cash flow statement. There are a few differences having to do with federal income tax deductibility but for our purposes the function and the form, in terms of arrangement and sequence, remain essentially the same. The real estate investment counterpart to the balance sheet is the deposit receipt used in the sale of real estate. In brief, the deposit receipt must set forth the price, less any loans, and the resultant equity or down payment, in the same manner that the ordinary business balance sheet sets forth the value of the assets less owed liabilities resulting in the company's net worth.

Here we introduce a third rule to those of arrangement and sequence, and that we'll call *juxtaposition,* which simply means placing certain figures next to, or near, other related figures.

Arrangement, sequence, and juxtaposition—we will use these terms throughout.

The Standard Analysis Form used in this text first *arranges* the data into three columns: Column I, called *static;* Column II, which shows *relationships;* and Column III, called *dynamic.* Note that Columns I and III, which contain dollar figures, are in logical *sequence,* with the largest figures (price and gross income, respectively) at the top. Too, the figures in each column are placed in *juxtaposition* to each other: the figure in Column I is on the same line as its counterpart in Column III, and they are joined by their percentage relationship in Column II.

The whole concept can be expressed as a matrix of threes: three columns across, three classes of capital structure, and three elements of cash flow.

A matrix of 3s.

	Column I *Capital*	*Column II* *Relationships*	*Column III* *Cash Flow*	
I	Price	Return on Income (ROI)	Income	I
II	*minus* Loan(s)	Constant Factor (K)	*minus* Loan Payments	II
III	*equals* Equity	Return on Equity (ROE)	*equals* Net Cash Flow	III

These broad topical groupings will be expanded, refined, and occasionally expressed in different terminology further on in this text, but their strategic relative positioning will never change.

Let's use some real numbers. Take a minute to refer to Chapter 27, where the Standard Analysis Form for a 50-unit apartment building is reproduced. This apartment building serves as a case study for this text, and you will find its figures used frequently throughout the book, beginning with this example:

Price	$	1,049,000
Loans	−	849,000
Equity		200,000

Gross income	$	154,000
Operating expenses	−	54,270
Net operating income		99,730
Loan payments	−	88,220
Net cash flow		11,510

Why not arrange these two sets of figures into columns in juxtaposition to each other so that each figure is lined up opposite the one in the other column to which it is related, like this:

Price	$	1,049,000	Gross income	$	154,000
			Expenses	−	54,270
			Net operating income		99,730
Loans	−	849,000	Loan payments	−	88,220
Equity		200,000	Net cash flow		11,510

This 3-column format will be used throughout the text.

We can even go one step further and measure the relationship between the two, expressed as a percentage; we'll put that percent into a third column, between the first two.

Column I		Column II	Column III	
Price	$ 1,049,000 ←	Gross multiplier 6.8 times →	Gross income	$ 154,000
			Expenses	54,270
	↖	Profit on investment 9.51% →	Net operating income	99,730
Loans	849,000 ←	Constant 10.39% →	Loan payments	88,220
Equity	200,000 ←	Return on equity 5.76% →	Net cash flow	11,510

Can you see how much closer you can come toward visual analysis—even instant analysis—when figures of the same class are always in the exact same place, with all key figures in the static column lined up opposite their related figures in the cash flow or dynamic column and the exact ratio, set out between them, linking them together? Even further, can you see how, even without being physically manifest, you could visualize the logical positioning of key figures and percentages in an oral or telephone negotiation?

Working with a consistent format allows you to visualize finance relationships during oral negotiation.

One of the essences of this book is to improve your ability not only to analyze, construct and restructure an investment, but to do it with maximum speed. Part of this speed will come with memorizing key ratios and simplified formulas, which in turn will enable you to perform certain calculations—perhaps "reckoning" sounds less imposing—in your head. In the practical world of business negotiating, there are times when precise figures are required, up to three and four decimals. For these, a calculator or computer are indispensable, and those techniques will be covered later. However, in many everyday instances what is required is a quick estimate of "ballpark" figures in order to take the property, or the prospective buyer or lessee, off the market, pending the more precise refinements of the three decimal computations.

Back to sequence, we may make still another observation: that the net operating income (NOI)* is the only *real* income the property owner or lessor has as return on investment (ROI) . . . *if* the property is free and clear of any loans. In most instances, however, the property is not free of debt but is encumbered with one or two or even several loans. Therefore, the net operating income (NOI) must serve *two* essential functions: to service the debt and provide return on the equity.

Here's where the concept of sequence comes in again. Normally, in working down from net operating income, you would subtract the loan payments first, and whatever is left is your return on equity (ROE). But who says it has to be done in this order? This is worth a brief moment's comment.

Loan payments or return on equity—which comes first?

Normally, a potential investment is presented with a stated selling price, which is subject to a loan (or loans), *after* payment of which—and *after* prior operating expenses—the return to the investor is residual. In the three-column example on page 16 above, the Column I figures would be multiplied from left to right by the rates in Column II to become dollar payments in Column III.

The method presented here is exactly the reverse. The investor's net cash flow is fixed *first,* at the *bottom* of the analysis sheet, and *then* the amount available for loan payments determined by simple subtraction (NOI minus cash flow). The resulting loan payment amount is then capitalized *from right to left*—again, this is the opposite of common practice—to determine the face value of the loan(s) which this dollar payment will support.

And the investor is in total control.

*Net operating income is the gross income less all operating expenses, before loan payments; all these elements will be discussed in detail in subsequent chapters.

To illustrate the process with the simplest of figures: In ordinary subtraction—say, 8 minus 5 equals 3—we envision it this way:

First, the large number	8
Second, the known subtracting number	− 5
Third, the difference	3

Would we not be just as correct to reverse the form, and put the known subtracting number, not directly under the larger number, but at the bottom, and then insert the answer in between, as:

First, the larger number	8
Third, the difference	− 3
Second, the known subtracting number	5

That may sound overly simple in theory, but the value in practice becomes apparent when we apply it to our 50-unit example. Our NOI, remember, has to service the loan, or loans, *and* the equity. But the sequence does not have to be, first debt service, and then equity return. We will reverse it: first, equity return, and then what is left for debt service. Carrying that process still further, if there were three loans, then the payment on one of the loans (any one of the three) would be subtracted from the total amount available for loans, leaving a balance which is obviously available for servicing the remaining two loans. Finally, still continuing our deductive reasoning, the payment of one of the two remaining loans may be subtracted from the balance, leaving the amount available for payment of the last loan. This is so vital to the analytic process that it's well worth demonstrating with some numbers.

A significant concept, demonstrated with our case study.

Example 1. In the 50 Unit Model Case Study, the NOI is $99,730. Assume the investor had $200,000 to invest and required 5.76% cash return. How much would the net cash flow have to be, and how much would be available for loan payments?

Procedure. Arrange in the three columns the figures you know to begin with, adding the remaining figures as you calculate them (follow the lettered sequence).

Column I			*Column II*		*Column III*	
Price	?				NOI	$ 99,730[A]
Loans	?				Payments	?
Equity	$ 200,000[B]	×	5.76%[C]	=	Spendable NCF	11,510[D]

If $11,510 must be reserved out of the $99,730 NOI, then by subtraction $88,220 will be left for loan payments. Extending our sequence then:

Column I			Column II	Column III	
Price	?			NOI	$ 99,730[A]
Loans	?			Payments	88,220[E]
Equity	$ 200,000[B]	×	5.76%[C]	NCF	11,510[D]

Example 2. Using the same example, assume all the facts are known except the payment on the second loan.

Procedure. Starting again, as always, with NOI $99,730, we drop down to the net cash flow (NCF) line, $11,510. By subtraction we derive $88,220 as the total amount available for loan payments. We know that the first loan requires a payment of $78,950. So by subtraction we can derive the amount available for the second loan payment:

When you start with the bottom line first, the investor remains in control.

$88,220 − $78,950 = $9,270

In outline form, the flow would appear as:

Column I	Column II	Column III		
		NOI		$ 99,730
		1st payment	$ 78,950	
		2nd payment	9,270	
		Total payments		88,220
		NCF		11,510

This same simple process works the same way when we need to determine the precisely correct loan or equity amount (Column I) when the cash flow figures (Column III) are known. It leads us to the technique of capitalization, which will be dealt with thoroughly in Chapter 15.

Let me repeat: doing mental calculations quickly—in the throes of verbal negotiation—is what this book is all about. And you *can* do it in your head if you use the three-column format that is the backbone of this text.

The telephone call brings an interesting offer; is it a good deal? Click on your mental picture of the three columns. As soon as you

Using our 3-column format to your advantage for quick mental calculations.

learn one figure in the ensuing discussion, mentally put it in its proper position; hold it there like a flashing neon in your mind as you continue with the conversation. If that first figure happens to fall in the right-hand column, you know you will have to work right to left, instead of the more familiar left to right. But you will not be dismayed by this "backward" approach, because you have long ago proved to yourself that the end result is the same.

LEFT TO RIGHT

	Column I		*Column II*			*Column III*
Price	$ 1,049,000	×	Cap rate*	9.51%	=	NOI $ 99,730
Loan(s)	849,000	×	K*	10.39%	=	K 88,220
Equity	200,000	×	ROE*	5.76%	=	NCF 11,510

RIGHT TO LEFT

Column III		*Column II*		*Column I*
$ 99,730	÷	9.51%	=	$1,049,000
88,220	÷	10.39%	=	849,000
11,510	÷	5.76%	=	200,000

OR, STILL RIGHT TO LEFT

Column I		*Column II*		*Column III*
$1,059,000	=	9.51%	÷	$ 99,730
849,000	=	10.39%	÷	89,220
200,000	=	5.76%	÷	11,510

*K = loan constant, whether dollar payment or percentage rate. ROE = return on equity. Cap rate = capitalization rate. All these terms will be explained fully later on in the book. For the moment, the concept of interrelationships is the important point.

At this point, let's summarize what we've learned so far. We first arrange our figures into three columns, each column set up in logical sequence, and the two complementary columns of cash flow (dynamic) and capital (static) placed in juxtaposition to each other so that the key figures in each are related to their counterpart in the other by a middle column of percentages.

This would be a strategic time to highlight the main motif of this book: the value of traditional, timeless form, over local and temporary substance. One of the principal shortcomings of investment textbooks, particularly in recent years, is the rapidity with which current interest rates, market return rates, rental and expense rates, *et al*, become obsolete and therefore meaningless, even misleading. This text will concentrate on form—problem solving formulas and techniques, which never change—while using currently prevailing dollar amounts principally for demonstration. Local, current dollar and rate levels are very simple to get. It only takes a few phone calls to the local tax assessor, an insurance agent, the utility companies and lending institutions, all easily found in a telephone directory. The timeless technique and formulas, of course, are not so easily looked up, and that's where this book comes in: sophisticated actuarial formulas simplified into easy to learn and use step-by-step procedures, using basic arithmetic.

Concentrate on mastering techniques, formulas, principles—these things do not change.

STANDARD INVESTMENT ANALYSIS FORM

The Standard Investment Analysis Form reproduced here was designed by me as a convenient way to assemble all the key analytical ratios in logical sequential order, with related capital and cash flow items juxtaposed. With this form, it is easy to grasp visually and quickly all the strategic ratios, including:

The Standard Investment Analysis Form contains all the relevant data, assembled into worksheet form.

- Operating expense items to gross income (income and expenses also by dollars and cents per square foot)
- Loan payments to gross income
- Net operating income (before loans) to gross income
- Net cash flow (after loans) to gross income
- First year mortgage principal paid to gross income
- Depreciation basis and first year calculation
- First year tax saving, or expense, to gross income
- Mortgage(s) to price
- Equity to price
- Gross multipliers of price to gross income

- Net operating income (before loans) to price
- Loan payment(s) to loan balance(s)
- Net cash flow to equity (before and after taxes)
- Net yield (net cash flow plus first year mortgage reduction) to equity before taxes
- Net yield (net cash flow, plus first year mortgage reduction, plus or minus taxes) to equity after taxes
- Recap of first year cash flow, tax saving or expense, and mortgage principal paid, to cash equity.

Note that every vital measurement is included, and that the format actually constitutes a computer program.

The form is a more detailed expansion of the basic matrix on page 23, where all the key elements of capital, cash flow, and ratios are matched in groupings of three—but extended to reflect even further the vital ratios. The capital structure column reflects the percentages of loan(s) and equity to the 100% price, and the cash flow column measures every income and outgo item as both percent of gross income, as 100%, and by dollars and cents per square foot.

RELATIONSHIP OF CAPITAL TO CASH FLOW BY ITEM

BEFORE TAX						
	COLUMN I *Capital (Static)*		**COLUMN II** *Relationship*	**COLUMN III** *Cash Flow (Dynamic)*		
100%	Price	$ ____	AGM ____ times	Gross income	$ ____	100%
				Less: Expenses	$ ____	____%
	Price	$ ____	Cap rate ____%	Net operating income	$ ____	____%
____%	Loan(s)	$ ____	K rate ____%	Annual constant	$ ____	____%
____%	Equity	$ ____	ROE ____%	Net cash flow	$ ____	____%
				Add: Mortgage principal paid	$ ____	____%
____%	Equity	$ ____	YOE ____%	Net yield	$ ____	____%
AFTER TAX						
____%	Equity	$ ____	ROE ____%	NCF ± taxes	$ ____	____%
____%	Equity	$ ____	YOE ____%	NCF ± taxes + mortgage principal	$ ____	____%

FIRST YEAR RECAP

		% to Equity
Net cash flow	$ ____	____%
Tax saving or (expense)	$ ____	____%
Total cash flow	$ ____	____%
Mortgage principal paid	$ ____	____%
Total yield	$ ____	____%

The Standard Investment Analysis Form, next page, assembles these relationships into a convenient working form.

STANDARD INVESTMENT ANALYSIS FORM

Folio____________

Type______________________ Pkg.______ Unf.______ Furn.______________ Listed Price $____________

Address______________________________ Est. Sq. Ft.______________ Cash $____________

Lot Size______________ Sq. Ft.____________ Zone____________ Age____________ Equity $____________

INDICATED PRICE AND FINANCING

100% **PRICE** $______________ ←(X)→ AGM

		Sq. Ft.	
ANNUAL GROSS RENTAL	$________		
TENANT CONTRIBUTIONS	$________		
ANNUAL GROSS INCOME	$________		100%
EXPENSES			
Taxes $________			
Insurance ________			
Utilities ________			
Trash ________			
Pool ________			
Gardening ________			
Elevator ________			
Res Mgr. ________			
Prop. Mgt. ________			
CAM ________			
HVAC ________			
Cleaning ________			
Leasing Fees ________			
Alterations ________			
Rep./Maint. ________			
Vacancy ________			
TOTAL EXPENSES	$________		
NET OPERATING INCOME (NOI)	$________		

(________% to Price) CAP RATE ←→ **NET OPERATING INCOME (NOI)**

LOANS:

CLASS	AMOUNT	ANNUAL CONSTANT (K)		INTEREST		PRINCIPAL
	$	%	$	%	$	$

TOTAL $____________ (________%) ←→ **ANNUAL CONSTANT** . . . . $____________

(________% to Cash) ROE ←→ **NET CASH FLOW** . . . . $____________

Plus EQUITY GAIN . . . . $____________

CASH $____________ (________% to Cash) YOE ←→ **NET YIELD** . . . . $____________

TAX SHELTER ANALYSIS — First Year

DEPRECIATION BASIS:

NET YIELD (Forward) . . . . $____________

Total Cost . . . . $____________

Less Land (________%) . $____________

Balance $____________

Furnishings . . . . $____________

Building Improvements $____________

YEARS	METHOD	%	
			$____________
			$____________

LESS TOTAL DEPRECIATION $____________

TAXABLE INCOME (LOSS) $____________

TAX SAVINGS @ ________% $____________

RECAP

	1ST YEAR	
	AMOUNT	% TO CASH
NET CASH FLOW		
TAX SAVINGS OR (Exp.)		
TOTAL CASH FLOW		
EQUITY GAIN		
TOTAL YIELD		

NOTES:

3.

Seven Key Investment Ratios

It is possible to boil the entire investment analysis process down into seven key ratios (relationship between key figures); five of these ratios occur before federal income taxes are applied, and two are after taxes. You will note that the procedure in the sixth and seventh ratios is the same as in the fourth and fifth, the only difference being that in the former the net cash flow (NCF) is either increased by taxes saved, or decreased by taxes paid. The ratios themselves are graphically depicted in the chart on page 27, and the concepts are explained here.

Ratio 1: gross income to price.

The **first ratio,** linking gross income with price, is called the annual gross multiplier (AGM); it is found by dividing price by income. For example, using the figures in the case study:

$$\$1{,}049{,}000 \div \$154{,}000 = 6.8$$

In other words, the price of the property is 6.8 times the annual gross scheduled income.

An aside: as a working rule of thumb, the AGM should be somewhere between 6 and 8 times the gross if the investment is being made for income, rather than buyer's hysteria or simply flight from the dollar.

Ratio 2: return on equity.

The **second key ratio**—the most vital of all—is known by two names: ROI (return on investment) and cap rate. The terms are synonymous, and describe the net profit on the total investment before financing. The term "return on investment" is simply descriptive; the "cap rate," short for *capitalization,* describes a process used to determine a viable selling price when NOI is known. For example:

NOI $99,730 ÷ cap rate .0951 = price $1,049,000

To put it another way, the cap rate is the backward function of the profit rate.

Ratio 3: loan amount to payment.

The **third key ratio** is the relationship between the face amount of the loan and its payment; this ratio is called the *annual loan constant* (K, for short) and can be expressed as a percentage. Again using our case study as an example: the total loan amount is $849,000 and the total loan payment is $88,220, so the constant is 10.39%.

The name "constant" derives from the fact the actual payment itself remains the same—constant—even though the balance due on the principal decreases with each payment.

Ratio 4: return on equity.

The **fourth key ratio** measures the net cash flow return on net equity investment—total investment *minus* loans. An example from our case study:

$11,510 net cash flow ÷ $200,000 equity = 5.76% return on equity (ROE)

Notice now that the original 9.51% return on the whole investment dwindled to 5.76% on the equity after loans. This is the direct result of the fact that the two loan payments—10.54% on the first and 9% on the second, averaging 10.39% on the total—are *higher* than the 9.51% return on the total investment if it had been bought for all cash. This is called negative, or *reverse leverage;* the opposite condition is called *positive leverage;* both will be explained in detail in Chapter 16.

Ratio 5: net yield, including mortgage reduction.

For the **fifth key ratio,** we add to the net cash flow the amount of the mortgage reduction in the first year, to arrive at what we call *net yield* (to distinguish it from net cash flow). Thus, in our example:

Net cash flow	$11,510
First year mortgage reduction	5,555
Net yield	17,065

The relationship of this net yield to the original equity is *yield on equity* (YOE)—the fifth ratio.

$17,065 ÷ $200,000 = 8.53% YOE

A word of caution here: the $5,555 loan reduction will be a profit *only* if the property is resold for at least what it cost. But the

SEVEN KEY RATIOS
FIVE BEFORE TAX plus TWO AFTER TAX

	COLUMN I *Balance Sheet* *Capital Structure* *Static*	**COLUMN II** *Relationship* *Capitalization Factor*	**COLUMN III** *Profit and Loss* *Cash Flow* *Dynamic*
		BEFORE TAX	
Ratio I	Price	Gross multiplier _________ times	Gross income
			(*less* Expenses)
II	Price	Cap rate/Return on investment (ROI) _________%	(*equals*) Net operating income (NOI)
III	Loan(s)	Constant (K%) _________%	(*less*) Annual constant (K$) Loan payments
IV	Equity	Return on equity (ROE) _________%	(*equals*) Return on equity (pretax) Net cash flow Net spendable income
			(*plus* Mortgage principal paid)
V	Equity	Yield on equity (YOE) _________%	(*equals*) Net yield on equity (pretax) (Net cash flow + mortgage principal, pretax)
		AFTER TAX	
VI	Equity	Return on equity (ROE) _________%	Net cash flow + tax savings (aftertax)
			(*plus* Mortgage principal paid)
VII	Equity	Yield on equity (YOE) _________%	Net yield on equity (aftertax) (Net cash flow + tax saving + mortgage principal)

estimate does have an indicative value, particularly when comparing one property with another.

These are the first five ratios, reflecting returns *before* taxes. The next two are *after* the effect of income taxes.

Ratio 6: net cash flow plus effects of income tax, to equity.

The **sixth ratio** increases the net cash flow by the amount of any tax savings, or decreases it by taxes paid out. In our example:

Net cash flow	$ 11,510
Tax savings	17,937
After-tax cash flow	29,447

The relationship of that after-tax cash flow (ATCF) to the original equity is the sixth ratio:

ATCF $29,447 ÷ $200,000 = 14.72% after-tax return on equity (ATROE)

Ratio 7: net cash flow, plus tax effects, plus mortgage reduction, to equity.

The **seventh ratio** adds to the ATCF $29,447 the same mortgage reduction of $5,555, producing the total after-tax yield (ATY) of $35,002. This after-tax yield, divided by the original equity, produces the after-tax yield on equity (ATYOE).

ATY $35,002 ÷ $200,000 = 17.5% ATYOE

These are the seven basic first-year ratios.

For full analysis, project these ratios over 10 years.

From here, the next extension to complete analysis is to project these ratios yearly over a period of years, usually 10 years by prevailing custom. At the end of the projected term, the property is resold—on paper—at the same price at which it was bought, or at whatever inflationary or deflationary price the prospective investor decides upon. I always make the first 10-year projection on the basis of resale at the same price as the purchase, on the theory that, particularly when comparing alternative investments, cranking in inflation or other adjustment factors simply complicates the analysis since all the properties would be subject to the same inflation. In addition, *outside* influences tend to obscure the purely *internal* profitability of each property as compared with others.

The word "internal" brings me to one of the profit measurement tests, called internal rate of return (IRR) which measures the exact net after-tax yield after an investment is operating for the given period of years, is resold at a given price, and all costs of sale, capital gains and tax preference taxes and loan balances are deducted. The other tests are net present value, payback and annualized net present value breakeven risk asorption. All these will be dealt with later.

CALCULATION OF RATIOS, USING 50-UNIT MODEL

RATIO	FORMULA	IN FIGURES
	BEFORE TAX	
I	$\frac{\text{Price}}{\text{Gross income}}$ = Gross multiplier	$\frac{\$1,049,000}{\$154,000}$ = 6.8%
II	$\frac{\text{Net operating income}}{\text{Price}}$ = Cap rate	$\frac{\$99,730}{\$1,049,000}$ = 9.51%
	$\frac{\text{NOI}}{\text{Cap rate}}$ = Price	$\frac{\$99,730}{.0951}$ = $1,049,000
III	$\frac{\text{Annual constant (K\$)}}{\text{Loan balance}}$ = Constant factor (K%)	$\frac{\$88,220}{\$849,000}$ = 10.39%
	$\frac{\text{Annual constant (K\$)}}{\text{Constant factor (K\%)}}$ = Loan balance	$\frac{\$88,220}{.1039}$ = $ 849,000
IV	$\frac{\text{Net cash flow}}{\text{Equity}}$ = ROE %	$\frac{\$11,510}{\$200,000}$ = 5.76%
	$\frac{\text{NCF}}{\text{ROE \%}}$ = Equity	$\frac{\$11,510}{.0576}$ = $ 200,000
V	$\frac{\text{NCF + Mortgage paid}}{\text{Equity}}$ = YOE %	$\frac{\$17,065}{\$200,000}$ = 8.53%
	$\frac{\text{NCF + Mortgage paid}}{\text{YOE \%}}$ = Equity	$\frac{\$17,065}{.0853}$ =$ 200,000
	AFTER TAX	
VI	NCF $\frac{\left(\begin{smallmatrix}+ \text{ Tax savings, } or \\ - \text{ Tax expense}\end{smallmatrix}\right)}{\text{Equity}}$ = ROE %	$\frac{\$29,447}{\$200,000}$ = 14.72%
	NCF $\frac{\left(\begin{smallmatrix}+ \text{ Tax savings, } or \\ - \text{ Tax expense}\end{smallmatrix}\right)}{\text{ROE \%}}$ = Equity	$\frac{\$29,447}{.1472}$ = $200,000
VII	NCF $\frac{\left(\begin{smallmatrix}+ \text{ Tax savings, } or \\ - \text{ Tax expense}\end{smallmatrix}\right)}{\text{Equity}}$ + Mortgage paid = YOE %	$\frac{\$35,002}{\$200,000}$ = 17.50%
	NCF $\frac{\left(\begin{smallmatrix}+ \text{ Tax savings, } or \\ - \text{ Tax expense}\end{smallmatrix}\right)}{\text{YOE \%}}$ + Mortgage paid = Equity	$\frac{\$35,002}{.1750}$ = $200,000

II.

Income and Expenses

4.

Income and Expenses

From an analyst's point of view, the only significant differences among apartments, commercial and industrial properties are in the nature and amounts of operating expenses. Once the expenses have been totaled and the net operating income calculated, all financing and equity ratios are practically identical.

But operating expenses, as we know, vary greatly from area to area and from day to day. There is simply no such thing as a uniform and precise table of expenses that would apply to all properties. I have tried here to give some notion of common ratios, and of expense and income characteristics, as a guideline for further investigation, but it's much more important to understand which *types* of expenses apply to the kind of property being considered, and to know some of the rule of thumb ranges within which those expenses should fall, in any particular geographic area at any particular time. Then, for specific figures, a few telephone calls to local banks, savings and loan associations, insurance companies, utility companies, property management firms, and county and city tax assessors can help you establish prevailing amounts. It's worth emphasizing: even though the size of the numbers changes, the vital interrelationships between expenses and income, and between expenses and square footage of the building, do not vary enough to preclude fairly accurate comparisons and assumptions in evaluating a potential investment.

If you learn basic rules of thumb about operating expenses, the changing dollar amounts can be accommodated.

In discussing the individual expense items below, I have used figures prevailing in southern California in 1980. Note that expenses are measured in two ways: as a percentage of gross rental income, and also in cents per square foot of rentable area. Of course, if you have one, it is easily converted to the other.

APARTMENT BUILDINGS

Rent-free apartment units are a thing of the past.

There was a time an investor could easily buy a four-unit apartment building, and live in one rent free, supported by the remaining three. With the rising cost of living, this "rent free unit" concept is no longer possible, as the multiplier of price to income and the interest rates for mortgage money have escalated.* As with almost everything else, investing in an apartment building is not as simple as it used to be. Nonetheless, I will try to give you some rule of thumb guidelines, as long as we both recognize that local investigation will be required.

The rise in foreign investment in U.S. property—a trend which shows no sign of abating—is a phenomenon the investment analyst must recognize, for its impact on our economy is profound. European investors, for instance, accustomed to interest rates and rental charges that are significantly higher than those in the U.S., are willing to sign leases, or buy property based on leases, which seem exhorbitant to the American investor. The gradual, cumulative effect on real estate prices is obvious.

Let me repeat: Before any investment or loan transaction is finalized, each expense item *must* be confirmed with the sources, whether they be local government (as in property taxes) or private suppliers. All can be verified and in some cases contract commitments made in escrow, subject to closing.

Even the rents should not be accepted without a signed form verifying the amount of rent, date paid to, any concessions, prepaid rent, security deposits, cleaning fees and whether refundable (check government regulations on mandatory refunds) by each tenant. This form is called a *writ of estoppel* or just estoppel. It means in plain language that the tenant is prevented (estopped) from making any contrary claim in the future.

INCOME

Rentals are almost always on a month to month basis, subject to increase with notice. This is partly because in inflationary times the owners are reluctant to stabilize the rental rates for months or years, and partly because in times of housing shortage the tenants are in little position to demand anything else. The exception is high-rent luxury units. Here tenants are usually much more sophisticated financially; also they often engage a professional interior dec-

*For the minimum number of units required to support full-time managers, see the section on "Resident Managers" below.

orator and have furnishings custom made for the unit, and therefore demand protection of at least a two- or three-year lease.

EXPENSES

As a general rule of thumb, apartment house expenses usually run between 35% and 38% of gross income, depending on the size of the project and local property taxes (which are usually the single largest expense item). At least you would know that total expenses would never be as low as 20% or as high as 60%.

A general guideline: total apartment expenses will be 35% - 38% of gross income.

PROPERTY TAXES Whatever else you may think about them, here we must look at property taxes as a very important expense item. In Chapter 11, under "Use of Tax Assessor Method," we go into the subject in detail. For now a useful rule of thumb which applies in many states (and did apply in California before Proposition 13) is that property taxes run between 3% and 3½% of market value. Stated another way, the tax cost will be between 18% and 20% of gross income, and around 40% of your *total* expenses.

INSURANCE Full fire and extended insurance coverage will range between 1½% and 2% of gross income. Another rule of thumb measurement is this: $2 to $2.50 per $1000 of market value when the value is 6 to 8 times the gross.

UTILITIES For years I made detailed breakdowns of water, gas and electricity expenses. Eventually I found that my estimates were not appreciably more accurate than grouping them all together as a percentage of gross income. Currently, utilities total 6% to 7% of income, up from 3% to 5% in the late '60s and early '70s.

TRASH Most cities have a public pickup service, charged with the water bill or other utility. In many instances, the service is not adequate and is supplemented with private contracts. A range of $15 per year per unit should be fairly close.

POOL For our purposes, the pool expense is limited to the inspection and superficial service contract, which averages $40 to $50 per month or $480 to $600 per year.

GARDENING The amount of this expense naturally depends on the amount of landscaping. Most units have minimum lawns and trees and can be handled for $60 to $75 per month or $720 to $900 per year. If the property was built as an FHA project, where literally acres of lawn were required, or if for esthetic reasons the building is set in a young forest, heaven help you.

PROPOSITION 13: Property Taxes in California

Before June 1978, property taxes in California averaged from 3% to 3½% of the market value of the property, and between 18% and 20% of gross income. In June 1978, the now-famous state ballot measure called Proposition 13 brought a drastic reduction. This, in essence, reduced and legally limited property taxes to 1% of market value as it existed in fiscal tax year 1975-76.

In application, it's not quite that simple. The law provides that local bonds and other assessment charges may be added to the 1%, which could amount to another ¼% or ½%. In addition, the 1% may be increased with the federal government's cost of living index, up to but not more than 2% per year, compounded, starting with the base year of 1975-76. In 1978, the base year tax figure would be multiplied by 6.12%, representing 2% per year compounded.

Far more reaching, however, is the phenomenon where local government bodies are devising new levies to replace the lost tax revenues, but calling them by different names. One city is attempting to pass a "square foot business" tax on offices. This is simply a charge paid by owner—and of course passed on to the tenants as additional rent—in proportion to the size of the building. Another city has already passed a fire department tax on all properties based on size, age and type of construction and the estimated amount of water and labor required to extinguish a fire. The concept is expected to be extended to other government services, and other cities.

Now this text is in no way concerned with political vagaries. What we must concern ourselves with is a realistic ratio of expected property taxes, as a major item of operating expense. Our rule of thumb here is that when the effects of local taxes are added, the effective property tax could come back to the pre-Proposition 13 level—or at least near to it: you should allow 8% to 10% of gross income for this item.

RESIDENT MANAGER This is one of the most frequently misunderstood and undervalued of all expenses. Too many apartment owners do not realize that a multi-unit building is tantamount to a retail store operation, which will not run itself and which constantly develops problems of equipment, personnel and clientele. The public simply cannot be left unattended.

The most common arrangement is a husband-wife team of managers. Usually the husband does light repairs that do not require a licensed professional and the wife does the renting and maintains tenant relations. The ideal management team has both mechanical and cleaning ability and pleasant, alert sales tact. The combination is not easily found, since the positions are after all not very high on the scale of career excitement. Very often, one or both are heavy drinkers with all the charm and efficiency that go with it.

Owners are finding increasingly that city and county employees make reliable managers, and are often mechanically handy as well.

The larger the apartment project, the more help will be required. After about 50 or 60 units, another assistant is needed for cleaning or engineer-grade repairs. All in all, full-time management is not really practical in buildings with fewer than 30 units because the dollar income is not sufficient to meet the salary needs of managers. Over that size, a reliable rule is to furnish a free apartment, usually near the entrance, and a salary of \$3 to \$5 per month per unit, or \$36 to \$60 per year per unit. Another guideline is that the salary and apartment should total between 4% and 5% of gross income. Where possible, the amount should be based on a guaranteed minimum plus bonus incentives for full occupancy (where that's a problem) or other economy achievements. Remember, the manager sets the tone of the class of tenants, and the entire character of the building, and compensation should not be skimped on if performance is expected.

To understand the size of apartment building required to support full-time resident management, we can use the process of capitalization effectively. If the management couple needed, say, salary plus apartment totaling \$9,000 per year (marginal in current economy) and that represented 5% of gross income, the gross would have to be \$180,000 year (\$9,000 ÷ .05 = \$180,000). If the average rental were \$300 per month, or \$3600 per year, then the required number of units would be 50. (180,000 ÷ \$3600 = 50.) Below this size, the owner must participate actively in management, and absorb at least half the maintenance costs. This means a resident part-time "monitor" manager compensated by some minor rent abatement.

ELEVATOR This is similar to the pool item in that it represents the service contract and light adjustments only. In the usual three- to four-story building, a fee of \$50 to \$75 per month or \$600 to \$900 per year is in line. In larger complexes, a few phone inquiries can guide you to a good estimate.

AIR CONDITIONING Only luxury units will have central air

conditioning; moderate-income properties will have separate window units, and low-income units have none. Estimates here require some phone inquiries. If the original vendor does not have a service contract, which can be obtained from the owner, outside estimates are difficult to pin down since they vary so widely depending on gas versus electric, etc. and repair shops prefer to charge by each call rather than by contract.

VACANCY The customary vacancy rate which you will find expounded in most textbooks as applicable for most parts of the country under normal conditions—if there is any such thing—is 5%. But some judgment must be used. If rents in a particular building are severely lower than the prevailing market rates, and haven't been raised in 5 years, you don't need a vacancy allowance. On the other hand, where rents have just been raised for the third time in the past year and are at or over the prevailing level, then the full 5% should be allowed. In California in 1980, vacancies are almost nonexistent; in fact, the better maintained buildings have waiting lists. Obviously, vacancy allowances under such conditions would be minimal.

MAINTENANCE This item, condensed under one embracing term, is really the total of more than one to two dozen items ranging from simple supplies of soap and buckets, all the way through minor and major repairs, to replacements of carpets, drapes, garbage disposals, water heaters and roof. Any reputable property management firm in your area will be willing to supply you with their checklist.

Here again, I dispensed with the detailed examination of each item when retrospective review of actual results over a number of years confirmed that, for preliminary analysis purposes, the total estimate of 7% of gross income was just as reliable—provided we're talking about *unfurnished* properties.

If the property is furnished, do not try simply increasing the maintenance allowance; instead adjust the rent down to pure real estate by deducting a value for furniture: I suggest $30 to $35 a month for one bedroom, $40 to $45 for two bedrooms, and $50 to $55 for three bedrooms, in the average middle class neighborhood. In luxury units, those figures could double, and in low-income units they could be halved. Now the rent schedule has been reduced to what is received for the nonperishable real estate—the land and buildings—for which a comparatively low return is reasonable. Furniture, on the other hand, is highly perishable, and should be recovered more quickly.

Another rent schedule adjustment is the removal of landlord-paid tenant utilities, for you can be sure the landlord has added a utility estimate to the normal rent. Some owners claim that by having a central, master meter, they get a lower "commercial" rate. This is true enough, but the saving is usually more than offset by the simple human trait of wasting what someone else pays for. If the tenant sees through the sham of "free utilities," and realizes that the rent has been increased to cover the cost, the tendency will be to get his money's worth by leaving the heat or air conditioning on and windows open, hot water running, lights on whether home or not, etc. The same reasoning on removing furniture charges from rent applies here also. Utilities are not real estate and to pay eight times the gross *including utilities* is the same as paying eight times the utility charges. In stark reality, the investor would be paying eight times for the dubious advantage of collecting each tenant's payment and mailing it to the utility companies!

In removing the charges from the rent, they must also be deducted from total utilities in the expenses, leaving only the general building share of utilities. This is not an easy estimate to make without knowing how much of the total is due to tenant use. One way is to use your own household average. Another is to take 10% of total expenses as attributable to the general building and deduct the excess as tenants' share. For accurate data, where the investment appears imminent enough to warrant closer investigation, the utility companies have source data that their customer service or public relations departments will be happy to provide.

PROFESSIONAL MANAGEMENT Fees range from a high of 7% of actual income to a low of 3%, depending upon the size and convenience of location of the property.

OFFICE BUILDINGS

Office buildings, of course, vary widely from older to newer, low rise to high rise, downtown to suburban, tower type to garden style. The comments here will be representative mainly of low rise (3 to 11 stories) and medium rise (17 to 21 stories) buildings, from new to post World War II vintage. Keep in mind that in all office buildings, provisions must be made for improvements and alterations for each new tenant. Leasing fees and janitorial contracts are also "givens" that you must allow for.

With office buildings, you have alterations, leasing fees, and janitorial expenses.

INCOME

Normally income is by lease arrangement, which ranges from short term of 3 to 5 years, to long term: 10 years for larger tenants, up to 20 years for institutional tenants such as banks, insurance companies, stock brokerage houses and the like. In view of expected continuance of inflation, building owners do not wish to be tied to any long-term agreements. See Chapter 5 for complete discussion of industrial and commercial leases.

EXPENSES

PROPERTY TAXES The discussion of the effects of California's Proposition 13 (see page 36) applies to office buildings as well as apartments. Under the taxation system in effect in most other states, taxes average $1 per square foot rentable per year. When rentals rise to a higher rate, the tax assessor raises the value of the property and hence the tax rate; normally then, the *ratio* of rent to tax does not change, whereas the tax per square foot will increase. The best source of continuing ratio studies is BOMA, Building Owners and Managers Association.*

The trend is toward *net leases,* where the tenant pays taxes, sometimes insurance and utilities, janitorial costs, etc.; or *gross leases,* with escalation provisions whereby the lessor pays the first year taxes (base year) and the lessee pays any increases.

RESIDENT MANAGER In smaller buildings, under 50,000 square feet, where there is no professional management service, a small office and a secretary/bookkeeper are sufficient. This item therefore represents the rental of the office, phone, utilities and salary of the employee.

PROPERTY MANAGEMENT Fees range from 4% to 6% of the gross income depending upon the size and location of the property. Leasing fees are not generally included in this item but treated as a separate expense (see earlier).

INSURANCE Estimate from $1.50 to $2.00 per $1000 of market value, or from 1.2% to 1.6% of gross income. At an average value-to-income multiplier of 8 times, you will see that the value and income percentages are related.

UTILITIES In larger, sealed buildings you can estimate 8% of gross income. In low rise, 2 and 3 story structures, where door and windows are often left open and other sealing insulation is generally inadequate, utilities can soar to 20% of gross income. In buildings and also geographical areas (such as Texas) where the owner absorbs all utility expenses through one water meter per building, the top figure is also encountered.

*Check your telephone directory for a local office, or write 1221 Massachusetts Avenue NW, Washington DC 20005.

ELEVATOR Costs will vary by height of building, from $100 a month for 6 stories, to many hundreds per month for high rise through skyscraper level. Best to get a local estimate.

AIR CONDITIONING First check with the previous owner to see if a service contract is in force; that will be your best way to estimate costs. If there is no contract, you will have to make a few inquiry calls, since charges vary widely depending on location and also on whether gas or electricity is used.

CLEANING Fees have increased steadily from an earlier range of $.02 to $.03 per month per rentable square foot, to a current spread of $.035 to $.05 per month, or $.42 to $.60 per year. When evaluating an office building for potential investment, take a look at its current cleaning contract: it's one indication of the caliber of tenants. Doctors, for instance, require thorough nightly cleaning. Light dusting, once or twice a week, vacuuming of carpets only, with infrequent shampooing, are signs of nonselective, low rent-paying tenants . . . or management fatigue.

LEASING FEES This fee, paid to the broker as a commission, is one of the differences from the normal expenses of an apartment. Normally, this fee will range from .5% to 1% of the gross income. Since the average lease term runs from 3 to 5 years, it should be expected that a certain percentage of tenants will change location either within or outside the building, or renew their lease. In any event, a leasing fee must be provided for.

To get a working estimate of leasing fees for totaling expenses, first make an assumption of what percent of tenants will change and multiply that percent by the prevailing leasing fees, which are easily obtainable from any broker. Currently in California they range from 5% to 6% for the first five years rental, 2½% to 3% for the second five years rental and 1½% to 2% thereafter. So, on the basis of 6% fee and a 10% estimated tenant change, then $.06 \times .10 = .006$, or .6% per year.

ALTERATIONS This is an even more important addition to the normal expenses of an apartment. When an apartment is vacated and rerented, washing and painting are required but not structural changes. Offices, on the contrary, are rarely rerented in the same form. Partitions must be removed and replaced; air conditioning ducts and vents and light fixtures must be moved; this necessitates removing and replacing ceiling tiles and floor covering, and so forth. Currently, in an average building, it costs about $10 per square foot to remove partitions and fixtures and another $15 to replace them; that means $25 per square foot each time the office is turned over.

This figure is often omitted from the seller's offering for two reasons, outside of dishonesty. The first is that it is forgotten. The second is that, technically, "expenses" include only repairs that *restore* property; whereas additions or structural alterations are *capitalized* and appear in the books not under expenses but under assets. Owners frequently forget to look at the assets account as well as normal expenses.

MAINTENANCE In the average type of office building being discussed here, the same 7% approximation for repairs and maintenance as in an apartment is feasible, plus from 1% to 2% for alterations.

In larger high rises, 40 to 100 stories, a much more complex classification of accounts is employed. For example, mechanical, engineering and plumbing (MEP) is one account; office administration is another. Since these skyscrapers rarely get out of the control of large institutions, the reader of this book is not very likely to encounter one. If the occasion arises, however, BOMA is an excellent reference source for comparisons or even consultation.

RETAIL STORES AND SHOPPING CENTERS

Generally, there are three classes of shopping centers:

- Individual stores up to small centers (5 acres).
- Medium-sized community shopping centers, up to 25 acres.
- Large regional shopping malls, up to 100 acres or more.

Each class, in turn, is composed of three kinds of tenants:

- The so-called *majors*—national chain stores with top credit ratings. They usually take up 70% of the gross leasable area (GLA).
- *Satellites*—medium-sized shops, such as women's fashion shops, that often are locally owned; they occupy about 25% of space (and also income).
- *Service shops*—dry cleaners, shoe repair, etc.—account for the remaining 5%.

You may be wondering why so much space—70%—is devoted to major stores. Mortgage lenders require a guaranteed minimum rent from them that is large enough to cover the principal and interest payments on their loan. On the other hand, major stores can demand low rental rates—precisely because they know they are needed for loan credit—so it takes a larger percentage of the total space to earn the dollar rental.

When evaluating a shopping center as an investment, remember to allow for two points. The landlord receives additional rent through the common area maintenance (CAM) charge, which is apportioned among the tenants on a square foot pro rata basis. There is also an additional expense item not encountered in other types of investment: the landlord is expected to cover 20% to 25% of the retail advertising and promotion fund, with the tenants contributing the balance.

Shopping centers bring unique expense/income items.

INCOME

For individual shops, income to the owner is usually by a straightforward lease for a certain cost per square foot. Currently these rates run from $.50 a month per square foot in the lower economic areas to $2 a month per square foot in upper-level areas*, and are increasing rapidly with inflation. Usually leases for this type property are for 3, 4 or 10-year terms.

In shopping centers, the most common leases are based on guaranteed minimum rent vs. percentage of sales. It works this way. Each kind of business has an optimum percentage of sales that can safely be paid in rent. They range from 1% for a supermarket to 10% for high markup specialty products, with an average of 3% to 4% for larger department stores and 6% to 8% for medium-sized retail shops.

If a retailer can pay 6% and can expect sales of $1,000,000 the first year, then the ideal rental would be $60,000 per year ($1,000,000 × 6%). The lessor, however, may require a guaranteed minimum of $72,000 per year as part of the lease. The retailer must pay the $72,000 minimum, even though in the first year it represents 7.2% of the sale volume. In later years, when the sales volume increases to, say, $1,500,000, the retailer pays the preferred sales percentage of 6%—which in this case would be $90,000. The overage of $18,000 (over the $72,000 guaranteed minimum) is additional income to the lessor.

EXPENSES

If you are dealing with a gross lease (when lessor pays basic expenses, usually taxes, insurance and outside maintenance), the costs range from 15% to 20% when property taxes are 1% or 1½% of market value, up to 25% to 30% of gross income where property tax is 3% or 3½%.

More common these days, however, for everything from a small

*On elegant Rodeo Drive in world-famous Beverly Hills, current rates are up to $10 per month per square foot.

individual shop to a mammoth shopping mall is the triple net lease: renter pays the big three expenses, so in effect there is no expense to the owner. In practice, the lessor pays the taxes, insurance and maintenance, and then bills each tenant in proportion to square footage.

Two other comments in connection with expenses:

Don't overlook vacancy allowances.

One concerns the question of vacancy allowances. Normally it is fruitless to attempt to provide for vacancies in the majors—sellers will not allow it and so any offer which contained such an allowance would be suspect and prohibitively below market value. For minor tenants, allow a vacancy rate of at least 5%. I suggest 10%, which will provide for the additional taxes you will have to contribute to cover the share of the missing tenant.

A charge should be made, too, for bookkeeping, mailing, telephoning, and, yes, dunning in connection with prorating charges to tenants. This has been frequently overlooked—to the investor's loss.

In terms of both income and expenses, the only real difference between smaller community shopping centers and large regional malls is one of size and complexity. And, as an aside, there is one trend characteristic of only the largest malls. Often the major stores build their own building on parcels of land in the center of the development, land they either purchase or lease from the developer. While the mall appears to be one entity, it is in reality several, with the developer owning only the minor groups of stores sandwiched between the majors. This brings in the need for cross parking agreements, called reciprocal easement agreements or REA.

NET LEASE AND THE LANDLORD'S NET INCOME

Some care must be exercised when evaluating the presentation of a net lease—one in which the tenants contribute expenses. There are three different methods by which a real estate analyst will receive the expense/income figures needed to compute the owner's net income. The first, showing only net expenses to owner, is totally inadequate and possibly misleading. The second, showing total operating expenses of the owner, less the tenants' pro rata contribution, is more revealing. The third, fully revealing as the second, simply rearranges the tenants' contribution as income, rather than expense deductions. This inversion is sometimes confusing at first. Note, however, that the owner's NOI is the same.

Net lease presentations do not tell the whole story; read them carefully.

For illustration of the three methods, let's use some numbers.

Example: Assume a gross rental of $100,000 a year. Property taxes were $10,000 in the base year, and have been raised last year to

$15,000. Insurance and maintenance costs were originally $5,000 and increased last year to $10,000. Under the terms of the lease, the lessor pays the base year expenses, and bills each tenant for prorated increases.

Set up in familiar outline form, we might think of the expense figures this way:

Total expenses this year		
Taxes	$ 15,000	
Insurance and maintenance	10,000	
Total		25,000
Less lessor's base year share		
Taxes	10,000	
Insurance and maintenance	5,000	
		15,000
Excess to be contributed by tenants		$ 10,000

Another way of looking at it is:

Total expenses		
Taxes	$ 15,000	
Insurance and maintenance	10,000	
Total expenses		25,000
Less amount contributed by tenant		
Taxes (excess)	5,000	
Insurance and maintenance (excess)	5,000	10,000
Landlord's net expenses		$ 15,000

The net income to the proposed investor might be presented thus:

Method I.	Gross rental	$ 100,000
	Less base year expenses	15,000
	Net operating income	85,000

This first net lease presentation is inadequate.

But if an offering were received in this latter form, as it frequently is, it would be inadequate: the true amount of taxes and other expenses is not revealed, nor how much the tenants are contributing. This means that, in case of a vacancy, the lessor not only loses the rental income, but must pay out of his own income the share of that tenant's contributions. Therefore, a better report would be our second method.

A more revealing net lease presentation, in 2 formats.

Method II.				
	Gross rental income			$ 100,000
	Taxes	15,000		
	Less tenant contribution	5,000		
	Net taxes		10,000	
	Insurance and maintenance	10,000		
	Less tenant contribution	5,000		
			5,000	
	Total lessor expenses			15,000
	Net operating income			85,000

Do you see how much more revealing that is? As a matter of fact, insurance and maintenance would ordinarily be shown as two separate items, but it was desired to make the point without burdensome detail.

Now the third and more advanced method simply rearranges the same figures but adds the tenant contributions to the *gross* rent, then subtracts all the expenses, to arrive at the NOI.

Method III.			
	Gross rental income		100,000
	Plus tenant contributions		
	Taxes	5,000	
	Insurance and maintenance	5,000	
	Total tenant contributions		10,000
	Total income		110,000
	Less operating expenses		
	Taxes	15,000	
	Insurance and maintenance	10,000	
	Total operating expenses		25,000
	Lessor's net operating income		85,000

Be sure you understand that inverting the normal order (adding the contributions first and then subtracting the gross expenses, instead of the other way around) results in the same net profit.

INDUSTRIAL PROPERTIES

Industrial properties range from older, center-city facilities to modern suburban landscaped parks. For our purposes, an "average" property, the one we're most likely to encounter, is of post-World War II vintage and ranges from 5,000 to 50,000 square feet.

INCOME

Typical leases on industrial properties range from 3 to 5 years for the oldest and smallest, up to 20 or 25 years for largest developments. Here are some rule of thumb rental charges:

If the property is	**the rental charge is**
up to 5,000 square feet, 20 to 30 years old	$.10 to $.15 per square foot per month
5,000 to 20,000 square feet, 10 to 20 years old	$.20 to $.30 per square foot per month
More than 20,000 square feet, 1 to 10 years old	$.30 to $.40 per square foot per month

EXPENSES

The trend today is toward net leases—where tenant pays some or all of the major expenses in proportion to leased footage—and so for all practical purposes there are no expenses to the lessor. In a triple net lease, tenant pays the big three expenses: taxes, insurance and maintenance; in a double net, tenant pays two, usually taxes and insurance. (See next chapter for more detailed discussion of industrial and commercial leases.)

In today's net leases, expenses are paid by tenants, not owners.

Where the property is under a gross lease, the following remarks will provide some rules of thumb.

TAXES A fair estimate of property tax costs, other than the 1% limitation in California*, is approximately 3% of the market value of land and building, or approximately 15% to 20% of the gross rent. Another measurement is about $.03 to $.04 per month per square foot.

OTHER EXPENSES For insurance and maintenance expenses, estimate about 5% of gross rent, or $.01 to $.015 per square foot per month.

This brings the total expenses under a gross lease to 20% or 25% of gross rent, or $.04 to $.055 per square foot monthly. In California, because of Proposition 13, these totals could be reduced as much as half.

*See page 36 for a discussion of the effects of Proposition 13 on California's property taxes.

5.

Modern Commercial and Industrial Leases*

While most apartment units are traditionally rented month to month, usually expressed as M/M, commercial and industrial properties are leased for periods of 3 to 25 years; smaller tenants from 3 to 5 years, larger tenants up to 25 years. The logic of this becomes apparent when it is recognized that the larger the tenant, the bigger the investment in interior improvements, fixturization, machinery and equipment requiring longer to amortize. Too, while landlords, especially in an inflationary period, are reluctant to commit themselves to current rental rates for any longer than necessary, the larger tenants carry more thump. In the case of large and financially responsible tenants, the landlord may need them to obtain, and assure payment of, the mortgage.

Two types of leases: net and gross.

Leases fall generically into two classes: gross and net. The gross lease is most widely understood, because financially it resembles the month to month rental of apartment units. The landlord collects a gross rental from the tenant, and out of it pays all expenses. The tenant pays only that gross sum, and nothing additional. The net concept is a little more complicated, and has several versions. Basically, in a net lease the tenant pays a base rent to the landlord and *also* pays some, or all, the expenses.

At the purest extreme is the triple net lease, commonly expressed as NNN. The three "nets" are property taxes, insurance and maintenance—in that order. In a triple net lease, the tenant pays the base rent and all three categories of expenses; the landlord has *no* operating expenses.** The triple net lease is also known as absolute

*One word of caution: these are practical business descriptions only, and make no pretense to legal interpretation. For that, you of course will seek out qualified legal counsel. This admonition applies to the entire content of this book, for the same sound reason.

**However, if the landlord borrows against the property, the landlord pays the loan payments out of his net rent.

net or bondable net. A pure (that is, unmodified) triple net lease cannot be cancelled nor can the rent be abated in the event of fire, flood, explosion, condemnation or similar events. No wonder it is sometimes referred to as a "hell and high water" lease. This kind of lease is practical only for major tenants.

There is a form known as modified net, in which the tenant pays all expenses as in the triple net, but which is not absolute and therefore not bondable. This modified version does provide for cancellation and for rent abatement should the property be rendered fully or partially unusable. This lease is more practical for smaller tenants.

Two other types of net leases are also written: the single net lease (N), in which the tenant pays one major expense, usually taxes; and the double net lease (NN), in which the tenant pays two expenses, usually taxes and insurance, and the landlord pays the third. The customary order, as we mentioned, is: taxes, insurance and maintenance—just remember your old friend TIM—but there's nothing to prevent the parties from changing the order and making a double net lease that calls for tenant to pay taxes and maintenance.

In the last several years, commercial and industrial landlords have turned more and more to net rather than gross leases. Primarily this is done to shift the burden of rising expenses to the tenant. An alternative arrangement that meets the same goal is a gross lease with an escalation clause calling for the tenant to pay any increases over base-year expenses as additional rent; the base year is usually the first year of the lease. These escalation clauses are also called "pass through" or "stops"; that is, the landlord's liability stops at the base year level.

Leases commonly have adjustment factors for increases in costs.

A third arrangement is one which allows for adjustment in the base rent as well as in the expenses. With the inflation rate continuing to rise, lessors are insisting on protecting their purchasing power, and are drawing up leases in which the base rent is tied to the consumer price index (CPI)* and adjusted every 3 or 5 years or—which is becoming more common every day—even yearly. Usually, as we noted earlier, this type of lease adjusts base rent only; in certain prime locations, however, it applies to the total rent—base plus expenses.

Here's a short example of how this is applied mechanically. Let's assume a lease with $1,000 per month as base plus $200 monthly expenses paid by tenant. Assume further that the base is subject to CPI adjustment yearly. The CPI table we're using showed the index on the beginning month at 180 points.

At the beginning of the second year the index rose to 198 points—an increase of 18 points. Note this is not an increase of 18

*The Bureau of Labor Statistics of the U.S. Department of Labor publishes two consumer price index tables: *All Urban Consumers* and *Clerical and Professional Workers.* Both are commonly used in this type of lease arrangement.

percent, but of *points.* The amount of increase is actually 10% over the original 180 points: 18 ÷ 180 = 10%. This 10% applied to the $1,000 base would raise the rent by $100, to $1,100.

The usual formula is:

18 ÷ 180 = 10% × $1,000 = $100 + $1,000 = $1,100

A simpler method is:

198 (new index) ÷ 180 (old index) = 1.10 × $1,000 = $1,100

A variation on the CPI-adjusted lease—and one that is espoused by tenants—calls for the adjustment to apply only to 25% of the base rent. The reasoning behind this is that most investments are financed 75% by a loan and only 25% by cash; since the loan payments are constant, only the return on the owner's 25% needs protecting. The value of the property, for borrowing or resale purposes, is increasing in proportion to the CPI. If rental income increases 10% every year in consonance with CPI, then the building's value increases 10% per year, so that it could be sold for twice its original value in 10 years. No analysis of projected income, loan value or resale price is possible without a clear understanding of the mechanical application and effects of escalation and CPI.

COMPUTING RENT CONCESSIONS

Like many other things in this world, the rental rates charged under commercial and industrial leases are often up for negotiation. If presented with an offer from a desirable tenant who asks for reduced rent, property owners would be wise to offer instead *free* rent for a specified period of time. The reason is that future resale value, and loan value, are computed on the basis of the scheduled rental rates; if you reduce the rent, you dilute this future value. The task of the analyst, when this question arises, is the fairly simple one of calculating the period of free rent that will equal the amount of rental discount agreed upon.

It is better to offer a period of free rent, than to agree to reduced monthly rental rates.

Example Space: 5,000 square feet
Term: 48 months
Scheduled rental: 5,000 sq. ft. @ $1.15 = $5,750 per month
Tenant's offer: 5,000 sq. ft. @ $1.00 = $5,000 per month

Procedure

Step 1. Extend scheduled rent for lease term.
Step 2. Extend tenant's offer rent for lease term.
Step 3. Subtract for difference.

Step 4. Divide difference by scheduled monthly rental; equals number of free rental months.

In Figures:

Step 1.	\$5,750 × 48 months = total rental	\$276,000
Step 2.	\$5,000 × 48 months = total rental	240,000
Step 3.	Difference	\$ 36,000
Step 4.	\$36,000 ÷ \$5,750 = number of free rental months	6.26

Alternative procedure using percents

Step 1. Divide lower rate by higher rate.
Step 2. Multiply lease term months by Step 1.
Step 3. Subtract Step 2 from total lease months to arrive at concession (free rent) months.

In Figures *(same example)*

Step 1. \$1.00 ÷ \$1.15 = 86.96%.
Step 2. 48 months × 86.96% = 41.74 months.
Step 3. 48 months − 41.74 months = concession months, 6.26.

The analyst may also be faced with the converse problem: when you know a lease is subject to a concession period, what is the effective, vs. stated, rental? Let's work one through, using the figures from the example above.

Procedure—*same as above.*

Step 1. Multiply the stated monthly rental by the number of actual payments.
Step 2. Divide that product by the total number of lease months.

In Figures

Step 1. \$5,750 × 41.74 months = \$240,000 total
Step 2. \$240,000 ÷ 48 months = \$5,000 effective rental
(\$5,000 per month × 12 months = effective annual rental \$60,000)

Another adjustment of base rent factor may arise out of the recent trend toward scarcity of mortgage loan funds. The lenders prefer variable to flat interest rates for business as well as single family residence loans. Investment property owners are reluctant to risk the unpredictability of future return inherent in variable loan terms. If new or rehabilitation construction should be materially diminished because of this conflict, it is possible the commercial and industrial lease of the future may contain still another adjustment passed on to the tenant along with CPI and operating expense escalation—that of increased mortgage interest.

INCOME/EXPENSE RATIOS[1]

TYPES OF INCOME		*APARTMENTS* M/M or 1-3 year lease			*OFFICES* 3-5 years 10 year lease average for large tenant	
Typical rental per square foot unfurnished[2]		*Low*	*Medium*	*High*	*Low*	*Medium*	*High*
	Monthly	$ .40	$ .60	$ .80	$ .60	$ 1.00	$ 1.50
	Yearly	$4.80	$7.20	$9.60	$7.20	$12.00	$18.00
Annual Expense per square foot	*Low*	$1.68	$2.52	$3.36	$2.16	$ 3.60	$ 5.40
	High	$1.82	$2.74	$3.65	$2.52	$ 4.20	$ 6.30
Typical expense ratio: % of Gross		35% - 38%			30% - 35% of gross lease		

[1]To avoid the unsettling appearance of a table with no numbers, I've included here reasonably current figures for southern California. A little local investigation would turn up comparable figures for other regions.

[2]All apartment units should be calculated as *unfurnished* by subtracting from the rental any additional charge for furniture. In the absence of accurate information, deduct the following approximations: one bedroom, $30-$35 a month; two bedrooms, $40-$45; three bedrooms, $50-$55.

INCOME/EXPENSE RATIOS

STORES					*INDUSTRIAL*			
Small 3-5 year lease			*Large* 10-25 year lease		*Small* 5-10 year lease		*Large* 10-25 year lease	
Low	*Medium*	*High*[3]	*Low*	*High*	*Low*	*High*	*Low*	*High*
$ .50	$ .75	$ 2.00	$ .25	$ .35	$ .20 gross	$ .50 net	$ .18 gross	$ .40 net
$6.00	$9.00	$24.00	$3.00	$4.20	$2.40 gross	$6.00 net	$2.16 gross	$4.80 net
$ .60	$ .90	$ 2.40	$ .30	$ .42	$ .24 if net		$ .22 if net	
$ .90	$1.35	$ 3.60	$ .45	$ .64	$ .36 no expenses		$ .32 no expenses	
10% - 15% of gross lease			10% - 15% of gross lease		10% - 15% of gross lease		10% - 15% of gross lease	

[3]A special exception is Rodeo Drive in Beverly Hills, which is higher than high: $10-$12 *per month.*

III.

Finance

6.

Loans: Types and Sources

Long-term real estate loans are secured by two different types of documents, called *mortgages* in some states and *deeds of trust* in others such as California. They differ mainly in method of foreclosure by the lender and redemption by the borrower (the right to pay delinquencies and reassume title to the property). Simply stated, the mortgage is a two-party agreement between lender and borrower; the deed of trust, commonly called trust deed, transfers the property title to a trustee who acts as a third party between lender and borrower. In event of default, the trustee usually has greater powers of foreclosure than a mortgagee (lender).

Different states also have varying periods of statutory redemption by the borrower after foreclosure. This period ranges usually from six months to one year except in Alabama and Arkansas which provide for two years. In California, there is one-year redemption only after judicial foreclosure, meaning by court action. When the trustee under a deed of trust exercises the "power of sale" provision in the deed of trust, the borrower does not have any period of redemption.

The sources of long-term loans throughout the country are many and varied. They include savings banks, such as in New York, as compared with savings and loan associations, as in California; insurance companies; pension funds; unions; religious and fraternal organizations; and some commercial banks, who prefer short-term rather than long-term loans but will occasionally accommodate a client.

Where to go for what kind of loan.

In general, savings banks and S&Ls are the best sources of apartment loans up to $1,000,000. Insurance companies are more at home with commercial and industrial loans from $500,000 to multi-millions. The same is true of unions and religious organizations.

Some of these institutions make their loan direct, but many prefer to be represented by mortgage loan correspondents who charge a fee of from ½% to 1½% of the loan amount.

The term of loans, with rare exceptions, is limited to a maximum of 30 years. One exception occurs when the institution resells a property it owns, usually the result of foreclosure—in which case it is not bound by laws governing lending for profit but is merely carrying back part of its own equity as part of the sale price. Another exception is FHA, HUD, VA, and other special purpose governmental agency-insured loans, which characteristically have a limit of 40 years.

The best source of a loan may be the seller.

An additional—and to the investor the most attractive—loan source is the seller, for several reasons. First, the seller is more motivated by the desire to *sell* than to make maximum interest profit. Consequently the interest rate is usually below that of an institutional lender. Further, a private seller rarely if ever charges "points," which mean percentages of the loan amount charged by institutions as their fee for making and processing the loan. These points are actually a form of increasing the lender's effective interest rate over the stated nominal rate and will be dealt with extensively later.

Another advantage of the seller acting as lender is that rarely, if ever, does the seller insert a provision for a penalty for prepayment of the loan before its stated maturity, as do all institutional lenders. These penalties range from a low of 2% of the loan balance at time of payoff to a high of one-half the annual rate, applied not to the balance at time of prepayment but to the *original* loan amount. In California, at least, this is more prevalent among savings and loan associations (S&Ls) than insurance companies.

In 1980, in California, commercial and industrial loans by insurance company lenders are at approximately 12%; loans by commercial banks are from 12% to 14%; loans on apartments, condominiums and single-family residences by S&Ls are from 12¼% to 13¾%.

Another loan form, usually up to 2 years, is the construction loan made by commercial banks mostly, but sometimes by the long-term lender as part of a package. Whereas the long-term loan is known popularly as "permanent" or "take-out," the construction loan has several names: interim, gap and bridge—describing its function as coming between the start of construction and the completion, at which point the permanent lender "takes out" the interim lender. As a touch of irony, a loan officer was quoted as telling a dinner gathering, "I *hate* the expression 'permanent loan.' "

The rates of interim loans, quite naturally, are higher than the permanent loan rates. They are usually quoted as so many points over prime. For instance, if the prime rate were 11%, the interim rate might be quoted at 14%, or 3 points over prime.

By state or federal law, lenders are limited to lending 75% or 80%

of the sale price—provided the lender's appraisal agrees with the price. If a sale price were $1,000,000, an 80% limit would permit a loan of $800,000. If, however, the lender appraised the property at only $900,000, the maximum loan would be only $770,000, regardless of the selling price. Lenders have another criterion to limit the maximum loan a property may carry, called debt service coverage (DSC) which is described later in the section on "How Lenders Determine Loan Amounts."

The maximum amount of loan is limited by law, and also by lenders' coverage needs.

So far we've talked of first lien loans, or senior loans. These are recorded by the lender and give the lender first claim to any proceeds of sale or foreclosure before the claims of other second, third, etc. lien loans—called junior loans—and also ahead of the equity owner, whose claim is last. These junior loans, like the senior loans, may be made in cash by a lender or carried back by the seller as part of the sale price.

When loans are made by a professional lender, they are termed "hard money" loans. Where carried back by the seller—since no cash is involved and the loan, after all, may represent the seller's profit rather than actual cost—the loans are termed "soft money" loans. The latter are also known as "purchase money" loans. This difference explains why the seller's carried back purchase money second loan almost uniformly bears a lower interest rate than the more secure first lien loan; the seller's prime objective is facilitating the sale rather than direct interest profit. Another, more subtle, reason for the seller to ease the terms of the purchase money loan is discussed under "Timing of Leverage" on page 118.

A second loan carried back by seller often has a lower interest rate.

An important difference between institutional first loans and seller's second loans is that the institutional first loans are payable over their stated term of, say, 25 or 30 years without obligation to prepay before; whereas seller's second loans are predominantly of the "balloon balance" type. A "balloon" is the unpaid balance of a loan sometime during its full term which is due in lump sum before the full amortization period. For example, a loan of $100,000 at 9% interest for 25 years is payable monthly at $840 per month. However, this loan contains a 5-year balloon, meaning that the full balance is due in one payment at the end of the fifth year. So, although the loan has the benefits of low, 25-year term payment, it really amounts to a 5-year loan. Obviously, the balloon payment is going to be not very much less than the original loan amount, since the early payments are practically all interest.

And it usually involves a balloon payment.

It is common practice for a balloon-type loan to be described as a "5 year" or "10 year" second, without mentioning that the period of time required for full amortization is 25 years. Many unwary buyers have fallen into this trap in the past, resulting in their losing the property or having to borrow at hard money rates to cover the balloon payment. For that reason, we stress in this text that the safest assumption to make is that any second or third balloon balance can be paid only by refinance of the underlying first loan.

Accordingly, the balloon date of any junior loan must be synchronized with the reducing of the balance of the senior loan. This will lead us to a simplified short-cut method of calculating the unpaid balances of any kind of loan, year by year, month by month, or at any selected future period.

Variable-rate loans allow the lender to adjust interest rate.

Still another loan variation is the "variable rate" type, in which the lender is allowed to change (raise or lower) the interest rate, but by no more than ¼% in any 6-month period (which amounts to a limit of ½% in any year) and in no event more than 2½% during the loan term. The reasoning here is that the lender will be more willing to make a long-term loan when the ability to raise interest rates provides some relief from inflation. On the other hand, the initial interest rate may be 1/8% or ¼% lower than the prevailing loan rate.

These loans have proved more acceptable to single family residence borrowers than to investment borrowers because of the uncertainty of projected return to the latter which could nullify the whole purpose of business property development. In turn, this could result in scarcity of available space with consequent further upward pressure on rental rates. A solution may be including in business property leases a provision passing on all, or a portion, of any mortgage interest increase to the tenant as another escalation, similar to those of CPI and operating expense increases.

Another type of loan being tried out in certain parts of the country (but not in California, yet) is the "step-up" kind, whereby a young couple may repay at less that the normal amount in their early, lesser-earning, years and eventually more than the normal amount on a graduated basis, in later years, as their earning powers increase.

A wrap-around loan encompasses a prior senior lien with a present junior, into one payment.

An intriguing loan concept imported from Canada in the 1940s is the all-inclusive security device. Descriptive of its function, it goes popularly by the name "wrap-around" (W/A). It is a junior, not senior, loan. It can take the form of a mortgage, trust deed, or land contract. Instead of a buyer taking over an existing loan balance and giving the seller a second lien for a remaining balance, the buyer gives the seller one larger lien which includes both balances. The seller collects one payment from the buyer, himself pays the payment due on the existing loan, and retains the balance as payment on his equity portion, which would ordinarily have been the second lien. So, the all inclusive lien "wraps around" the existing lien, or liens, and its excess over the existing balances becomes the seller's "equity." Therefore, if there were one prior loan, the seller's equity would be tantamount to a second loan. If there were a prior first and second loan, the seller's equity would be equal to a third loan, and so on.

ALL INCLUSIVE SECURITY DEVICE (AISD) Or WRAP-AROUND (W/A)

The wrap-around loan, either land contract or mortgage, is used to achieve three different objectives:

1. To provide a bonus yield to the seller in proportion to the amount by which the interest rate paid by the buyer to the seller exceeds the interest rate paid by the seller to the underlying lender under his existing loan terms.

2. To enable a new lender to realize a higher yield on the new money advanced over the rate paid by the borrower, in proportion as the new rate paid by the borrower exceeds the rate of the existing loan which the new lender wraps around. Here, the new lender benefits exactly as does the seller.

3. To avert triggering the provision of IRS Section 453 Installment Sales whereby any "excess of existing loan balance over adjusted tax basis" in the year of sale becomes part of the maximum 30% cash that the seller may receive. In other words, where a seller carries back a wrap-around loan that includes the existing loan, then any excess of the existing loan over the property's tax basis is not recognized as cash received by the seller.

a) Estate of Lamberth, 31 TC 302 (1958);

b) United Pacific Corp. 39 TC 721 (1963).

In California, property may be transferred by *grant deed*, whereby title is given to the buyer; or by *land contract*, whereby the seller retains the title until some designated date or performance, and the buyer has an *equitable interest* in the property. In the case of the land contract, the terms "buyer" and "seller" are not used; the buyer is called the "vendee" and the seller the "vendor."

Brokers are advised never to attempt to influence clients as to which type of wrap instrumentation to use, or to draw one up. Both for protection of the broker's license, and moral obligation not to endanger clients, the problem may be handled by words to this effect: "The parties have agreed to enter into an all inclusive security device to be prepared by their respective legal counsel."

Let's take a wrap-around example in figures. First, the normal sale:

Assume		
	Sale price	$ 100,000
	Down payment	20,000
	Balance	$ 80,000
	Existing first loan	65,000
	Purchase money second loan	$ 15,000

Here, the buyer gives the seller the second lien for the balance of the purchase price still owing after the down payment. Now then, let's assume that to take advantage of Section 453, the parties agree to a wrap-around (W/A) loan. The structure would look like this:

Sale price	$ 100,000
Down payment	20,000
All inclusive land contract by vendee to vendor	$ 80,000

On the vendor's books, the $80,000 would be separated into the vendor's remaining obligation to the underlying existing lender, and his own contract equity:

All inclusive contract	$ 80,000
Underlying existing loan	65,000
Vendor's equity	$ 15,000

Now suppose the payments on the first loan were $6,500 per year, and on the vendor's equity $1,500 per year. The vendee would make one payment of $8,000 ($6,500 + $1,500) to the vendor; the vendor would pay $6,500 to the underlying lender, and retain the $1,500 balance as return on his equity.

Let's expand the structure, visually:

Wrap-around (W/A)	$ 80,000	Paid by vendee	$ 8,000
Existing loan	65,000	Paid by vendor	6,500
Vendor's equity	$ 15,000	Retained by vendor	$ 1,500

There are, then, three levels of different elements within the one instrument, and three elements in the one payment received by the vendor: the amount he receives, the amount he pays out, and the amount he retains. Of the three elements, the existing loan balance and payment (as well as interest rate and due date) have to be known or the wrap-around would have no basis for existence.

These are the mechanics of structuring loans. To calculate the *yield* on the three elements requires familiarity with the band of investment theory and mortgage/equity techniques, covered in detail in Chapter 17. With these mathematical tools in hand, you can apply the shortcuts to yield calculation described in that chapter.

DUE ON SALE CLAUSES

A frequent provision in institutional loans is the right of the lender to call the loan due at once whenever the property changes hands from the original borrower. This right is called by various names, including *due on sale, acceleration* and *alienation.* The due on sale clause is less common, but not unknown, in purchase money loans carried back by the seller as part of a sale.

In a landmark California Supreme Court decision in October 1974, in the case of Tucker *vs.* Lassen, it was held that the sale of property under all inclusive land sales contract does not invoke the due-on-sale clause in state-chartered institutional loans *unless* the lender can prove being "harmed" by such sale. In August 1978, in the case of Wellenkamp *vs.* Bank of America, the same decision was held to include sales by an all inclusive trust deed, again affecting only state-chartered institutions. At date of this writing, federal institutions assert they are not subject to California jurisdiction and, therefore, continue to invoke the due-on-sale clauses in their loans.

7.

Loan Constants Explained

Every lender has two absolute requisites: return *of* capital and return *on* capital. These two elements are combined in one payment called a constant; the amortization portion of this loan payment is the return of capital and the interest portion is return on capital.

The term *constant*, called K for short, is used to describe the actual dollar amount of the loan payment (K$) *and also* the percent of the constant dollar amount to the loan balance (K%). The distinction between the two would be clear from the context of their use. A reference to "K 88,220" in conversation would obviously not be a percentage rate; conversely, if you heard "K 10.39" you would recognize it as a percentage.

The loan constant is both the dollar amount of the loan payment, and the percentage of that payment to loan total.

The term itself comes from the fact that the *amount* of the loan payment remains constant throughout the life of the loan, although the balance on the loan principal decreases with each payment. Another way to look at it: with each successive payment, the portion of the payment which is interest gets smaller and the portion which is principal gets larger.

There are several shortcut methods to calculate the amount of loan reduction at every stage during the term of the loan, and these we shall come to. For now, a quick, if not strictly accurate, way to compute the interest payments is to multiply the loan balance by the interest rate, and subtract that amount from the constant.

A quick way to compute the portion of the payment which is interest.

For example, let's use the figures in our model case study. The interest rate on the first loan is 10%. Then $749,000 × .10 = $74,900, which, subtracted from the $78,950 constant leaves $4,050 representing the principal, or amortization portion. (The actual figures in the model are slightly different because the interest is compounded monthly.)

Similarly, multiply the second loan by its interest rate of 8% for the rounded interest amount: $100,000 × .08 = $8,000. Thus the constant of $9,270 less $8,000 interest leaves $1,270 as principal. (Again the slight difference in the model represents monthly compounding.) So that the total loan reduction in the first year is $5,320 (actually, $5,555).

Let's see how the K factor applies. Turn to the loan amortization schedule at the end of this book; look up 9¾% interest and 25-year term. The K is seen to be 10.7%. With a loan of $300,000, then:

$300,000	×	constant rate (K)	10.70%	=	constant	$ 32,100
$300,000	×	interest rate	9.75%	=	interest	$ 29,250
$300,000	×	amortization	.95%	=	amortization	$ 2,850

Still using the loan amortization schedule, note that as the remaining term of the loan diminishes, the K factor increases.

Remaining Term	*End of Year (EOY)*	*Constant* (K$)		*Constant* (K%)		*Balance*
25	0	$32,100	÷	10.70	=	$300,000
24	1	32,100	÷	10.81	=	296,947
23	2	32,100	÷	10.93	=	293,687
. . .	. . .	32,100		. . .		. . .
15	10	32,100	÷	12.72	=	252,356

In the above example, when the same constant payment is divided (capitalized) at an increasingly higher K factor, the loan balance decreases correspondingly.

Interest rate, constant, and term—if you know two, you can always find the third.

The two out of three principle which we encounter throughout this book applies very handily to constants:

- If the interest rate and constant are known, simply scan the book to find the years under which the constant appears.
- If the interest rate and years are known, find the constant where the two intersect.
- If the years and constant are known, scan the book to find the interest rate at which the constant appears.

SHORTCUT CALCULATION OF BALLOON BALANCES

It is possible to calculate balloon balances for any number of years quickly. All that is necessary is to subtract the balloon period of years from the *currently* remaining term of the loan, and divide the constant dollar payment by the K factor for the *resulting* remaining term. The quotient will be the unpaid (balloon) balance. Let's do a sample problem or two.

Problem: Using the above schedule, what will be the balloon balance at the end of 10 years?

Procedure

Step 1. Currently remaining term 25 years
Less balloon period 10 years
Resulting remaining term 15 years

Step 2. K factor for 15 years remaining = 12.72%

Step 3. Constant \$32,100 ÷ K .1272 = balloon balance \$252,358

When there is a second loan over the first, the safest assumption is that the balloon of the second must be paid out of the proceeds of refinancing the first at the time the second loan balloon is due. This means synchronizing the payoff of the second loan with that of the first. In brief, the process is: the unpaid balances of both are projected for several periods and the periods compared until the first loan, if refinanced back to its *original amount,* would provide sufficient proceeds to pay off the second loan balance.

Timing the payoff of a balloon balance to coincide with refinancing a first loan.

Example The first loan of \$500,000 is payable monthly at \$61,000 per year total for 25 years, including interest at 11.5% per year (K = 12.2%). A second loan of \$67,100 is payable monthly at \$7,247 per year total at 9% interest per year, with a balloon balance due in 6 years. Original constant \$7,247 ÷ \$67,100 = K 10.8%.

Problem Will the first loan balance be reduced sufficiently in 6 years so that its refinance will produce enough cash proceeds to pay off the second balloon? If not, then how many years will be required to do so?

Procedure Project the payoff schedule of both loans, starting with 5 years as a test and continuing for as many additional years as necessary.

Step 1. Compute second loan balance for years 6 through 10, as a trial. First, determine the full amortization period in order that the balloon periods (number of years) may be deducted from the beginning term to arrive at the remaining term K factors.

Step 2. Scanning the loan amortization schedule in payment book we find K 10.8% under 20 years.

Step 3. Subtract each balloon period, successively, from the original 20 years to get remaining terms.
20 − 6 = 14 years 20 − 7 = 13 years 20 − 8 = 12 years
20 − 9 = 11 years 20 − 10 = 10 years

Step 4. Find in payment book the K for each of the remaining terms at 9%.
K for 14 years = K 12.59%
13 years = K 13.08%
12 years = K 13.66%
11 years = K 14.36%
10 years = K 15.21%

Step 5. Divide the constant $7,247 by each K to arrive at loan balance.
Remaining Years:
Year 14. $7,247 ÷ 12.59% = $57,562 balance
Year 13. $7,247 ÷ 13.08% = $55,405 balance
Year 12. $7,247 ÷ 13.66% = $53,053 balance
Year 11. $7,247 ÷ 14.36% = $50,467 balance
Year 10. $7,247 ÷ 15.21% = $47,646 balance

Step 6. Next, project the first loan in same manner. However, now that the procedure has been established, the format may be condensed considerably, as follows (EOY = end of year and BOY = beginning of year):

K for each remaining term at 11.5% is:
19 years = K 12.98%
18 years = K 13.18%
17 years = K 13.42%
16 years = K 13.70%
15 years = K 14.02%

EOY	*BOY*	*K$*		*K%*		*Balance*
6	19	$61,000	÷	12.98	=	$469,954
7	18	61,000	÷	13.18	=	462,823
8	17	61,000	÷	13.42	=	454,546
9	16	61,000	÷	13.70	=	445,256
10	15	61,000	÷	14.02	=	435,093

Year	*First loan proceeds*	−	*Second loan balance*	=	*(Deficit) or margin of coverage*
6th	$30,046		$57,562		($27,516)
7th	$37,177		$55,405		($18,228)
8th	$45,454		$53,053		($ 7,599)
9th	$54,744		$50,467		$ 4,277
10th	$64,907		$47,646		$17,261

Clearly, the second loan balloon could not be covered in 6 years, but could be in the 9th year.

This introduces my own rule in timing balloon due dates: The balloon date should not fall due until the first loan proceeds cover not just the balloon balance, but *1.25 times* the balloon. There may be unforeseen fees or other premiums required, added to the balloon amount; again, in a tight money market, the first loan may not be refinanceable to its full original amount. Because of this unpredictability of future money market conditions, I advise you never to follow another popular fallacy fraught with danger: that of projecting inflation increases in the property value, with a resulting increased loan ratio, which appears to greatly hasten the date of feasible ballooning of the junior loan. Always assume refinanceability of the first at its original rate. Even that cannot be absolutely assured, as history has proved. Hence my 1.25 to 1 requirement.

I recommend that the timing of the payoff allow for 1.25 times the balloon amount.

Using the figures from the above example, and applying this 1.25 test, we can see that 10 years would be required, not 9.

> The 9th year balloon is $50,467 × 1.25 = $63,084; and first loan proceeds are only $54,744.
>
> But the 10th year balloon is $47,646 × 1.25 = $59,558, which is amply covered by the first loan balloon of $64,907.

To use the loan payment book as an analysis tool, sometimes you have to turn a question around. If the question posed is "How much will be paid off in 10 years?" you need to reverse it to "What will the balance be in 10 years?" If you are asked "How many years are required to reduce the loan by $64,907?" you must switch it around to "How many years are needed for the loan to be reduced to $435,093?" The reason for this is: the loan payment schedule is arranged on the basis of *remaining* term, not on years elapsed. Therefore, the elapsed period must always be subtracted from the current remaining term.

In the above example:

$500,000 − $64,907 = balance $435,093

$61,000 ÷ $64,907 = K factor 14.02%

Scanning the payment book, 14.02% appears at 10 years.

In conclusion, you can see that the laborious step-by-step procedure outlined may be greatly condensed in actual practice, once it is known. An even quicker method of computing balloon, using only factor percents, is explained on page 162.

Your loan payment book is a remarkably handy device for this calculation.

HOW LENDERS DETERMINE MAXIMUM LOAN AMOUNTS

Every lender recognizes—as every investor should—that net operating income (NOI) must serve two functions: (1) provide funds for paying off the loan, and (2) provide cash flow return on equity (ROE). If too much is spent on one, too little is available for the other.

A lender may require that net operating income be a set amount higher than loan payment.

The lender protects his position by requiring what is called debt coverage (DC); *i.e.,* the NOI must be a certain percentage higher than the loan payment. In effect, this says that the loan payment may be no more than a certain percent of the NOI. The most common debt coverage factors are 1¼ to 1 and 1½ to 1; in other words, the NOI must be 1¼ times or 1½ times the loan payment. Stating it the other way around, the loan payment may be either 80% or 66⅔% of NOI. (The reciprocal of 1.25 is 80%, the reciprocal of 1.50 is 66⅔%; see page 69.)

As an example of a quick estimate of a maximum attainable loan, assume an NOI of $1,800,000, loan terms of 12% for 25 years (K 12.64%) and a lender debt coverage policy of 1.25 to 1.

NOI $1,800,000 ÷ 1.25 ÷ .1264 = $1,139,240 loan (rounded)

Or, using the DC reciprocal, 80%:

NOI $1,800,000 × .80 ÷ .1264 = $1,139,240 loan

For visual speed, mentally structure the operation like this, following the A/B/C sequence and using our three column format:

		NOI	$1,800,000^{A}
Loan $1,139,240^{D}	K .1264^{C}	80%	$1,440,000^{B}

Still quicker, since the prevailing K factor will be known before encountering the exact NOI in various transactions, capitalize the K factor by 80% first, then divide any NOI amount by the quotient. Using the figures above:

.1264 ÷ 80% = 15.8%

In visual form, from right to left:

Loan $1,139,240^{C} = K 15.8^{B} ÷ NOI $1,800,000^{A}

For a quick estimate of market value, capitalize the $1,139,240 loan at the common mortgage ratio of 75% of price:

$1,139,240 ÷ .75 = estimated value $1,518,980.

RECIPROCALS

Reciprocals are found by dividing any number into 1. The reciprocal of a whole number must be a decimal; the reciprocal of a decimal must be a whole number. The value of reciprocals, in analysis, is that the same answer may be obtained by *multiplying* by one reciprocal or *dividing* by the other, and vice versa. To make quick mental calculations, pick the one which is easier to work with. For example, rather than capitalize a cash flow of $300,000 by 12.5%, it would be easier, especially in oral negotiation, to multiply by the reciprocal 8%.

$300,000 ÷ .125 = $2,400
$300,000 × .08 = $2,400

For a reverse example, $490,000 is more easily divided by 7 than multiplied by its reciprocal .142857.

$490,000 ÷ 7 = $70,000
$490,000 × .142857 = $70,000

The reciprocals of all numbers up to at least 12 should be memorized for speed calculations.

Reciprocal of	2 = 1/2 = .50	Conversely,	1/.50 = 2
	3 = 1/3 = .33 1/3		1/.333 = 3
	4 = 1/4 = .25		1/.25 = 4
	5 = 1/5 = .20		1/.20 = 5
	6 = 1/6 = .167		1/.167 = 6
	7 = 1/7 = .142857		1/.142857 = 7
	8 = 1/8 = .125		1/.125 = 8
	9 = 1/9 = .111		1/.111 = 9
	10 = 1/10 = .10		1/.10 = 10
	11 = 1/11 = .09		1/.09 = 11
	12 = 1/12 = .083		1/.083 = 12

8.

Wrap-Around Financing

The term "wrap-around" is the common parlance nickname for all-inclusive security devices (AISD), which may take the form of a mortgage (AIM), a trust deed (AITD), or land contract (AILC). It is a document that wraps around an existing loan or loans and is used by sellers and lenders. In the case of a sale, the seller may include the amount that would ordinarily be a second loan in a larger loan which includes the amount of the underlying first loan as well as the second. This device should not be used to circumvent a "due on sale" provision* in an existing first loan, without advice of counsel.

As preparation for the shortcut techniques that follow, you might find it helpful to first turn to Chapter 17, where the techniques will be explained in greater detail.

A valid application of the wrap-around (W/A) lies in its ability to afford the seller a larger return on his equity (what would ordinarily be a second loan) than the rate charged on the overall W/A, by virtue of the profit he realizes on the difference between the W/A rate and that of the underlying loan, as will be demonstrated below.

In every such transaction the questions posed to the vendor, vendee and broker are two—or, more precisely, either one of two. They arise out of the need to provide a return on the vendor's equity.

1. If the payment, and the interest rate included, on the total W/A are determined first, possibly by the vendee's offer, then the question to be answered is, what is the vendor's return, both in dollars and interest rate, on vendor's equity?

2. If, on the other hand, the vendor stipulates his required return in dollars, and the rate of interest to be included, then the question

*See page 62.

is, what must be the dollar payment, and interest rate included, on the total W/A?

The answers to these questions have been thought to require the use of very sophisticated mathematical formulae and complex calculations. But they don't. They can be reduced to the four simple arithmetic functions of add, subtract, multiply and divide, which we all understand. Some of us have less native flair for and have had less exposure to figures, it's true. But we can all reason, and all the procedures that follow—in fact, all of them throughout the text—are well within the ability of the reader to comprehend and use, with just enough interest and patience.

Example 1. Using interest only.

Sale	$100,000
Cash down	10,000
Balance (Wrap-around)	90,000 × 9% = $8,100
Underlying loan	60,000 × 8% = 4,800
Purchase money equity	30,000 × 11% = 3,300

Reconciliation

$60,000 × 9% = $5,400 − $4,800 = $600 override
$30,000 × 9% = $2,700 vs $3,300 = $600 proof

Override of wrap-around rate over underlying loan rate is added to the return on equity, raising the equity rate proportionately in the ratio of the underlying loan to equity. In the above example, the underlying loan ratio to equity is 2:1. Therefore the override of the 1% excess of wraparound rate is equal to 2% added to the equity rate.

Use of the wrap-around to equity ratio.

A faster and more flexible approach is to use the ratio of the total W/A to the equity, rather than the ratio of the underlying loan to equity. Thus in the above example, while the ratio of underlying loan to equity is 2:1, the W/A to equity ratio is 3:1. Using this ratio makes it possible to use the speed technique detailed in "Extended Applications of Mortgage-Equity Technique," page 136, and to adapt the technique to W/A calculation. Two yield problems are encountered:

- What is the yield rate on the vendors (seller's) equity when the W/A rate is known?
- What is the yield rate on the total W/A when the required equity yield rate is known?

Calculating the yield when the wrap-arond rate is greater than the underlying rate.

Remember that the underlying (existing) loan terms are always known, or there would not be a wrap-around. Now, let's demonstrate the step-by-step solution to both types of problems, using the figures from Example 1 above. First, for positive leverage (W/A rate is greater than the underlying rate).

Problem: Find the vendor's equity rate.

Step 1. Divide the W/A by the equity to get the ratio.

$90,000 ÷ $30,000 = ratio 3

Step 2. Subtract the underlying rate from the W/A rate to find the upper spread.*

9% − 8% = upper spread 1%

Step 3. Multiply Step 2 by Step 1 to find the lower spread.*

1% × 3 = lower spread 3%

Step 4. Add Step 3 to the underlying rate to arrive at answer, the equity return rate.

8% + 3% = equity rate 11%

Problem: Find the W/A rate.

Step 1. Divide the W/A by the equity to get the ratio.

$90,000 ÷ $30,000 = ratio 3

Step 2. Subtract the underlying rate from the equity rate to get the lower spread.

11% − 8% = lower spread 3%

Step 3. Divide Step 2 by Step 1 to find the upper spread.

3% ÷ 3 = upper spread 1%

Step 4. Add Step 3 to the underlying rate to arrive at answer, the W/A rate.

8% + 1% = W/A rate 9%

Using the same situation to demonstrate negative leverage.

Then, to demonstrate negative leverage (W/A rate is less than the underlying rate), we'll reverse the above example so that the W/A rate is 8% and the underlying rate is 9%.

Problem: Find the vendor's equity rate.

Step 1. Divide W/A by the equity to get the ratio.

$90,000 ÷ $30,000 = ratio 3

Step 2. Subtract the W/A rate from the underlying rate to get upper spread.

9% − 8% = upper spread (−1%)

Step 3. Multiply Step 2 by Step 1 to find the lower spread.

−1% × 3 = lower spread (−3%)

Step 4. Subtract Step 3 from the underlying rate to find answer, vendor's equity rate.

9% − 3% = equity rate 6%

---

*The upper spread is the difference between the W/A rate and the underlying loan rate: 9% − 8% = upper spread 1%. The lower spread is the difference between the equity rate and the underlying loan rate: 11% − 8% = lower spread 3%. The use of upper and lower spreads is dealt with in more detail in Chapter 17.

Problem: Find the W/A rate.

Step 1. Divide the W/A by the equity to get the ratio.
$90,000 ÷ $30,000 = ratio 3

Step 2. Subtract the equity rate from the underlying rate to find the lower spread.
9% − 6% = lower spread (−3%)

Step 3. Divide Step 2 by Step 1 to find the upper spread.
−3% ÷ 3 = upper spread −1%

Step 4. Subtract Step 3 from the underlying rate to find the answer, the W/A rate.
9% − 1% = W/A rate 8%

The technique works equally with interest only or with constants (K) including principal and interest. The only further step required when the rate is a K instead of pure interest is that of scanning a loan payment book to find the interest rate where the loan term is known, or the loan term where the interest rate is known.

The procedure is the same when the constant factor, rather than interest, is used.

Example 2. Using principal and interest (K) to find seller's equity yield rate.

In this example let's assume the underlying loan was originally 8% for 25 years. It's now 10 years old with 15 years remaining. The leverage is positive as in Example 1. A loan payment book shows that an 8% loan over 15 years has a constant of 11.47%. Still using 9% for the W/A rate, it is customary to write the W/A for the same term as the underlying, and the constant factor, per loan payment book for 9% over 15 years is 12.18%. The seller's yield can be found in either dollar figures, or just K factors.

In dollars:

W/A	$ 90,000	×	12.18%	=	Debt service	$ 10,962
Underlying	60,000	×	11.47%	=	Debt service	6,882
Equity	30,000	×	?	=	Debt service	4,080

Divide $4,080 by $30,000 = K 13.60%. Scanning the payment book under 15 years we find 13.60% between 10 7/8% and 11%; interpolate* that to 10.9% and round off to 11%—just as in Example 1, using interest only.

In factors:

100%	W/A	12.18%
67%	Underlying	11.47%
33%	Equity	?

Using our formula:

Step 1. 100% ÷ 33% = Ratio 3

*See page 167 for rate book interpolation procedure.

Step 2. 12.18% − 11.47% = Upper spread .71%
Step 3. .71% × 3 = Lower spread 2.13%
Step 4. 11.47% + 2.13% = Equity K 13.60%

In the payment book, K 13.6% at 15 years = interest 11%.

USE BY LENDER

These same principles apply to a loan refinance negotiation whereby a lender can realize a much higher effective return on the new funds advanced ($30,000 in above example) while increasing the underlying rate by only a fractional proportion of the true effective rate. Thus in the above example, while the lender increased his $60,000 loan to $90,000 at a new rate of 9%, he actually realizes a return of 10.9% on the $30,000 of new funds advanced.

An interesting variation arises when the cash flow available for total debt service is fully absorbed by the existing (underlying) loan, a phenomenon of increasing frequency. The approach here is to wrap-around the existing loan with total debt service on the wrap-around limited to that of the underlying loan, but with an increased wrap-around interest rate. This will then result in a larger wrap-around balloon balance at the time the underlying is fully paid out, as the next example shows, because when the interest yield exceeds available cash flow to pay it, the unpaid interest is added to the principal balance and compounded in each succeeding period!

Example 3. When interest rate exceeds constant cash flow.

Assume an original 7%/25 year loan of $300,000 payable at an annual constant of $25,470 ($300,000 × K .0849), with balance after 15 years (10 years remaining) of $182,712 ($25,470 ÷ K .1394). Wraparound mortgage is written for, say $215,500 at the same constant $25,470 but at a higher interest rate of 8.5%. Consequently, the constant factor is 11.82% ($25,470 ÷ $215,500 = .1182).

Arranged in order, the figures appear:

		K	*Interest*		
W/A	$ 215,500	.1182	.085	Constant	$25,470
Existing loan	$ 182,712	.1394	.07	Constant	$25,470
Seller's equity	$ 32,228	-0-	.1699*	NCF	-0-

Then* .085	−	.07	=	.015	Upper spread
.015	×	6.6588	=	.09988	Lower spread
.07	+	.09988	=	.1699	Return on equity

*See in Chapter 17, "Mortgage Equity Technique," how equity interest rate becomes .1699 by applying W/A-to-equity ratio (215,500 ÷ 32,228 = ratio 6.6588) to interest differential (W/A 8.5% less existing loan 7% equals spread of 1.5%) and adding the product to the existing loan rate.

Scanning the loan payment book under 8.5% interest, the factor 11.82% appears under a remaining life of 15 years. Therefore, at the end of 10 years, when the underlying is paid out, the wrap-around will have a balloon balance of $103,542 ($25,470 ÷ K 24.62% factor for 5 years remaining). Thus, even though the cash flow is insufficient to afford an income to the seller during the life of the underlying mortgage, the seller may still realize a deferred net benefit in form of the balloon, which could be discounted if desired to a present cash value.

INTERPOLATION

At this point a brief outline of the interpolation procedure will surely be helpful. It consists simply of finding the proportionate point between a higher and lower rate book factor of a particular factor which is your target. (See page 167 for more detailed explanation.)

How to interpolate between two rate figures in payment book.

Example. You wish to know the interest rate represented by a constant factor of 10.49% for 25 years. In your payment book under 25 years, you note that the K factor for 9¼% is 10.28 and for 9¾% is 10.70. Interpolating the intermediate interest rate is accomplished with the following formula:

Interest Rate	*%*	*Rate Book Difference*	*Target Rate Difference*
Lower rate	9.25	.1028	.1028
Higher rate	9.75	.1070	.1049
Difference	.50	.0042	.0021

Your target factor equals .0021 ÷ .0042 or one-half of the total .50% difference between the high and low interest rates, or .25%. Add this to the lower rate and your target factor turns out to indicate an interest rate of 9½% for 25 years. Stated as a formula, the figures above look like this:

$$\frac{.0050 \times .0021}{.0042} + .0925 = 9.50\%$$

You might find it handy to jot the above example and this arrangement of figures in your payment book for quick reference.

WRAP-AROUND CASE HISTORY

The accuracy of the four-step shortcut method of calculating yield demonstrated earlier in this chapter can be proved by subjecting the figures to an intensive, 10-year internal rate of return* projection.

*See Chapter 22 for complete discussion of internal rate of return method of yield measurement.

A lender is approached by the owner of a 4-year-old successful shopping center for refinancing. The existing loan rate is 8¼%; the current new loan rate is 12%. The borrower does not wish to pay the higher interest on his existing balance, but the lender must realize 12% on the amount of additional money advanced. The problem is solved by a wrap-around loan at an overall rate considerably less than current market, but which will yield 12% to the lender on the new money advanced. The facts are as follows:

Market value of the property	$ 10,000,000
Proposed wraparound loan (75%)	7,500,000
Terms: 30 years, 9% interest, K 9.66 annual payment, balloon due in 10 years	724,160
Existing loan balance	6,123,000
Terms: 24 years remaining, 8¼% interest. Annual payment K 9.58%	586,700
New money advanced (lender's equity in wrap-around)	1,377,000
Wrap-around annual payment	724,160
Existing loan payments	586,700
Cash flow on lender's equity (K 9.98% on $1,377,000 equity)	$ 137,460

Normally, computing the net yield to the lender would require extensive mathematical projections of interest and principal payments, balloon balances and use of present value tables applied to both payments and balance. This can all be averted by the simple use of the four-step shortcut, whereby the W/A to equity ratio is applied to the excess of W/A interest over the underlying interest rate to produce the equity interest rate.

To calculate net yield, let's see our 4-step shortcut in action.

I. Shortcut Method

Balance		*Rate %*
$7,500,000	W/A	9.00
6,123,000	Underlying	8.25
$1,377,000	Equity	?

Step 1. Divide W/A by equity to find ratio.

$7,500,000 ÷ $1,377,000 = 5.4466

Step 2. Subtract underlying rate from W/A rate to find upper spread.

9.00% − 8.25% = .75%

Step 3. Multiply Step 2 by Step 1 to find lower spread.

.75% × 5.4466 = 4.08495%

Step 4. Add Step 3 to underlying rate to find equity interest rate.

8.25% + 4.08495% = 12.34%

II. Long Method A: Using K Factors

First, calculate 10-year balloons on W/A, underlying and equity. (Note that the equity balloon is always the difference between the W/A total and the underlying loan.)

Step 1. W/A Loan: 30 years less 10 years = 20 years remaining. The K factor for 9% at 20 years is 10.8%.

Step 2. Underlying loan: 24 years less 10 years = 14 years remaining. The K factor for 8.24% for 14 years is 12.07%.

Step 3. Calculate the equity balloon:

W/A payment $724,160 ÷ 10.8% = balloon	$6,705,185
Underlying payment $586,700 ÷ 12.07% = balloon	4,860,812
Therefore the equity balloon is the difference	1,844,373

Step 4. Using the above information, we are now ready to calculate the IRR.

IRR Calculation

Try 12%:	Equity payment	137,460 ÷	.1722	(K, 10 years)	= $	798,258
	Balloon $	1,844,373 ×	.321973	(Table 4, 10)	=	593,838
				Total		$ 1,392,096
Try 13%:	Equity payment	137,460 ÷	.1792	(K, 10 years)	=	767,076
	Balloon $	1,844,373 ×	.294588	(Table 4, 10)	=	543,330
				Total		$ 1,310,406

The IRR will now be found by interpolation of the above trial rates:

Interpolation

Lower	.12		1,392,096		1,392,096	
Higher	.13		1,310,406	Target	1,377,000	
Difference	.01	÷	81,690	×	15,096	+ .12 = 12.2% IRR

II. Long Method B: Using the monthly tables instead of K factors

Using Table 5 monthly factors and Table 4 annual factor, the process is the same and the results are similar.

W/A payments	$ 724,160	÷	12 months =	$60,347
First loan payments	586,700	÷	12 months =	48,892
Equity payments	137,460	÷	12 months =	11,455

10 Year Balloon Computation

60,347 ×	111.144953	(Table 5, 9%, 240 months)	=	$ 6,707,264
48,892 ×	99.44652	(Table 5, 8¼%, 168 months)	=	4,862,139
11,455				1,845,125

IRR Calculation

At 12%	11,455 ×	69.700522 (Table 5, 120 months)	=	$798,419	
	1,845,125 ×	.321973 (Table 4, 10 years)	=	594,080	$1,392,499
At 13%	11,455 ×	66.964435 (Table 5, 120 months)	=	767,078	
	1,845,125 ×	.294588 (Table 4, 10 years)	=	543,552	$1,310,630

Interpolation

Lower .12		1,392,499		1,392,499	
Higher .13		1,310,630	Target	1,377,000	
Difference .01	÷	81,869	×	15,499	+ .12 = 12.2% IRR

You can see that the *annualized K factor* (12 monthly compoundings) applied to annual payments produces the same result and requires less time and effort.

Finally, note that with a rate of 12.2% and a K factor of 9.98%, which is *less* than the interest, the equity balloon after only 10 years, $1,845,125, will *exceed* the original equity of $1,377,000, an increase of *34%*. In the hands of professionals, this is not too rare, and sometimes serves the purpose of obtaining control of a property at a lesser cash flow than would be necessary to completely service a purchase money loan. However, when the full payment (cash flow) is less than the interest by *oversight,* the result can be damaging, even disastrous.

The minor difference between the 12.34% arrived at by the shortcut method and the 12.2% by the long computation, due to rounding, is more than offset by the speed and convenience afforded.

9.

Add-on Interest Loans

What is the effective (true) rate of interest on an installment loan when the interest for the entire period and on the entire original loan is deducted (discounted) in advance? The answer is best understood (not just memorized) by making two proportions and multiplying them together. The first fraction (proportion) represents the total dollar interest paid in advance (numerator) divided by the original loan amount (denominator). The second fraction represents the number of first year payments (numerator) divided by the average number of payments plus 1 (denominator).

Example: Loan amount \$5,000 at 10% interest discounted in advance, payable monthly over 3 years (36 months).

Step 1. Derive first fraction:
Numerator = Loan \$5,000 × Rate 10% × 3 years = \$1,500
Denominator = Original loan amount \$5,000
Numerator ÷ Denominator (\$1,500 ÷ \$5,000) = 30%

Step 2. Derive second fraction:
Numerator = Number of first year payments = 12
Denominator = *Average* number of payments + 1 = 18.5 (37 ÷ 2)
(Loan outstanding one-half the full term)
Numerator ÷ Denominator (12 ÷ 18.5) = .6487

Step 3. Multiply to derive effective rate:

First fraction	×	*Second fraction*	=	*Effective rate*
.30	×	.6487	=	19.46%

Visually, the formula appears as:

$$\frac{\text{Total interest paid}}{\text{Original loan amount}} \times \frac{\text{Number of first year payments}}{\frac{1}{2}\,(\text{Total monthly payments} + 1)} = \text{Effective rate}$$

$$\frac{\$5{,}000 \times 10\% \times 3}{\$5{,}000} \times \frac{12 \text{ months}}{\frac{1}{2}\,(37 \text{ months})} = \text{Effective rate}$$

$$\frac{\$1{,}500}{\$5{,}000} \times \frac{12}{18.5} = \text{Effective rate}$$

$$30\% \times .6487 = 19.56\%$$

In actual practice, having a fraction as the denominator of another fraction, as in $\frac{12}{\frac{1}{2}\,(37)}$ is considered poor arithmetic form. It is easily corrected by multiplying both numerator and denominator by 2 so that the original numerator is doubled without changing the value of the fraction.

Thus $\frac{12}{1/2\,(37)}$ or $\frac{12}{18.5}$ becomes $\frac{24}{37} = .6487$

So the original formula would appear:

$$\frac{\text{Total interest paid}}{\text{Original loan amount}} \times \frac{\text{Twice the first year payments}}{\text{Total monthly payments} + 1} = \text{Effective rate}$$

10.

Loan Points: Understanding and Using Them

It may be easy enough for a salesperson or broker to explain what a loan point is. It may be more difficult for him to analyze the impact of loan points on the effective interest rate of a loan. And what if he actually has to convert points to interest and interest to points? There are certain formulas which will enable the analyst to calculate exactly how loan points affect a loan.

A point is 1% of the face amount of the loan. Two points on a $100,000 loan, for instance, would represent 2%, or $2,000.

Loan points are lump sum interest payments made when the loan is granted.

This money, which is considered interest, is paid to the lender at the time the loan is granted. Obviously, interest paid in a lump sum at the beginning of a loan term must have the effect of raising the actual or effective interest cost over the stated or nominal rate. This has several implications.

Formerly, points were popular with buyers as a way to realize an extraordinary tax deduction in the year paid. Homebuyers still receive this benefit. However, effective January 1976, this tax advantage was qualified considerably by the Tax Reform Act of 1976. This act provides that, except for single-family homes used as the taxpayer's principal residence, loan points must be amortized over the term of the loan. If the loan were for, say 120 months, the points, prorated at 1/120th each month, would be deductible in the year of sale only to the extent of the number of months left in that year. Some tax advisors, therefore, are advocating using the largest possible number of points and closing in the earliest part of the tax year to gain the largest tax writeoff in the purchase year.

But it is no longer a full tax deduction, except for homebuyers.

Other advisors are seeking alternative deductions. One such alternative is to adjust the loan: to reduce the principal amount of purchase money mortgage carried back by the seller, and hence the price, and to raise the interest rate. Thus at the end of the loan term the same number of dollars would be paid, but a larger portion would be deductible as interest by the buyer. In such a case, of course, the seller would realize a lower capital gain but a higher ordinary taxability on the annual interest, to which he would have to agree.

So when points are involved, loan terms are often adjusted for maximum tax benefit.

The details of the tax advantages of adjusting the loan, rather than adding points, are beyond the scope of this chapter. Our focus here is the mechanical procedure for correct adjustment of the loan amount. However, the question of reducing the loan amount is closely related in principle to the question of points and interest rates. It is really the other side of the coin of the procedure we will be exploring in this chapter: how the relationship between points and effective interest rates can be calculated.

To calculate this adjustment, we must understand the relationship between points and effective interest rate.

A salesperson who encounters points must be able to answer the most common question that arises: "When points are quoted by a lender, what is the true rate of interest?" Or, conversely, "If it is desired to realize a higher effective rate of interest, how many points should be charged?"

The loan constant is such a vital ingredient in the loan point formulas that a quick review is in order. The constant, you will remember, is the annual payment of both principal and interest. The term can mean either the dollar payment, or the percent that this dollar value bears to the face amount of the loan. For example, in the loan payment book, a loan of $50,000 at 10% for 25 years is payable at $5,455 a year. This latter figure is the *dollar* constant. The constant *factor* is 10.91%, found by dividing $5,455 by $50,000.

The value of knowing the dollar constant and the constant factor is that the procedure can be reversed. The loan balance can be determined if only the annual dollar constant is known, by dividing (capitalizing) the dollar constant by the constant factor. For instance, in the case above, the constant factor for a 25-year loan at a 10% interest rate is always 10.91%. If you know that these are the terms and that the dollar constant is $5,455, you can simply divide $5,455 by 10.91% to arrive at a loan amount of $50,000.

One more point must be made before the formulas for calculating loan points and effective interest rates are given. The K factor of any loan *increases* as the interest rate rises and the payoff period shortens. It *decreases* as the interest rate diminishes and the payoff term lengthens. This is verifiable in the loan payment tables (see Appendix). It will become clear if you locate and identify each of the constant factors in the payment table as you follow the examples given.

Example I. What does a lender do when he wishes to realize an effective interest rate higher than the face amount on a loan? He simply divides the dollar constant of the face loan by the constant factor of the loan at the higher interest rate. This produces a smaller loan amount which is subtracted from the larger face-rate loan. The difference is collected from the borrower as points.

Calculating how many points to add to obtain a higher effective rate of interest.

For instance, suppose a lender is giving a loan of $100,000 at 9% for 25 years. The K factor with these terms is 10.08%. The dollar constant is $10,080. The lender wants to realize an actual interest rate of 9-1/8%. The K factor for a loan at 9-1/8% for 25 years is 10.18%. What percentage of points would the lender charge?

Procedure

Step 1. Divide the lower rate payment by the higher rate factor.

$$\frac{\$10{,}080}{.1018} = \$99{,}018$$

Round off to $99,000.

Step 2. Subtract the resulting lower loan amount from the original loan. The difference equals the dollar amount of points.

$$\begin{array}{r} \$100{,}000 \\ -\ \ 99{,}000 \\ \hline \$\ \ \ 1{,}000 \end{array} \text{ points}$$

Step 3. If the percentage of points is desired, divide the points by the original loan.

$$\frac{\$1{,}000}{\$100{,}000} = 1\% \text{ of the loan as loan points}$$

Example II. Sometimes the suggestion to add points originates with the borrower. For example, suppose a developer is building a tract of homes. By the time he is ready to take down his permanent loan commitment for the purchasers of the completed homes, the market interest rate has risen ¼%, from 8¾% to 9%. His competition will come on the market just a little earlier with their 8¾% commitment, which was firmed up before the rise. His problem is that he will be advertising a 9% loan, with higher monthly payments than his competition. Not a bright outlook for a fast close-out. However, understanding the function of points, he could approach his lender and suggest a "buy down" of the loan rate. In other words, he would offer the lender additional points in exchange for a reduction of the permanent loan interest rate from 9% to 8¾%.

Calculating points needed to create a lower effective interest rate.

How would he know how many points to add? Here is how the points would be calculated. Assume each loan as $60,000, payable monthly for 30 years. The face interest rate is 8¾, but an effective rate to the lender of 9% is desired. First, look up the K factors for a loan with these terms. K for 9% interest rate is 9.66%. K for 8¾% is 9.45%, with constant payments amounting annually to $5,670. Then follow the same procedure that was used with Example I.

Procedure

Step 1. Divide the lower rate annual payment by the higher rate factor to obtain the lower effective loan.

$$\frac{\$5{,}670}{.0966} = \$58{,}696$$

Step 2. Subtract the resulting lower loan from the original loan amount to arrive at the dollar amount of points.

$$\begin{array}{r} \$\ 60{,}000 \\ -\ \ 58{,}696 \\ \hline \$\ \ \ 1{,}304 \end{array} \text{ points}$$

Step 3. To express the points that will be charged as percentage, divide the dollar amount of the points by the original loan amount.

$$\frac{\$1{,}304}{\$60{,}000} = 2.17$$

Rounded off, this means that by paying 2 points on the loan, the effective interest rate will be raised to 9%. As a convenient generalization, in the interest rate range from 8 to 10% and the term range of 20 to 30 years, each 1 percentage point is approximately equivalent to 1/8% in interest; 2 percentage points to ¼% interest, and so on. The developer must, of course, either add the additional cost of points to the sale price or take it out of his profit or do both. But his ads will now bring in the traffic.

It is thus possible in this manner for one competitor to undersell another in the matter of loan terms. Still further, when you stop to realize the favorable capitalization effect for the seller of a lower loan constant, you see that a buyer might be interested to know whether the loan on a property he is acquiring may indeed have been "bought-down" by the seller, at his ultimate expense.

This could be reflected in one of three ways. To illustrate them, let us assume a $700,000, 30-year loan at 9¾% interest rate. It is brought down with points to an effective interest rate of 9¼%. The K factor with the higher interest rate is 10.31%; the constant payment is $72,170. At the lower interest rate, the K factor is 9.888%; the constant payment is $69,160. The difference in K factors is .43%; the difference in constant payments is $3,010.

In the first instance, the loan itself might be raised by capitalizing the original constant by the lower K factor. Dividing the original constant $72,170 by .0988, we arrive at a new loan amount of $730,466. Here the difference in annual loan payments of $3,010 is equal to an additional $30,400 in loan value, a ratio of 10.1215 to 1. (10.1215 is the reciprocal of the lower K factor of 9.88%.)

Second, the loan amount might be kept the same at $700,000 but the dollar constant might be reduced to $69,160. This would increase the cash flow available for servicing a larger secondary loan.

If that constant rate were 9%, the second loan would be raised 11.11 times $3,010 or $33,441. (Again, 11.11 is the reciprocal of 9%.)

Or third, in still another variation, the $3,010 might be added to return on equity (ROE) which at, say, 8% would justify a higher down payment by $37,625 ($3,010 × .125, the reciprocal of 8%). The seller would gain directly only by the excess of such price increase over the cost of the points. Psychologically, however, the more attractive rate is usually interpreted as reflecting a higher opinion of value on the part of the lending institution than is actually the case, thereby enticing the buyer to bid higher for the property.

Example III. When the points are known and the effective interest rate is sought, simply reverse the first procedure shown in Example I. For instance, a buyer obtains a 25-year loan of $100,000 at 9% interest. He must pay one point up front, which comes to $1,000. The buyer asks you what the effective interest rate is. You know that the dollar constant with these terms is $10,080.

Calculating the effective interest when amount of points is known.

Procedure

Step 1. Subtract the dollar amount of points from the original loan amount.

$$\begin{array}{r} \$100{,}000 \\ -\quad 1{,}000 \\ \hline \$\ 99{,}000 \end{array}$$

Step 2. Divide the dollar constant at the lower face interest rate by the reduced loan amount obtained in Step 1. This will produce a higher K factor.

$$\frac{\$10{,}080}{99{,}000} = .1018$$

Step 3. Scan the payment book under the remaining years of the loan term to find the interest rate under which the higher K factor appears. Under 25 years, the K factor .1018 appears under 9-1/8% interest rate. This is the effective interest rate when one point is paid.

Example IV. The problem here is to adjust a loan amount to provide the same amount of dollars paid, but more interest and less principal. Assume a price of $500,000 with the seller carrying a purchase money loan for $150,000 at a nominal interest rate of 8% for 12 years. It is now desired to raise the interest rate to 10% while lowering the loan amount so that the total dollar amount paid back by the buyer remains the same. The K factor for 8% for 12 years is 12.99%; the dollar constant is $19,485. The K factor for 10% for 12 years is 14.35%.

Adjusting the loan to raise interest but retain dollar payment.

Procedure

Step 1. Divide the original constant dollar payment by the higher rate K factor. The answer is the lower loan amount desired.

$$\frac{\$19{,}485}{.1435} = \$135{,}784$$

The adjusted loan amount is $135,784.

Step 2. Now for the proof. At 8% interest rate:

Loan amount	$ 150,000
× K factor	.1299
Dollar constant	$ 19,485
× 12 years	× 12
Total paid	$ 233,820

At 10% interest rate:

Loan amount	$ 135,784
× K factor	.1435
Dollar constant	$ 19,485
× 12 years	× 12
Total paid	$ 233,820

So the total dollars paid remain unchanged although the loan, and price, are lower. However, the interest vs. principal changes as follows:

	8%	*10%*
Total paid	$ 233,829	$ 233,820
Original loan	150,000	135,784
Interest paid	$ 83,820	$ 98,036

Now that the formulas have been demonstrated and proven using dollar amounts, we are ready for still further timesaving devices. That is, we can arrive at the same answers by using nothing more than our K factors and the loan payment tables.

A shortcut way of determining points needed to raise effective interest rate.

Look back to Example I in which we computed the amount of points necessary to achieve a higher effective interest rate. Instead of having to first multiply the loan by 10.08%, the K factor, to get the dollar constant $10,080 and then dividing $10,080 by the higher rate K of 10.18%, the whole computation can be done using only the K factor.

Procedure

Step 1. Divide the original K by the higher rate K.

$$\frac{.1008}{.1018} = 99\%$$

Step 2. Subtract the quotient from 100%. The difference equals the percentage of points.

$$\begin{array}{r} 100\% \\ -99\% \\ \hline 1\% \end{array}$$

Step 3. For the dollar amount of the point, multiply the loan amount by the points percentage.

$$\begin{array}{r} \$100{,}000 \\ \times \quad .01 \\ \hline \$ \quad 1{,}000 \end{array}$$

The dollar amount of one point is $1,000.

You can see now what was meant when we mentioned earlier that this lowering of the loan amount was the other side of the points coin. When points are calculated, the reduction of the loan is an indirect effect. The borrower is in essence receiving the whole loan and then giving back the amount of the points. In Example IV, the reduced loan amount is actual, in lieu of points. In some instances a combination will be indicated and may be effected easily by applying the same procedure.

In Example III, the figuring with the dollar amounts can also be eliminated. Again, we have a 25-year loan at 9% interest rate. The buyer is paying one point. The problem is to determine the effective interest rate. Instead of first multiplying the loan amount by the points percentage to get the dollar amount (remember that lenders quote points, not in dollars, but in percent), then subtracting the dollar points from the original loan, we use only the K factors.

Using K factors to determine effective interest rate.

Procedure

Step 1. Subtract the points percentage from 100%.

$$\begin{array}{r} 100\% \\ -1\% \\ \hline 99\% \end{array}$$

Step 2. Divide the original K by the difference found in Step 1. The quotient is the K for a higher interest rate.

$$\frac{.1008}{.99} = 10.18\%$$

Step 3. Scan the payment tables under the number of years of the loan to find the interest rate under which the higher K appear. In this case, 10.18% for 25 years appears under 9-1/8%. That is the effective rate.

Let's see how quickly and easily the problem in Example IV dissolves. There we wished to raise the interest rate without disturbing the dollar amount of the loan.

Procedure

An easy method for keeping dollar amount the same while raising effective interest rate.

Step 1. Find the factors in the payment tables for both interest rates for the number of years of the loan. Looking at the terms of Example IV, we find the K factor for a 12-year loan with an 8% interest rate is 12.99%. The K for a 12-year loan at 10% is 14.35%.

Step 2. Divide the lower rate K by the higher rate K. The quotient will be less than 100%.

$$\frac{.1299}{.1435} = .905226$$

Step 3. Multiply the original loan amount by the percentage found in Step 2. The answer will be the new and smaller amount of the loan.

$$\begin{array}{r} \$150{,}000 \\ \times .90522 \\ \hline \$135{,}784 \end{array}$$

Or lowering it.

Just for exercise, suppose the situation were reversed. Suppose the original loan were $135,784 at 10% and either the buyer or seller wanted a lower interest rate but the same dollar cash payments. Then we'd simply invert the K factors when dividing in Step 2. Multiplying in Step 3 would then raise the loan amount.

Step 2. $\frac{.1435}{.1299} = 1.1047$

Step 3. $\begin{array}{r} \$135{,}784 \\ \times 1.1047 \\ \hline \$150{,}000 \end{array}$

The total sum of payments would not be disturbed, as the following calculations show.

	Loan Amount	×	*K Factor*	×	*Years*	=	*Dollar Constant*
At 10%	$135,000	×	.1425	×	12	=	$233,820
At 8%	$150,000	×	.1299	×	12	=	$233,820

One last word remains to be said. If you find that the use of factors seems a little strange, try employing them in sample problems. With practice, they will become a natural part of your work.

11.

Leasing as a Financing Tool

A leasehold is created when one party owns a building (called leasehold or leasehold improvement) situated on land owned by another party, to whom the building owner is paying rent under a ground lease. When the ground lease expires, the land use, and *all improvements on it,* revert to the landowner.

At the end of a ground lease, your building becomes the property of the landowner.

Under our income tax system, large landowners are finding it increasingly difficult to sell their holdings outright, and consequently long term ground leases are becoming more prevalent.

Contrary to a rather popular fallacy, the investor should be aware that from the standpoint of real value, there is no substitute for ownership. Ownership is ownership: renting is renting. The fallacy goes that a long-term lease, say 99 years, is tantamount to ownership since the day of reckoning, when the land—and all improvements on it—will revert to the landowner, is so far off. To dispel this thinking as briefly as possible let's construct a time diagram of a $1,000,000 building on leased land for 99 years.

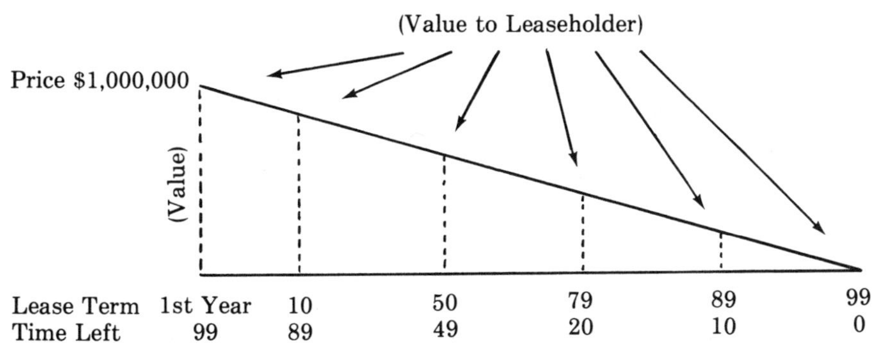

Beware: long term leasing is not the same as owning.

Without becoming lost in figures, it is obvious that each time the original leaseholder sells the improvement, the time left on the lease is shorter. Working backward, the buyer of the improvement in the 89th year has only 10 years to recoup his investment and show a profit. A prospective mortgage lender has only 10 years to be repaid. Such a position is clearly untenable. In the 79th year, the parties have only 20 years. Slightly less untenable. With a little reflection it becomes evident that somewhere along the line a leaseholder is going to be unable to sell or finance the property, and therefore be the one to lose it entirely to the ground owner. Which means that each successive purchaser to whom the original leaseholder offers the property must consider his own future plight, or the resistance on the part of the investor to whom he, in turn, must offer it. In addition, of course, there is the loss of opportunity to benefit by the market appreciation of the land.

There are admittedly certain income tax advantages in that all of the ground rent is tax deductible whereas the principal repayment portion of the loan for the land value is not deductible. Another theory is that the equity investment is reduced by the land value, thereby increasing the investor's leverage and requiring less cash. This is dubious in light of the ability—and the practice—of a seller to raise the price of the leasehold to the value of both land and building by manipulation of capitalization factors (see Chapter 16 on leverage).

Add to present operating expenses a reserve fund for replacement of the building.

The present chapter deals with the mechanics of providing for the building owner's ultimate loss of the leasehold improvement. In essence, we do this by adding to the operating expenses a reserve fund for replacement of the building at the end of the lease.

To see how this process works, let's assume an office building on a 60-year ground lease, with a gross annual income of $1,762,000 and net operating income, after all expenses and ground rental totaling $837,445, of $924,555. Assume further that the negotiated cap rate, based on a normal fee simple transaction, is 9.08%.

Since the building improvement (called the leasehold) will revert to the ground lessor in 60 years, the leaseholder must include in his calculations an amortization (or recapture) factor. Rather than divide the building value by 60 years and subtract 1/60th each year, the amortization may be accomplished with less impact on the cash flow by use of a sinking fund factor found in Table 3 under a reasonable interest rate of, say, 6%. In this example, the Table 3 factor at 6% for 60 years is .001876, or .19% rounded.

Ordinarily, the value of the leasehold would be multiplied by this factor and the dollar reserve added to expenses. However, at this stage in the analysis the building value has not yet been determined. This is accomplished by adding the sinking fund factor to the normal cap rate, resulting in an adjusted cap rate (9.08% + .19% = 9.27%). Increasing the cap rate, of course, has the effect of lowering the capitalized value, just as reducing the cap rate raises the value.

STANDARD INVESTMENT ANALYSIS FORM

Folio__________

Type__________ Pkg.______ Unf.________ Furn.__________ Listed Price $__________

Address__________ Est. Sq. Ft.__________ Cash $__________

Lot Size__________ Sq. Ft.__________ Zone__________ Age__________ Equity $__________

INDICATED PRICE AND FINANCING

		$	Sq. Ft.
	ANNUAL GROSS RENTAL	$	
	TENANT CONTRIBUTIONS	$	
100% **PRICE** $________ ←(X)→ AGM	**ANNUAL GROSS INCOME**	$	100%
	EXPENSES		
	Taxes $		
	Insurance		
	Utilities		
	Trash		
	Pool		
	Gardening		
	Elevator		
	Res Mgr.		
	Prop. Mgt.		
	CAM		
	HVAC		
	Cleaning		
	Leasing Fees		
	Alterations		
	Rep./Maint.		
	Vacancy		
	TOTAL EXPENSES	$	
(______% to Price) CAP RATE ←→	**NET OPERATING INCOME (NOI)**	$	

LOANS:

CLASS	AMOUNT	ANNUAL CONSTANT (K)		INTEREST		PRINCIPAL
	$	%	$	%	$	$

TOTAL $________ (______%) ←→	**ANNUAL CONSTANT**	$
(______% to Cash) ROE ←→	**NET CASH FLOW**	$
	Plus EQUITY GAIN	$
CASH $________ (______% to Cash) YOE ←→	**NET YIELD**	$

TAX SHELTER ANALYSIS — First Year

DEPRECIATION BASIS: **NET YIELD (Forward)** .... $

Total Cost .... $__________

Less Land (______%) . $__________

Balance $__________

Furnishings .... $__________

Building Improvements $__________

YEARS	METHOD	%	
			$
			$

LESS TOTAL DEPRECIATION $

TAXABLE INCOME (LOSS) $

TAX SAVINGS @______% $

RECAP

	1ST YEAR	
	AMOUNT	% TO CASH
NET CASH FLOW		
TAX SAVINGS OR (Exp.)		
TOTAL CASH FLOW		
EQUITY GAIN		
TOTAL YIELD		

NOTES:

ABBREVIATIONS USED IN THIS TEXT

AGM	annual gross multiplier
AILC	all-inclusive land contract
AIM	all-inclusive mortgage
AISD	all-inclusive security device
ANPV	annualized net present value
ATCF	after-tax cash flow
ATROE	after-tax return on equity
ATY	after-tax yield
ATYOE	after-tax yield on equity
BOMA	Building Owners and Managers Association
BOY	beginning of year
Cap	capitalization
CAM	common area maintenance
CPI	Consumer Price Index
DC	debt coverage
DSC	debt service coverage
EOY	end of year
FMRR	financial management rate of return
GLA	gross leaseable area
I	income (cash flow)
IRR	internal rate of return
K	constant
K%	constant rate (percentage)
K$	constant dollar payment
M-E	mortgage-equity
MEP	mechanical, engineering, plumbing
N	net
NCF	net cash flow
NN	double net
NNN	triple net
NOI	net operating income
NPV	net present value
PV	present value
R	rate of yield
REA	reciprocal easement agreement
ROE	return on equity
ROI	return on investment
TD	trust deed
TIM	taxes, insurance, maintenance
V	value
W/A	wrap-around
YOE	yield on equity

Calculating the amount of reserve needed.

First, the normal net operating income is capitalized by the adjusted cap rate to arrive at the leasehold value. Then, the value is multiplied by the sinking fund factor to determine the dollar amortization reserve. Thus, NOI $924,555 ÷ adjusted cap rate 9.27% = leasehold value $9,973,625. (This would ordinarily be rounded to $9,973,500 or even $9,975,000 in practical business, but for example purposes the actual amount will be retained for accuracy.) Then, the value $9,973,625 × the sinking fund .19% = $18,950, amortization reserve. The total expenses now read $856,395 ($837,445 + $18,950) and the NOI becomes $905,605 gross rent ($1,762,000 − $856,395).

Note now that capitalizing this adjusted NOI by the original, or normal, cap rate will produce the same value, as did capitalizing the normal NOI by the adjusted cap rate. Stated differently, dividing the smaller profit by the larger factor brings the same result as dividing the larger profit by the smaller factor. So,

$924,555 ÷ 9.27% = $9,973,625, and
$905,605 ÷ 9.08% = $9,973,625.

In this way, the investor preserves the required normal cap rate of 9.08% after providing for leasehold amortization. Reverting to the original cap rate of 9.08% offers the added advantage that the mortgage and equity components, together with their respective debt service (mortgage) and net cash flow (equity), may be calculated quickly, as in the Standard Analysis Form, page 24.

To summarize step-by-step:

Step 1. Normal cap rate 9.08% plus Table 3 factor .19% = adjusted cap rate 9.27%.

Step 2. Normal NOI $924,555 ÷ 9.27% = value $9,973,625.

Step 3. Value $9,973,625 × Table 3 factor .19% = 9.27% = amortization reserve $18,950.

Step 4. Normal operating expenses $837,445 plus reserve $18,950 = adjusted expenses $856,395.

Step 5. Gross income $1,762,000 less $856,395 = adjusted NOI $905,605.

Step 6. $905,605 ÷ normal cap rate 9.08% = value $9,973,625.

Now, using the mortgage-equity technique, we can proceed to the next phase, called cash distribution, which uses the above factors to break down the total value and ROE into dollar amounts of loan(s), equity, loan payments and net cash flow as they would normally appear on our analysis worksheet.

Example (Now capital figures are rounded into 00's)

Step 1. Price $9,973,600 × .75% = loan amount $7,480,200

Step 2. Price $9,973,600 × .25% = equity amount $2,493,400

Step 3. Loan $7,480,200 × K .1044 = $780,935

Step 4. Equity $2,493,400 × ROE .05% = net cash flow $124,670

Assembled into our standard format the process appears as follows, starting with dividing, from right to left, the NOI \$905,605 by .0908 to arrive at the market value \$9,973,600. Then multiply the price by the mortgage ratio, 75%, to get the mortgage dollar amount, \$7,480,200. This amount in turn is multiplied by the K factor, 10.44% to find the debt service \$780,935, which subtracted from the NOI \$905,605 leaves the NCF \$124,670, which is 5% of the equity \$2,493,400 (\$124,670 ÷ \$2,493,400 = 5%). Here's how it looks, with letters indicating the sequence of operation.

100%	\$ 9,973,600[C]	Cap	9.08[B]	\$ 905,605[A]
75%[D]	7,480,200[E]	K	10.44[F]	780,935[G]
25%	\$ 2,493,400[J]	ROI	5.00[I]	\$ 124,670[H]

USE OF TAX ASSESSOR METHOD TO VALUE NET IMPROVEMENT

We are all reasonably familiar with the way property tax calculation works. The assessor is required by local law to assess the property, for tax purposes, at a certain percentage of its real market value. Then the tax rate, also set by law, is applied to that assessed value. So, for example, in an area where the tax rate is \$12 per \$100 of assessed value, and the assessment rate is 25% of market value, then the tax on a \$100,000 property would be \$3,000.

\$100,000 market value × 25% assessment rate = \$25,000 assessed value

\$25,000 × 12% tax rate = \$3,000 property tax.

However, the calculation need not proceed just this way. Instead of multiplying a *portion* of the market value by the *full* tax rate, we get the same result if we multiply the *full* market value by a *portion* of the tax rate.

Just as \$25,000 [one fourth of \$100,000] × 12% = \$3,000
So \$100,000 × 3% [one fourth of 12%] = \$3,000

Tax assessor uses this principle to fix market value for a building still under construction.

When the building is new or even under construction, actual market value is not yet known, so the assessor must use an adjusted capitalization factor to ascertain the market value of the building. To do this, he uses the same simple principle used in amortizing a leasehold improvement above. Here's the step by step procedure:

Step 1. Deduct all operating expenses, *except* property tax, to arrive at a pre-tax net operating income.

Step 2. Next, add the fraction of the tax rate (3% above) to the normal cap rate for the type of property involved, which we'll pretend is 8%.

Step 3. Then divide the pre-tax NOI by the compound adjusted cap rate, 11% (8% + 3%), which will determine the fair market value of the property.

Step 4. Now multiply the market value by the tax rate *fraction* (3%) to get the tax dollar amount.

Step 5. For proof, deduct the tax amount from the pre-tax NOI, then divide the after-tax NOI by the normal tax rate (8%) to arrive at the same market value as above.

Different parts of the country have various combinations of assessed valuation and tax rates, but the process works the same. Suppose an area assessed property at 35%, and the tax rate were $11 per $100, or 11%. Then, 35% × 11% = 3.85% assessor's ajustment factor. Or, an assessed valuation of 30%, and tax rate of $13 per $100, or 13%. Then, 30% × 13% = 3.9% assessor's adjustment factor.

In California, after the passage of the landmark Proposition 13, property taxes are limited by law to a flat 1% of market value. Under this circumstance, the 1% would be added to the normal cap rate, the pre-tax NOI divided by the compounded rate, and the resulting market value would be multiplied by the 1% to get the dollar tax.

Just for practice, suppose the following case:

Step 1.	Annual scheduled gross	$ 100,000
	Expenses before taxes	25,000
	Pre-tax NOI	$ 75,000
Step 2.	Assessed valuation percent of market value	28%
	Local tax rate per $100 of assessed valuation	$14
	Or, $14 × 28% = assessor's adjustment factor	3.92%
	Add normal cap rate	8.50%
	Adjusted cap rate	12.42%

Step 3.	(Pre-tax NOI) $75,000 / (Adjusted cap rate) .1242	= Market value	$ 603,865
Step 4.	$603,865 × .0392	= Property tax	$ 23,672
Step 5.	Proof	Pre-tax NOI	$ 75,000
		Less tax	23,672
		Normal NOI	$ 51,328
	(Normal NOI) $51,328 / (Normal cap rate) .085	= Market value	$ 603,865

Another practical aspect of understanding the technique of fractionalizing the tax rate by the proportion of assessed valuation to market value, as above, is that the dollar tax amount may be divided (capitalized) by the fractioned rate to find the market value on the tax assessor's books.

For example, in the immediately preceding case, if it were known that the taxes were \$23,672, the market value, at least in the assessor's opinion when he last appraised the property, may be found very quickly by dividing (capitalizing) \$23,672 by .0392 (\$23,672 ÷ .0392 = \$603,865). In California, since Proposition 13, the market value can be figured visually as 100 times the tax, since the tax is 1% of the value. More realistically, since bonds and assessments may be included in property tax, the figure of 1.25% is used instead of the flat 1%. Therefore multiply the dollar tax by 80, since 80 is the reciprocal of 1.25%, or divide the dollar tax by 1.25%.

12.

Leasehold Estate: How to Compute and Discount

When a property is leased by a tenant (lessee) at a fixed rental which is below the present realizable market rate, the fixed lease rental is called the contract rent or contract rate, and the market rate is called the economic rent or economic rate. When the economic rent is higher than the contract rent—i.e. when the lessee could sublease the premises at a higher rent than the current lease rental—the potential excess is called a leasehold estate. The lessee, for the balance of the lease term, has two alternate leasehold estate opportunities:

When you sublease a property for higher rent than your original lease, you have created a leasehold estate.

1. He can sublease the property at the higher economic rent, in which case he becomes a sublessor, and enjoy the benefits of the net difference in income.
2. He can capitalize the differential amount of rent into a cash capital asset.

As a matter of fact, he could compromise, and take part of the rental differential as net income over his contract rent, and capitalize the balance. This capitalization of excess of economic over contract rent is called "key money" or, in marketplace parlance, "selling the key."

Let's take an example. A lessee signed a lease 5 years ago, when rents were low. The 15-year contract rent under the lease is $10,000 per month. The currently prevailing rental rates make the economic rent for the property $15,000 per month. The lessee's banker (or broker) informs him that money is currently worth 10%. The lessee sublets the property (he now becomes a sublessor) to another tenant (who becomes the sublessee) for $15,000 per month for the 10 years remaining on the lease.

You can receive excess income each month, or "sell the key" in one lump sum.

Now the sublessor has a choice. He can enjoy a net leasehold estate in the form of $5,000 per month, $60,000 per year, for the remaining 10 years of his lease. Or he can "sell the key." To do so he will capitalize (divide) the annual $60,000 by the constant factor for 10% at 10 years, which is 15.86%, to find the present value of the future stream of income, $378,310 ($60,000 ÷ .1586 = $378,310). So the sublessor sells the key to the sublessee for the lump sum of $378,310 and the sublessee takes over the lease at the same contract rent of $10,000.

Or some combination of the two.

Suppose the sublessee did not have $378,310 in cash. The parties could get together and agree on a compromise combination of some higher rent payments and some key money.

For example, if the sublessee had $151,324 in cash, then he could "buy down" the excess rent by the amount of which $151,324 is the present value at 10% for 10 years. This may appear to be very "mathematical" but in reality it's only a reverse switch on the capitalization process by which we obtained the $378,310. We got that by dividing the excess rental by the constant factor.

We can do that backward, can't we, and *multiply* the *present value quotient* by the constant?

If $60,000 ÷ .1586 = $378,310
then $378,310 × .1586 = $60,000

Since that's true, and the whole present value figure can be multiplied by the constant factor to get the annual excess rent, then why can't *any part of* the present value be multiplied by the same constant factor to get *a part* of the annual excess rent? Let's see. If we subtract the $151,324 that's available in cash from the total present value of $378,310, the difference is $226,986:

Total present value	$ 378,310
Less cash available	151,324
Net difference	$ 226,986

In other words, the $151,324 is the key money that represents a certain amount of annual rent. How much? *Multiply* it by the constant factor, 15.86%.

Step 1. $151,324 × .1586 = $24,000 rental per year (round)
Step 2. Subtract

If the total annual excess rental is	$60,000
And cash of $151,324 is the present value of	24,000
Then the additional rent to be paid each month over the contract rent, every year, is	$36,000
Divided by 12 is, monthly,	$ 3,000

This is such a valuable and timely process, it is worth another approach for practice.

Same example. Suppose the sublessee wished to pay only $2,700 per month as excess rent (the amount is not important; the formula is) and settle the difference of $3,300 by key money. The question for us is, how *much* key money?

First, always convert monthly payments, whether rental or loan payments, or whatever, to annual payment. So, $2,700 per month equals $32,400 per year.

Step 1. Subtract

If the total annual excess rent is	$60,000,
And sublessee wishes to pay only	32,400,
Then the net difference to be settled by key money per year is	$27,000

Step 2. Divide (capitalize)

$27,600 ÷ .1586 = present value $174,023 key money

The mathematical key is superbly simple, and important to understand.

There are two important lessons here. First, note the versatility inherent in all multiplication and division problems: the division process can be reversed by multiplication, and the multiplication process can be reversed by division, using the same numbers.

The second is that, in the above example, the key money (present value of future payments) is treated *exactly* the same as the principal balance of a loan, and the rental payments treated *exactly* the same as loan payments. Thus, the present value in either case is *multiplied* by the appropriate constant factor to determine the amount of dollar payments (annually), and in reverse, the dollar payments of either nature are *divided* by the constant factor to determine the present value.

For more drill on this simple but highly strategic fundamental function, see the "2 × 3 = 6" example which is expanded upon in page 115.

13.

Sale Leaseback: Setting the Rent

A sale leaseback (or purchase leaseback; the terms are identical) differs from an ordinary purchase of land in this way: Instead of the buyer improving the ordinary purchase of land with a building to be leased to a user, in a sale-leaseback the ultimate user first develops his own property, sells it to an investor and leases it back simultaneously. From the viewpoint of the seller-lessee the transaction is a *sale*-leaseback; from the viewpoint of the buyer-lessor it is a *purchase*-leaseback.

The most simplistic method of calculating the rent over the lease term is to treat the investment as a loan and amortize it over the term using monthly Table 6 (Installment to Amortize $1) for the monthly rent, or using the loan payment book constant (K) factor for the annualized rent.

Calculating the leaseback rent by amortizing the full investment over term.

Example. A supermarket buys land at $300,000, improves it with a $1,200,000 building, and sells the $1,500,000 package to an investor, leasing it back for 25 years. Money is currently worth 12%.

Procedure A: Using monthly Table 6 for monthly rent
Value $1,500,000 × Table 6, 300 months .010532 =
monthly rent $15,798 × 12 = year's rent $189,576

Procedure B: Using annualized loan constant (K)
Value $1,500,000 × K .1264 = year's rent $189,600

The difference of $24 year ($189,600 vs. $189,576), due to rounding, is inconsequential.

A more conservative approach, from the lessee's standpoint, would be to recognize that the land will revert to the lessor at the end of the lease term, and therefore only the building value should be amortized and interest paid only on the land.

Example: Using monthly Table 6 for monthly rent:

Building	$1,200,000 × Table 6, 300 months .010532 =	building rent	$ 12,638
Land	$300,000 × 1% (12% ÷ 12 months) =	land rent	3,000
		Total monthly rent	$ 15,638
		Yearly rent	$ 187,656

The latter case is calculated exactly like a loan which is to be partially amortized over the term with a balloon payable at the end.

Alternatively, amortizing only the building value.

Still more conservatively, and still from the lessee's viewpoint, it could be held that the building will have some salvage value at the end of 25 years, and that the land will increase in value over the same term. Therefore, only the portion of the building which will deplete in value should be amortized, with interest only on the residual values:

At end of 25 years, building salvage value, say,	$200,000
At end of 25 years, land value	400,000
Total reversion to lessor	$600,000

Original value $1,500,000 − $600,000 = amount to be amortized $900,000.

Therefore: Using monthly Table 6 for monthly rent:

$900,000 × Table 6, 300 months .010532 =	$ 9,479
$600,000 × 1% (12% ÷ 12 months) =	6,000
Total monthly rent	$ 15,479
Total yearly rent	$185,748

You can see that the differential is slight, amounting to the spread between the total constant and the interest rate only. With high current interest rates such as the 12% used here, the difference is only .000532 per month (K .010532 vs. interest .01).

It is also demonstrated that mathematical formulae and tables only reflect and serve human judgment, and are not intended as replacements.

14.

Fragmenting Real Estate Investments

SEPARATING LAND FROM IMPROVEMENT

Fragmenting, sometimes called fractioning, means separating the elements of land and building. The building owner leases the land back, whereupon the building becomes a leasehold, or leasehold improvement. Often, it is the lender of the building mortgage that buys the land and leases it back to the leasehold owner.

Fragmenting works to best advantage in times when mortgage repayment constants are lower than the overall cap rate, producing positive leverage. In current times of negative leverage, when loan repayment rates exceed the cap rate, it is of value primarily to developers, since their return on cost, before market value markup, is as high as, or higher than, permanent loan constant rates.

Assume a shopping center with the following income and costs:

Costs	Land	$ 2,000,000
	Building	8,000,000
	Total cost	10,000,000
	Net operating income	$ 1,200,000

If the developer's cap rate is 12% on his cost and the retail market value, when sold as a going center, is 10%, the values appear as:

Developer's cost: NOI $1,200,000 ÷ Cap rate .12 = Cost value $10,000,000

Retail fair market value: NOI $1,200,000 ÷ Cap rate .10 = Retail value $12,000,000

As a general observation, capitalized economic value will usually be 14% to 20% higher than cost.

OTHER FINANCING VARIATIONS

Let's assume some market conditions as a foundation for speculating on several methods of financing the project. Assume that prevailing mortgage terms for a quality development are:

1. 75% of land and building market value at 10¼%, 30 years (K 10.6%).
2. 75% of unsubordinated land leasehold improvement at 10-5/8, 32 years (K 11%) with 25 year balloon.
3. 90% of land value at 10%, 40 years with 25 year balloon (K 10.2%).
4. Land lease rates range between 9% and 11%. We shall use 10%.

Example 1. Straight sale with 75% first mortgage

Buyer's return on equity

Price	$ 12,000,000	Cap	10.00%	NOI	$ 1,200,000
75% loan	9,000,000	K	10.62%	Constant	955,800
Equity	3,000,000	ROE	8.14%	NCF	244,200

Developer's return on cost equity

Cost	$ 10,000,000	Cap	12.00%	NOI	$ 1,200,000
75% loan on market value	9,000,000	K	10.62%	Constant	955,800
Cost equity	1,000,000	ROE	24.40%	NCF	244,200

Example 2. Land sold off, and leased back by the developer—unsubordinated.

Sometimes the developer creates a land-holding entity and owns both land and improvements. Both the land fee and the leasehold improvement are separately mortgaged.

Total cost	$ 10,000,000	Cost cap 12.0%	NOI	$ 1,200,000
Land	2,000,000	Leased at 10.0% a year	Ground rent	200,000
Leasehold	8,000,000	Adjusted cap 12.5%	Adjusted NOI	1,000,000

The leasehold mortgage is repayable at K 11%. The land mortgage is repayable at K 10.2%. The leasehold is capitalized at 10.5%. The returns appear as follows:

The developer's leasehold estate is:

				NOI $	1,200,000
				Ground rent	200,000
Leasehold Value $	9,500,000	Cap	10.5%	Adjusted NOI	1,000,000
75% loan	7,100,000	K	11.0%	Constant	781,000
Equity	2,400,000	ROE	9.1%	NCF	219,000

The mortgage rate (10-5/8%) is higher because the land is not subordinated to the loan so that in case of foreclosure, the lender could reposses only the improvement, not the land. Further, the lender would then be obligated to pay the ground rent.

The developer's return on the leasehold cost is:

Improvement cost $	8,000,000	Cost cap rate	12.5%	Adjusted NOI $	1,000,000
Leasehold loan	7,100,000	K	11.0%	Constant	781,000
Developer's cost equity	900,000	ROE	24.3%	NCF	219,000

The developer's land position is:

Land cost $	2,000,000			10% rental income $	200,000
Land loan 90%	1,800,000	K	10.2%	Constant	183,600
Land equity	200,000	ROE	8.2%	NCF	16,400

Developer's total return on both equities

Leasehold equity $	900,000	ROE	24.3%	NCF $	219,000
Land equity	200,000	ROE	8.2%	NCF	16,400
Total equity	1,100,000	ROE	21.4%	NCF	235,400

Example 3. Sale leaseback, with land subordinated to leasehold loan.

When the landowner is the leasehold developer, subordination is no problem. If the landowner is a different party, there must be a special inducement to take the risk of losing the land to the lender in event of leasehold foreclosure. This inducement may be higher rent, or outside additional collateral, or minimal risk if the lessee is a rated national corporation where the risk of bankruptcy is almost nil. Subordination may also be the only way a landowner can attract a developer in order to turn tax payment outlay into rental income.

The chief impact of land subordination on financing leverage stems from the lender's willingness to lend on the total land and building value even though the borrower owns only the leasehold. Too, the developer's equity contribution is sharply reduced.

Using the same above example, the equity and return are:

Total cost	$ 10,000,000	Cap	12.0%	NOI	$ 1,200,000
Land cost	2,000,000	Leased at	10.0%	Gross rent	2,000,000
Leasehold cost	8,000,000	Adjusted cap	12.5%	Adjusted NOI	1,000,000
75% loan total value	7,500,000	K	11.0%	Constant	825,000
Leasehold cost equity	500,000	ROE	35.0%	NCF	175,000

Leasehold market value capitalized at 10.5% for resale:

				NOI	$ 1,200,000
				Gross rent	200,000
Leasehold fair market value	$ 9,500,000	Cap	10.5%	Adjusted NOI	1,000,000
Loan 75% of total	7,500,000	K	10.6%	Constant	795,000
Leasehold equity	2,000,000	ROE	10.25%		205,000

Note that the mortgage rate is at normal fee loan rate, rather than the higher unsubordinated land rate.

So the developer either has 35% return on his net cost equity, or a profit of $1,500,00 ($2,000,000 market equity less $500,000 cost equity).

Example 4. Joint venture by sale of developer's total cost equity, which becomes a minor percent of resale market value equity.

In this example, the developer's entire cost equity—100%—is sold as a 33⅓% interest in projected market value when the net operating income is capitalized at 10%.

Market value	$ 12,000,000	Market value cap	10.0%	NOI	$ 1,200,000
75% loan	9,000,000	K	10.6%	Constant	954,000
Market value equity	3,000,000	ROE	8.2%	NCF	246,000
Cost	$ 10,000,000	Cap cost	12.0%	NOI	$ 1,200,000
Loan on market value	9,000,000	K	10.6%	Constant	954,000
Cost equity	1,000,000	ROE	24.6%	NCF	246,000

You can see that the developer's total cost equity ($1,000,000) is equal to one third of the capitalized market value equity of $3,000,000. These percentages between joint venturers vary anywhere from 25%/75% to 50%/50%.

Fragmenting is a flexible financing tool, with endless variations.

The possibilities of further fragmenting are limitless when the money market is favorable; that is, when loan repayment is less than the cash flow before financing.

Fragmenting can extend to leases as well, with loans made against leases, subleases, sub-subleases, etc. You are encouraged to use your imagination to devise methods of separating every element of investment which can be sold or financed individually.

Remember, the seller of property is still the most reasonable lender.

SEPARATING REALTY FROM BUSINESS

Another form of fragmenting is the allocation of values between a going business, and the real estate premises it occupies, when both are owned by the same person. Frequently, the owner attempts to sell both together as a package.

The objection to this is twofold: first, rarely does a buyer of a business have the capital to buy real estate at the same time; even rarer is the real estate investor who wishes to acquire or operate the business. Second, the consolidation obscures the individual value of each component, precluding accurate evaluation. The solution is to assume that each will be sold to a separate party, with the business operator leasing the premises from the real estate investor.

Fragmenting also applies to separation of real estate and business enterprises.

Suppose a rather commonplace example of a going restaurant offered for sale, including the premises it occupies, for a price of $2,550,000 total. The restaurant does a volume of $2,400,000 with a net profit of 10% of sales, or $240,000 a year.

In addition to a physical appraisal of the real estate, its economics will depend on the net rental it can generate from its tenant, which is capitalized at a prevailing cap rate to arrive at market value. Restaurants classically can pay 6% of sales as rental for premises; in this example that would be $144,000 year ($2,400,000 × .06 = $144,000). (Businesses generally can pay anything from 6% to 10% for rent.)

Real estate leased to a low-range credit operation such as a restaurant must earn 12% net income. (The sounder the credit of the tenant, the lower the required cap rate would be.) Investors in a *business,* as distinct from real estate, generally require a net return of 20% to 25% on their invested capital (not to be confused with net profit on sales). Therefore, a shortcut estimate of the purchase price of a business is 4 times (25%) to 5 times (20%) the net profit in sales.

On the above facts, then, the original owner, whom we'll call A, sells the real estate to investor, B, for a price calculated by capitalizing the 6% of sales, $144,000, by the required real estate investment net income of 12%, or $1,200,000 ($144,000 ÷ .12 = $1,200,000). A third party, C, purchases the restaurant business from A at a price calculated at 4 times (25% return) the net profit on sales of $240,000, or $960,000 (4 × $240,000).

So that A finally realized:

Sale of business	$ 960,000
Sale of real estate	$ 1,200,000
Total sale value	$ 2,160,000

B ends up with leased property:

Value $ 1,200,000 Cap 12% NOI $ 144,000

C owns a restaurant operation:

Value $ 960,000 Net profit 25% NOI $ 240,000

Some interesting variations can arise. For one, there could be mortgages involved. Suppose A's property is encumbered with a $400,000 mortgage payable at $45,840 a year, which is a K rate of 11.46%, including interest at 8.5% a year, with 16 years to go. A sells to B for $500,000 cash down and carries back a wrap-around for $700,000 at a constant of 12.74%, including interest at 10.25% a year, or $89,180 a year (which indicates a term of 16 years, if you scan the loan payment book under 10.25% interest).

The net payment to A, then, is $43,340 ($89,180 − $45,840 = $43,340). Then, $43,340 ÷ W/A equity $300,000 = K 14.45%. The interest yield could be found by scanning the loan payment book under 16 years, indicating approximately 12.5%.

Or the same result could be achieved by using the shortcut mortgage-equity ratio technique (see Chapter 17).

W/A total $700,000 @ K .1274
Existing balance $400,000 @ K .1146
Equity $300,000 @ K ?

The upper spread .0128 (.1274—.1146) when multiplied by the W/A to equity ratio of 2.333 ($700,000 ÷ $300,000 = 2.333) equals the lower spread .02986 (.0128 × 2.333). This, added to the existing loan K .1146, equals the cash flow (K) to the equity of .1445 (.1146 + .02986 = .1445). Scanning the loan payment book at 16 years, the nearest constant to .1445 is .1449 opposite 12.5% interest. Close enough.

Further, A could sell the business to C on terms of $360,000 cash, and carry a note for the $600,000 balance payable at 14% interest for 6 years. In the loan payment book, the K factor for 14%, 6 years is 24.73%, so the payment is $148,380 a year ($600,000 × .2473 = $148,380) payable $12,365 a month ($148,380 ÷ 12 = $12,365).

Still further, B may not wish the risk of leasing direct to C, an unknown, and prefer to require A to master lease the premises and sub-lease to C. A agrees, in order to induce B to buy the real estate, but insists on a rental cap rate of 11% instead of 12%, in deference to his higher credit responsibility than that of C. His rent to B then is $132,000 a year; A then sub-leases to C at 12%, or $144,000 a year. The positions of the parties, then, are:

Party A: Income—Before and After

Before Transaction

Profit from business operation	$ 240,000	
Less existing mortgage payment	− 45,840	
Net income		$ 194,160
Net income gain		$ 9,560

Plus income from reinvestment of $860,000 cash received

After Transaction

W/A mortgage from B	$ 700,000	@ K $ 89,180		
Less: existing mortgage	400,000	@ K 45,840		
W/A equity		$ 300,000		@ K $ 43,340
Note from C		600,000		@ K 148,380
Total notes and mortgages		$ 900,000		
Total income from loans				@ K $ 191,720
Rent from C			$ 144,000	
Rent to B			− 132,000	
Net rent income				$ 12,000
Total income after transaction				$ 203,720

Party A: Equity—Before and After

Before transaction

Total original value	$ 2,160,000	
Less existing mortgage	400,000	
Net equity		$ 1,760,000

(Net income $194,160 ÷ $1,760,000 = 11.03%)

After transaction

W/A from B	$ 700,000		
Existing mortgage	400,000		
W/A equity		$ 300,000	
Note from C		600,000	
Total loan equities		$ 900,000	
Cash down from C	360,000		
Cash down from B	500,000		
Total cash		860,000	
Total loans and cash			$ 1,760,000

(Net income $203,720 ÷ $1,760,000 = 11.58%)

Plus income from reinvestment of $860,000 cash received.

Party B—Equity and Return

Price $	1,200,000	Cap	11.00%	Net rent from A $	132,000
W/A	700,000	K	12.74%	Constant	89,180
Equity $	500,000	ROE	8.56%	NCF $	42,820

Party C—Equity and Return

Price $	960,000	Cap	25.00%	Operating net $	240,000
Note to A	600,000	K	24.73%	Constant	148,380
Cash $	360,000	ROE	25.45%	ROE $	91,620

(Note that the $144,00 rent paid to A is an operating expense, deducted before the $240,000 net.)

The lease of A between the two parties, B below and C above, is called a *sandwich lease* (the meat between the bread slices of B and C). The sub-lease from C to A is called the *top lease,* while B is the fee owner.

The possibilities for innovation continue. Party A, collecting a higher rent from C ($144,000) than is paid to B ($132,000) has a yearly profit of $12,000 and has thereby created a leasehold estate (see Chapter 12) which A may enjoy as an annual annuity or capitalize to a cash asset. If the lease term were 10 years and the market value of money were 12%, then A could sell (discount) his leasehold for $69,686 cash by dividing $12,000 by the loan payment book K factor of 17.22% for 12%, 10 years ($12,000 ÷ .1722 = $69,686). To be more precise, since rent is paid in advance, the K factor could be adjusted from arrears to advance by dividing it by the base rate and then dividing. The base rate 1.01 ($1 plus the first month's interest rate) divided into K .1722 = K .1705; therefore, $12,000 ÷ .1705 = cash value $70,381.

Alternatively, for practice, the reciprocal of the K factor (monthly Table 5: present value of $1 per period) could be adjusted to advance payment by multiplying it by the base rate 1.01 and their adjusted factor multiplied by the *first month's* (not annual) rental:

Table 5: 12%, 10 years, monthly = 69.700522
69.700522 × base rate 1.01 = 70.39753
70.39753 × $1000 month = $70,398

(The small $19 difference is not material.)

Unless the amounts are very large, or the term very long, the simple K factor is amply practicable in everyday business.

Just to point the way to the endless fragmenting possibilities, A could sell his $70,381 estate for, say, $20,000 cash down, and carry a note secured by the lease for the $50,381 balance at a given interest and principal payment. He could then sell that note to a speculator, discounted at a higher interest rate to show the speculator an attractive profit commensurate with the risk. Or, A could reduce the required discount rate by further securing the loan with outside collateral. That note in turn, secured by the $50,381 loan, could be discounted at a still higher speculative rate, with a portion of cash down, and the balance carried as a third loan, secured by the prior second loan, and on and on.

Similarly, C could increase the business net profit, sell it at a gain, and sub-sublease the premises to the new operator at a higher rent than the $144,000 called for by the lease with A, thereby creating his own sub-subleasehold estate, with all the potential variable benefits above described.

In these times of hard to get and high interest rate mortgage money, the emphasis is being placed more and more on using the lease as a financing instrumentality. It opens the way to a new world of chain financing and consecutive subordinations, whereby prior lenders will subordinate their positions to a later lender, only because the funds advanced by the latter at a critical time could avert default on the former's loan because of lack of funds to cure a business adversity.

Using a lease as a financing device is a creative solution in tight money market.

The key throughout is converting future cash flows to cash assets at present value.

FINANCING CONDOMINIUM CONVERSIONS

The implications of the condominium concept are more legal than financial, and therefore largely outside the basic aim of this text. For a fuller study, you should investigate the many excellent books and periodical articles on the subject. A few observations on the fundamental condominium characteristics will lay the foundation for a brief explanation of the financing procedures involved.

The condominium is a combination of fee ownership title to a cubicle of air (called air rights) and joint ownership title to the land. That is, each unit owner has fee to his particular building suite, but shares the land title proportionately with all the other unit owners in joint tenancy.

A condominium project may be constructed as such from inception, or converted from an existing rental property. When the project is originally developed, the financing is similar to that of a rental project; a construction, or interim, loan is obtained until completion, which is replaced or "taken-out" by a permanent or "take-out" long-term mortgage loan. The only variation is that in the case of a rental property, one permanent loan is issued to the owner. In the condominium project, the total loan amount is divided into separate loans to each unit owner exactly as if the unit were a single-family residence.

When a rental property is converted, it almost always requires extensive renovation to comply with governmental requirements such as privacy of entry, additional parking, insulation, fireproofing, etc. Now the financing is a little more complicated.

If there is an existing mortgage loan, its terms forbid any

substantial modification, sometimes referred to as "gutting" of the building; also, removal of the tenants, either temporarily or permanently, obviously endangers payment of the loan.

Converting apartments to condominiums calls for special financing arrangements.

This gave rise to another type of loan, the bridge loan, which is merely another version of the interim construction loan. As its name implies, it bridges the gap from rental to condominium by paying off the existing permanent loan and then advancing further funds in stages as the conversion construction progresses. Upon completion, it is replaced by individual permanent loans to each consumer who purchases a completed unit.

In a simple illustration, imagine an 80-unit apartment with a value of $4,000,000 ($50,000 average per apartment) subject to an existing mortgage balance of $2,500,000. The conversion will require $1,000,000 in remodeling for conversion to condominiums to be sold at $75,000 each, for a total value of $6,000,000 (80 × $75,000).

A permanent lender will lend 80%, or $60,000, to each unit buyer; each buyer will put 20%, or $15,000, cash down, for a total of $1,200,000 (80 × $15,000). Thus the acquisition at $4,000,000 plus the renovation cost of $1,000,000 will represent a total cost to the converter of $5,000,000. Resale to consumers will total $6,000,000 leaving $1,000,000 profit.

The existing loan balance of $2,500,000 must be replaced with a more flexible bridge loan of $2,500,000 to be increased during progress to $3,500,000. Upon completion, it will be paid off ("taken-out") in stages by the $60,000 loan to each consumer purchaser, or a total of $4,800,000 (80 × $60,000), giving the converter net loan proceeds of $1,300,000 ($4,800,000 − $3,500,000).

Having paid $1,500,000 cash to acquire the project ($4,000,000 − $2,500,000 loan), the converter's final cash position is:

By Cash Flow			
80 units × $15,000 down per resale =		$ 1,200,000	
80 loans × $60,000 =	$ 4,800,000		
Less bridge loan	3,500,000		
Net proceeds		1,300,000	
Total cash received			$ 2,500,000
Original Cash Down:			
Acquisition price		$ 4,000,000	
Less existing loan		2,500,000	
Cash investment			$ 1,500,000
Net cash profit			$ 1,000,000
By Total Values			
Resale value			$ 6,000,000
Acquisition cost		$ 4,000,000	
Plus renovation cost		1,000,000	5,000,000
Profit on project			$ 1,000,000

In visual diagram, the transaction progresses like this:

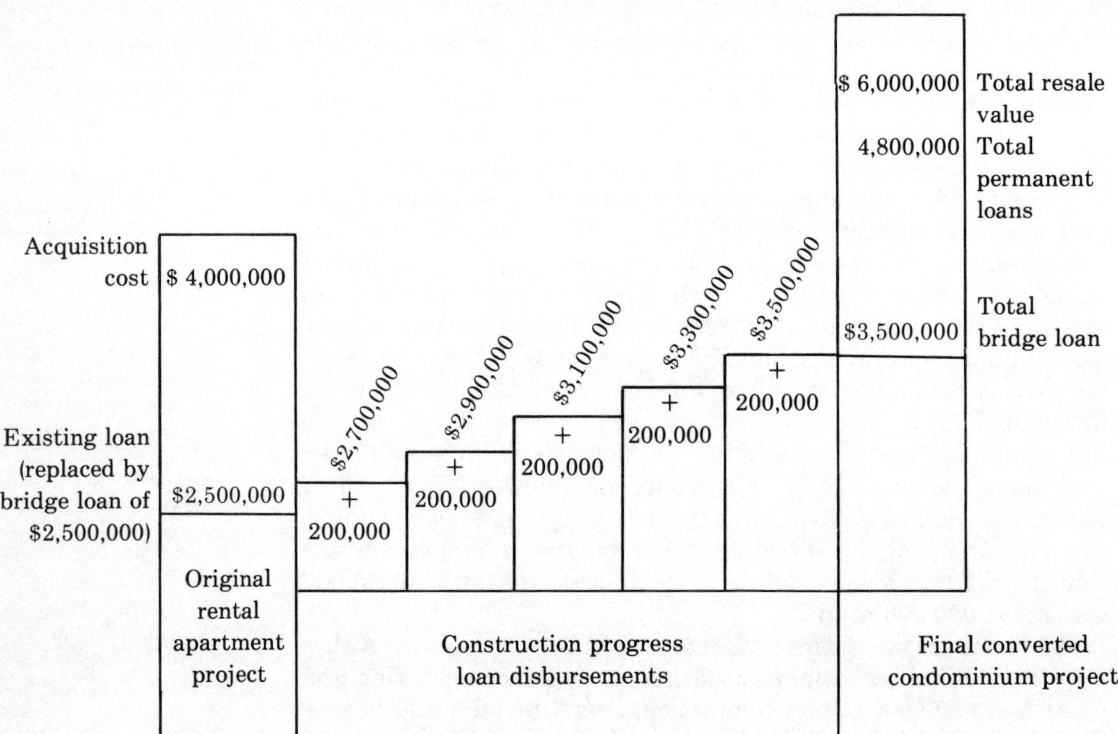

The condominium concept has been most practicable as living units, expanding to a smaller extent to industrial plant complexes and only recently, to an even smaller degree, office buildings. The reason is that to be enforceable, and to be insurable, and particularly transferable, the fee title to each unit, delineated by imaginary boundary lines in the air, must remain static. This is easiest in apartments, which when sold, require only surface repair, not structural changes in size or shape. Industrial plants share this quality to a large degree.

Office suites, by contrast, change fluidly in both size and shape with every successive re-tenancy, by the very nature of each tenant's office layout requirement. This renders air right boundaries impracticable. However, a compromise solution is to sell each full floor as a separate condominium unit, whereupon each floor owner could partition and lease any number of suites desired. Subsequent repartitioning would not disturb the air-right integrity of the full floor unit.

IV.

Appraisal Techniques and Tools

15.

Capitalization Applications

Capitalization is defined as "the art of converting a cash flow, or an annuity, into its capital sum, or lump sum present value." It's the process you use to determine the amount of money you need to invest in order to realize a desired rate of return when the dollar cash flow is known.

Capitalization converts cash flow into the corresponding capital amount.

It is accomplished by dividing a cash flow amount by a given interest rate to find the corresponding capital sum of which the cash flow represents the return at that interest rate. It is the reverse of multiplying the capital sum by the interest rate to find the equivalent cash flow.

Example. If a bond of $10,000 multiplied by 6% interest equals $600 cash flow, conversely the $600 divided (capitalized) by 6% interest equals the $10,000 bond price. Instead of "bond," we could have been talking about "purchase price," "loan balance" or "investment equity."

Capitalization is an indispensable tool for determining with precision:

Using figures from our case study to demonstrate the many uses of cap rate.

- The purchase price, at a given rate of return on investment (ROI) when the net operating income (NOI) is known.
  NOI $99,730 ÷ Capitalization rate (Cap rate) 9.51% = price $1,049,000
- The amount of equity to be invested in order for a dollar amount cash flow to represent a desired rate of return (ROE).
  NCF $11,510 ÷ ROE 5.76% = equity $200,000
- The amount of loan(s) that can be supported by the available cash flow for principal and interest payments (constant).
  Annual constant (K) $88,220 ÷ K 10.39% = loan(s) $849,000

- The amount of expenses, at a given expense-to-gross ratio, when the net operating income (NOI) is known. The net income is divided (capitalized) by the complement of the expense *percent;* this will produce the total dollar gross rent. The net is then subtracted from the gross to find the dollar expense.

  NOI $99,730 remains after expenses of 35.2% (dollar amount unknown).

100%	−	35.2%	=	complement	64.8%
$ 99,730	÷	64.8%	=	gross rent	$ 154,000
$154,000	−	$99,730	=	expenses	$ 54,270

- The amount of commissions payable, at a given rate, when the net sales price is known.

  Assume resale price at $1,049,000 *net* after payment of commission of 6%:

100% − 6%	=	complement	94%
$1,049,000 ÷ 94%	=	gross price	$1,115,957
$1,115,957 − $1,049,000	=	commission	$66,957

The familiar I/R/V formula is based on principle of capitalization.

The capitalization principle is the basis for the classic appraisal formulas that measure the relationship between income, which is any cash flow including loan payments (I), the yield rate (R), and value (V). These formulas are:

$V = \frac{I}{R}$ Value equals income divided (capitalized) by the yield rate.

$R = \frac{I}{V}$ Rate equals income divided by value.

$I = V \times R$ Income equals value multiplied by rate.

The point to remember is that I, the cash flow, is always the numerator; it is divided by R to find V, or by V to find R. This is because I is the product of the factors V and R, and every product can be divided (capitalized) by either of its factors to find the other. This relationship can be expressed graphically:

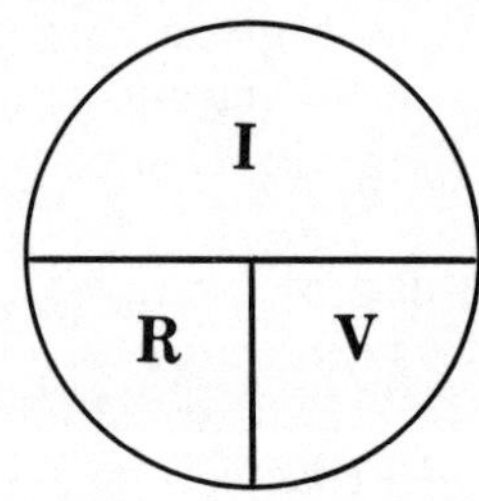

It may help further, in view of the isolated I, to remember your old friend Irv, the Private I:

Now let's apply this relationship to the three-column format used throughout this book. Reviewing quickly, the left column represents capital, the right column cash flow, and the middle column a percentage relationship between the two; when any two are known, the third can be found. The I/R/V relationship can also be expressed in this three-column format; V is the left-hand or capital column; I is the right-hand or cash flow column; and R is the percentage or middle column.

Capital	%	Cash Flow
V	R	I
?	R	I

Solve for unknown by capitalization.

In investment analysis, we frequently start with the right (I) and middle (R) columns as the known figures, and the left column (V) the unknown. In these instances, our solution is not by multiplication but by division—*capitalization.*

This concept is so important to recognize that it will not be amiss to presume with a most elementary example of 2 × 3 = 6.

I would hesitate to introduce such a simplistic example in a work of this kind, if it were not for a phenomenon I've witnessed many times in the years of teaching this course since 1965 on the various University of California campuses. The math and finance majors, upon first hearing this example, have manifested varying degrees of amusement from smirks to paroxysms of hilarity. Then, when a practical problem was outlined to which the solution lay in recognition and application of this same 2 × 3 = 6 principle, it was not recognized until cited and demonstrated. So, with your indulgence, we'll spell it out and demonstrate how it relates.

2 X 3 = 6
A simple example for a critical principle.

Whenever two or more numbers are multiplied to equal a third, they are called *factors,* and the third is called the *product.* It is also true that the product can be divided by either factor (assuming two in our application) to arrive at the other factor:

Just as 2 × 3 = 6,
So, 6 ÷ 2 = 3,
And 6 ÷ 3 = 2.

This means that each *factor* is also a *divisor,* and the *product* is a *dividend.* Memorize these terms, and practice their application, using various combinations of numbers, until the double identities become automatic. Further, you must be able to read the equation *three ways,* whether it's on one line such as 2 × 3 = 6, or in fraction form such as $\frac{6}{2} = 3$.

On one line, 2 × 3 = 6 (from left to right)
Read it also: 6 divided by 3 = 2 (from right to left)
Read it also: 6 divided by 2 = 3

In fraction form, $\frac{6}{2}$ = 3 (from left to right)

Read it also: 6 divided by 3 = 2 (right to left)
Read it also: 3 × 2 = 6 (right to left)

Now another rule emerges: The *divisor* (2) and the *quotient* (3) are factors of the *dividend* (6). Suppose now that any one of the three elements instead of a real number was a strange symbol, such as *x* or *y*. You could use this principle to find the unknown amounts.

Example 1. $\frac{x}{2} = 3$ Since the divisor (2) and quotient (3) are factors of the dividend (6) then x = 6 (2 × 3 = 6).

Example 2. $\frac{6}{y^3} = 3$ Since the dividend (6) is also the product of the divisor and quotient (3) then $y^3 = 2$ because the product may be divided by either factor to get the other. Thus, $\frac{6}{2} = 3$, just as $\frac{6}{3} = 2$.

Example 3. $\frac{6}{2} = (1 + i)^{10}$ Since the divisor (2) and the quotient $(1 + i)^{10}$ are factors of the product (6) and a product may be divided by either factor to arrive at the other, then $(1 + i)^{10} = 3$.

$\frac{6}{2} = 3$

If we now bring in our familiar three columns, the association becomes clear:

	Column I		*Column II*		*Column III*
As,	Static	×	Relationship	=	Dynamic
or,	Structure	×	Percent	=	Cash Flow
So,	Price	×	Cap Rate	=	NOI
	Loan	×	Constant %	=	Constant $
	Equity	×	ROE %	=	Net Cash Flow
Just as,	2	×	3	=	6

Or, shown in reverse,

Column III		*Column II*		*Column I*
Dynamic	÷	Relationship	=	Static
Cash Flow	÷	Percent	=	Structure
NOI	÷	Cap Rate	=	Price
Constant $	÷	Constant %	=	Loan
Net Cash Flow	÷	ROE	=	Equity
6	÷	3	=	2

In each case, Columns 1 and 2 are factors of Column 3. Column 3 is always the dividend and the factors always divisors.

Conclusion. There are three items in every equation above. When any two are known, then by either simple multiplication or division (capitalization) the third can be found.

Our columnar format sets up equations in 3s. When you know two items, you can always find the third.

Thus, if the dollar amount available for loan repayment in Column III and the prevailing constant percent factor in Column II were known, as

Column I			*Column II*		*Column III*
Loan	?	×	Constant 12.35%	=	Constant $ 247,000

then the loan amount can be easily ascertained by dividing (capitalizing) Column III by Column II because it is recognized visually that Column II is one of the factors of Column III and therefore Column III may be capitalized by Column II to arrive at Column I:

Column I			*Column II*		*Column III*
Loan	$ 2,000,000	×	Constant 12.35%	=	Constant $ 247,000

Remember to read the equation backwards, from right to left, in order for the visual arrangement not to be disturbed. Thus, Column III $247,000 ÷ Column II 12.35% = Column I $2,000,000. This way, in oral negotiation, you are in position to add any of three cap rate components (price, cap rate, ROI) to their slots above, or any of the three ROE components (equity, ROE%, NCF) below. Your negotiating power is now greatly enhanced.

This two out of three principle is not restricted to the above ratios. The same principle works in using the loan payment book for shortcut calculation of interest rate, term of years or loan amount. The book itself contains the three elements of interest rate, term of years and constant factor, so any one can be found when the other two are known. Using the book this way, and recognizing the basic principle, is so profoundly simple, and such a handy device, that I feel it's worth repeating here, although it is also covered in other portions of this text.

This also works for the three elements in the ever-handy payment book.

16.

Leverage: Multiplying Your Dollars

In an analyst's vocabulary, leverage has two meanings: one deals with the ability to swing a large investment in relation to the cash available for equity, and the other refers to the advantage or disadvantage of borrowing, from the point of view of equity return.

The first version can be best described by an example of a property bought for $100,000, with 10% ($10,000) cash down and the balance in loans. If the property appreciates in value by only 1% of the total price, that's $1,000—which is equal to an *equity* gain of 10% ($1,000 ÷ $10,000).

Leverage expresses the relationship between profit rate and loan payment factor.

The second, and even more strategic, is the effect on equity return of the difference between the rate of return before financing (capitalization rate), and constant rate of repayment of borrowed money (K factor). When the constant loan repayment rate is less than the cap rate, the result is called *positive leverage.* When the constant loan repayment rate is greater than the cap rate, the result is called *negative leverage,* or *reverse leverage.*

Consider the following situation. A property costing $100,000 has a net operating income (NOI) of $10,000 or 10%. A loan of $50,000 is obtained at a constant repayment of $4,500 a year. The constant *rate* (K) is therefore 9% ($4,500 ÷ $50,000). Of the $10,000 NOI, $4,500 goes as loan payment, leaving $5,500 as return on equity (ROE). The cash equity is $50,000 and the ROE is 11% ($5,500 ÷ $50,000).

Expressed in our three-column format it looks like this:

Price	$ 100,000 ←	Cap rate	10% →	NOI	$ 10,000
Loan	50,000 ←	K	9% →	Constant	4,500
Equity	$ 50,000 ←	ROE	11% →	Net cash flow	$ 5,500

This is positive leverage—the return on equity is actually higher *after* the loan than before. This is because every dollar borrowed costs less to repay than the investment brings in. And here's the moral of the story: Even if the investor had available the full $100,000 in cash, it would be more profitable to put $50,000 down on *two* investments of $100,000 each and borrow the difference. Then the total $100,000 equity would return $11,000, or 11% whereas the original one investment bought for cash generated only $10,000, or 10%. It's almost like alchemy.

The magical effect of positive leverage.

This advantage occurs only when borrowed-money rates are low in relation to investment property earnings, such as in a buyer's market. When the conditions are the opposite—high money rates and seller's market—borrowing has an adverse effect on equity return. Let's see how it works, using the same example and the same 10% cap rate but a loan constant rate of 11%. The constant repayment is therefore $5,500 a year, leaving only $4,500 as return on equity, or 9% ($4,500 ÷ $50,000). Here's the negative, or reverse, leverage, in our format:

Price	$ 100,000	← Cap rate	10%	→	NOI	$ 10,000
Loan	50,000	← K rate	11%	→	Constant	5,500
Equity	$ 50,000	← ROE	9%	→	Net cash flow	$ 4,500

It is worth emphasizing that this computation is made with the NOI, and not gross income.

If we were considering an apartment or office building and the expense ratio were, say, 40%, then the complete figures would appear:

					Gross rent	$ 16,667	100%
					Expenses	6,667	40%
Price	$ 100,000	← Cap rate	10%	→	NOI	$ 10,000	60%
Loan	50,000	← K	11%	→	Constant	5,500	
Equity	$ 50,000	← ROE	9%	→	Net cash flow	$ 4,500	

The leverage effects are greatly amplified when the mortgage/equity ratio is increased to the actual market maximum of 80% for conventional institutional first mortgage loans.

At 80% for example, the ROE would be reduced to 6%:

Price	$ 100,000	← Cap rate	10%	→	NOI	$ 10,000
Loan	80,000	← K	11%	→	Constant	8,800
Equity	$ 20,000	← ROE	6%	→	Net cash flow	$ 1,200

When seller is the lender, the application of leverage is particularly important.

Incidentally, the ability to foresee the net result to ROE before working out the example is a most valuable tool and is explained at length in the chapters on wrap-around financing and extensions of mortgage equity techniques.

True, there is not much, if any, control over prevailing rates by lending *institutions*—but there is another source through which the above principles may be applied by either buyer or seller. That source is the seller, who frequently carries back a portion of the sale price in some form of junior lien, such as second or third mortgage, trust deed, or seller's equity in an all-inclusive security device.

These loans are known as "purchase money loans" and also as "soft money" as opposed to "hard money" loans from an outside lender. The purchase money loan does not involve an actual cash advance, and often represents all or a portion of the seller's profit, rather than actual cost, in the property being sold. Remember: whereas the whole objective of the institutional lender is to earn as much interest as possible, the seller has another motivation—to facilitate the sale, or to enhance the selling price. Therefore, the purchase money loan may be substituted for all or a portion of the institutional loan at a more favorable rate of repayment—in other words, to offset the effect of a negative leverage.

If, in the negative leverage example above, the borrower's request for the institutional loan was reduced from 80% to 70%, and the difference carried back by the seller at a constant of 9%, compared with the institution's 11%, the saving of 2% on the $10,000 difference ($200), would raise the ROE by 1% ($200 ÷ $20,000), or up from 6% to 7%. Especially in larger transactions, this could make the difference in effecting the sale.

TIMING THE LEVERAGE

Most of us are familiar with the concept that price and terms are the two sides of the same coin. The easier the terms, the higher the price; the tighter the terms, the lower the price. This leads us to wonder, "To what extent is a property priced on its intrinsic value, quality of location, etc. and to what extent on the terms?" Stated more pointedly, "How much is a buyer paying for land and building value, and how much is he paying for financing terms?"

It's probably safe to say that in any transaction one party is bound to be more knowledgeable than the other, whether by virtue of inherent endowment, education or experience. For this reason, it is essential to wise buying or selling of investment property to realize that there are two phases of leverage timing: one *before* the sale, which gives the advantage to the seller, and one *after* the sale, which benefits the buyer.

Keeping in mind that commercial properties are frequently sold on the basis of cap rate, let's take a very basic example. A property has an NOI (right column) of $48,000. On an all-cash transaction, a buyer pays $480,000, so that his cap rate is 10% ($48,000 ÷ $480,000 = 10%). Under our visual system of arrangement it would be written:

Price $480,000 ⟵ 10% ⟶ NOI $48,000

Is $480,000 the true value? Suppose he resells to an investor at a cap rate of 8%, which makes the price (not value, necessarily) $600,000 ($48,000 ÷ .08 = $600,000).

Just for argument's sake, let's go the other way and say the money supply tightened; the same property may have to be sold, or valued by a lender as basis for a loan, at a cap rate of 12%, in which case the price is $400,000 ($48,000 ÷ .12 = $400,000). So on an all-cash basis the *same* property is worth from $400,000 to $600,000—quite a substantial variance.

Now let's see what terms could do. Take the first example of $480,000 price and 10% cap rate; let's assume a 75% loan at a 10.1% constant (9½% interest rate over 30 years). It would look like this:

Price	$ 480,000	×	10.0%	Cap	=	NOI	$	48,000
Loan	$ 360,000	×	10.1%	K	=	Constant	$	36,360
Equity	$ 120,000	×	9.7%	ROE	=	NCF	$	11,640

Now what happens if the seller carries back a second trust deed (or mortgage) loan of $50,000 at an 8% constant?

Price	$ 480,000	×	10.0%	Cap	=	NOI	$	48,000
First loan	360,000	×	10.1%	K	=	Constant		36,360
Balance	$ 120,000	×	9.7%	ROE	=	Balance	$	11,640
Second loan	50,000	×	8.0%	K	=	Constant		4,000
Equity	$ 70,000	×	10.9%	ROE	=	NCF	$	7,640

The ROE increases from 9.7% to 10.9%.

The dollar amount of the increase is $850—the difference between the original ROE of 9.7% and the seller's second loan constant of 8% on the $50,000 second loan:

	$ 50,000	×	9.7%	=	Constant	$ 4,850
Less	$ 50,000	×	8.0%	=	Constant	$ 4,000
Difference			1.7%			$ 850

And, $850 ÷ $70,000 = 1.2%, just as 10.9% − 9.7% = 1.2%.

But the seller didn't carry back the second loan to increase the buyer's return, but rather to enhance the market value of his property. So, instead of passing the $850 along to the buyer, the seller stabilizes the 9.7% return to the buyer ($70,000 × 9.7% = $6,790), subtracts it from the balance after payment of the first loan,

$11,640, leaving a net balance of $4,850 available for payment of the second loan, instead of only $4,000. Capitalizing the $4,850 by the 8% constant rate of the second loan equals a loan amount of $60,625. Adding the equity, the second loan and first loan brings the total price to $490,625.

Now the seller—having read this book—puts each figure into its sequential position (follow the letters) and calculates the problem quickly. Remember?

First, he establishes the all-important NOI, $48,000, in its slot at the top of the right column, then inserts the *known* first loan and equity figures in their respective positions through equity, multiplies equity by 9.7% to arrive at NCF, subtracts that from the balance to find the constant on second loan, capitalizes $4,850 at 8% from right to left, producing the amount of second loan, then simply adds up equity and second loan, for an interim balance of $130,625, which added to first loan totals the price:

Price	$ 490,625[M]			=	NOI	$ 48,000[A]
First loan	360,000[B]	×	10.1%[C]	=	Constant	36,360[D]
Balance	$ 130,625[L]				Balance	$ 11,640[E]
Second loan	60,625[K]	×	8.0%[J]	=	Constant	4,850[I]
Equity	$ 70,000[F]	×	9.7%[G]	=	NCF	$ 6,790[H]

Just to complete the offering, he could have continued with cap rate 9.8% ($48,000 ÷ $490,625 = 9.8%) and interim equity return 8.9% ($11,640 × $130,625 = 8.9%). If the seller had capitalized the second loan at a still lower rate, say 7%, the second would be $69,286, and the price $499,286. This is how leveraging *before* the sale—offering attractive terms—actually benefits the seller by raising the price.

On the other hand, sometimes the buyer is the more astute. He first establishes a lower price by offering a high retirement rate on the second loan; then in escrow finds reasons not to approve contingencies (thereby giving him the right to cancel the offer), *unless* the seller eases the second loan rate without raising the price. Most sellers, inexperienced in the effects of capitalization, would not recognize this strategy.

Here's how it could work. Assume that in the above case, the buyer had agreed to the 8% constant on the second loan and then in escrow for some reason prevailed upon the seller to reduce the payment to 6% interest only. This would increase the NCF to the buyer and raise his ROE. The buyer could then capitalize that extra cash flow and sell the property, either in escrow or directly after, at a profit.

For practice let's follow the lettered sequence through to buyer's increased ROE of 11.43%.

						NOI	$ 48,000[A]
First loan	$ 360,000[B]	×	K	10.10%[C]	=	Constant	$ 36,360[D]
						Balance	$ 11,640[E]
Second loan	$ 60,625[G]	×	K	6.00%[H]	=	Constant	3,638[I]
Equity	$ 70,000[F]	×	ROE	11.43%[K]	=	NCF	$ 8,002[J]

Up to this point, the buyer has increased his cash flow by $1,212—the 2% saving on the second loan payment:

Second loan at	8%	$ 60,625	×	8%	=	$ 4,850
Less Second loan at	6%	$ 60,625	×	6%	=	$ 3,638
Difference				2%		$ 1,212

If he was willing to accept 9.7% ROE on his original offer, that can be assumed to be the going market rate. Therefore, he can capitalize the $8,002 new cash flow at 9.7%, which would support an equity of $82,495 ($8,002 ÷ .097 = $82,495). He can sell that equity to a third party buyer in cash, or he could create a third loan by capitalizing the excess cash flow of $1,212.

Take the alternatives one at a time. First, a cash profit, starting with equity. Pick up where we left off:

Equity	$ 70,000[A]	×	ROE	11.43%[B]	=	NCF	$ 8,002[C]

Now here, as we continue to think in terms of arrangement, after multiplying $70,000 by 11.43% to get $8,002, we now want to capitalize $8,002 by the lower rate of 9.7%, which ordinarily would appear as:

$8,002 ÷ 9.7% = $82,495 Equity

But we want to maintain our format, and always have the cash flow to the right and the structure to the left. What if we simply think backward, and place the $8,002 in its normal NCF position, divided (capitalize) the $8,002 from right to left, and just drop each number into its respective slot? Following our arrangement pattern, we place the $8,002 to be capitalized right below the $8,002 product of multiplication, and trace the sequence:

Starting equity	$ 70,000[A]	×	ROE	11.43%[B]	=	NCF	$ 8,002[C]
Final equity	82,495[F]	×	ROE	9.70%[E]	=	NCF	$ 8,002[D]
Profit	$ 12,495[G]						

Then the buyer has created a cash profit in escrow of $12,495—a markup of 17.9%. The second alternative is to take a third loan for the profit:

Starting equity	$ 70,000[A]	×	ROE	11.43%[B]	=	Net cash flow	$ 8,002[C]
Third loan	12,495[I]	×	K	9.7%[H]	=	Constant	1,212[G]
Final equity	$ 70,000[D]	×	ROE	9.7%[E]	=	Net cash flow	$ 6,790[F]

The progression from $8,002 to the final equity then around the Horn to the third loan was for drill practice, because in some cases there may be still further alterations. For instance, suppose the return on the equity and the K on the third loan were not the same? In order to get a still higher resale price, what happens if the third had payable interest of only 6%? The capitalization would then be:

Starting equity	$ 70,000[A]	×	ROE	11.43%[B]	=	Net cash flow	$ 8,002[C]
Third loan	20,200[I]	×	K	6.00%[H]	=	Constant	1,212[G]
Final equity	$ 70,000[D]	×	ROE	9.7%[E]	=	Net cash flow	$ 6,790[F]

Another variation: suppose the buyer elected to take a part of the markup in cash and part in paper, even at the same 9.7%? For example, the buyer wishes to mark the equity up 10%, or $7,000 to realize a 9.7% cash flow on the $77,000, and capitalize the remaining cash flow into a third loan at the same 9.7%. The process, step-by-step, would be:

Starting equity	$ 70,000[A]	×	ROE	11.43%[B]	=	Net cash flow	$ 8,002[C]
Third loan	5,495[I]	×	K	9.7%[H]	=	Constant	533[G]
Final equity	$ 77,000[D]	×	ROE	9.7%[E]	=	Net cash flow	$ 7,469[F]

Remember, the amounts of the percentages used here are not necessarily realistic in many parts of the country, or the world for that matter—nor need they be. The *method* is the important thing, because the relationship of numbers will never change.

17.

Mortgage-Equity Technique:
A Modern Method for Constructing an Accurate Capitalization Rate

When a financial package is being put together, several terms tend to come up: band of investment . . . mortgage/equity ratio . . . composite cap rate . . . weighted average. All these terms are really only different names for the same procedure. More exactly, the mortgage/equity technique is a modern refinement of band of investment, and both are used to produce a composite capitalization rate. All are based on the principle of weighted average.

Mortgage-equity technique, properly applied, serves both lender and investor.

The band of investment is a method of constructing a precise cap rate which will produce a price which will assure each lender, and the equity investor, of their required rate of payment. In other words, every lender has two variables to consider; first, the ratio of the loan to the total price; second, the interest rate and principal amortization rate required for repayment. The equity investor also has a required rate of return.

Since each element of loan and equity represents a varying ratio to the total price, the required return to each must be weighed in proportion to its respective contribution to the total. This is the principle of "weighted average," which, being a composite of the varying proportionate rates, is actually the exact capitalization rate which will convert a net operating profit into its corresponding market value.

When the price is thus determined, it can be translated into specific dollar amounts of loans and equity by multiplication by the proportion of each. Similarly, the dollar payments to each are found by multiplication by their respective percentage rates. This will be demonstrated below.

BAND OF INVESTMENT

As a foundation for clear understanding, let's clarify the term "band of investment." Think of a band as a layer of borrowed money or equity money. And think of a total investment as a stacking of such borrowed and equity bands, each bearing a different interest rate (equity return is actuarially called "market interest"). For example:

	Ratio	*Interest Rate*
First loan	70%	9%
Second loan	10%	7%
Cash equity	20%	8%
Total	100%	

If each interest rate is multiplied by the ratio of its respective element to the whole, a weighted index figure is arrived at. For example:

Ratio		*Interest*		*Weighted Index*
.70	×	.09	=	.063, or 6.3%

Deriving a composite capitalization rate.

When these weighted indices are totaled, the resulting sum is called the weighted average or, what is more important to us as analysts, the composite capitalization rate. Thus:

	Ratio		*Rate*		*Weighted Index*		
First loan	.70	×	.09	=	.063,	or	6.3%
Second loan	.10	×	.07	=	.007,	or	.7%
Equity	.20	×	.08	=	.016,	or	1.6%
Composite capitalization rate (weighted average)							8.6%

We use this weighted average (cap rate) to capitalize any net operating income (NOI) to determine fair market value. So that if the NOI were, say, \$86,000, the value would be capitalized as:

$$\frac{\text{NOI} \quad \$86{,}000}{\text{Cap rate} \quad .086} = \$1{,}000{,}000 \text{ fair market value}$$

And with it, determining value, or price.

To summarize: the band of investment uses a weighted average, called cap rate, to divide into NOI to determine value.

To simplify this illustration, so far we have dealt with interest only. As a matter of practice, another qualifying element usually is added: a factor for "recapture" of the asset (*physical* depreciation, as distinct from *book* depreciation). Suppose the building, net of land, equaled 80% of the investment and was projected to be worth zero in 25 years. A simple calculation would be a straight line factor: 80% decline = 3.2% per year (100% ÷ 25 years = 4% × 80% = 3.2%). Now add this 3.2% to the original 8.6% cap rate for an adjusted cap rate of 11.8%. But to actually do this would so depress the value of the property that a purchase offer could never be accepted.

A more practical approach is to multiply the 80% asset by a 25-year sinking fund factor at the prevailing market interest rate. Let's assume an interest rate of 9%; in any compound interest table reference, we find that its factor is 1.1806%. Thus, 80% × 1.1806% = .95%. The adjusted rate is now 9.55% (8.6% + .95%). And that changes our market value:

NOI $86,000 ÷ Cap rate .0955 = $900,525 Fair market value

Note the important principle demonstrated here. To provide for future *depreciation,* the cap rate is *increased;* for future *appreciation,* the cap rate is *reduced.* That is, a sinking fund factor is either added to, or subtracted from, the base cap rate. This use of a sinking fund factor becomes the connecting link in the transition from the original band of investment theory to the more modern version called the mortgage-equity technique. It came about this way.

How the contemporary M-E technique originated.

Prior to the 1930s, mortgages were not amortized, as they are today, but payable interest only. When legislation in the '30s required amortization in addition to interest, L.W. Ellwood, actuarial vice president of New York Life Insurance Company, reasoned that the sinking fund factor, *which represents the amortization portion of the loan constant,* approximates the "recapture" (depreciation) factor; therefore, the use of the loan constant, in computing weighted averages, should replace the combination of interest and recapture factor to determine the cap rate. This is particularly true since mortgage financing is the rule rather than the exception in real estate investment, and the amortization factor is unavoidable.

If we assume that in the example above the first loan at 9% was for 25 years, the annual constant (K) would be 10.07% (9% interest plus 1.07 amortization, or sinking fund factor), then this same example would emerge with the same cap rate as follows:

Ratio		*K Rate*			*Weighted Index*		
.70	×	K	.1007	=	.0705,	or	7.05%
.10	×	K	.09	=	.009,	or	.90%
.20	×	ROE	.08	=	.016,	or	1.60%
		Mortgage-equity cap rate =					9.55%

Thus, the pure band of investment theory evolved into the more modern mortgage-equity technique, substituting *loan constants* for *interest only plus recapture.* The exact coincidence of recapture and amortization rates was purposely oversimplified, in order for the principle of comparison to emerge without undue complication. Now, by knowing the prevailing loan terms (K factors) and equity return rates (ROE) we can construct a scientifically accurate cap rate with which to instantly capitalize net operating income (NOI) into a market value, without juggling a mass of figures.

The next step is to convert these ratios into dollar amounts. This

With cash distribution, we convert ratios into dollars.

procedure is called "cash distribution." First, capitalize the value: $86,000 ÷ .0955 = $900,524 fair market value. Now multiply the value by the ratios of loans and equities to find the dollar amounts:

%		
100	Value	$ 900,524
70	First loan	630,367
10	Second loan	90,052
20	Equity	180,105

Then multiply the loans by their respective constants (K factors) and the equity by the ROE percent, and your entire cash flow projection is complete*:

%								
100	Value	$ 900,524	×	.096	=	NOI		$ 86,000
70	First loan	630,367	×	.1007	=	K	$ 63,478	
10	Second loan	90,052	×	.09	=	K	8,105	71,583
20	Equity	$ 180,105	×	.08	=	ROE		$ 14,417

Suppose now that the seller, carrying the second loan, would accept a constant payment of 8.5% instead of the 9% shown. In that case, the $8,105 which is available to service that loan in the above cash flow projection could be capitalized to $95,353 ($8,105 ÷ .085 = $95,353) instead of $90,052, which would also increase the value. Each of the loans, and the equity, could be raised or lowered similarly, simply by altering the appropriate factor as a capitalizing rate.

This is a valuable opportunity to make another essential observation. We have seen how the dollar constant loan payments, and dollar return on equity, are obtained by multiplying the principal of the loan and of the equity by their respective percentage factors. More importantly, however, the *procedure can be reversed,* which is more frequently encountered. That is, when the amount of cash flow available for either debt service or equity return is known, and the K *rates* and ROE *rate* are known, then the principal amounts of loan and equity may be determined by capitalization of the *dollar payment* amounts by the rates.

Another use of capitalization.

Example.	If	$ 630,367	×	.1007	=	$ 63,478
	Then	63,478	÷	.1007	=	630,367
Again.	If	$ 90,052	×	.09	=	$ 8,105
	Then	8,105	÷	.09	=	90,052

This vital principle is worth special emphasis at this stage because it is key to whole vistas of instant, even mental, calculation of cap rates, loan constants and equity returns. At the risk of over-

*Small differences are due to rounding. In actual practice, the figures would be rounded even more, at least to the nearest hundred.

simplifying (I have found in years of teaching that the obvious and simple is often overlooked or forgotten) let me demonstrate the principle by using a simple equation, which, though elementary, parallels our figure relationships exactly. Let's consider the equation: 3 × 2 = 6. Since both 3 and 2 are factors of 6, then 6 may be divided by either of its factors to determine the other.

Again, our simple
2 X 3 = 6
clarifies a vital concept.

By the same principle, using the second loan from the earlier illustration in place of the 3 × 2 = 6:

Principal		*Rate*		*Constant*
$90,052	×	9%	=	$8,105

In this case, because they are joined by a multiplication sign, both the principal ($90,052) and the rate (9%) are factors of the constant ($8,105). Consequently, the constant may be divided by either factor to learn the other:

$8,105 ÷ .09 = $90,052 $8,105 ÷ $90,052 = 9%

Earlier we used three different elements in the same type of equation—ratio, K rate and weighted index. Using the figures for the first loan:

Ratio		*K Rate*		*Weighted Index*
70%	×	10.07	=	7.05%

Again, the ratio and K rates, being joined by a multiplication sign, are factors of the weighted index. It is critically important to recognize this. When, as is so frequently the case, we have determined the weighted index and the ratio, we can automatically resolve the K rate or the ROE by remembering this simple relationship.

The weighted index can be separated into its components: another 2 out of 3 process.

If the rate is a constant, and not interest only, you can use a loan payment book as a tool for quick calculation. That valuable little book, remember, contains the three essentials: interest rate, term of years, and K rate. If you know two, which you usually do, you can always find the third by scanning. (See Chapter 20 for other examples and uses.)

While we're on this subject of capitalizing a product by one of its factors in order to determine the other factor, there is another very valuable and timely application using the same principle. It arises when, as part of a sale, the seller carries back an all-inclusive instrument in which he wants a *higher* than market rate of interest on his *equity* while at the same time offering the buyer a *lower* than market rate on the *total* loan.

Using capitalization to construct a seller's all-inclusive loan.

The Realtor can encounter this situation from two different directions. First, if the seller's required yield on his equity is fixed, what compromise rate on the all-inclusive will result in such a yield after servicing the underlying loan? From the opposite viewpoint, if the overall rate is fixed, what will be the yield on the seller's equity?

Let's take an example. A commercial property is sold on the following terms:

Price	$ 466,500
Cash down	100,000
Balance	$ 366,500
Existing loan balance	258,000
Seller's equity	$ 108,500

The existing loan was originally $300,000, payable $27,810 per year, including 8% interest, for 25 years. It was made 8 years ago, so it has 17 years to go.* The K factor for 7% at 17 years is 10.78%, so the present balance is computed: $27,810 ÷ .1078 = $285,000.

Determining the overall rate when equity yield is fixed.

An all-inclusive security device is decided upon, and let's say the first question posed to the realtor is: What shall be the overall rate if the seller fixed his equity yield at 10.5% to be amortized over the remaining term of the existing first loan, 17 years? The loan payment table reveals the K factor to be 12.64% for 17 years at 10.5% interest. Therefore, the constant payment on seller's equity is $13,714 ($108,500 × .1264 = $13,714).

The next step is to lay out the known figures, in order to highlight the unknown:

			K Rate		*Constant Payment*
All-inclusive	$ 366,500		?		?
Existing loan	258,000	×	10.78%	=	$27,810
Seller's equity	$ 108,500	×	12.64%	=	$13,714

It becomes readily apparent that the all-inclusive constant has to be the sum of the two known constants, or $41,524 ($27,810 + $13,714).

We know that $41,524 must amortize the $366,500 over 17 years, since both the existing loan and seller's equity, which are the components, amortize in that period, so all that remains to be determined is the interest rate.

First find the K factor: $41,524 ÷ $366,500 = .1133, K for 17 years. Then simply scan your payment book under 17 years. K 11.33% is located at 8¾%—so you have found the all-inclusive yield rate.

Or the opposite problem: calculating yield when rate is fixed.

On the other hand suppose the realtor is asked the reverse question: If the overall rate had been fixed first at 8¾%, say by the buyer, then how would the yield be figured on the seller's equity? Reverse the above procedure.

In the loan payment book, the K factor for 17 years at 8¾% is 11.33. Therefore the all-inclusive constant is $41,524 ($366,500 × 11.33% = $41,524). Laying out the figures will highlight the known and unknown figures:

*Note that the dollar constant is divided (capitalized) by the K factor for the years *remaining*, in this case 25 − 8 = 17.

			K Rate		*Constant Payment*
All-inclusive	$ 366,500	×	11.33%	=	$41,524
Existing loan	258,000	×	10.78%	=	$27,810
Seller's equity	$ 108,500		?		?

This time the seller's equity constant is the difference, or $13,714 ($41,524 − $27,810). Again find the factor: $13,714 ÷ $108,500 = 12.64% K for 17 years. In this instance, the payment book, under 17 years, indicates that a 12.64% constant will yield 10.5% on the seller's equity.

Another observation that seems simple but is just as often overlooked, is that the cap rate, as a weighted average, is a sum of component weighted indices. Therefore, when you know the cap rate and one component, you can extract the weighted index of the other. Then the K rate can be determined by factoring, as in our 3 × 2 = 6 equation.

When the components of cap rate are isolated, the K rate can be easily figured.

For analysts, the moral is: always arrange your figures in equation form. After that, it's all downhill.

Let's work one through. Take a proposed sale at a cap rate of 9.3%; the buyer, who requires 7% ROE, will put 25% cash down. What loan terms must be obtained? First, lay out the known factors:

	Ratio %	*K and ROE %*	*Weighted Index %*
Price	100	9.3	9.3
Loan	?	?	?
Equity	25	7.0	?

You can quickly see that the loan ratio has be to 75%. Then, having determined the equity index as 1.75% (25% × 7% = 1.75%), you can see that we could back into the K rate for the loan by subtracting 1.75% from 9.30% to get the loan index, 7.55%. Then, by dividing 7.55% by the loan ratio, 75%, you can get the loan K rate: .0755 ÷ .75 = .1007. Finally, in your payment tables you can find various combinations of interest and term years for which 10.07% is exactly or very close to the K rate.

K%	*Interest Rate %*	*Years*
10.07	8½	22
10.09	8-7/8	24
10.08	9	25
10.08	9-1/8	26

Now, let's apply this instant cap rate tool to some practical cases.

Try an example.

A chain supermarket is offered at $1,300,000, all cash, at an annual triple net rental of $120,250 for 25 years. Your buyer has $325,000 cash and requires 8% ROE. Your problem: What terms are needed on a first loan for the balance, and how to find it without trial and error calculations?

First, reduce your known facts to factors.

$120,250 rent ÷ $1,300,000 price = 9.25% cap rate
$325,000 cash ÷ $1,300,000 price = 25.00% cash ratio

Second, arrange your figures into mortgage/equity order. (With very little practice, you can do this in seconds.)

	Ratio %		*Rate %*		*Index %*	
Total	100	×	9.25	=	9.25	Weighted average (cap rate)
Cash	25	×	8.00	=	?	
Loan	?		?		?	

Immediately, you see that the loan ratio would have to be 75%. Next, the 25% cash ratio × 8% ROE equals 2% weighted index. Therefore, the cap rate of 9.25% less 2.00% equals 7.25% weighted index. Your formula now looks like this:

	Ratio %	*Rate %*	*Index %*
Total	100	9.25	9.25
Cash	25	8.00	2.00
Loan	75	?	7.25

Your question now is how to quickly convert the 75% loan ratio and 7.25% weighted index into the loan K rate. Remember 3 × 2 = 6. So, divide the 7.25% by the 75%; .0725 ÷ .75 = 9.67% K rate. In most instances, you will know your prevailing loan terms and without referring to the tables could recognize the 9.67% constant as ranging from 8.5% for 25 years to 9% for 30 years.

The reverse approach: calculating return on equity when terms are set.

Let's reverse the problem and say that the loan terms were fixed at 9% for 28 years. Your problem now is: What ROE will the buyer receive? First, you know (or find in your payment book) that the constant for 9% at 28 years is 9.8%. Arranging your ratio and rate figures you find:

	Ratio %		*Rate %*		*Index %*	
Total	100	×	9.25	=	9.25	Cap rate
Loan	75	×	9.8	=	7.35	
Cash	25	×	?	=	?	

Subtracting the weighted index of a 75% loan with a 9.8% constant, which is 7.35%, from the cap rate of 9.25%, leaves a weighted index of 1.90% for the 25% cash ratio. Now divide the 1.90% by the 25%; .0190 ÷ .25 = ROE 7.6%. So we can quickly see that our buyer's 8% requirement will not be met without renegotiation of the price, rental or loan terms, which may not be possible. Are we out of business? Not by a long shot!

We have so far applied our deductive reasoning process to every component of our three-column formulae except one—the ratio column. Aristotle taught that the key to solution of a problem lies in first analyzing the problem, then reducing it to its smallest elements. Let's do that here.

The return on the investment has shrunk from 9.25% *before* financing to 7.6% *after* financing. Obviously the financing is causing *negative leverage.* That is, the loan costs more than the investment earns. Specifically, the K rate exceeds the cap rate: 9.8% vs. 9.25%.

If the loan equaled 100% of the investment, the investor would actually be cash out of pocket. But the loan is 75%, so the investor is losing on only the major portion, with the net effect that his ROE is reduced.

Overcoming negative leverage by controlling loan and equity ratios.

Since the more you borrow, the more you lose, the conclusion is inescapable—borrow less. The question is, how much less. One approach is trial and error: decreasing the loan ratio and increasing the equity ratio in gradual steps. Fortunately, a faster and more precise formula for measurement and correction is available.

First, by how much does the K rate exceed the cap rate?

K rate	.0980	
Cap rate	.0925	
Negative difference	.0055	(above the loan)

Next, by how much does the K rate exceed the ROE?

K rate	.0980	
ROE	.0760	
Negative difference	.0220	(below the loan)

The difference below the loan is greater than the difference above the loan. How much, exactly?

$$\frac{\text{Below the loan} \quad .0220}{\text{Above the loan} \quad .0055} = 4 \text{ times}$$

Here's a key clue. Why 4 times? The answer must lie in the relative ratios of loan and equity. We're interested primarily in the equity, so let's measure that:

Total investment 100% ÷ Equity ratio 25% = 4 times.

(Remember, your actual problems will not always be in such visible proportions; hence the detailing.)

It is apparent that *the difference between the K rate and cap rate (above the loan) is magnified between the K rate and ROE (below the loan) by the ratio of total investment to equity.* In other words, the basic negative leverage above the K rate of .0055, when magnified by the total investment-to-equity proportion of 4 times, equaled a loss below the loan of .0220. So if the equity were larger, then the .0055 would be multiplied by a smaller ratio number, and the loss below would be less than .0220. How much less do we need? We find that out by subtracting the investor's required ROE from the K rate:

K rate	.0980
Required ROE	.08
Visible difference	.018

Back now to our 3 × 2 = 6. If earlier .0055 × 4 = .0220, and .0220 ÷ .0055 = 4 times, ergo, by substitution: .0180 ÷ .0055 = 3.27 times. Thus the total investment must be 3.27 times the equity, or reciprocally the equity must be 30.6% of the total investment (1.00 ÷ 3.27 = 30.6%). And there's the answer! To receive an 8% ROE, the investor must increase his equity to 30.6%, reducing his borrowing to 69.4%.

Now the investment, restructured, appears:

	Ratio %		*K rate, ROE %*		*Weighted Index*
Loan	69.4	×	9.8	=	6.80
Equity	30.6	×	8.	=	2.45
Cap rate	100.	×	9.25		9.25

Q.E.D. The explanation is longer than the performance.

We can restate the process in summary outline:

Where the leverage is negative:

Procedure

Step 1. Subtract cap rate from K rate. This measures the negative leverage. (If the leverage is positive, reverse the subtraction.)

Step 2. Subtract the required ROE from the K rate. This indicates the below the loan loss.

Step 3. Divide Step 2 by Step 1. This is the correct ratio of total investment to equity.

Step 4. For equity percentage, divide 100% by ratio found in Step 3.

In Figures (using above example):

Step 1. K .0980 − cap rate .0925 = .0055

Step 2. K .0980 − ROE .0800 = .0180

Step 3. $\frac{.0180}{.0055}$ = 3.27 times

Step 4. $\frac{1.00}{3.27}$ = .306 Equity ratio

Actually, Step 3 could be inverted to eliminate Step 4 because: .0055 ÷ .0180 = .306 directly. Note that if the leverage is *positive* (the cap rate is *greater* than the K rate) the subtraction in Steps 1 and 2 will be reversed—always the smaller subtracted from the greater.

With these factors, and local rules of thumb, you can do an analysis in record time.

An interesting aspect of this system of factors is that it enables you to utilize economically the many facts about the current market in your particular area that you use every day without being consciously aware—rules of thumb.

The average investor will accept as little as zero return on equity up to approximately $500,000 cash (at 25% down, indicating a price of $2,000,000). This is a reflection of the seller's market whereby there are more investors in competition to buy than there are available properties. As the property increases in price, necessitating wealthier, and concomitantly more professional, investors, either individual or institutional, the required return demands increase proportionally, up 7% or 8%, which seems to be the maximum attainable.

So, given only the scheduled annual gross income, a scientific cap rate and one or more alternatives may be formulated in an instant, and the entire investment, including price and terms, may be structured in minutes.

An example of quick calculations.

I'll prove it. Let's assume a long distance call comes to you, collect (as usual) involving possible sale of a six-story office building. The only information your informant knows for sure is the scheduled annual gross income, which we'll call $1,470,000.

In your area, and at that time, you know that institutional loans are available at 11% interest for 30 years at 75% of selling price; the seller will carry a second loan at a constant of 10% including 9½% interest, and your investor wants 7% return on equity. You also know that an office building expense ratio is 35%; certain rules of thumb you have at your fingertips always.

Very quickly, on a scratch pad, you jot down the net operating income at 65%, or $955,500 (note the shortcut: 100% − 35% expenses = 65% NOI). K for 11% for 30 years is 11.43%. Then just as quickly, you assemble your mortgage-equity ratios, constants and return on equity.

	Ratio %			*%*	*Index %*
First loan	75	×	K	11.43	8.57
Second loan	10	×	K	10.00	1.00
Cash down	15	×	ROE	7.00	1.05
			Composite cap rate (weighted average)		10.62

Next, capitalize the NOI to obtain price: $955,500 ÷ .1062 = price $8,997,195. Normally, the price would be rounded to, say, $9,000,000 but strict accuracy will probably be more helpful for explanation purposes.

Again on the phone (collect!) your client wants the dollar figures—which he can understand—instead of percent factors. The work of a moment, with a calculator handy. Let's do it, and assemble it for typing at the same time:

						Gross	$ 1,470,000
						Expenses	514,500
Price	$8,997,175		Cap	.1062		NOI	$ 955,500
First loan	[75% of price $8,997,175]						
	$6,747,881	×	K	.1143	= $ 771,283		
Second loan	[10% of $8,997,175]						
	$899,718	×	K	.10	= 89,972		
Total loans	$7,647,599	×	K	.1126	=		$ 861,255
Cash down	[15% of $8,997,175]						
	$1,349,576	×	ROE	.07	=	NCF	$ 94,245

Note that $1,349,576 multiplied by ROE 7% is actually $94,470, or $225 more than the cash flow column of $94,245. The minor difference is not significant, especially since in reality price and loan numbers are generally rounded off anyway.

At this juncture, stop and imagine another phone call, using a different gross and the terms prevailing in your area; do the operation and time yourself; you are sure to be pleasantly surprised.

Back to our example, you can see how quickly you could lower the cap rate (raise the price) by reducing the first loan to 70% and raising the second loan to 15%, thereby reducing the cap rate to 10.55% and consequently raising the price by $56,697 to $9,056,872.

Example.

							Index
First loan	70%	×	K	.1143	=		8.00
Second loan	15% ~~10%~~	×	K	.10	=		1.50
Cash	15%	×	ROE	.07	=		1.05
Price	100%					Cap	10.55

NOI $955,500 ÷ Cap rate .1055 = Price $9,056,872

These are only some of the many uses of these principles of mortgage-equity capitalization in particular and weighted averages in general. With reflection, and practice, you will surely find that these principles and reasoning processes will improve your ability not only to *analyze,* but to *restructure* and *control* any investment transaction, and in less time . . . which still is money.

EXTENDED APPLICATIONS OF MORTGAGE-EQUITY TECHNIQUES

There are four extensions of the mortgage-equity techniques that are extremely useful and time-saving both in value analysis and in wrap-around financing. They provide an instant solution to four everyday problems involving determination of yield where two factors are known and a third is to be sought.

Problem 1. When the cap rate and K rate are known, what is the ROE rate?

Problem 2. When the K rate and ROE rate are known, what is the cap rate?

Problem 3. When the cap and ROE rates are known, what is the K rate?

Problem 4. When the cap, K and ROE rates are all fixed, what is the correct proportion of equity to price?

The solutions require introduction to three additional simple terms—upper spread, lower spread and total spread. The terms come from their visual position in our arrangement of figures. See Examples 1 and 2 below.

The upper spread is simply the difference between the cap and K rates, as:

Cap rate	10%
K rate	9%
Upper spread	1%*

The lower spread is the difference between the K rate and the ROE rate, as:

K rate	9%
ROE rate	13%
Lower spread	4%*

The total spread is the difference between the cap rate and ROE rate, as:

Cap rate	10%
ROE rate	13%
Total spread	3%*

The spreads are always used in conjuction with the price-equity ratio, or the mortgage-equity ratio, and are either multiplied or divided by whichever ratio applies, as shown below.

Example 1. Positive Leverage

Price	100%	@	Cap rate	10%		Total spread 3%
				(1%)	Upper spread	
Mortgage	75%	@	K rate	9%		
				(4%)	Lower spread	
Equity	25%	@	ROE rate	13%		

Price-equity ratio = 4 (100% ÷ 25% = 4)
Mortgage-equity ratio = 3 (75% ÷ 25% = 3)

Following our diagrammed example, let's track through the step-by-step procedure for each problem.

Determining the ROE rate.

Problem 1: Find the ROE rate.

Step 1. Divide the price by the equity to find the price-equity ratio (100% ÷ 25% = ratio 4)

Step 2. Subtract the K rate from the cap rate to find upper spread (10% − 9% = upper spread 1%).

Step 3. Multiply Step 2 by Step 1 to find the lower spread (4% × 1% = lower spread 4%).

Step 4. Add lower spread to K rate to find ROE rate (4% + 9% = ROE 13%).

---

*These spread figures will most frequently be found in decimals rather than round, but the principle is more easily understood using round numbers.

Determining cap rate.

Problem 2: Find the cap rate.

Step 1. Divide the price by the equity to find the ratio (100% ÷ 25% = ratio 4).

Step 2. Subtract the K rate from the ROE rate to find the lower spread (13% − 9% = lower spread 4%).

Step 3. Divide Step 2 by Step 1 (4% ÷ 4 = upper spread 1%).

Step 4. Add upper spread to the K rate to find the cap rate (1% + 9% = cap rate 10%).

Determining K rate.

Problem 3: Find the K rate.

Step 1. Divide the *mortgage* by the equity to find the *mortgage-*equity ratio (75% ÷ 25% = ratio 3).

Step 2. Subtract the cap rate from the ROE rate to find the total spread (13% − 10% = total spread 3%).

Step 3. Divide Step 2 by Step 1 (3 ÷ 3% = upper spread 1%).

Step 4. Subtract Step 3 from the cap rate to find the K rate (10% − 1% = K rate 9%).

Determining correct equity percent.

Problem 4: Find the correct equity percent.

Step 1. Subtract the K rate from the cap rate to find the upper spread (10% − 9% = upper spread 1%).

Step 2. Subtract the K rate from the ROE rate to find the lower spread (13% − 9% = lower spread 4%).

Step 3. Divide the upper spread by the lower spread to find the correct equity percent (1% ÷ 4% = 25% equity percent).

Example 2. Negative Leverage (K rate higher than cap rate)

Price	100%	@	Cap rate	9%		Total spread −3%
				(−1%)	Upper spread	
Mortgage	75%	@	K rate	10%		
				(−4%)	Lower spread	
Equity	25%	@	ROE rate	6%		

Price-equity ratio = 4 (100% ÷ 25% = 4)
Mortgage-equity ratio = 3 (75% ÷ 25% = 3)

Following this example, here are the step-by-step procedures for each problem when negative leverage exists.

Problem 1: Find the ROE rate.

Step 1. Divide the price by the equity to find the price-equity ratio (100% ÷ 25% = ratio 4).

Step 2. Subtract the cap rate from the K rate to find the upper spread (9% − 10% = upper spread −1%).

Step 3. Multiply Step 2 (−1%) by Step 1 (4) to find the lower spread (−1% × 4 = lower spread −4%).

Step 4. Subtract Step 3 (−4%) from the K rate (10%) to find the ROE rate (10% − 4% = 6%).

Problem 2: Find the cap rate.

The same problem, now with negative leverage.

Step 1. Divide the price by the equity to find the price-equity ratio (100% ÷ 25% = price-equity ratio 4).
Step 2. Subtract the ROE rate from the K rate to find the lower spread (10% − 6% = lower spread −4%).
Step 3. Divide Step 2 (−4%) by Step 1 (4) to find the upper spread (−4% ÷ 4 = upper spread −1%).
Step 4. Subtract Step 3 (−1%) from the K rate to find the cap rate (10% − 1% = cap rate 9%).

Problem 3: Find the K rate.

Step 1. Divide the *mortgage* by the equity to find the *mortgage-equity* ratio (75% ÷ 25% = mortgage-equity ratio 3).
Step 2. Subtract the ROE rate from the cap rate to find the total spread (9% − 6% = total spread 3%).
Step 3. Divide Step 2 by Step 1 to find the upper spread (3% ÷ 3 = upper spread 1%).
Step 4. Add Step 3 to the cap rate to find the K rate (9% + 1% = K rate 10%).

Problem 4: Find the correct equity percent.

Step 1. Subtract the cap rate from the K rate to find the upper spread (10% − 9% = upper spread 1%).
Step 2. Subtract the ROE from the K rate to find the lower spread (10% − 6% = lower spread 4%).
Step 3. Divide the upper spread by the lower spread to find the correct equity percent (1% ÷ 4% = equity percent 25%).

When the buyer requires a higher ROE yield rate, but the cap and K rates are not negotiable, then the only remaining solution is for the buyer to reduce the degree of negative leverage by increasing the equity percent. Your problem is to determine how much.

Assume that in the above example the buyer requires 7% ROE instead of the 6%. How much does he have to pay down (equity percent)?

Step 1. Subtract the cap rate from the K rate to find the upper spread (10% − 9% = upper spread 1%).
Step 2. Subtract the required ROE rate from the K rate to find the lower spread (10% − 7% = lower spread 3%).
Step 3. Divide Step 1 by Step 2 to find the correct equity percent (1% ÷ 3% = equity percent 33⅓%).

Now, prove it. If the equity is 33⅓% at ROE 7%, then the mortgage must be 67%, at K 10%, so that when the investment is assembled in our arrangement:

Price	100%	@	Cap	9%	=	9.00
Mortgage	67%	@	K	10%	=	6.70
Equity	33%	@	ROE	7%	=	2.30

APPLICATION TO WRAP-AROUND FINANCING

To substitute a wrap-around for the above examples, simply envision the W/A as 100% instead of price; the underlying loan as the mortgage; and the seller's equity as the equity. In other words, deduct the buyer's cash equity from the price, then the W/A becomes the 100%:

		%
Selling price	$ 120,000	N/A
Buyer's equity	20,000	N/A
W/A balance	100,000	100%
Underlying loan	75,000	75%
Seller's W/A equity	$ 25,000	25%

Then in the foregoing terminology,

Cap rate	becomes	W/A K
K	becomes	Underlying K
(Buyer's) Equity	becomes	(Seller's) Equity

In Step 3 of the last example, the same formula would be labeled:

Formula Title	*W/A Title*	*Ratio*	*Rate*		*Weighted Average*
(Price)	W/A	100%	(Cap) W/A	9%	9.00
(Mortgage)	Underlying	67%	(K)	10%	6.70
(Equity)	Equity	33%	(ROE)	7%	2.30

See Chapter 8 for full discussion of wrap-around financing.

18.

Introduction to the Six Investment Tables

The mounting rate of technological advances in our exciting computer age, combined with increasingly complex income tax implications, are offering a greater challenge than ever to the progressive investment property Realtor to have at his command a sound knowledge of practical mathematics to maintain his position in the forefront of providing real estate investors with maximum opportunity for capital enhancement, both before and after income tax effects.

Specifically, there are six actuarial formulae which are invaluable tools for coping professionally with such common problems as mortgage and lease discounting, and calculating future loan balances and, increasingly, with more advanced tax-oriented evaluation techniques.

Fortunately, the analyst has in his possession a valuable master key with which to unlock the values of these formulae, without embarking on a career as a mathematician but by using only the simple process of logical deduction. This key is the familiar payment book (Financial Constant Percent Amortization Tables), and its annual constant factor.

The loan payment book is the key to using 6 investment formulas.

Keep in mind, as we go through the six formulae, that while the explanation seems extensive, each formula can be reached through simple steps.

Here then, are the six formulae, with their formal titles and actuarial symbols as they appear in most standard statistical and financial texts.

1. Amount of 1 at Compound Interest $(1 + i)^n$
2. Final Value of Annuity (or Amount of Annuity of 1 at End of Each Period)

$$\frac{(1 + i)^n - 1}{i}$$

3. Sinking Fund Factor (Reciprocal of 2) $\frac{i}{(1+i)^n - 1}$
4. Present Value of 1 at Compound Interest (Reciprocal of 1) $\frac{1}{(1+i)^n}$
5. Present Value of 1 Per Annum (or Present Value of Annuity of $1 at End of Each Period) (Reciprocal of 6; also known as Inwood Coefficient)

$$\frac{1 - \frac{1}{(1+i)^n}}{i}$$

6. Annuity Which 1 Will Buy (or Periodic Payment Required to Amortize $1 and Interest)

$$\frac{i}{1 - \frac{1}{(1+i)^n}}$$

$(1 + i)^n$ the symbol for compound amount, is basis for all 6 formulas.

A vital observation at this point: all these formulae are merely varied combinations of subtracting and dividing the key symbol for compound amount, Table 1 $(1 + i)^n$, so let's simplify that first, by listing its elements separately:

1 = Principal of $1. The secret of all financial actuarial formulae is to reduce all problems to $1 and parts of $1, which, based on 100 cents, are at the same time percentages. Then these ratios and percentages are applied to the dollar amount of the problem at hand. In this symbol, the $1 is deposited (or invested) for a number of months, quarters, or years, (known as conversion periods).

+ i = The rate of interest, to be compounded at the end of each conversion period.

n = Number of periods; it is a multiplier of the figure it modifies.

Thus $(1 + i)^n$ is read, "$1 plus interest rate per conversion period (year, in our example) compounded *n* times," or using real numbers, say, 8% for 25 years, $(\$1 + .08)^{25}$, reads "$1 + 8% interest compounded annually for 25 years."

Note further that the simple elements of $1 and *i* (for interest rate) within the parentheses, are the same which outside the parentheses are applied in simple patterns of subtraction and/or division.

Table 2 is reciprocal of Table 3.

Table 2, final value of annuity, is self-explanatory; it represents the accumulated value of regular periodic deposits of $1, plus compounded interest. It functions as the reciprocal of the next formula, (3), and is useful in speed loan payoff calculations, among others.

Table 3 is the sinking fund.

Table 3, the sinking fund formula, as its name suggests tells us how much to deposit periodically at any given rate of interest so that the sum of deposits plus compounded interest will equal a required amount at a future date, say a roof replacement or retirement of a trust deed balloon. It also constitutes the first loan payment principal, which added to the interest rate composes the constant payment.

Example: If a $10,000 loan is repayable principal and interest at $1,000 per year, at 9%, then $900 would be interest and $100 principal, or sinking fund. Thus, as a factor, it will be shown as the decimal .10 per $1. In the next example of 10.91%, the interest is 10.00% and the balance of .91% is the principal, or sinking fund.

Present value, Table 4, means the value at the *present* time of money due at a *future* date. It is the reciprocal of Table 1.

Table 4 is reciprocal of Table 1.

Example.

$1 compounded at 8%, 2 years $(1.08)^2 = \$1.166$

Present value $\frac{1}{(1.08)^2}$ or $\frac{1}{(1.166)} = 85.7\%$

$1.166 × 85.7% = Present value $1.000

(Difference $.166 = compound discount)

Be careful not to confuse this present value formula, which is based on a *single $1* left for a number of periods, with the present value of annuity (5), which is based on a continual *series* of deposits of $1.

Table 5 asks the question, "How much would I invest today to receive a yearly income of $10,910 for 25 years?"

Table 5 is the present value of annuity.

It answers with a present value of the expected future gross contract income, in the form of a factor by which the periodic (in this case, yearly) income is multiplied.

Example. To receive the above gross return of $272,750 payable $10,910 per year for 25 years, including interest compounded at 10%, the correct investment would be $10,910 × 9.1659, or $100,000.

Table 6 is the one most frequently used although perhaps not recognized. *It is the principle upon which our payment book is based.* It is really the reciprocal of its cousin (5), which is the present value of the aggregate payments of principal and interest computed by formula #4.

Table 6, reciprocal of 5, is the basis of the loan payment book.

The original function of this formula, before its adaptation for loan amortization, was to answer the question, "If I invest $1 today at a given interest rate, compounded annually, how many payments of how much money, including principal and interest, would I receive?" It is the converse of the question answered by Table 5. Here Table 6 provides the answer in the form of an annual constant factor.

Example. $1 invested at 10% for 25 years will return at an annual constant rate of 10.91% or $.1091. Thus, $100,000 invested @ 10% for 25 years, will return $10,910 per year ($100,000 × 10.91%) × 25 years, equals gross contract $272,750.

To understand how a lending institution uses these companion formulae in originating loans, think of the lender as an investor who invests in (lends to) the borrower.

The difference between the gross income of $272,750 and its present value, $100,000 is called the compound discount (interest profit):

Gross income ($10,910 year × 25)	=	$ 272,750
Present value ($10,910 × 9.1659)	=	100,000
Compound discount (interest profit)	=	$ 172,750

A word about using the payment book, and then to solution of the formulas.

The monthly payments opposite a graduated scale of loan amounts are only a subdivision, as a convenience for payment, of the true basis of the book's values—called the annual constant. This is the percentage obtained by dividing the annual payments of principal and interest by the face amount of the loan:

Example. A loan of $100,000 at 10% for 25 years:

Annual payment = $10,910

$$\frac{\$10{,}910}{\$100{,}000} = 10.91\% \text{ Annual constant}$$

It is imperative, since the values in the book are related to *all* the formulae by the annual constant factor, that only that figure be used.

The payment book is based on annual constants; if your book shows monthly amounts, you must convert.

The newer payment books have the annual constant factor set forth as reproduced elsewhere in this text. The older books show the monthly dollar payment for the dollar amounts of loans. When using those books, a shortcut method of finding the annual constant is to read the monthly payment factor opposite the loan amount of $12,000 and move the decimal point one place to the left, which by a coincidence, becomes the annual rate per $100. For example:

8% 25 year column, opposite $12,000, adjusted by moving decimal = 9.27

6% 10 year column, opposite $12,000, adjusted by moving decimal = 13.33

7.5% 30 years column, opposite $12,000, adjusted by moving decimal = 8.40

9% 20 year column, opposite $12,000, adjusted by moving decimal = 10.80

Thus to quickly find the annual payments on a loan at 9% for 20 years, multiply the loan amount by the annual constant factor of 10.80%. (Memorizing the more frequently used can save a lot of time.)

Let's now read and analyze our key Table 6 before applying it to unlock all the others:

$$\frac{i}{1 - \frac{1}{(1+i)^n}} = \text{Annual constant, or}$$

$$\frac{\text{Interest rate}}{\text{Compound discount}} = \text{Annual constant}$$

Applying numbers to Table 6 formula demonstrates how it works.

Step 1. We know that the Annual Constant, at 10% for 25 years = 10.91%. Substituting, then, the figures we know for symbols,

$$\frac{.10}{1-\frac{1}{1+.10)^{25}}} = 10.91\%$$

Having two known numbers, we can now solve the unknown value of the compound discount.

$$\$1-\frac{\$1}{(1+i)^{25}}$$

At this point we should review a principle with which we are all familiar, although we may not be aware of its mathematical name—that of reciprocal numbers.

For example, we know that just as 1 ÷ 4 = .25, so 1 ÷ .25 = 4. In other words, if 4 were the unknown number, it could be found by dividing 1 (the dividend) by .25; or, if .25 were the unknown number, it could be found by dividing 1 by 4. The principle, then, is that reciprocal factors are counterparts of each other, and each may be found by dividing a common dividend by the other. In actuarial math, that common dividend is always number 1.

Returning to the formula, we see that the interest rate, .10, is the dividend, and that both the annual constant (.1091) and the compound discount, $1-\frac{1}{(1+.10)^{25}}$ are reciprocal divisors of the dividend .10.

So that, if $.10 \div \left(1-\frac{1}{(1+i)^{n}}\right) = .1091$

it follows, that .10 ÷ .1091 = .91659.

Now we know all the factors, and can reassemble the formula:

$$\frac{.10}{.91659} = .1091$$

The compound discount symbol $1-\frac{1}{(1+.10)^{25}}$ is thus evaluated as .91659.

Step 2. Next, we must determine the value of $\frac{1}{(1+.10)^{25}}$ (the present value symbol).

If $1-\frac{1}{(1+.10)^{25}}$ is worth .91659 (read Present Value subtracted from $1 equals .91659) then it follows that the opposite is true, that .91659 subtracted from $1 equals $.08341, thus:

if	$ 1.00000	then	$ 1.00000
	− .08341		− .91659
	.91659		.08341

We have now solved Table 4: The present value of \$1 at 10% for 25 years = \$.08341.

Step 3. Continuing our deductive reasoning, we see that the symbol for present value of \$1 $\frac{1}{(1+.10)^{25}}$ is composed of \$1 divided by the symbol for the amount of \$1 compounded at 10% for 25 years, $(1 + .10)^{25}$.

If $\frac{1}{(\$1+.10)^{25}}$ = .08341, it follows that

$$\frac{1}{.08341} = 11.98897$$

We have now solved Table 1: The amount of \$1 compounded at 10% for 25 years = 11.98897.

Solving Table 2.

Step 4. We are ready now to solve Table 2 $\frac{(1+i)^n - 1}{i}$,

or, in the figures of this example $\frac{(\$1+.10)^{25} - \$1}{.10}$.

If $(\$1 + .10)^{25}$ is worth \$11.98897,
then $(\$1 + .10)^{25} - \$1$ = \$10.98897
Using known figures, then, the formula becomes:

$$\frac{10.98897}{.10} = 109.8897$$

We have now solved Table 2: The final value of \$1 per annum compounded at 10% for 25 years = \$109.8897.

Solving Table 5.

Step 5. Lastly, we come to Table 5, the present value of \$1 per annum, $\frac{1 - \frac{1}{(1+i)^n}}{i}$ which, after Table 6, is perhaps the most frequently required in the analyst's daily routine.

Before undertaking its resolution into figures, look carefully: it is simply Table 6 inverted. That is, it is the reciprocal of 6. Let's read the formula:

$$\frac{1 - \frac{1}{(1+i)^n}}{i} = \text{present value of \$1 per annum}$$

or, $\frac{\text{Compound discount}}{\text{Interest rate}}$ = Present value of \$1 per annum

We have already convered both the compound discount and interest rate into figures, when resolving Table 6 above.

Therefore:

$$\frac{\text{Compound discount}}{\text{Interest rate}} = \frac{.91659}{.10} = 9.1659$$

We have now solved Table 5: The present value of \$1 per annum compounded at 10% for 25 years = $9.1659.

The annual constant payment of principal and interest, on a 10%/25 year loan in any principal amount, when multiplied by this factor, will produce the present value of the loan.

Observe, now, that because Tables 6 and 5 are reciprocals, and therefore the factors 10.91% and $9.1659 are reciprocal, the same result can be obtained by capitalizing by 10.91% as by multiplying by $9.1659 (allowing for the fractional differential caused by the rounding of the book's factors).

So, to find a present value of $1 annuity (Table 5), instead of converting your annual constant into its reciprocal by dividing into 1, simply capitalize your rental or loan payment figure by the annual constant factor.

Now, not to confuse you with too many technical details, but just so you'll be aware of it, the actuarial formulae are based on what is known as ordinary annuity, as differentiated from annuity due; the former, such as loan payments, include interest payable through the *end* of each period, while the latter, such as lease rental, is paid *in advance* and therefore does not accrue interest in the last period. The correct present value factor to use in case of lease discount is the one for 1 year less than the actual terms, plus $1. However, the difference is fractional and since the time-saver method being advanced in this chapter is for estimating only, the same formula as that used for loan discounting will serve the purpose. Where a written estimate is involved, the qualifying phrase "subject to actuarial adjustment (in escrow)" would cover.

You can now solve any of the 6 formulas, step by step.

In summation, the above process, stripped of the need for extended explanation, can enable you to derive any of the formulae in moments, in one to five simple dividing or subtracting steps in the following order:

Step 1. Divide interest rate by constant and you have the value of the *compound discount.*

Step 2. Subtract value of compound discount from $1 and you have *present value of $1* (Table 4).

Step 3. Divide $1 by the answer to Step 2 and you have the *amount of $1 at compound interest.*

Step 4. Subtract $1 from the answer to Step 3 and you have the *compound discount of $1.*

Step 5. Divide the answer to Step 4 by the interest rate and you have the *final value of $1 annuity.*

And to find the *present value of $1 per annum,* requires only one step—divide $1 by the annual constant factor and you have the present value factor (or simply capitalize the income [loan payment] directly by the annual constant factor).

The sinking fund is just as easy. Subtract the interest rate from the constant. The remainder is the sinking fund.

I should like to share with you one more time-saver. To find the amount of a loan paid off at the end of any given number of years,

Using this process to find the balance remaining on a loan.

divide the present annual constant, minus the interest rate, by the balloon-period annual constant, minus the interest rate.

Example. To find the balance at the end of 10 years, of a 10.25% loan of $100,000, payable $11,112 per year:

($11,112 ÷ $100,000 = 11.12%)

	Present K	*10-Years K*
Annual constant	11.12	16.03
Less interest rate	10.25	10.25
Amortization	.87	5.78

then $\frac{.87}{5.78}$ = 15.1% paid off.

100% − 15.1% = 84.9% balance remaining

$100,000 × 84.9% = $84,900 balance 10 years.

Even quicker, if the original term of years is known, the balance in dollars after any number of years may be determined by subtracting the elapsed years from original term to arrive at the remaining life. Then, divide the annual *dollar* loan constant by the constant *factor* for the remaining life to get the dollar unpaid balance. This is very useful in quickly calculating second trust deed balloon balances.

Example. 10.25%, 25 year loan of $100,000, payable $11,112 year. Find balance at end of 10 years.

25 years − 10 years = 15 years remaining.
Constant factor for 15 years = 13.08%.
$11,112 ÷ 13.08% = $84,954 balance at end of 10 years.
Then, $100,000 − $84,954 = $15,046 paid off.

With a little reflection and experimentation, you will find that the above applications are only a sampling of the questions that can be resolved in a trice with only Table 6 itself, once its relationship to companion tables is understood.

The tables have been presented above in the order in which they could be devolved from the most complex (loan repayment) down to their simplest common factor (compound amount of) by subtraction and division, as an educational exercise.

In practice, they are assembled in different order, and can be marshalled into helpful groups as:

By Time Value

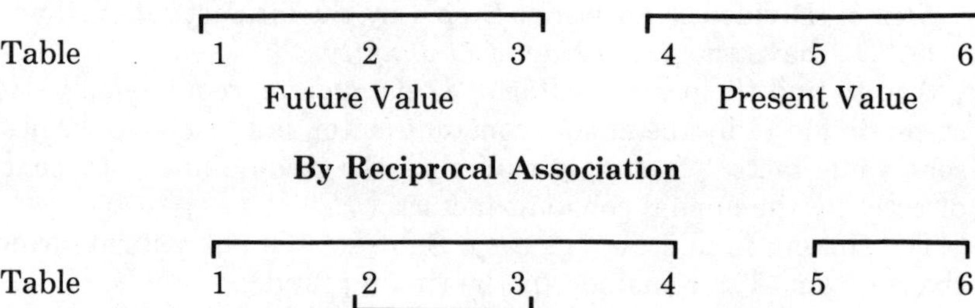

SINKING FUND

The sinking fund, or Table 3, is a very strategic figure and serves many purposes.

The most recognized use is to indicate the amount that must be deposited in each conversion period (monthly, quarterly, semiannually or annually) which, together with compound interest will equal a desired future sum.

Using Table 3 to figure amount you must deposit to derive a future sum.

Example. A bond issue of $500,000 must be redeemed in 60 months. A savings and loan institution pays 6% interest, compounded monthly. What amount must be deposited monthly?

Table 3: 6%, 60 months = .014333

$500,000 × .014333 = monthly deposit	$ 7,166.50
Total of actual deposits ($7,166.50 × 60) =	$ 429,990.00
Plus compound interest	70,010.00
Target amount	$ 500,000.00

Another, less widely recognized use is in amortization of loans, where the sinking fund constitutes the principal in the loan constant. When a loan is advanced, remember, the two objectives are return *of* capital (principal) and return *on* capital (interest). The lender simply adds the sinking fund factor to the effective interest rate to construct the monthly constant.

Table 3 is also helpful in structuring loan amortization.

Example. A loan of $100,000 is repayable in 300 months (25 years) including interest at 10% per year (.008333 per month). The sinking fund, Table 3, for 300 months is .00753. Adding the two together, we find the constant.

Interest	.008333
Principal	.000753
Constant	.009086

This leads to a useful shortcut computation, bypassing a rather involved mathematical formula demonstrated in a later chapter.

At any given interest rate, the payments on a short-term loan are naturally higher than on a long-term loan. Since the interest rate can't change, it is only the principal amortization portion, or sinking fund, which changes. Therefore, if it is desired to amortize only a percent of the total loan in a given period of years, just separate the interest from the principal, multiply the principal by the percent to be amortized, and add the product back to the interest for the adjusted constant.

Example. A loan of $100,000 at 10% is to be only 60% amortized over a 25-year period, leaving a $40,000 balloon balance. What should the monthly constant be?

Step 1.	Table 3, 10%, 300 months	.000753
Step 2.	.000753 × 60% =	.000452
Step 3.	Add the interest rate	.008333
Step 4.	Adjusted monthly constant	.008785

$100,000 × .008785 = $878.50 per month

Proof by alternate method.

Step 1. Divide the loan into the percent to be amortized, and the percent balloon.

Step 2. Multiply the percent to be amortized by the monthly constant from Table 6.

Step 3. Add one month interest on the balloon balance to Step 2.

In figures.

Step 1. $100,000 × 60% = $60,000
$100,000 × 40% = $40,000

Step 2. $60,000 × Table 6 .009087 = monthly constant $545.22

Step 3. $40,000 × .00833 = one month interest 333.32

Monthly payment $878.54

The sinking fund, while constituting the return-of-capital portion of the constant, is actually an interest figure itself. It is determined by dividing the effective interest rate from the first conversion period, by the total compound interest for any given period. The latter is known as $S^n - 1$. S^n is the compound interest plus the original $1 deposit, which is Table 1. $S^n - 1$ is the interest alone, minus the $1.

Example. In the monthly tables for 9%, 25 years, the effective rate is .0075 (.09 ÷ 12 = .0075). Table 1 for 25 years (S^{25}) = 9.408414. $S^n - 1$ = 8.408414. The fraction of the two, .0075 ÷ 8.408414 equals .000891, which can be seen to be Table 3, the sinking fund, for 25 years. The symbol for this equation is

$$\frac{i}{(S^n - 1)} = \frac{1}{S_{\overline{n|}}}$$

indicating that the sinking fund, Table 3, is the reciprocal of Table 2, symbolized as $S_{\overline{n|}}$

The constant (Table 6) is constructed by adding the effective

rate	.007500
to the sinking fund	.000891
total constant (check, Table 6)	.008391

The numerator, .0075, represents 100% or the whole number 1. Substituting 1 for .0075 in the above fraction, we have what will be recognized as the reciprocal of $S^n - 1$:

$$\frac{1}{S^n - 1} = .118928 \text{ reciprocal}$$

Adding back the original 1 deposit, we have 1.118928. Multiplying this $S^n - 1$ reciprocal plus 1 by the effective rate .0075 results in the Table 6 constant, .008391 (1.118938 × .0075 = .008391).

In classicial mathematics, this would be expressed in the formula

$$\frac{1}{(S^n - 1)} + 1\ (i) = K$$

In figures: $\frac{1}{8.408414} + 1 = 1.118928 \times .0075 = .008391$

In the above example, it will be seen that the interest rate, by being multiplied by a number larger than 1, establishes the sinking fund by creating a constant larger than the interest rate, by the amount of the sinking fund. Thus, if the effective rate .0075 is deducted from the constant .008391, the sinking fund emerges as .00891. This leads to the practical application of reducing only a portion of a loan in a given period.

Since using 1, or 100%, as the numerator produces the constant that will retire 100% of the loan in a given period, then substituting a smaller percent than 100 as the numerator will produce a constant that will retire only a corresponding percent of the loan.

To reduce the above loan by only 40% in the same 25-year period then, the formula is (P = percent):

$$\frac{P}{S^n - 1} + 1\ (i) = K$$

In figures:

$$\frac{.40}{8.408414} + 1\ (i) = 1.04756 \times .0075 = .007857$$

CONVERSION OF TABLES FROM ORDINARY ANNUITY TO ANNUITY DUE, USING THE BASE RATE

The six tables are computed on the basis of interest in arrears, or at the end of the conversion period (month, quarter, half year or year) as in the case of a mortgage loan. This is known as an *ordinary annuity.* Rent, however, is normally paid in advance; therefore, for the first period, no interest is earned. This is called *annuity due.* A visual diagram will help.

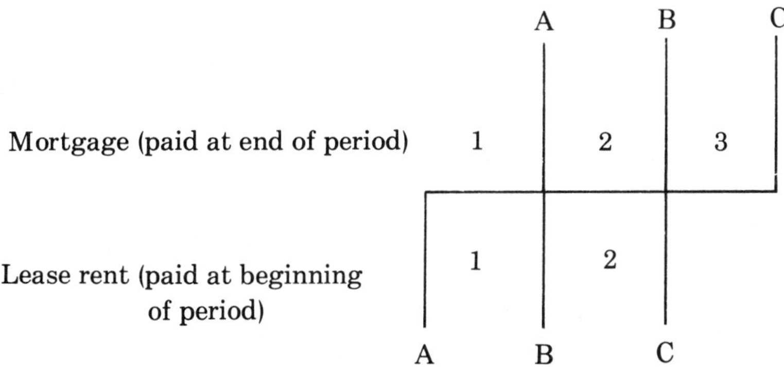

In both cases there are three *payments,* but the mortgage has three interest-earning *periods,* whereas the lease rent has only two.

There is a very simple way in which the six tables can be converted to annuity due. The very first effective interest rate, plus $1, appears at the top of Table 1 for every nominal interest rate and every conversion frequency. This is the **base rate**. Take 9% for example, for each conversion frequency:

First Table 1 figure,	monthly, is	1.0075
First Table 1 figure,	quarterly, is	1.0225
First Table 1 figure,	semi-annually, is	1.045
First Table 1 figure,	annually, is	1.09

To convert any table, either multiply (M) or divide (D) by the base rate as follows:

Table 1	*Table 2*	*Table 3*	*Table 4*	*Table 5*	*Table 6*
D	M	D	M	M	D

Notice that the respective reciprocal tables—Table 1 and Table 4; Table 2 and Table 3; Table 5 and Table 6—are treated oppositely. Where Table 1 is divided, Table 4 is multiplied, and so forth. This makes it a snap to memorize these conversion processes—which you must do.

19.

Practical Applications of the Six Tables

Here we will work out examples for each of the six tables, using 9% in each case.

1. Table 1—Compound Amount of $1

This is the basic principle on which your savings account is compounded at the bank or savings and loan (if it is compounded monthly, that is).

Example:

Deposit at 9% compounded monthly for 5 years	$ 10,000
Table 1 factor 9% for 5 years	1.5657
$10,000 × 1.5657 = compounded amount	$ 15,657

In other words, $10,000—or anything—compounded monthly for 5 years at 9% will expand to a little more than 1½ times itself. The table could also be used to calculate populations, cost of living, in fact anything expected to grow.

2. Table 2—Accumulation of $1 Per Period

Similar to Table 1 but instead of a single sum deposit, a series of equal deposits is envisioned. For example, if you deposited $100 per month at 9% compounded monthly, your balance at the end of 5 years could be calculated using Table 2, which shows the factor for 9% for 5 years is 75.424.

$100 × 75.424 =	$ 7,542.40
Your deposits, $100 × 60 months =	$ 6,000.00
Compound interest earned	$ 1,542.40

This table has other uses, too. In Chapter 27 it is seen that a loan payoff may be quickly projected by multiplying the first month amortization by Table 2 for 12 months, giving effect to the fact that each month the interest on unpaid balance diminishes, and the amortization increases (compounds) correspondingly. Table 2 does that compounding. If the first month payment of a loan is $500, then the amount paid off at the end of 12 months would be, not 12 times $500, but compounded, as:

Table 2, 9% for 12 months = 12.5076
$500 × 12.5076 = $6,253.80 paid in 12 months

3. Table 3—Sinking Fund

This table is the reciprocal of Table 2. Where Table 2 tells how much a periodic deposit or payment will grow to, Table 3 tells how much *less* than the desired final amount may be deposited in order to achieve the final amount when compound interest is added. It is most useful for meeting some future obligation, such as a bond issue that must be redeemed, or a note balance coming due.

It is actually the principal portion of loan repayments. The lender desires two things: to obtain return *of* the loan capital, and return *on* the loan. The latter is accomplished by assigning an interest rate. To accomplish the former, the lender adds to the interest rate, the sinking fund factor shown in Table 2 for the given interest rate and term. Together, they constitute the loan constant factor.

Example. What are the monthly payments for a 9% loan of $20,000 repayable in 60 equal installments?

First month interest rate $\frac{.09}{12}$ = .0075
Table 3 sinking fund factor 9%, 60 months = .01325
Total loan repayment constant .02075

In dollars:

$ 20,000	×	.0075	=	$ 150.00	interest
$ 20,000	×	.01325	=	$ 265.00	principal
$ 20,000	×	.02075	=	$ 415.00	constant

To prove that $265 will return the capital in 60 months, multiply by the Table 2 factor for 9% for 60 months, 75.424: $265 × 75.424 = $20,000. For return *on* capital:

$415 constant × 60 months = Total paid	$ 24,900
Less original loan	20,000
Return *on* lender's capital	$ 4,900

For a more everyday example that's closer to home, assume a new roof will cost $20,000 in 5 years. The question would be, "How much should be deposited every month, compounded monthly at 9% to equal $20,000?"

$20,000 × Table 3, 9% for 60 months, .01325 = $265.00

Now look at the compounding effect.

Total amount compounded =	$ 20,000
Actual deposits $265 × 60 months =	15,900
Interest profit	$ 4,100

Note that multiplying the Table 3 periodic deposit by Table 2 for the same period (60 months in the above example) produces the total target amount, including the compound interest.

Table 2, 75.42 × $265 deposit = $20,000

More than one table may be needed for the solution of any problem. Suppose it was reasoned that, with inflation at the rate of, say, 9% per year compounded, the roof will cost considerably more than $20,000 5 years from now. The question, "How much more?"

First, multiply by Table 1.

Table 1, 9% for 60 months = 1.5657

$20,000 × 1.5657 = $31,314 cost in 5 years

Next, find the sinking fund deposit at 9% monthly needed to meet the cost of $31,314.

Cost $31,314 × Table 3 .01325 = monthly deposit $414.91.
Round $415.

4. Table 4—Present Value Reversion of $1

There are two kinds of present value: one for a single sum due in the future (this table), and the other for a level stream, or series of payments over a period of time (Table 5, to follow).

Table 4 is the reciprocal of Table 1. Where Table 1 *adds* interest to an amount deposited at the *start* of a period (like a bank deposit), Table 4 *deducts* compounded interest for an amount to be collected at the *end* of a period.

The most common application we encounter is a note to be paid in a lump sum at the end of a period of time. If this note is offered for purchase, the question is, how much should be paid for the note if the price is to earn a certain interest rate compounded monthly for the buyer? Table 4 charges the note backward (*discounts*) for the interest the buyer loses by having to wait for payment.

Assume a $5,000 note due in 5 years. The buyer's money is worth, in his opinion, 9% compounded monthly. Table 4 says that $1 due in 60 months at 9% is worth today $.638699, or 63.87%. Therefore any amount of dollars may be multiplied by that factor for $1. So, $5,000 × .638699 is worth *today* $3,319.35.

Purchase price means present value, and present value means price.

Another version of this same principle will be used when we discount future income *which is not level but uneven,* so that each year's income must be calculated separately as single sums, and then totaled.

Table 5—Present Value of $1 per Period

Table 6—Installment to Amortize $1 (Loan Repayment Constant)

Table 5 converts monthly payments of a given principal and interest into the corresponding principal loan amount. It is the reciprocal of Table 6, which converts a principal amount into equal monthly payments of principal and interest.

Problem. We are considering a $200,000 loan at 9% interest for 10 years payable monthly (120 months). What will the monthly payments be?

Procedure. *Divide* the loan amount by Table 5. The Table 5 factor at 9%, 120 months is 78.941692.

$200,000 ÷ 78.941692 = $2533.58 monthly payments

We could also do the same problem using Table 6.

Procedure. *Multiply* the loan amount by Table 6. In Table 6, the factor for $1 is .012667. If $1 is to be repaid at $.012667 a month, then $200,000 must be repaid at 200,000 times that, or $2,533.40 a month (200,000 × .012667).

Or, the opposite problem can also be quickly calculated, with either Table 5 or 6.

Problem. If the monthly payment is known, how do we find the loan amount? (Same figures as above.)

Procedure. *Multiply* the monthly payment by Table 5.

$2533.40 × 78.941692 = $200,000 loan amount

Procedure. Or *divide* the monthly payment by Table 6.

$2533.40 ÷ .012667 = $200,000 loan amount

Another example: A couple wants to establish an annuity for their parents for 10 years; they have $200,000 to deposit with an insurance company that can invest it at 9% compounded monthly. The question is, how much could be paid to the parents monthly, including interest and return of principal, before the $200,000 fund is depleted?

An annuity, remember, functions much like a loan. Just as a lender "invests" in the borrower, our couple invests in an insurance company. So the solution to this problem uses the same process as the example just above; Tables 5 or 6 again.

Procedure. *Divide* the fund amount by Table 5 (78.941692).

$200,000 ÷ 78.941692 = $2533.40 monthly annuity.

Procedure. Or, *multiply* the fund amount by Table 6 (.012667).

$200,000 × .012667 = $2533.40 annuity.

Now let's use Table 5 to solve the problem in reverse. If we know that $2,533.40 is payable every month for 120 months at 9%, then what must the loan balance, or equity fund, be?

Table 5, 9%, 120 months = 78.9417.

That is, every $1 paid monthly is worth 78.9417 times itself, or $78.94 rounded. Therefore, $2,533.40 must have a capital value of:

$2,533.40 × 78.9417 = $200,000.

Or, using the reciprocal Table 6 (.012667):

$2533.40 ÷ .012667 = $200,000

Since in financial analysis the *annualized* total of monthly payments is used, it is faster to use the annualized constant factor (K) found in the ordinary loan amortization book, described in Chapter 20. For instance, in the above example (where K 9%, 10 years is .1521), the annualized annuity is $30,400 × 80 (2533.40 × 12).

Procedure. *Multiply* the fund amount by K.

$200,000 × K .1521 = $30,400.80

Procedure. Or, *divide* the annuity by K.

$30,400.80 ÷ K .1521 = $200,000 (round)

HOW TO USE THE LOAN PAYMENT BOOK TO FIND EACH OF THE SIX COMPOUND INTEREST TABLES.

The payment book, which is portable, can be used to replicate the 6 tables, which are not.

The loan payment book is small and easily portable, whereas the tables are bulky and best suited to use in an office. On the many occasions when the tables are not accessible, it will be helpful to know how to convert the basic loan constant factor, or K factor, which is actually the sixth table, into each of the other five. It's especially handy with the two most frequently used: Table 1, Compound Amount of $1, and its reciprocal, Table 4, Present Value of $1.

Before proceeding, remember that the payment book constant is the *annualization* (not annual) of 12 monthly compoundings, not just one compounding in the annual table factor. This is because the annual Table 6 is based on the entire loan being outstanding for the full year, and the payment made in one sum at the end. The interest, of course, must be earned on the entire balance for the year. When payments are monthly, on the other hand, the loan balance is being diminished each month, so that the interest is computed each month on a declining balance, resulting in a lower amount of effective interest by the year end.

Therefore, the analyst must choose between applying the *monthly* Table 6 factor to the *monthly* payment, or the annualized total of monthly rate (12 times the *monthly* Table 6 factor) to the annualized total of payments. For example, payments of $1000 per month equal $12,000 per year. So then $1000 is divided by the monthly Table 6 factor to find the loan amount, or the $12,000 total is divided by the payment book K factor, which is equal to 12 times the *monthly* Table 6 factor, not the single payment *annual* Table 6.

There is frequently a slight difference between the K figures and the table, which appears at first glance to be significant. However, if you round back the third and fourth decimal, the difference is miniscule. Certainly for the tolerance required in investment analysis, especially preliminary analysis, the difference is inconsequential. For example, deducting the nominal interest rate of 10% (rather than the exact effective rate that results from 12 monthly compoundings) from the K factor for 25 years, 10.91, leaves an annualized sinking fund of .0091 (.1091 − .1000 = .0091).

Dividing .0091 by 12 months =	.000758
The monthly Table 3 factor is	.000753
Difference	.000005

With that explanation, let's list the conversions. For a vehicle of orientation, we'll use a common 10% interest rate and a 25-year term.

1. To find the sinking fund—Table 3.

The K is composed of interest and sinking fund; therefore, subtracting the interest leaves the sinking fund.

In symbol: K − i = Table 3 or sinking fund.

In figures: .1091 − .10 = .0091

2. To find the compound amount of $1—Table 1.

Divide K by the Table 3 sinking fund.

In symbol: $\frac{K}{K - i}$ = Table 1, compound amount of $1

In figures: $\frac{.1091}{.0091}$ = Table 1 factor, 11.989

The monthly Table 1 figure is	12.0569
K conversion	11.9890
Difference	.0679

3. To find the present value of $1, or single sum reversion—Table 4.

Divide Table 3, sinking fund, by K.

In symbol: $\frac{K - i}{K}$ = Table 4, PV of $1

In figures: $\frac{.0091}{.1091}$ = Table 4 factor, .083497

Note that, since they are reciprocals, if you had the Table 1 figure, 11.989, then Table 4 factor, .0834097 could be found by inverting Table 1, or dividing it into 1: (1 ÷ 11.989 = .0834097). Conversely, the Table 4 factor .0834097 could be divided into 1 to find Table 1: (1 ÷ .0834097 = 11.989).

4. To find the accumulation of $1—Table 2.

Divide 1 by the sinking fund, Table 3.

In symbol: $\frac{1}{K - i}$ = Table 3, sinking fund

In figures: $\frac{1}{.1091 - .10} = \frac{1}{.0091}$ = Table 2, 109.89

Monthly Table 2 factor, 1326.83 ÷ 12 months =	110.57
Difference	000.68

This process was simply finding the reciprocal of Table 3. Visually, you could deduct the interest rate .10 from K .1091, and see .0091. Then divide .0091 into 1 = 109.89.

5. To find the present value of $1 per period—Table 5.

Divide 1 by K.

In symbol: $\frac{1}{K}$ = Table 5, PV of 1 per period

In figures: $\frac{1}{.1091}$ = Table 5 factor, 9.1659

Monthly table factor 110.047 ÷ 12 months =	9.1706
Difference	.0147

Note again, this is simply finding the reciprocal of Table 6. Since the same answer found by *multiplying* by one reciprocal component may be found by *dividing* by the other component, why not skip converting K to PV of $1 per period (Table 5) and simply divide the problem dollar payment by K right off?

Example. A 10-year loan at 10% interest is payable $660.83 per month, or $7,930 per year. What is the balance?

The easiest method is to divide (capitalize) the annualized payment by K for 10% at 10 years, which is .1586. Then, $7,930 ÷ .1586 = $50,000 balance.

To use the monthly Table 5 factor it would be necessary to divide the annual payment, $7,930, by 12 to find the monthly payment, since only *monthly* payments may be multiplied or divided by monthly factors, and *12 months annualized* payments can be multiplied or divided only by *annualized* factors.

Thus	Table 5, 10%-10 year monthly factor =	75.671	
	$7,930 ÷ 12 months =	$ 660.83	month
	$660.83 × 75.671 =	$ 50,000.00	
But easier	$7,930 ÷ K .1586 =	$ 50,000.00	

20.

Shortcut Uses of the Ordinary Loan Amortization Book

The loan payment book, which is in actuality one of the six standard compound interest tables (Table 6), has locked in its formula all the elements of the other five tables. Therefore, all the solutions to present and future values that are made possible by use of all six tables can be achieved in seconds using only the small, convenient loan payment book.

Two varieties of loan payment book.

There are two varieties of such books in circulation. One lists the actual dollar payments per month for loan amounts in gradations of $100. The other, more modern, type lists the annual constant percent factor by which any loan amount may be multiplied to find the dollar payment per year. By this time you have probably noted that I prefer using the annual constant factors, but don't despair if you have one of the earlier types of loan payment books—you can easily convert the tables. Compare these two samples, using an example of a $100,000 loan at 10% for 25 years.

Type A. Dollar Amount Payment Book

Monthly Payments Necessary to Amortize a 10% Loan

Term	*2 Years*	*3 Years*	*etc.*	*10 Years*	*25 Years*
Amount					
$ 100	$ 4.62	$ 3.23		$ 1.33	$ .91
200	9.23	6.46		2.65	1.82
etc.					
1,200	55.38	38.73		15.86	**10.91**
12,000	553.74	387.21		158.59	109.05

Type B. Payment Book Using Constants

Constant Annual Percent Needed to Amortize a Principal Amount
Calculated on an annualized monthly payment basis.
Divide by 12 to determine monthly payment.

Interest Rate	*2 Years* %	*3 Years* %	*etc.*	*10 Years* %	*25 Years* %
7	53.73	37.06		13.94	8.49
7¼	53.87	37.19		14.09	8.68
7½	54.00	37.33		14.25	8.87
7¾	54.14	37.47		14.41	9.07
8	54.28	37.61		14.56	9.27
etc.					
10	55.38	38.73		15.86	**10.91**

Notice that, by a coincidence of numbers, the dollar amount monthly payment in Type A for a $1,200 loan, $10.91, is the same figure as the annual constant factor for 10% in Type B. In other words, for any given interest rate or term of years, the monthly payment per $1,000 for a $1,200 loan will always be the same as the annual constant factor per $100 for that interest rate and term of years.

Some Type A editions skip from a $1,000 loan to a $1,500 loan, so no $1,200 loan line is available. In that case, note above that the monthly payment for a $12,000 loan is simply 10 times the figures for a $1,200 loan. Therefore, all that is necessary is to move the decimal of the $12,000 loan payment one place to the left. This is really dividing by 10. Thus, 109.05 becomes 10.91.

Another way to find the constant factor when the loan amount and annualized payment are known is to divide the payment by the loan amount. Thus, $149,243.67 ÷ $1,367,953 = 10.91%.

The advantage of using annual constant factors is speed and simplicity. To figure the payment on an odd amount loan, such as $1,367,953 for example, would involve adding together a lot of smaller loan payments, since no book goes above either $20,000 or $100,000. Whereas using 10%/25 years, the loan amount could be multiplied by one factor, 10.91%, to arrive instantly at the payment: $1,367,953 × .1091 = $149,243.67 per year.

We'll use a 10%/25-year loan for these examples.

All examples will be based on 10%/25 years so that you can follow the step-by-step procedures without a payment book. The same solutions apply to any combination of interest rate and term of years.

Problem I. How to find a balloon balance, in dollars.
Assume a $200,000 loan, 10%, 25 years. K 10.91%. Balloon due in 5 years. $200,000 × K .1091 = $21,820 annual payment total.

Find balloon balance in dollars.

Procedure

Step 1. Subtract balloon period from full term to arrive at remaining term.

Step 2. Find constant factor for remaining term by intersecting interest rate and years.

Step 3. Divide annual dollar payment by remaining term constant percent (K). Quotient is the dollar balloon balance.

In Figures

Step 1. 25 years − 5 years = 20 years remaining.

Step 2. Constant factor for 10%, 20 years = 11.59%.

Step 3. $21,820 ÷ .1159 = balloon balance $188,266.

Find balloon balance in percent.

Problem II. How to find a balloon balance, in percentage.

Procedure.

Step 1. Subtract balloon period from full term to arrive at remaining term.

Step 2. Find constant factor for remaining term.

Step 3. Divide full term factor by remaining term factor. Quotient is the *percent* balloon balance.

In Figures

Step 1. 25 years − 5 years = 20 years remaining.

Step 2. Constant factor for 10%, 20 years = 11.59%.

Step 3. .1091 ÷ .1159 = 94.133% balloon balance. $200,000 × .94133 = $188,266 balance (compare with above).

Find term of years.

Problem III. How to find the term of loan in years when loan amount, interest rate and annual payment are known.

Procedure

Step 1. Divide annual payment by loan amount to find constant percent.

Step 2. Scan payment book under the interest rate, across the term of years to find the nearest term at which the constant percent is found.

In Figures

Step 1. $21,820 ÷ $200,000 = constant factor 10.91%.

Step 2. At 10% interest rate, constant 10.91% appears at 25 year term.

When the factor is between the factors for two different years, visual interpolation is generally sufficient. For example, if a target factor of 10.96% fell between the constants of 11.01% for 24 years and 10.91% for 25 years, then the difference between the lower 10.91 and the larger 11.01 equals .10; the difference between the lower 10.91 and the target 10.96 equals .05, which is half the difference between the extreme rates; therefore, the term of the loan will be halfway between 24 and 25 years, or 24 years and 6 months.

It really wouldn't be significant if the difference were not exactly half the spread. When such accuracy is required, see the section on Rate Book Interpolation in Chapter 20.

Problem IV. How to find the interest rate when the loan amount, annual payments and term of years are known.

Find interest rate.

Procedure

Step 1. Divide the annual payment by loan amount to find the constant factor.

Step 2. Scan the payment book under the term of years to find the interest rate at which the constant factor appears.

In Figures

Step 1. \$21,820 ÷ \$200,000 = 10.91%.

Step 2. At 25 years, constant 10.91 appears opposite 10% interest rate.

One word of caution here: many of the calculations that real estate investment analysts require can be performed as estimates, good ballpark numbers, at least in the early stages of negotiation. In the case of interest rates, however, close is not good enough; you must be exact, for the rate is the rate. Therefore, when solving for interest rates, if you do not find the precise figures in the tables, you must perform a mathematically accurate interpolation; a visual interpolation is not sufficient. See page 167 for the formula.

Problem V. How to determine term of years required to reduce a loan to a given amount.

How long to reduce a loan?

We'll use the same example with a target payoff of 6%. *(Note: Always convert the percent paid off to the percent remaining by subtracting payoff percent from 100%, because the payment book is constructed on the basis of remaining term.)*

Procedure

Step 1. Subtract 6% from 100% = 94% balance.

Step 2. Divide (capitalize) the constant for the original term by the balance percent, to arrive at a larger factor. *(Note: Dividing any number by less than 100% always results in a higher number.)*

Step 3. Scan the payment book under the interest rate to find the term of years nearest to which the larger factor appears.

Step 4. Subtract remaining term from original term. Difference is the payoff term required.

In Figures

Step 1. 100% − 6% = 94%.

Step 2. .1091 ÷ .94 = .1160 constant factor.

Step 3. At 10% interest rate, 11.59% appears under 20 years. Close enough.

Step 4. 25 years − 20 years = 5 years payoff term.

Find the yearly payment needed to pay off a loan.

Problem VI. How to find the annual constant payment required to amortize a portion of a loan, leaving a balloon balance.

Example. An original loan of $1,500,000 at 10% for 25 years is to be reduced by 60% ($900,000) leaving a 40% ($600,000) balloon due at the end of 25 years.

There are two methods.

Method A: *Separate portion to be amortized from the balloon amount.*

Procedure

Step 1. Subtract balloon from original amount.

Step 2. Multiply the amortized portion by the K factor.

Step 3. Multiply the balloon balance amount by one year's interest.

Step 4. Add Step 2 and 3 for the annual constant payment.

In Figures

Step 1.	$1,500,000 − $600,000 =	$ 900,000
Step 2.	$900,000 × K .1091 =	98,190
Step 3.	$600,000 × .10 =	60,000
Step 4.	Total yearly constant	$ 158,190

Method B: *Reduce the principal portion of the K factor to the percent to be amortized.*

Procedure

Step 1. Subtract nominal interest rate from K factor for interest rate and term given to get principal.

Step 2. Multiply principal by percent of investment to be amortized.

Step 3. Add product from Step 2 to interest rate.

Step 4. Multiply original loan by Step 3 to arrive at adjusted *annual* constant payment.

In Figures

Step 1. Constant (K) .1091 − .10 = principal .0091.

Step 2. .0091 × .60 = adjusted principal .00546.

Step 3. .00546 + .10 (interest rate) = adjusted constant .10546.

Step 4. $1,500,000 × .10546 = annual constant $158,190.

The difference of $54 between $158,190 and the $158,136 you get using monthly Table 6 (.0003) below is not significant, particularly compared to speed and ease of calculation.

Same problem, using monthly Table 6 for comparison, and the same two methods.

Method A: *Separate portion to be amortized from the final balloon amount.*

Procedure

Step 1. Subtract balloon amount from original loan.

Step 2. Multiply the amortized portion by monthly loan constant (Table 6) for the interest rate and term given.
Step 3. Multiply balloon amount by one month's interest.
Step 4. Add Steps 2 and 3 for the total monthly constant payment.

In Figures

Step 1. \$1,500,000 − balloon \$600,000 = amortized \$900,000.
Step 2. \$900,000 × .009087 (Table 6 for 300 months)
= \$ 8,178 per month
Step 3. \$600,000 × .008333 (10% ÷ 12 months)
= 5,000 per month
Step 4. Total monthly constant \$ 13,178 per month
Step 4. Total yearly constant \$158,136

Method B: *Reduce the sinking fund (principal) portion of the monthly loan constant (using monthly Table 6 constant, .009087).*

Procedure

Step 1. Subtract first month's interest from monthly loan constant to get first month's principal.
Step 2. Multiply principal by percent of loan to be amortized.
Step 3. Add Step 2 product back to first month's interest to get adjusted constant.
Step 4. Multiply original loan amount by Step 3.

In Figures (same example)

Step 1. .009087 (Table 6 for 300 months) − .008333 (interest) = .000754 principal.
Step 2. .000754 × 60% (to be amortized) = sinking fund .0004524.
Step 3. .008333 + .0004524 = adjusted constant .0087854.
Step 4. Loan \$1,500,000 × .0087854 = monthly
constant \$ 13,178
annual constant \$158,136

Note that Method A, calculating the two elements separately, proves the accuracy of Method B. These two methods may be used in sale-leaseback rental calculations where only a portion of the investment (usually the building improvement) is to be amortized, since the land (plus any building salvage value) will revert to the lessor at the end of the lease term (see Chapter 11).

Problem VII. How to calculate annuities.

Your handy loan payment book can also be used as a tool when planning an annuity (a deposited fund which disperses payments over a period of months or years). Because annuities are usually thought of as retirement income plans, you may wonder why it's included in a text on real estate analysis. Look on it as a bit of mind-stretching, if you will. What I hope to show is that it provides a new

Planning an annuity gives insight into loan mechanics.

insight into the basic workings of a loan payment (composed of principal and interest); the problems of one are the problems of the other. Typical questions about annuities fall into the same categories as questions about loans: What interest rates? What dollar amounts are possible? What size fund must be deposited to provide a given income? How long will the income last before the fund is depleted?

Take a typical annuity question. A daughter wants to establish an annuity for her parents of $1,000 per month for 10 years. She can earn 10% on invested funds. The question: How much does she have to deposit to earn a $1,000 monthly payment, representing principal and interest, for 10 years?

Procedure

Step 1. Look up the constant factor for 10%, 10 years.

Step 2. Divide the *annual* total of payments by that factor to find the investment fund needed.

In Figures

Step 1. The constant for 10%, 10 years = 15.86%. (See sample payment book pages in Appendix A.)

Step 2. $12,000 year ÷ 15.86% = required deposit $75,662.

Let's look at the alternate problem. How many years would $75,662 support annuity payments of $1,000 a month before the fund is exhausted, if invested at 10%?

Procedure

Step 1. Divide the *annualized* payments by the fund to find a constant factor.

Step 2. Scan the payment book at 10% interest to find the term of years nearest to which the factor appears. That is how long the fund will last.

In Figures

Step 1. $12,000 ÷ $75,662 = constant 15.86%.

Step 2. At 10% interest, 15.86% appears under 10 years.

Another alternate problem: At what interest rate must a fund of $75,662 be invested to provide $1,000 per month principal and interest annuity payments for 10 years, at which point the fund would be exhausted?

Procedure

Step 1. Divided the *annualized* total of payments by the fund amount to find a constant factor.

Step 2. Scan the payment book under the term of years to find the interest rate nearest to which the factor appears.

In Figures

Step 1. $12,000 ÷ $75,662 = constant 15.86%.

Step 2. Under 10 years, the constant 15.86% appears opposite 10% interest rate.

If it fell between two interest rates, either interpolate (see below) or use the nearest even constant and multiply the fund by it to slightly adjust the monthly payments.

COMMON PROBLEMS REQUIRING INTERPOLATION OF RATE BOOK FIGURES

Procedure

Interpolating between two payment book rates.

Step 1. Subtract *lower* rate from *higher* rate in rate book.
Step 2. Subtract *lower* rate from problem rate.
Step 3. Divide problem rate difference (Step 2) by rate difference (Step 1) to get percent.
Step 4. Apply percent to difference in element being solved for:
- Amount of loan
- Rate of interest
- Term of years

Example I. To Solve for Amount. Loan is payable $164.20 month @ 9% for 17 years. What is principal owing? Or, what amount loan will that pay off?

Rate book shows:

	Amount	*Payments*	
Lower	$ 17,000	$ 163.00	$ 163.00
Problem	?		164.20
Higher	17,500	167.80	
Difference	$ 500	$ 4.80	$ 1.20

$$\frac{1.20}{4.80} = 25\%$$

Difference in loan amount, $500 × 25% = $125. Therefore, lower rate book amount, $17,000 + $125 = $17,125.

Example II. To Solve for Rate. Borrower can pay $424.38 per month for $50,000 loan for 30 years. What would the interest rate be?

Rate book shows:

	Percent	*Payments*	
Lower	9.50	$ 420.43	$ 420.43
Problem	?		424.38
Higher	9.75	429.58	
Difference	.25	$ 9.15	$ 3.95

$$\frac{3.95}{9.15} = .43$$

Difference in book rate .25% × 43% = .001075. Therefore, lower book rate .0950 + .0011 = .0961.

Example III. To Solve for Term. The second trust deed of $18,500 is payable at $512.00 per month at 9%. How many years and months?

			Payments @ 9%	
4 years	=	48 months	$ 460.38	$ 460.38
Problem		?		512.00
3 years	=	36 months	588.30	
Difference		12 months	$ 127.92	$ 51.62

$$\frac{51.62}{127.92} = 40\%$$

Rate book difference 12 months × 40% = 4.8 months.

48 months (the longer term) − 4.8 months = 43.2 months, or 3.6 years.

To refine: 360 days × .6 years = 216 days ÷ 30 days = 7.2 months

To refine further: .2 months × 30 days = 6 days

Finally, then, we have assembled this exact term:

3 years, 7 months, 6 days.

Note this important exception: Term and payment constant do not vary directly, but inversely. That is, as the loan is reduced, the remaining term of years decreases in numbers but the amount of payment required grows larger.

Therefore, when an interpolation amount exceeds the payment for the longer term of years, it is progressing in trend from the longer period toward the shorter. So when making the interpolation, we subtract from the longer period, rather than adding to the shorter period. In the example above, the target amount of $512 is progressing from the low of $460.38 to the higher of $588.30, or from 48 months toward 36 months. Therefore, by adding it to the low dollar amount, it is progressing away from the longer term toward the shorter term.

For a more complete explanation of the interpolation procedure, see page 186.

ENRICHMENT

A look at the math formulas which are the foundation of the payment book shortcuts.

As enrichment for the more inquiring reader, and also to demonstrate again the time and effort saving value of the shortcuts presented in this text, the following classical mathematic formulae are presented and solved in steps. First we'll apply the classical math formula to Problem VI on page 164, to better appreciate the efficiency of the loan payment book shortcuts.

The formula produces the *yearly* K, but uses the *monthly* Sn because the loan will be paid monthly, requiring 12 interest compoundings per year.

P = Percent paid off; (60%)
Sn = Table 1, Compound Amount of \$1 (at 10%, 25 years, monthly = 12.056944)
Sn − 1 = 12.056944 − 1 = Compound Amount of \$1 less the original \$1 deposit (11.056944)
I = Nominal interest rate (10%)

The formula, applied to Problem VI on page 164.

$$\left(1 + \frac{P}{Sn - 1}\right) I = K \text{ (per year)}$$

It is read "One plus the quotient of the percent to be paid off, divided by the net compounded interest (Sn − 1), times the interest rate (I) equals the necessary loan constant (K)."

In Figures

$$\left(1 + \frac{.60}{11.056944}\right) \times .10 = K \text{ per year } .105426$$

(1 + .05426) × .10 = K per year .105426
Annual K: \$1,500,000 × .105426 = \$158,139
Monthly K: \$158,139 ÷ 12 months = \$13,178

Another important formula, also possible to solve speedily with the loan payment book, is:

HOW TO FIND THE PERCENT OF LOAN PAID OFF IN ANY GIVEN PERIOD

First let's introduce the equations used.

$$\frac{K}{I} - 1\ (Sn - 1) = P$$

The essence of the formula is that the percent of loan paid off is equal to the same percent of compound interest earned (Sn − 1) which percent is determined by the $\frac{K}{I} - 1$ part of the formula.

It is read: "The loan constant (K) divided by the nominal interest rate (I) less 1, times the compound amount of \$1 (Table 1) less the original \$1 deposit, for the given time period (Sn − 1), equals the percent paid off (P)."

The underlying mathematical process that leads to this formula is that the first principal payment portion of a loan constant constitutes the sinking fund factor found in Table 3. This factor, when multiplied by the reciprocal Table 2 Annuity factor for the given time period, equals the percent of a loan paid off in that period.

The algebraic procedure for determining how much of a loan will be paid off in a given period.

At the top of each table (see at the end of this text) is the symbol describing the table's function. Table 1, for example, is symbolized as Sn. Sn, in turn, represents the fundamental interest compounding process upon which all six tables are based, $(1 + i)^n$. It is read "The original deposit (\$1) plus the interest rate (i) multiplied by itself for a given number of compounding periods (n)." For example,

\$1 deposited in a savings account and compounded monthly at 9% for 96 months (8 years) would amount to \$2.048921.

Now, if it were desired to ascertain just the total accrued interest, net of the original \$1 deposit, the symbol would be modified to read Sn − 1, or more basically $(1 + i)^n - 1$ and the amount of interest only would be \$1.048921. The Table 2 symbol is based on that same Sn − 1, or (1 + i) − 1 which is capitalized at the given interest rate (i), and reads:

$$\frac{Sn - 1}{i} \quad \text{or} \quad \frac{(1 + i)^n - 1}{i}$$

Its reciprocal Table 3 sinking fund factor uses the same symbols, but inverted:

$$\frac{i}{Sn - 1} \quad \text{or} \quad \frac{i}{(1 + i)^n - 1}$$

In both it can be seen that the principal deposit, \$1, is extracted from the compounding, and the interest rate and the compounded total interest divided into each other as indicated in each table symbol.

So the first step is to multiply the symbol for the sinking fund (Table 3) by that of the annuity (Table 2) and reduce them to a working equation which will establish the percent by which the compound interest (Sn − 1) is to be multiplied.

Since Sn, or $(1 + i)^n$ and (Sn − 1), or $(1 + i)^n - 1$ are the essential factors of both tables, it is then necessary to find the value of each. This is achieved by dividing the Table 6 constant (K) symbolized as

$$\frac{1}{a_{\overline{n}|i}}$$

by the same constant but less the interest (which is recognized as the sinking fund) and is symbolized logically as

$$\frac{1}{a_{\overline{n}|i}} - i$$

When the percent has been arrived at by Tables 2 and 3, and the value of $(1 + i)^n$ established, the formula is ready for solution.

Example. Assume a 9%, 20 year loan (K 10.8%). What percent (P) is paid off in 8 years (96 months)?

Sn, or $(1 + i)^n$ for 96 months is	2.048921
(Sn − 1), or $[(1 + i)^n - 1]$ for 96 months is	1.048921

Procedure

Step 1. Multiply Table 3 (Sinking Fund) by Table 2 (Annuity of \$1).

$$\left(\frac{i}{(1+i)^n - 1}\right)\left(\frac{(1+i)^{96} - 1}{i}\right) = P$$

Step 2. Cancel out i as numerator and denominator. Annuity divided by sinking fund = P.

$$\frac{(1+i)^{96} - 1}{(1+i)^n - 1} = P$$

Step 3. Convert sinking fund to reciprocal to determine percent of interest earned.

$$\frac{1}{(1+i)^n - 1} \times (1+i)^{96} - 1 = P$$

Step 4. Recognize that $[(1+i)^n - 1]$ equals (Sn − 1), or the aggregate compounded interest for ^{n} periods. Therefore, it is necessary to find the value of $(1+i)^n$ first, then subtract original deposit (1) to isolate interest only.

Step 5. Define value of $(1+i)^n$.

$$\frac{\dfrac{1}{a_{\overline{n|}\,i}}}{\left(\dfrac{1}{a_{\overline{n|}\,i}} - i\right)} = (1+i)^n$$

That is, $\left(\dfrac{1}{a_{\overline{n|}\,i}} - i\right)$ equals Table 6 − i, or Installment to Amortize $1 less interest, or K − i which is the *sinking fund.*

In Figures

Step 6. Substituting figures, to prove symbols, using above example of 9%, 20 years (K 10.8%).

$$\frac{\dfrac{.108}{12 \text{ months}}}{\dfrac{.108}{12 \text{ months}} - \dfrac{.09}{12 \text{ months}}}$$ Eliminate common 12's:

$$\frac{.108}{.108 - .09} = \frac{.108}{.018} = 6$$

Therefore, $(1+i)^n = 6$, so that $[(1+i)^n - 1]$ *must equal* 6 − 1, or 5.

Step 7. And the reciprocal evolved in Step 3 $\dfrac{1}{(1+i)^n - 1}$

therefore, equals $\dfrac{1}{5}$ which is .20.

Step 8. So that $\frac{1}{(1 + i)^n - 1} \times (1 + i)^{96 \text{ months}} - 1$ as in Step 3 is equal to $.20 \times [(1 + i)^{96 \text{ months}} - 1]$.

Remember that $(1 + i - 1)^{96 \text{ months}}$ is the same as $(Sn - 1)^{96 \text{ months}}$.

So if (Sn − 1) at 9% for 96 months is 1.048921, then .20 × 1.048921 *must equal 20.98% meaning the loan is 20.98% paid down.* Finally, \$500,000 loan × 20.98% = \$104,892 paid off.

The original formula, then, could be seen to work as follows.

$$\left(\frac{K}{I} - 1\right) \times \quad (Sn - 1) \quad = P$$

$$\left(\frac{.108}{.09} - 1\right) \times \quad (1.048921) \quad = P$$

$$(.2) \qquad \times \quad (.1048921) \quad = P.\ 20.98\%$$

SAME FORMULA, USING THE PAYMENT BOOK FORMULA

A simpler version of the same procedure.

Since the loan amortization book is more convenient to carry around, the following is an easier method. The book is based on remaining balances rather than amounts paid off, so the problem is simply reversed from "how much is paid off?" to "what will the balance be after the given amount is paid off?" The above example would be restated to "What will be the balance after 8 years?" The difference between the original loan and the balance after 8 years is the amount paid off. Using the same 9%, 20 year example as above,

Step 1. Subtract balloon period from full amortization term:

20 years − 8 years = 12 years remaining

Step 2. Divide original 20 year K factor (.108) by K factor for 9%, 12 years (.1366) to find the remaining balance: .108 ÷ .1366 = .79063, or 79.06% of the original loan is the balance remaining after 8 years.

Step 3. Subtract from 100% to find the percent paid off: 100% − 79.06% = 20.94% paid off.

21.

Reversion and Income Stream: How to Find Each When the Other Is Known

Another frequent analytical problem involves finding the required resale reversion when the income stream is known, in order to realize a given yield.

HOW TO FIND THE AMOUNT OF REVERSION REQUIRED WHEN THE INCOME STREAM IS KNOWN

Method A: Final Value Annuity Approach
Formula

$$V\left[(1+i)^n - I\ \frac{(1+i)^n - 1}{i}\ (1+i)\right] = \text{required reversion}$$

The formula is composed of these basic elements:

V = The value, or purchase price.

$(1+i)^n$ = The compound amount of \$1, or Table 1.

I = The known income, expressed as a percent of the investment.

$(1+i)$ = The base rate, which is the original deposit of \$1 plus the first period portion of the interest rate.

$\frac{(1+i)^n - 1}{i}$ = The accumulation of \$1, or Table 2.

To read the formula, the amount of reversion will equal the original investment (V), multiplied by the difference (−) between the total compounded amount of the investment $(1+i)^n$ and the accumulated total of the income stream $\left[(I)\ \frac{(1+i)^n - 1}{i}\right.$ multiplied by the base rate $\left.(1+i)\right]$ to adjust the tables to advance, rather than arrears, payments, as explained on page 152.

The formula is more readily recognized if presented as:

(value × Table 1), less (income × Table 2 × base rate) = reversion

Since the whole theory of factors is to compute every problem in terms of $1 and then apply the resulting factor to the actual dollar amount of the problem, the dollar rental income is reduced to a factor by dividing it by the value and the formula assembled in terms of $1 factors, as:

(Table 1 factor) less (income factor × Table 2 factor × base rate), the resulting factor of which is then multiplied by the dollar amount of value.

To grasp the concept, remember that the two future benefits of the investment are the income stream and the reversion. If the income stream is known, then the reversion must be equal to the total benefit less the income benefit.

The basic relationship between reversion and income stream.

Problem. Take the example of a $1,000,000 investment that must achieve a total yield over 20 years of 10%. The rental income is $7,000 per month in advance. What price (reversion) must it sell for? First, since the tables are all in decimal form, compute the dollar rental into a decimal as well.

$7,000 ÷ $1,000,000 = .007

Table 1 tells us that in 240 months at 10% $(1 + .00833)^{240}$, an original investment will have compounded to 7.328073 times itself. That total will be made up of the accumulated compounded rent and the final resale reversion.

The monthly rent accumulation is found by multiplying it by the Table 2 factor, which for 10%, 20 years (240 months) is 759.36883. Then, since rent is paid monthly in advance, the Table 2 factor must be adjusted by multiplying by the base rate of 1.008333. Then, 759.3683 × 1.008333 = 765.969. The rent factor .007 × 765.696 = 5.3599.

Remember that the base rate may be applied to the Table 2 factor first and then the rent factor multiplied by the product, or applied first to the rent factor and the Table 2 factor multiplied by that product. Or the total compounded rent could be computed in dollars, and the *dollar* total multiplied by the base rate.

Now, if 7.328073 is the total, and of that, the rent factor amounts to 5.3599, then the reversion factor must be the difference, or 1.9682. The original investment (V) multiplied by that factor equals the percent of required reversion: $1,000,000 × 1.9682 = reversion $1,968,200.

In dollars, then, the formula becomes:

$1,000,000 [7.328073 − (.007 × 759.3683 × 1.00833)], or
$1,000,000 [7.328073 − (5.359873)], or
$1,000,000 (1.968200) = required reversion $1,968,200

In outline form, for easier reference:

Procedure

Step 1. Divide periodic income by original equity (price) to find amount per $1 (factor).

Step 2. Multiply Table 2 factor for final value by base rate (to convert ordinary annuity factor to annuity due).

Step 3. Multiply Step 1 by the product of Step 2 to find the income factor.
Step 4. Deduct Step 3 from compound amount of $1 factor for the investment period, Table 1, to find reversion.
Step 5. Multiply original equity by the difference found in Step 4.

In Figures

Step 1. $7,000 ÷ $1,000,000 = .007.
Step 2. 759.3683 × 1.00833 = 765.969.
Step 3. .007 × 765.969 = 5.3599.
Step 4. 7.328073 − 5.3599 = 1.9682.
Step 5. $1,000,000 × 1.9682 = $1,968,200.

Method B: Present Value Capitalization Approach

Another valuable observation is that every present value (original equity or purchase price) is really composed of two present values; one of the income stream, and the other of the final resale reversion. Therefore, if one of the present values is known, the other may be found by simple subtraction.

If the income present value is known, and subtracted from the total present value, then the remaining present value must be capitalized by the factor for the present value of $1 reversion, which is Table 4. If, in reverse, the reversion present value is known, and subtracted from the total, then the remaining income present value must be regarded the same as repayment of a loan, and multiplied by the installment to amortize $1 factor, which is Table 6. This latter table in some books is titled "Annuity Which $1 Will Buy," but it's the same table.

Second technique uses present, rather than future, values to arrive at same solution.

Therefore, whereas the first solution used the *future* value differential technique, the same answer may be found using the *present* values of Table 5 for the income stream (present value of $1 per period) and Table 4 for the reversion (present value of $1 reversion).

Procedure

Step 1. Multiply Table 5 factor by base rate to convert ordinary annuity to annuity due.
Step 2. Multiply periodic dollar income by adjusted factor found in Step 1 to find present value of the income.
Step 3. Deduct the Step 2 product from original equity to find present value of the reversion.
Step 4. Capitalize the difference found in Step 3 by Table 4 factor to find the dollar amount of required reversion.

In Figures

Step 1. 103.6246 (Table 5 for 10%, 240 months) × base rate 1.00833 = 104.4878, annuity due Table 5 factor.
Step 2. $7,000 × 104.4878 = $731,415 present value of income.
Step 3. $1,000,000 less $731,415 = $268,585 present value.
Step 4. $268,585 ÷ Table 4 factor .136461 = $1,968,200 reversion.

A more economical business form of presentation is suggested, as:

Step 1.	Original equity	$ 1,000,000
Step 2.	Less present value of income at 10%, 240 months, ($7,000 × Table 5 103.6246 × base rate 1.00833) =	731,415
Step 3.	Present value of reversion	$ 268,585
Step 4.	$268,585 ÷ Table 4 .136461 = reversion	$ 1,968,200

A shorter procedure, using our payment book.

Same example, using the loan payment book. First, adjust the monthly income to annual. $7,000 per month × 12 = $84,000 per year. The K factor for 10%, 20 years is .1158. The base rate is 1.00833. Adjust the K factor to annuity due by dividing it by the base: .1158 ÷ 1.00833 = .11484. Also, convert the K factor to Table 4 to capitalize the present value of the reversion. This is really quite simple once it becomes familiar to you (see Chapter 19 under "How to Use the Loan Payment Book to Find Each of the Six Compound Interest Tables."). Divide the sinking fund by the K:

$$\frac{K - i}{K} = \frac{.1158 - .10}{.1158} = \frac{.0158}{.1158} = \text{Table 4, } .13644$$

Procedure

Step 1. Divide the first year income by the adjusted K to find the present value of the income stream.
Step 2. Deduct Step 1 from the original equity to find the present value of the reversion.
Step 3. Capitalize the difference found in Step 2 by Table 4 to arrive at the reversion.

In Figures

Step 1. $84,000 ÷ adjusted K .11484 = $731,450.
Step 2. $1,000,000 − $731,450 = PV of reversion $268,550.
Step 3. $268,550 ÷ Table 4, .13644 = $1,968,264 required reversion.

Note: The reversion arrived at using the monthly tables = $ 1,968,200
The reversion arrived at using the payment book = $ 1,968,264

Sometimes the above problem is reversed: the amount of reversion is known, and the required income stream must be determined.

HOW TO FIND THE REQUIRED INCOME STREAM WHEN THE REVERSION IS KNOWN

You need to know that Table 6, 10%, 20 years = .00965, and the base rate = 1.00833.

Procedure. *Using monthly tables.*

Step 1. Multiply the dollar reversion by Table 4 to find its present value.

Step 2. Deduct Step 1 from original equity to find present value of periodic income.
Step 3. Divide Table 6 by the base rate to adjust to annuity due.
Step 4. Multiply the present value found in Step 2 by the adjusted Table 6 to find the required income.

In Figures

Step 1. \$1,968,200 × Table 4, .136461 = \$268,583 present value of reversion.
Step 2. \$1,000,000 − \$268,583 = \$731,417 present value of income.
Step 3. Table 6, .00965 ÷ base rate 1.00833 = .00957.
Step 4. \$731,417 × .00957 = \$7,000 required income.

In Business Form

Original equity	\$1,000,000
Less present value of reversion at 10%, 240 months (\$1,968,200 × Table 4, .136461)	268,583
Present value of required income	\$ 721,417

Then \$731,417 × adjusted Table 6, .00957 = \$7,000 required income.

Same example, using payment book. Here K 10%, 20 years = .1158. Divided by base rate of 1.00833 adjusts to annuity due. K converted to Table 4:

$$\frac{K - i}{K} = \frac{.0158}{.1158} = \text{Table 4, .13644}$$

Procedure. *Using payment book.*

Step 1. Multiply the dollar reversion by Table 4 to find its present value.
Step 2. Deduct Step 1 from original equity to find the present value of the income stream.
Step 3. Multiply Step 2 by the K factor (adjusted by the base rate to annuity due) to find the required income.

In Figures

Step 1. \$1,968,200 × Table 4, .13644 = \$268,541 present value of reversion.
Step 2. \$1,000,000 − \$268,541 = \$731,459 present value of income.
Step 3. \$731,459 × adjusted K .11484 = \$84,000 required annual income. And \$84,000 ÷ 12 months = \$7,000 required monthly income.

V.

Measurement of Yield: Alternate Methods

22.

Internal Rate of Return: Purpose and Calculation

The internal rate of return (IRR) technique is simply the process of discounting the future benefits of income and final reversion down to a present value equal in amount to the original investment. It is based on the true value of money. A dollar in hand today is worth more than a dollar payable at a later date because the recipient is not able to invest it at interest until it is received. Therefore, for each period he has to wait for the money, he deducts the interest lost. As a result of discounting the sum by the interest not earned, for each period of waiting, the present value is less than the future value by the accumulated compounding of interest.

IRR technique discounts from future value of money the interest not earned in the present.

Two present value tables that provide the factors by which the interest is deducted (discounted) are:

(a) When the future benefit is paid in a single sum, with no interim payments, use Table 4, called Present Value of $1 Reversion.

(b) When the income stream is paid equally in each period, use Table 5, called Present Value of $1 Per Period.

Here's how it works. The future benefits are discounted at two or more rates, by trial and error, until one rate produces a present value figure which is less than the original investment, and the other a figure greater than the original investment. The correct yield rate is then somewhere between the trial rates, and is found by interpolation.

For example, assume a purchase price of $100,000, an income stream of $9,000 per year and a reversion of $78,000 at the end of 10 years. Discounting the income and the reversion (future benefits) at 7%, the present value would be approximately $103,000, which is higher than the original investment. Therefore, the discount rate

It uses a process of interpolation.

must be too low. At 8%, the present value comes to approximately $97,000, which is lower than the original investment, indicating that the discount rate is too high. By interpolation, the original investment, $100,000, lies halfway between the higher and lower discounted values and therefore, the true yield rate lies halfway between 7% and 8%, or 7.5%.*

In the following examples, it will be seen that the IRR, where the present value (price) is known and yield rate is sought, is exactly the reverse of the calculation of present value when the yield rate is known. Note, too, that the future benefits of income plus reversion are *treated the same* whether they constitute (a) constant payments and balloon payment of a loan, (b) rental payments and final reversion of land and improvements of a lease, or (c) cash flow and resale reversion proceeds of an income property.

First the mathematical formula will be analyzed as to its elements and function, then demonstrated as applied to even and uneven income streams, using loan payments and rent income examples.

Since interest declines each year, as well as depreciation if on an accelerated basis, the after-tax cash flow will vary from year to year even if the rental stream is level throughout the period. Therefore, the mathematical formula evaluates the present value of each annual cash flow as a separate reversion, and adds to the accumulated total of these flows the final reversion as follows.

First, meet the formula.

$$\sum_{t=1}^{n} \frac{R1}{(1+i)^t} + \frac{R2}{(1+i)^t} + \frac{R3}{(1+i)^t} \ldots + \frac{R^n}{(1+i)^n} = IRR$$

$\sum_{t=1}^{n}$ = Greek letter Sigma, or S, for "summation" of the basis on which the formula to follow is conducted.

n = the final period

t = one period

R1, 2, etc. = each annual after-tax cash flow

Rn = the final reversion

$(1 + i)^t$ = the compound amount of 1 (Table 1) for each year

$(1 + i)^n$ = the same table for the final year

Note that when $(1 + i)^t$ or $(1 + i)^n$ is used as a denominator, the fraction really equals the present value of 1, or Table 4, since numerators of fractions may be added. For example:

$$\frac{1}{4} \times 100 \text{ is the same as } \frac{100}{4};$$

$$\frac{1}{4} \times 100 = 25; \quad \frac{100}{4} = 25$$

*The formula for exact interpolation is covered on page 186.

Likewise, the present value of $1, $\frac{1}{(1+i)^n} \times \text{Rent}$ is the same as

$$\frac{\text{Rent}}{(1+i)^n}.$$

Now, using the after-tax cash flow of the 50-unit model example, the first trial rate 5% formula becomes:

$$\sum_{t=1}^{n}$$

$$\frac{\$29{,}447}{(1.051182)} + \frac{\$27{,}894}{(1.104941)} + \frac{\$26{,}369}{(1.161472)} +$$

$$\frac{\$24{,}864}{(1.220895)} + \frac{\$19{,}624}{(1.283359)} + \frac{\$119{,}165}{(1.283359)} = \$204{,}472 \text{ present value at } 5\%$$

Note again that

$$\text{Table 1} \quad \frac{\$29{,}447}{1.051162} = \$28{,}014$$

just as

$$\$29{,}447 \times \text{Table 4}, .951328 = \$28{,}014$$

so that the formula is really a totaling of successive annual Table 4 present values.

Where the income stream is level, then a still briefer formula is:

$$Po = R \times a_{\overline{n}|i} + \frac{Pn}{(1+i)^n}, \text{ where}$$

Po = Present value at start
R = Periodic income stream (first period)
$a_{\overline{n}|i}$ = The symbol for Table 5, present value of $1 per period
Pn = Final reversion
$(1 + i)^n$ = The symbol for Table 1, compound amount of $1, at a given interest rate for *n* periods.

Referring to Table 5 (monthly) for 5% at 5 years we see that the symbol $a_{\overline{n}|i}$ is abbreviated to $a_{\overline{n}|}$ but is the same.

For 5% at 5 years (60 months) $a_{\overline{n}|i}$ = 52.990706, meaning that the income stream has a present worth of approximately 53 times the first monthly payment.

Assuming the above first year dollar income remained level each year at $2,453.92 per month ($79,447 ÷ 12 months in order to use the monthly Table 5 factor), and the fifth year reversion was the same, $119,165, then the process is simply:

$$Po = \$2{,}453.92 \times 52.990706 + \frac{\$119{,}165}{1.283359}, \text{ or}$$

$$Po = \$130{,}035 + \$92{,}854$$

$$Po = \$222{,}889$$

As explained on pages 142-143, Table 5 is the reciprocal of Table 6, so that the same answer is obtained by dividing by one or multiplying by the other, and the ordinary loan amortization book constant factors are the annualization of the monthly Table 6 factors, (see page 157). Therefore, the above example could have been solved more quickly by dividing the annual total of monthly income $29,447 by the annualized loan constant 22.65% (monthly Table 6 .018872 × 12) and the process appears as:

$$Po = \$29{,}447 \div .2265 + \frac{119165}{1.283359}$$

$$Po = \$130{,}009 + \$92{,}854$$

$$Po = \$222{,}863$$

The $29 difference is due to rounding and is inconsequential.

Again, I want to stress that the mathematical formulae are presented for the more inquiring scholar and to establish the authenticity of the more practical arithmatic solutions. They are further offered as encouragement toward pursuit of higher knowledge. However, they are not requisite to solving everyday business problems.

COMPUTATION OF IRR ON BALLOON NOTE

Three ways to compute the balloon amount, and then translate to present value.

First, the amount of the balloon must be computed. There are three alternative methods of arriving at a balloon balance, all of which are outlined for their educational value. The third method, using the loan payment book, is the quickest and most convenient since the small book is easier to carry about than the bulkier tables.

Note that in most instances when a note is to be discounted, the periodic payments (monthly usually) are given, as well as the interest rate, but not the exact balloon amount. Also, the period of payments is given, but not the total period required to fully amortize the loan if there were no balloon.

In the first method, the full amortization period is not required, only the number of payment periods. In the next two approaches the full amortization period is first ascertained, and then the balloon balance found by scanning the tables, or loan book, as the case may be.

Example. A loan balance of $350,000 is payable $2,600 a month including 7% interest for 8 years at which time the then unpaid balance (balloon) is due and payable. The loan is offered for purchase at $284,500.

Method I. Using monthly tables.

Step 1. Multiply the monthly payment by the monthly present value of $1 per period (Table 5) for the remaining term, at the loan interest rate.

Step 2. Subtract answer from present balance.

Step 3. Divide the difference by the present value reversion of 1 (Table 4) for the remaining term at the loan interest rate. The answer is the balloon balance.

In Figures

Step 1.	$2,600 month × Table 5, 8 years 73.347569	= $190,704
Step 2.	$350,000 − $190,704	= $159,296
Step 3.	$159,296 ÷ Table 4, 8 years .572139	= $278,579 balloon

Explanation of the formula. Since there is a balloon, then obviously the $2,600 per month does not retire the entire loan balance, but only a portion. The size of this portion is determined by Step 1. If only a portion of the loan is being paid off, then the remaining portion is not. Step 2 isolates this unamortized portion. If the $350,000 entire balance is the present value of both the monthly income stream *and* the balloon, and Table 5 tells us that $190,704 is the present value of the *income stream,* then the remainder of the $350,000 balance, $159,296, must be the present value of the *balloon.*

The factor for PV reversion of $1 may be used to capitalize a present value as well as to discount a future benefit.

Example. If $278,597 × Table 4 .572139 = $159,296
Then in reverse, $159,296 ÷ Table 4 .572139 = future benefit $278,597

Method II. Using monthly tables. Find the full amortization term, then subtract the balloon period to find the remaining term after the balloon date.

Step 1. Divide loan balance by the monthly payment, to get the factor for present value of $1 per period (Table 5).

Step 2. Scan Table 5 under the interest rate to find the year nearest to which that factor appears. (Interpolate if necessary for strict accuracy; however, visual estimate is generally close enough.)

Step 3. Subtract the balloon period from the indicated full term. The difference will be the remaining term of the loan after the balloon date.

Step 4. Multiply the monthly payment by the factor for the remaining term. The answer is the balloon.

In Figures (same example).

Step 1. $350,000 ÷ $2,600 = 134.62 times.

Step 2. Nearest factor in monthly Table 5 is 134.513 at 22 years. Close enough.

Step 3. 22 years full term − 8 balloon period = 14 years remaining.

Step 4. The Table 5 factor for 14 years is 106.906075 × \$2,600 = \$277,956 balloon. (*Note:* this method's balloon is within \$641, or .002%, of the first method's balloon, \$278,597.)

Method III. Using loan payment book.

Step 1. Divide *annual* payments by the loan balance to find the K factor.

Step 2. Scan the payment book under the interest rate to find the years nearest to which the K appears. (Visual interpolation is generally close enough.)

Step 3. Subtract the balloon period from the full term to find the remaining term after the balloon date.

Step 4. Divide the *annual total* of payments by the K factor for the remaining term found in Step 3.

In Figures

Step 1. \$2,600 × 12 = \$31,200 year ÷ \$350,000 = K 8.91%.

Step 2. Nearest payment book factor is 8.93%, at 22 years. Close enough.

Step 3. 22 years − 8 years = 14 years remaining.

Step 4. The payment book K factor for 14 years is 11.23%. \$31,200 ÷ .1123 = \$277,827 balloon. (Again, this is accurate within \$129 (.0005) of Method II, and \$770 (.003) of Method I.)

Final IRR solution requires interpolating two trial rates.

Find the IRR using some trial rates to discount future income and balloon to the amount of original price, or equity, as the target value. Try higher and lower rates until the target price of \$284,500 is bracketed above and below. The bracket rates do not have to be within fractions of the target rate, but may be widely divergent. The wider spread, say 3% to 5% apart, reduces the number of efforts to bracket the target between. Try 9% and 12% using monthly Table 5 for the monthly income and monthly Table 4 for the balloon.

At 9%

Income \$2,600 × 68.258438 (Table 5, 96 months) =	\$ 177,472
Balloon \$278,597 × .488061 (Table 4, 96 months) =	\$ 135,972
Present value at 9%	\$ 313,444

At 12%

Income \$2,600 × 61.527703 (Table 5, 96 months) =	\$ 159,972
Balloon \$278,597 × .384722 (Table 4, 96 months) =	\$ 107,182
Present value at 12%	\$ 267,154

INTERPOLATION PROCEDURE

The 9% present value is higher than the actual price of \$284,500, which means that the \$284,500 is a better buy and therefore the yield must be higher than 9%. By the same token the 12% present value is lower, meaning that the purchase price, being higher, will earn less than 12%. The object now is to find where, proportionately, between the bracket rates is the actual target price. Three columns are best for this interpolation:

1. One column measuring the spread between the bracket rates;
2. A second column measuring the spread between the lower rate discount and the higher rate discount;
3. A third column measuring the spread between the lower rate discount and the target price.

Inspection of the Tables 4 and 5 will reveal that the interest rate and its dollar present value vary *inversely;* that is, the higher the rate the lower the dollar value; conversely, as the rate goes down, the value goes up.

Putting the lower rate at the top is usually more convenient because the discounted value of the lower rate is higher than that of the higher rate (important to understand and remember). Therefore, the subtraction of the dollar figures is more natural.

	I	*II*		*III*
Lower rate	9%	$ 313,444		$ 313,444
Higher rate	12%	$ 267,154	(Target)	$ 284,500
Difference	3%	$ 46,290		$ 28,944

The actual yield rate will fall proportionately between the bracket rates, as the target excess over the lower rate value falls proportionately between the higher and lower bracket rate values.

Procedure

Step 1. In Column I, subtract the lower rate from the higher.

Interpolation, step by step.

12% − 9% = 3% difference

Step 2. In Column II, subtract the lower rate value from the higher.

$313,444 − $267,154 = $46,290

Step 3. In Column III, subtract the target value from the lower rate value.

$313,444 − $284,500 = $28,944

Step 4. Divide the smaller difference in Step 3 by the larger in Step 2 to get the percent of the target spread to the total bracket spread.

$28,944 ÷ $46,290 = 62.53%

Step 5. Multiply the bracket rate difference (Step 1) by this percent.

.03 × .6253 = 1.88%

Step 6. Add Step 5 to the lower rate to find the actual internal rate of return (IRR).

.09 + .0188 = IRR 10.88%

Here's a convenient and compact form for interpolation.

Format

$$\frac{\text{Rate difference} \times \text{Target difference}}{\text{Bracket value difference}} = \_\_\_\% + \text{Lower rate } \_\_\_\% = \_\_\_\% \text{ IRR}$$

In Figures

$$\frac{.03 \times \$28{,}944}{\$46{,}290} = 1.88\% + .09\% = 10.88\% \text{ IRR}$$

23.

Net Present Value

An alternate test to IRR to determine whether an investment meets a yield criterion is the net present value (NPV) approach. In simplest terms, it discounts the future benefits of income and/or reversion, at the required yield rate. Then the initial cost (present value) is deducted from the discounted value. If the remainder is zero or greater, the investment is acceptable. If less than zero, it is rejected. It differs from the IRR approach only in that the IRR forces the remainder to zero, using trial rates and interpolation:

NPV compares investment cost to discounted future income.

$$\sum_{t=1}^{n} \frac{Rt}{(1+i)^t} - C = O = IRR$$

The NPV approach, on the other hand, just deducts the original investment from the discounted present value of the cash flow to discover the net profit or loss:

$$\sum_{t=1}^{n} \frac{Rt}{(1+i)^t} - C = NPV$$

Stated another way, the NPV method indicates only yes or no while the IRR continues through to the exact rate.

And produces a clear yes or no answer.

Example of ranking alternate investments by NPV

	Investment A			*Investment B*		
Year	*Net Cash Flow*	*10% Discount*	*PV*	*Net Cash Flow*	*10% Discount*	*PV*
1	\$ 1,000	.905	\$ 905	\$ 3,000	.905	\$ 2,715
2	\$ 2,000	.819	\$ 1,638	\$ 3,000	.819	\$ 2,475
3	\$ 3,000	.742	\$ 2,226	\$ 3,000	.742	\$ 2,226
4	\$ 4,000	.671	\$ 2,684	\$ 3,000	.671	\$ 2,013
5	\$ 5,000	.608	\$ 3,040	\$ 3,000	.608	\$ 1,824
Totals	\$15,000		\$ 10,493	\$15,000		\$ 11,23 (11,253)
Less original investment			\$ 11,000			\$ 11,000
Net present value			(\$ 493)			\$ 23 (253)

In theory, Investment A would be rejected because the net present value is less than the original cost; Investment B would be accepted because the net present value is greater than the cost. (The numbers might seem impractical to you, but the *process* is the same no matter what.) To determine how much higher than 10% the Investment B yield is, a trial and error process is undertaken, as in the IRR example, page 186.

IRR and NPV are two ways to answer the same question: will the proposed investment produce the desired yield?

NPV is also useful in ranking competing investments. In short, the greater the excess of discounted present value over the original cost, the relatively more attractive the investment.

Another difference between IRR and NPV is that NPV applies the *same rate* to two or more different cash flows from *different properties,* as in the above example; whereas IRR applies two or more *different* trial *rates* to the cash flow from *one* property, as in the 50 Unit Case Study.

RELATIONSHIP OF PRESENT VALUE DISCOUNT AND INTERNAL RATE OF RETURN

A frequent real estate transaction is the discounting—buying at less than face value—of documents such as leases and mortgages.

The problem is posed one of two ways. Most commonly, the buyer or broker is asked to make an offer of price. The buyer must have in mind a rate of interest yield he wants. The document is then purchased at whatever price will yield that rate. The price is determined by consulting a present value table which provides a factor for the rate and term of the investment.

In reverse, the document may be offered at a stated price, and the buyer or broker must calculate what the yield rate would be. This is a little more complicated and requires the internal rate of return process.

The techniques of finding the present value when the desired rate of yield is known, and finding the yield when the original investment or price (present value) is known, are two sides of the same coin. The only variation is that finding the present value at a given rate involves multiplying future benefit by one rate; finding the rate involves multiplying by two trial rates and interpolating the difference. The following example will emphasize the relationship of the two techniques. In the first case, the present value is sought. In the second case, the value is known, and becomes the basis for finding the rate.

Example I. When the desired rate is known and the price is sought.

Assume \$30,000 loan at 7½% for 24 years, with a 10 year balloon, payable \$225 a month, K = 9%.

Problem: What is the present value at 10%?

Use this data:

Table 5 for 168 months, 7½% = 103.826706
Table 5 for 120 months, 10% = 75.671163
Table 4 for 120 months, 10% = .369406
K for 14 years, 7½% = .1156
K for 10 years, 10% = .1586

Procedure

Step 1. Determine amount of balloon.
Step 2. Find PV (present value) of income stream.
Step 3. Find PV of balloon (reversion).
Step 4. Add both PVs.

In Figures

Step 1.	\$225/month × 103.826706	= \$ 23,361	10th year balloon
Step 2.	\$225/month × 75.671163	= \$ 17,026	PV income
Step 3.	\$23,361 × .369406	= \$ 8,630	PV reversion
Step 4.	\$17,206 + \$8,630	= \$ 25,656	Discounted PV at 10%

Alternative Method, using payment book and *annualized* payments:

Step 1. \$2,700 yr. ÷ .1156 ($K^{14\text{ yr.}}$ @ 7½%) = \$ 23,356 10th year balloon
Step 2. \$2,700 yr. ÷ .1586 ($K^{10\text{ yrs.}}$ @ 10%) = \$ 17,024 PV reversion
*Step 3.** \$23,356 × .36948 $\left(\frac{K - i}{K}\ 10\text{ yr.}\right)$ = \$ 8,630 PV reversion
Step 4. \$17,024 + 8,630 = \$ 25,654 Discounted PV at 10%

Example II. When the price (present value) is known and the yield rate is sought. *Use same figures as in Example I.*

Problem: If bought at \$25,656 what is IRR?

Use this data:

Table 5 for 120 months 9% = 78.941692
Table 5 for 120 months 12% = 69.700522
Table 4 for 120 months 9% = .407937
Table 4 for 120 months 12% = .302994

Procedure

Step 1. If not known, determine amount of balloon (assume known as \$23,361).
Step 2. Select higher and lower trial rates, say 9% and 12%.

*Here, $\frac{K - i}{K} = \frac{.1586 - .1000}{.1586} = \frac{.0586}{.1586} = .36948$, which is Table 4, 120 months, 10%.

Step 3. Multiply monthly payment Table 5, 120 months for both rates.

Step 4. Multiply balloon reversion by Table 4, 120 months for both rates.

Step 5. Interpolate resulting factors.

In Figures

Step 1.	\$225 month × 78.941692	=	\$ 17,762
Step 2.	\$23,361 × .407937	=	9,530
			\$ 27,292 PV at 9%
Step 3.	\$225 month × 69.700522	=	\$ 15,683
Step 4.	\$23,361 × .302994	=	7,078
			\$ 22,761 PV at 12%

Interpolation

Lower	9%	\$ 27,292		\$ 27,292
Higher	12%	22,761	(Target)	25,656
Difference	3%	\$ 4,531		\$ 1,636

$\frac{.03 \times 1,636}{\$4,531}$ = .0108 + lower rate .09 = IRR 10.08%, round 10.1%

24.

Financial Management Rate of Return

A criticism of IRR and NPV is that they merely discount any negative cash flow in future periods at the same rate as applied to positive income; whereas in fact, the losses are out of pocket, and so must be considered a *100% loss,* not discounted. Whenever you project a loss in any future period, you have two ways to provide for it: (1) the present value of such amounts should be added to the original purchase equity, as though deposited at interest to accumulate the amount of the loss, or (2) the loss amount should be deducted from the previous period(s) of positive cash flow, and banked at interest to be available in the future loss period. In either case, the projected yield of the future positive cash flows is diminished, resulting in a more realistic yield rate.

A negative cash flow in future is deducted from present income by FMRR process.

In practice, the second method, deducting the loss from previous period income, is preferred. The technique used to accomplish this is called financial management rate of return (FMRR), demonstrated here.*

Step 1. Separate positive from negative cash flows.
Step 2. Multiply positive flows by Table 1 for the number of periods *until* the next negative flow. For example, if the

*One word of encouragement for the novice: Don't be unduly intimated by these sophisticated refinements; astronomical numbers of transactions were made before they were discovered.

first (or next) negative occurs in the fourth year, then compound the first year positive for three years (years minus the final loss year), the second year positive for two years (4 − 2) and the third year positive for one year (4 − 3). If the next negative after the fourth year negative occurs in the ninth year, then the positive flows are compounded from the fifth (the first positive) for four years (9 − 5), the sixth for three years (9 − 6), etc.

Step 3. If the accumulated positive compounded amounts are greater than the negative, the positive excess is included as part of the total reversion. If the negative flow exceeds the accumulation of positive flows the discounted net excess of negative is added to the original investment. This has the effect of depositing that amount at interest to be compounded until it equals the full amount of negative flow in the given year.

Step 4. In any year where both a positive and negative occur, the net excess of either becomes that year's flow. This would happen where the last year cash flow were negative, but the property were sold that year with a positive cash reversion.

Step 5. When the total compounded positive reversion is determined—which is the future value—and the total original investment, including addition of discounted negative flows, is determined—which is the present value—then the present value is divided by the future value, resulting in a decimal. This decimal is the present value of 1, or Table 4, factor for the number of total years involved, at a certain interest rate. That rate is found by scanning the interest rates under the given number of years, until the interest rate is found nearest to which the Table 4 factor appears. If the factor falls between two interest rates, interpolate.

Consider the following combinations of positive and negative cash flows. Use a rate of interest realizable in an ordinary savings and loan account, say 7%, which is called a "safe rate." To be strictly accurate, the six compound interest tables, including Tables 1 and 4 used below, are compounded in arrears, so that the first year positive income would be assumed to be deposited at the year end, and consequently accrue no interest. Similarly, the positive flows in later years would be compounded for one year less than is shown. However, the illustration is less complicated, and requires fewer periods to bring out the principle by accruing interest from the beginning of each year. In any event, the difference is not material in everyday business application.

Safe rate 7% monthly

I. First and last period positive.

	Table 1		*Table 4*	
1.	$ 5,000 1 year = 1.07229 = $5,361			
2.	($ 2,000)	2 years .869712	=	($ 1,739)
3.	(3,000)	3 years .811079	=	(2,433)
4.	(4,000)	4 years .756399	=	(3,026)
5.	$20,000 1 year = 1.07229 = $21,446			($ 7,198)

Total negative present value	($ 7,198)
Less prior year positive compounded	5,361
Net negative to equity	($ 1,837)
Add to original investment	10,000
Total adjusted equity	$11,837
Fifth year positive reversion	$21,500 (rounded)

Total equity divided by total reversion:

$$\frac{\$11{,}837}{\$21{,}500} = .55056 = \text{Table 4, 60 months est. 12\% FMRR}$$

Table 4, 60 months 12% = .55045

To illustrate more fully, let's consider two additional variations frequently encountered in investment analysis.

II. Third period negative; first two and last three years positive.

	Table 1					*Table 4*	
1.	$ 4,000	2 years	1.149806	$4,599			
2.	5,000	1 year	1.072290	5,362	$ 9,961		
3.	($ 14,000)	3 years				.811079	($ 11,355)
4.	$ 7,000	3 years	1.232926	$8,631			
5.	8,000	2 years	1.149806	9,199			
6.	9,000	1 year	1.072290	9,851	$27,681		

Third year negative	($ 11,355)
Less prior 2 years' positive compounded	9,961
Net negative, added to original equity	($ 1,394)
Original equity	11,000
Adjusted original equities	12,394
Last three years' positive, compounded	$ 27,681

Total equity divided by total reversion:

$$\frac{\$12{,}394}{\$27{,}681} = \$4{,}477 = \text{Table 4, 60 months approx. 14.5\%}$$

Table 4, 60 months 14% = .437109

15% = .4323

III. No income for two years, negative in third year, positive reversion fourth and fifth year.

	Table 1					*Table 4*	
1.	-0-	-0-		-0-			
2.	-0-	-0-		-0-			
3.	($ 4,000)	3 years				.816298	($ 3,265)
4.	$ 2,000	2 years	1.149806	$2,300			
5.	20,000	1 year	1.072290	21,446	$23,746		

Total third year negative flow to original equity ($ 3,265)
Add original equity 10,000
$ 13,265
Total positive flow PV $ 23,746

$\frac{\$13,265}{\$23,746}$ = .559 = Table 4, 60 months approx. 11¾% FMRR
Table 4 11¾% = .5573

Some authorities maintain that, in view of the varying periods of income and outgo of funds (monthly rents and loan payments, but yearly insurance premiums and semi-yearly property taxes, etc.) the annual conversion period should be used and is more convenient. I do not disagree. (To illustrate both, examples 1 and 3 use the monthly period, example 2 the annual.) On that basis, the first year net income would not be compounded, nor the last year. In fact, each year's income would be compounded for one period less.

However, the above method brings out the number of compoundings from negative to negative, and from the last negative until the last payment with less complications. The actual difference in return would not be significant.

25.

Payback Method

The payback method is used to determine how many periods (years, in this example) it will take for the investor's original investment to be returned. The technique involves adding the cash flows until a total is reached which is more than the original investment. From that total, we subtract the previous year total which is less than the original investment, so that the original investment is bracketed between. The time period required, then, will be the lesser number of years plus a percent of the next year, as will be borne out in the following examples.

The payback method pinpoints how long before original investment is recovered.

There are two approaches. The first totals the actual cash flows at full value. The second, more accurately recognizing the time value of money, discounts the cash flows to their present values at the investor's desired rate of interest.

In order to conserve space, the cash flows used are considerably higher and the time periods shorter than they would be in normal experience. The objective is to illustrate the principle with the least complication of excess figures.

Problem. How many years are required for an original investment of $150,000 to be paid back?

Method I. Cash flows at full value.

Assume the following:

Years	*Cash Flow*	*Cumulative*
1	$48,200	$ 48,200
2	43,500	91,700
3	44,300	136,000
4	51,700	187,700
5	47,600	235,300
6	54,400	289,700

Procedure

Step 1. Accumulate the cash flows, as above, until visually the original investment falls between a larger and smaller amount. You can see here that $150,000 falls between the third and fourth years' totals.

Step 2. Subtract the smaller from the larger total.

$187,700 − $136,000 = difference $51,700

Step 3. Find the difference between the lesser total and the original investment.

$150,000 − $136,000 = difference $14,000

Step 4. Divide this difference by the later year's cash flow to find what percent of the year it represents.

$14,000 ÷ $51,700 = 27.1% of the fourth year

Therefore, the payback period is more than three years and less than four years. To be more accurate, 27.1% of a year equals 3.24 months (12 months × .271 = 3.24 months). So the payback period is 3 years, 3.24 months.

Method II. Same example, using discounted present values.

Year	*Cash Flow*		*Table 4 @ 12%*		*Present Value @ 12%*	*Cumulative*
1	$48,200	×	.892857	=	$43,036	$ 43,036
2	$43,500	×	.797194	=	$34,678	$ 77,714
3	$44,300	×	.711780	=	$31,532	$109,246
4	$51,700	×	.635518	=	$32,856	$142,102
5	$47,600	×	.567427	=	$27,010	$169,112
6	$54,400	×	.506631	=	$27,561	$196,673

Procedure—same as above.

Step 1. It can be seen that $150,000 falls between the fourth and fifth year totals.

Step 2. Compute the difference.

$169,112 − $142,102 = $27,010

Step 3. Compute the difference between the lesser total and the original investment.

$150,000 − $142,102 = $7,898

Step 4. $7,898 ÷ $27,010 = 29.2% of the fifth year.

So payback is 4 years and 3.5 months.

You may have recognized by now that the difference between the longer and shorter period totals is exactly the last year cash flow. Now that the principle is made, Step 2 may be eliminated for convenience.

Annualized Net Present Value (ANPV)—Income Loss Absorption Test.

Calculating how low cash flow could drop, and still yield acceptable return.

As a further test, the NPV may be annualized to determine how much each annual cash flow could diminish and still meet the desired yield rate. It is done merely by multiplying the NPV (total of present values less the original investment) by the Table 6 factor for the given rate and years. In other words, treating the NPV total as if it were a loan, to find the annual constant payment, which is the counterpart of the annual cash flows in this exercise.

The annualized NPV figure represents the amount by which each annual cash flow could be reduced and still equal the desired yield rate. Stated another way, the annualized NPV constitutes the safety margin over the minimum income requirement for the yield rate to remain intact.

Example. Let's use the same $150,000 original investment, and assume that the investor requires 12% yield. By how much could the annual cash flow fall, and still return the 12%?

Step 1. Calculate the net present value. (Refer back to page 198 for the annual and cumulative totals of the $150,000.)

Cumulative total for 6 years	$ 196,673
Original investment	150,000
Net present value	$ 46,673

Step 2. Annualize the NPV by the Table 6 factor for the period (6 years) and the desired yield (12%), which is .243226.

$46,673 × .243226 = annualized NPV $11,352

Therefore, each annual cash flow could diminish by $11,352 and still return 12% to the investor.

VI.

Federal Income Taxes

26.

Federal Income Taxes

As emphasized in the Introduction, this book endeavors as much as possible to confine itself to timeless formulae and procedures, rather than temporary conditions, such as income tax laws and regulations which change frequently. The subject of taxes cannot be completely ignored, however, because of their vital impact on real estate income. The following, then, is included more for illustration of method of computation and helpful arrangement of figures than as an in-depth instruction in currently prevailing rates.

In this chapter we will particularly focus our attention on three elements of the federal tax code:

- depreciation (Section 167)
- recapture (Sections 1245–1250)
- capital gain (Section 1201)

Please note this important caution: The information in this chapter is presented as helpful business guides *only*. In this intricate and highly volatile subject, you must rely *only* on the counsel of an attorney or accountant.

For substantive advice on tax matters, you must consult an attorney or accountant.

Section 167 of the Internal Revenue Code of 1954, as amended, provides for a reasonable deduction every year, over the useful life of assets used for the production of income, for the exhaustion, wear and tear, and obsolescence of these assets. Land is not depreciable; therefore, real estate cost must be allocated between land and improvements, to establish a basis for the latter.

The Code has been amended many times, most sweepingly by the Tax Reform Acts of 1969, 1976 and 1978. As an overview, the

Changes in tax laws have affected handling of depreciation and capital gain.

results of the various amendments and reforms have been to curtail the amount of depreciation that may be taken each year, to recapture an increasing portion of accelerated depreciation as ordinary income (100% taxable) rather than long term capital gain (40% taxable) and to impose additional "preference" taxes on gain upon disposition of the property. The limitations on depreciation and capital gain can be traced broadly over the periods: 1954 through 1963; 1964 through 1969; 1970 through 1975; and post 1975. For purposes of visual comprehension, the subject will be under two major headings: "Methods Allowable" and "Treatment Upon Disposition." Under each grouping, a further classification will outline the differences between nonrealty (Section 1245) and realty (Section 1250) according to whether the property is new or used and, in the case of realty, whether nonresidential or residential.

METHODS ALLOWABLE

Nonrealty (Section 1245)

New, with life of 3 years or more, any accelerated method.

Used, maximum 150% declining balance.

Realty (Section 1250), separated into residential and nonresidential as follows:

Residential (80% or more of income must be from residential each year).

New: S/L to maximum 200% DB, or SYD

Used: S/L to maximum 125%, minimum term 20 years

Nonresidential

New: S/L to maximum 150% DB

Used: S/L only

HOW TO CALCULATE THE VARIOUS STRAIGHT LINE AND ACCELERATED METHODS.

For those of you who may be rusty on arithmetic, the following steps may be helpful:

Straight Line Divide 100% by number of remaining years to find rate. Then multiply building (net of land) by rate.

Example		
	Value of property	$ 100,000
	Less land	20,000
	Net improvement	$ 80,000

Remaining life, 25 years

100% ÷ 25 = 4% per year

$80,000 × .04 = $3,200 per year depreciation

Accelerated Same as above, except raise the straight line rate by allowable percentage.

Example 1 If used residential – allowable rate = 125%
Thus: 4% × 125% = 5%
$80,000 × .05 = $4,000, first year depreciation
$80,000 – $4,000 = $76,000
$76,000 × .05 = $3,800, second year depreciation
Etc.

Example 2 If new commercial or industrial – allowable rate = 150%
Thus: 4% × 150% = 6%
$80,000 × .06 = $4,800, first year depreciation
$80,000 – $4,800 = $75,200
$75,200 × .06 = $4,512, second year depreciation
Etc.

Sum of Years Digits (SYD) (allowable only on new residential income). Add years of remaining life consecutively to arrive at denominator. The numerator will be the number of years remaining, which will decline by one consecutively, resulting in a lower percentage each year.

Example Remaining life, 25 years
Adding years consecutively equals 325, denominator
First year rate is 25 ÷ 325 = 7.69%
Second year rate is 24 ÷ 325 = 7.38%,
Etc.

An easy formula for determing the denominator is to multiply the sum of the lowest and highest years by the total number of years and divide the product by 2:

Formula $\frac{n(l + h)}{2}$ = denominator

n = total number of years
l = lowest year
h = highest year

So that, in example of 25 years, the figures would appear as:

$\frac{25\ (l + 25)}{2} = \frac{650}{2}$ = 325, denominator

First year depreciation = 25 ÷ 325 = 7.69%, etc. as above

TREATMENT UPON DISPOSITION: Long Term Capital Gain vs. Recapture

Section 1245, Nonreal Estate. Depreciation is all recaptured as ordinary income (up to total gain realized) regardless of holding period.

Section 1250, Depreciable Real Estate. Depreciation taken on *nonresidential* property, such as office buildings, factories, etc., is subject to recapture of all *additional* (excess over straight line) depreciation, regardless of holding period.

Recapture on *residential only* is computed as follows:

I. First, starting 1/1/76:
   1. Holding period 1–12 months: all depreciation.
   2. Holding period over 12 months: all excess.

II. Second, 1/1/70 through 12/31/75:
   1. Holding period 1–12 months: all depreciation.
   2. Holding period 13–100 months: all excess.
   3. Holding period 101–200 months: all excess less 1% for each month over 100.

III. Third, 1/1/64 through 12/31/69:
   1. Holding period 1–12 months: all depreciation.
   2. Holding period 13–20 months: all excess.
   3. Holding period 21–120 months: all excess less 1% for each month over 20.

Note that the *latest* depreciation is recaptured *first* (post 1975); then if there is still unabsorbed gain, the next period back ('70–'75); if there is still unabsorbed gain, then the previous period ('64–'69).

Example. Assume a holding period of 9 years (108 months) from 1/1/68 through 12/31/77.

Total depreciation taken	$ 100,000
Less S/L	80,000
Excess depreciation	20,000
Portion taken in period post 1975	4,000
Portion taken in period 1/1/70 through 12/31/75	6,000
Portion taken in period 1/1/68 through 12/31/69	10,000

Now let's compute the appropriate applicable percentages by subjecting each period's excess to the required holding periods.

	I		*II*		*III*	
Required maximum holding period	NA		200[1]		120[2]	
Actual holding period			108		108	
Recapture %	100%		92%		12%	
Excess taken	$ 4,000		× $ 6,000		× $ 10,000	
Recaptured as ordinary income	4,000		5,520		1,200	
× Tax bracket (70%)	70%		70%		70%	
Tax payable	$ 2,800	+	$ 3,864	+	$ 840	= Total $7,504

[1]Minimum 100 months
[2]Minimum 20 months

How tax is figured on long term capital gain, and recaptured excess depreciation. Assume a sale of $400,000 with an adjusted tax basis of $238,000 and accelerated depreciation taken as in above example. Taxpayer in maximum 70% bracket. Mortgage balance $190,500.

		Tax Calculation			*Cash Proceeds*
Gross sale		$400,000			$400,000
Costs of sale (8%)		32,000			32,000
Net sale		368,000			368,000
Adjusted tax basis: (Original purchase price less depreciation taken)		238,000			
Realized gain		130,000			
Less Section 1245 recapture	-0-				
Less Section 1250 recapture:					
1. Post 1975	$ 4,000				
2. 1/1/70 - 12/31/75	5,520				
3. 1/1/64 - 12/31/69	1,200				
Total recapture		10,720	× 70% = tax	$ 7,504	
Net long term gain		119,280			
Taxable 40%		47,712	× 70% = tax	$ 33,398	
Total tax					40,902
Balance					327,098
Mortgage(s) balance					190,500
Net after tax proceeds (reversion)					$136,598

ADDITIONAL TAXES AS OF TAX REFORM ACT OF 1978

With the 1978 Tax Reform Act, there are five basic federal income taxes payable by individuals and four payable by corporations:

Individuals

1. Ordinary income tax
2. Capital gains tax
   a. Short term
   b. Long term
3. Minimum tax
   a. Add-on preference tax
   b. Alternative minimum tax

Corporations

1. Ordinary income tax
2. Capital gains tax
   a. Short term
   b. Long term
3. Add-on preference tax (*note:* no alternative minimum tax)

TAX RATES FOR INDIVIDUALS

Federal income tax rates for individuals.

Ordinary income. Maximum 50% tax rate on "personal services" or "earned" income (salary, commissions, etc.). Maximum 70% on non-earned income (dividends, rental, interest, etc.).

Capital gains income.

Short term gains (property held for 1 year or less) are taxed at ordinary rates.

Long term gains (property held for more than 1 year) are taxed on only 40% of the total gains; 60% is excluded from ordinary income tax but the excluded portion is included in the alternative minimum tax calculation. Prior to the 1978 Reform Act, the excluded 60% was also subject to the add-on preference tax, but this requirement was eliminated by the 1978 Act.

Example.

Total long term capital gain	$ 200,000
Less 60% exclusion	120,000
40% taxable at ordinary rates	$ 80,000

Since the maximum ordinary rate is 70%, applied to 40% of the long term gain equals 28% (70% × 40% = 28%). The effective maximum tax on the entire long term gain may thus be expressed as 28%.

Minimum tax. To correct inequities in tax laws whereby certain taxpayers, because of tax shelters, paid little or no ordinary tax, two additional taxes were enacted to which all taxpayers, including individuals, corporations, estates and trusts, are subject.

Add-on preference tax. A number of income items were identified as "preference" items and subjected to a minimum tax of 15% applied to their excess over the *greater* of (1) $10,000 or (2) one half of the taxpayer's regular income tax.

Of all the items listed as preference items, only one directly affects real estate: the excess of accelerated depreciation over straight line. Note again that since the 1978 Reform Act, the 60% long term capital gain exclusion is no longer a preference item.

Example. Assume a taxpayer had regular income tax payable of $44,000 and excess depreciation and other non-real estate preference items totaling $60,000.

Total preference items	$ 60,000
One half of the regular tax	22,000
(greater than $10,000)	
Taxable at 15%	$ 38,000
Preference tax payable	$ 5,700

Alternative minimum tax. This tax includes the 60% long term capital gain tax exclusion which must be added to the taxpayer's regular tax (after the exclusion) and subject to the following alternative tax rates. Taxpayers must pay the higher of the two computed taxes.

Example. Assume a taxpayer had earned taxable income of only $20,000 but long term capital gains totaling $400,000, of which 60% ($240,000) is excluded from ordinary taxes and 40% ($160,000) is taxable.

Ordinary Tax Calculation

Earned taxable income	$ 20,000	
Net taxable gain income	160,000	
Taxable ordinary income		$ 180,000
Tax liability on $180,000		75,000

Taxpayer must then compute alternative minimum tax, adding back to ordinary income the 60% long term gain exclusion.

Taxable ordinary income	$ 180,000
Add capital gain exclusion (60% × $400,000)	240,000
Alternative minimum taxable income	$ 420,000

Alternative Tax Rates

	Income	*Rate*
First	$ 20,000	exempt
Next	$ 40,000	10%
Next	$ 40,000	20%
Over	$100,000	25%

Taxpayer's Alternative Tax Calculation

Bracket	*Taxable Income*	*Tax Rate*	*Tax*
	$420,000		
$0 - 20,000	20,000	exempt	0
	400,000		
$20,000 - 60,000	40,000	10%	4,000
	360,000		
$60,000 - 100,000	40,000	20%	8,000
Over $100,000	320,000	25%	80,000
Alternative minimum tax			$92,000

Summary

Alternative tax	$ 92,000
Ordinary tax	75,000
Excess	$ 17,000

Since the alternative minimum tax exceeds the ordinary tax, the taxpayer must pay the higher amount, $92,000.

Note that excess depreciation, while a "preference" item, is not included in the alternative minimum tax. For example, using the above figures:

Item	*Taxable as Preference*	*Taxable as Alternative*
Excess depreciation	$60,000	No
Excluded 60% of long term gain	No	$240,000

Shortcut: If the alternative taxable income exceeds $100,000, multiply the total taxable income by 25% and subtract $13,000 from the total tax. In the above example: $420,000 × 25% = $105,000, less $13,000 equals tax of $92,000, the same as in the detailed calculation.

Federal income tax rates for corporations.

TAX RATES FOR CORPORATIONS

Ordinary Income. Under the 1978 Tax Reform Act, corporate tax rates range from 17% on the first $25,000 of income to a maximum of 46% of income over $100,000, as follows:

Taxable Income		*Tax Rate*
First	$ 25,000	17%
Second	$ 25,000	20%
Third	$ 25,000	30%
Fourth	$ 25,000	40%
Over	$100,000	46%

Example. Assume ordinary taxable income of $225,000.

	Taxable Income	*Rate*	*Tax*
	$225,000		
Less	25,000	at 17%	$ 4,250
	200,000		
Less	25,000	at 20%	5,000
	175,000		
Less	25,000	at 30%	7,500
	150,000		
Less	25,000	at 40%	10,000
	125,000	at 46%	57,500
		Total tax	$ 84,250

Shortcut: If taxable income exceeds $100,000, multiply taxable income by 46% and subtract $19,250. In the above example, $225,000 × 46% = $103,500, less $19,250 = $84,250 total tax.

Capital gains. Short term gains are taxed at ordinary rates. Long term gains are taxed at a flat 28% to conform with maximum tax on individuals.

Add-on preference tax. 15% of the greater of (1) $10,000 or (2) the *entire* regular tax.

When a property is sold, care should be taken to structure the transaction to attain the desired tax result: the sale could be either taxable, non-taxable, or partially both. The following chart points out how the gain *realized* (also called indicated or potential) may become *recognized* (taxable), or *deferred* (non-taxable), or partially both.

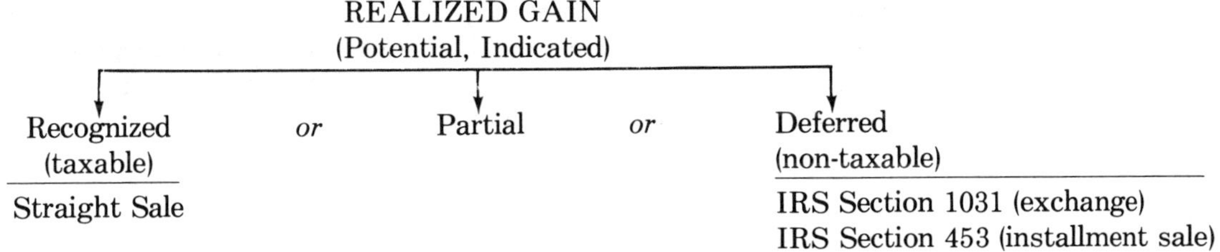

SECTION 1231: ASSETS

Real property held for use in taxpayer's business, or for rental income, and not for sale or trade, qualifies for especially advantageous tax treatment. All net gains (if held for 1 year by 1978) are treated as long term gains, and all losses as ordinary losses, without limitation as in the case of capital assets.

DEPRECIATION NOTES

Change of Method. Since 1/7/74 taxpayers may change their depreciation method, particularly from accelerated to straight line when the accelerated amount drops below straight line, and assume IRS consent. Section 167(e)(3).

Any other method may be used which does not result in greater depreciation during the first two thirds of the life of the property than under the double declining method. Section 167(b)(4); Reg. 1.167(b)-4.

Useful Life. The period of expected *usefulness to taxpayer*—not possible longer physical or economic life. Massey Motors Inc., v. US (1960) 5 AFTR 2d 1780 364 US 92. Also: Hertz Corp. v. US (1960) 5 AFFTR 2d 364 US 122 Reg. 1.167 (a)-1(b).

PARTNERSHIPS*

In the case of a limited partnership, the most popular tax shelter investment vehicle, each partner's proportionate share of *partnership debt* is treated the same as a contribution of cash (Sec. 752(a) IRC) thereby increasing the partner's tax basis and permitting tax losses to be deducted in excess of actual cash investment.

Where there is no personal liability by any partner (non-recourse),

*Courtesy: "The Strategy of Tax Shelter" by Benjamin Benson, C.P.A., in *The Journal of Accountancy,* July 1975.

then all partners share in the liability for tax purposes (IRC Reg. 1.752-1(e)). Most *permanent* loans are written this way.

Most importantly, any decrease in such debt is treated as distribution of cash to the partner (IRC Sec. 752(b)). This occurs upon sale, withdrawal, foreclosure, gift or abandonment, whereupon the partner would realize taxable income to the extent that the debt exceeds adjusted tax basis even though no cash is received. Such income would be capital gain except for the portion of excess depreciation, which would be subject to recapture as ordinary income. This should be kept in mind when contemplating accelerated depreciation of highly leveraged investments.

VII.

Case Study

27.

Model Case Study: 50-Unit Apartment Building

Hypothesis. A 50-unit unfurnished apartment building purchased on basis of 5.76% cash flow ($11,510) by buyer in 60% bracket, held for five years, then resold at same price as purchased.

Objective. To note after-tax benefits over and above operational cash flow, and to provide basis for study of resourceful methods of increasing income, and/or restructuring financing, employing techniques of mortgage-equity ratios (band of investment), capitalization, wrap-around (all-inclusive) security devices and leveraging.

Normally, income projections are made for a holding period of 10 years; for the sake of brevity, we've used 5 years here. The principle is the same, the numbers are fewer. This means that our rate of return will be unrealistically low, because we haven't allowed for the normal appreciation period.

Method.

First, prepare first year analysis form to structure acceptable expense ratios, finance leverage, cash flow and tax shelter.

Second, construct working schedules as follows:

- *Schedule 1.* Depreciation
- *Schedule 2.* Loan Amortization for Both Trust Deeds
- *Schedule 3.* After-Tax Cash Flow
- *Schedule 4.* Calculation of After-Tax Cash Reversion Upon Five-Year Resale
- *Schedule 5.* Calculation of Internal Rate of Return (IRR) and Net Present Value (NPV)

STANDARD INVESTMENT ANALYSIS FORM

Folio ______

Type 50 Units - Pool Pkg. ___ Unf. 50 Furn. ______ Listed Price $ ______
Address Los Angeles Est. Sq. Ft. 45,000 (net) Cash $ ______
Lot Size ______ Sq. Ft. ______ Zone ______ Age ______ Equity $ ______

INDICATED PRICE AND FINANCING

			Sq. Ft.	
	ANNUAL GROSS RENTAL	$ 154,000	3.42	
	TENANT CONTRIBUTIONS	$ - 0 -		
100% PRICE $ 1,049,000 ← (6.8 X) AGM →	ANNUAL GROSS INCOME	$ 154,000	3.42	100%
	EXPENSES			
	Taxes	$ 10,490	.23	6.8
	Insurance	2,310	.05	1.5
	Utilities	7,410	.165	4.8
	Trash	780	.017	
	Pool	480	.011	
	Gardening	480	.011	
	Elevator	600	.013	
	Res Mgr.	7,080	.157	4.6
	Prop. Mgt.	6,160	.137	4.0
	CAM			
	HVAC			
	Cleaning			
	Leasing Fees			
	Alterations			
	Rep./Maint.	10,780	.24	7.0
	Vacancy	7,700	.171	5.0
	TOTAL EXPENSES	$ 54,270	1.21	35.2
(9.51 % to Price) CAP RATE ← →	NET OPERATING INCOME (NOI)	$ 99,730	2.22	64.8

LOANS:

%	CLASS	AMOUNT	ANNUAL CONSTANT (K)		INTEREST		PRINCIPAL	Sq. Ft.	%
71.4	1st	$ 749,000	10.54 %	$ 78,950	10.0 %	$ 74,715	$ 4,235	1.75	51.3
9.5	2nd	100,000	9.27	9,270	8.0	7,950	1,320	.21	6.0
80.9									

%					Sq. Ft.	%
80.9	TOTAL $ 849,000	(10.39 %) ← →	ANNUAL CONSTANT	$ 88,200	1.96	57.3
		(5.76 % to Cash) ROE ← →	NET CASH FLOW	$ 11,510	.26	7.5
			Plus EQUITY GAIN	$ 5,555	.12	3.6
19.1	CASH $ 200,000	(8.53 % to Cash) YOE ← →	NET YIELD	$ 17,065	.38	11.1

TAX SHELTER ANALYSIS — First Year

DEPRECIATION BASIS: | **NET YIELD (Forward)** $ 17,065 | .38 | 11.1

Total Cost	$ 1,049,000
Less Land (20 %)	$ 209,800
Balance	$ 839,200
Furnishings $500 ea	$ 25,000
Building Improvements	$ 814,200

YEARS	METHOD	%	
4	S/L	25	$ 6,250
25	125%DB	5	$ 40,710

		Sq. Ft.	%
LESS TOTAL DEPRECIATION	$ 46,960	1.04	30.5
TAXABLE INCOME (LOSS)	$ (29,895)	.66	19.4
TAX SAVINGS @ 60 %	$ 17,937	.40	11.6

RECAP

	1ST YEAR AMOUNT	1ST YEAR % TO CASH
NET CASH FLOW	$ 11,510	5.76
TAX SAVINGS OR (Exp.)	17,937	8.97
TOTAL CASH FLOW	29,447	14.72
EQUITY GAIN	5,555	2.78
TOTAL YIELD	35,002	17.50

NOTES:

1st TD 10% - 30 years (K 10.54%)
2nd TD 8% - 25 years (K 9.27%)
Balloon due 10 years

SCHEDULE I: Depreciation
Shortcut method of computation

Step 1. Divide 125% by the number of years to find rate.
125% ÷ 25 = 5% rate on declining balance

Step 2. Multiply the improvement (net of land) by 5% to find first year depreciation.
$814,200 × 5% = $40,710

Step 3. Multiply $40,710 by the complement of 5% (100% − 5% = 95%) as a constant multiplier:

	First year	$ 40,710
95% × $40,710 =	Second year	38,675
95% × 38,675 =	Third year	36,741 etc.

Years	*Building at 5% DB*	*Furniture at 25% S/L*	*Combined Total*	*Building Only Excess over S/L*			*Section 1250 Years*
1	$ 40,710	$ 6,250	$ 46,960	$ 40,710 −	$ 32,568 =	$ 8,142	1/1/76
2	38,675	6,250	44,925	38,675 −	32,568 =	6,107	1/1/77
3	36,741	6,250	42,991	36,741 −	32,568 =	4,173	1/1/78
4	34,904	6,250	41,154	34,904 −	32,568 =	2,336	1/1/79
5	33,156	—	33,156	33,156 −	32,568 =	588	12/31/80
Totals	$184,186	$25,000	$209,186	$184,186	$162,840	$21,346	

Building S/L = $814,200 × 4% = $32,568

Note: All excess depreciation over S/L after 1975 is 100% recapturable. For partial recapture in holding periods before January 1, 1976, see page 206.

SCHEDULE II: Loan Amortization
First Trust Deed

Step 1.	Monthly K = $78,950 / 12	= $	6,579
Step 2.	First month interest = $749,000 × .10 / 12	=	6,242
Step 3.	First month principal	=	337
Step 4.	Annualized by Table 2, 12 months 10% = 12.565568 × 337	=	4,235 First Year
Step 5.	Multiplied by Constant Table 1, 12 months 10%		
	1.104713 × $4,235	= $	4,678 Second Year
	1.104713 × 4,678	=	5,168 Third Year
	1.104713 × 5,168	=	5,710 Fourth Year
	1.104713 × 5,710	=	6,307 Fifth Year
	Total amortization		$ 26,098
	Original loan amount		$749,000
	Balance EOY 5		$722,902

Annual breakdown of principal and interest for calculation of after-tax cash flow.

Years	*K*	*Principal*	*Interest*	*EOY Balance*
0				$749,000
1	$78,950	$4,235	$74,715	744,765
2	78,950	4,678	74,272	740,087
3	78,950	5,168	73,782	734,919
4	78,950	5,710	73,240	729,209
5	78,950	6,307	72,643	722,902

Second Trust Deed

Step 1. Monthly K = $\frac{\$9{,}270}{12}$ = $ 773

Step 2. First month interest = $\frac{\$100{,}000 \times .08}{12}$ = 667

Step 3. First month principal = 106

Step 4. Annualized by Table 1, 12 months 8% = 12.449926 × $106 = 1,320 First Year

Step 5. Multiplied by Constant Table 1, 12 months 8%

1.083000 × $1,320 = $ 1,430 Second Year
1.083000 × $1,430 = 1,548 Third Year
1.083000 × 1,548 = 1,677 Fourth Year
1.083000 × 1,677 = 1,816 Fifth Year

Total amortization	$ 7,791
Original amount	$100,000
Balance EOY 5	$ 92,209

Annual breakdown of principal and interest for calculation of after-tax cash flow.

Years	*K*	*Principal*	*Interest*	*EOY Balance*
0				$100,000
1	$9,270	$1,320	$7,950	98,680
2	9,270	1,430	7,840	97,250
3	9,270	1,548	7,722	95,702
4	9,270	1,677	7,593	94,025
5	9,270	1,816	7,454	92,209

SCHEDULE III: After-Tax Cash Flow

There are two ways to compute taxable income—or loss. The first, the most commonly used, takes a straight deduction of both interest and depreciation from net operating income. The second, while it appears on the surface more complex, is actually quite a bit more convenient, for it eliminates one tedious step. The background is this: real estate *analysis* is usually done on the "cash" accounting system, and therefore amortization is deducted (as a real cash expenditure) but depreciation is not. But when it comes time to calculate *taxes* on the income from real estate investment, the accrual accounting system is normally used, and in that system depreciation *is* deductible but amortization is not. To do tax calculations using the information at hand usually involves two separate computations. But in the second method explained here, you merely make a shortcut conversion.

You will note as we outline the two methods that only the first two columns differ; the remaining five columns are identical, including the resulting after-tax NCF.

Method I. Using the "accrual" method of accounting in which both interest and depreciation are deducted from net operating income to determine taxes payable (or refundable).

Year	*NOI*	−	*Total Interest*	−	*Depreciation*	=	*Taxable or (Refundable)*	× 60% =	*Tax Saving or (Payable) at 60% Bracket*	+	*NCF*	=	*After Tax NCF*
1	$99,730		$82,665		($ 46,960)		($29,895)		$17,937		$11,510		$29,447
2	99,730		82,112		(44,925)		(27,307)		16,384		11,510		27,894
3	99,730		81,504		(42,991)		(24,765)		14,859		11,510		26,369
4	99,730		80,833		(41,154)		(22,257)		13,354		11,510		24,864
5	99,730		80,079		(33,156)		(13,523)		8,114		11,510		19,624
					($209,186)								

Method II. Using a shortcut conversion from cash accounting to accrual. Briefly, this conversion technique takes the amortization payment, which had been deducted to arrive at the net cash flow, and adds it back, since it cannot be counted a *tax* deduction. This produces the same total as if only interest (which *is* tax deductible) had been deducted. To demonstrate the principle using sample figures:

NOI $99,730 − interest $82,665 = $17,065

NCF $11,510 + amortization $5,555 = $17,065

In this time-saving method, the cash flow projection does double duty: it capitalizes the value of the property, and adapts taxable income computing.

Year	*NCF*	+	*Amortization*	−	*Depreciation*	=	*Taxable or (Refundable)*	× 60% =	*Tax Saving or (Payable) at 60%*	+	*NCF*	=	*After Tax NCF*
1	$11,510		$5,555		($ 46,960)		($29,895)		$17,937		$11,510		$29,447
2	11,510		6,108		(44,925)		(27,307)		16,384		11,510		27,894
3	11,510		6,716		(42,991)		(24,765)		14,859		11,510		26,369
4	11,510		7,387		(41,154)		(22,257)		13,354		11,510		24,864
5	11,510		8,123		(33,156)		(13,523)		8,114		11,510		19,624
					($209,186)								

SCHEDULE IV: Calculation of After-Tax Cash Reversion Upon Five-Year Resale at Original Price (6% Cash Flow)

	Tax Basis			*Cash Proceeds*
Sales price	$ 1,049,000			$1,049,000
Less sales cost (6%)	62,940			62,940
Net price	$ 986,060			$ 986,060
Less adjusted tax basis:				
Cost less depreciation				
$1,049,000 − $209,186	839,814			
Indicated gain	$ 146,246			
Less recapture:				
Section 1245	25,000	@ 60% = Tax	$ 15,000	
Section 1250	21,346	@ 60% = Tax	12,808	
Total recapture	$ 46,346			
Net long term gain	$ 99,900			
Taxable 40%	39,960	@ 60% = Tax	23,976	
Total tax payable				51,784
Balance				$ 934,276
Less trust deed balances		First $722,902		
		Second 92,209		815,111
Net cash reversion				$ 119,165

Section 1245: Gain on disposition of Section 1245 property is treated as ordinary income up to the lower of (1) the gain realized or (2) the amount of depreciation. The amount of gain in excess of depreciation still qualifies as capital gain.

The actual procedure is more complicated and involves "recomputed basis" of interest only to accountants. For our purposes as investment analysts the item, in over-simplified form, is included only to demonstrate the function.

Section 1250: See Chapter 26 for detailed explanation. The assumption here is that the holding period 1/1/76 to 12/31/80 covered five years wherein *all* excess depreciation is recaptured 100%.

SCHEDULE V: Calculation of Internal Rate of Return (IRR)

TRIAL DISCOUNT RATES, TABLE 4

Year	*Cash Flow and Reversion*	5%		6%	
1	$ 29,447	.951328 =	$ 28,014	.941905 =	$ 27,736
2	27,894	.905025 =	25,245	.887186 =	24,747
3	26,369	.860976 =	22,703	.835645 =	22,035
4	24,864	.819071 =	20,365	.787098 =	19,570
5	19,624	.779205 =	15,291	.741372 =	14,549
5 Reversion	119,165	.779205 =	92,854	.741372 =	88,346
			$204,472		$196,983

Interpolation

Smaller rate	.05	$ 204,472		$ 204,472
Larger rate	.06	196,983	Target	200,000
Difference	.01 ÷	$ 7,489	×	$ 4,472 + .05 = 5.6% IRR*

Alternative Interpolation Method

$$\frac{.01 \times \$4,472}{\$7,489} + .05 = 5.6\% \text{ IRR*}$$

Net Present Value (NPV)

If the investor required a minimum of 5% ROE, the investment would pass because the discounted present value *exceeds* the purchase price equity:

Cash flow and reversion discounted at 5%	$ 204,472
Actual purchase price equity	200,000
Net present value	$ 4,472

If the investor required a minimum of 6% ROE, the investment would *not* pass because the discounted present value is *less* than the purchase price equity:

Cash flow and reversion discounted at 6%	$ 196,983
Actual purchase price equity	200,000
Deficit net present value	($ 3,017)

The normal breakeven projection period for internal rate of return and net present value is 10 years. However, for brevity, 5 is used here simply to demonstrate the procedures.

The difference between this apartment building example and a commercial or industrial project exists primarily in the nature and ratio of operating expenses; from NOI onward, the financing and analytical formulas are the same.

EFFECTS OF INFLATION

Finally, the low 5.6% IRR reflects the conservative approach of ignoring any rise in rates or market appreciation. For example, applying a 10% annual inflation rate, the first year's after-tax net cash flow would increase as follows:

*Note that the low return is due to the short holding period, and elimination of any market value appreciation for breakeven and strictly internal analysis.

Gross rental income $154,000 × 1.10 =	$ 169,400
Operating expenses $54,270 × 1.10 =	59,697
Net operating income =	109,703
Loan constant payments	88,220
Net cash flow before taxes	21,483
Add first year principal paid	5,555
Net yield	27,038
Depreciation first year	(46,960)
Taxable (loss)	(19,922)
Tax saving @ 60%	$ 11,953

Compare this first year summary with that at the bottom of the analysis work sheet:

	Case History Worksheet		*Adjustment for 10% Annual Inflation*	
NCF	11,510	5.76%	21,483	10.74%
Tax savings	17,937	8.97%	11,953	5.98%
Total cash	29,447	14.72%	33,436	16.72%
Mortgage principal	5,555	2.78%	5,555	2.78%
Total yield	35,002	17.50%	38,991	19.50%

In 10 years, at 10% inflation, the gross rent would have doubled to $308,000. If sold at the same multiplier as that of the purchase, the resale would be doubled as well: $308,000 × 6.812 = $2,098,000, and the IRR and NPV would naturally be considerably more encouraging.

However, for purposes of comparing several investments, increasing the net income of each for inflation would give each the same external advantage over its own internal attributes, and only complicate the analysis without further benefit.

VIII.

Appendix

A.

Six Compound Interest Tables

These compound interest tables are available in interest rates ranging from 3% to 30%, in gradations of ¼%. They are computed for four basic conversion periods: monthly, quarterly, semiannually, and annually. In real estate, with rare exceptions, the most frequent conversion period for both rental income and loan repayment is monthly.

Representative tables for the interest rates used in the examples in this book are reproduced here. They all include the four conversion periods except the rates over 12%, which come only in the annual mode.

The four conversion periods, using a 10% nominal rate, are:

Annual	10.0%	One time per year
SemiAnnual	5.0%	Two times per year
Quarterly	2.5%	Four times per year
Monthly	.8333%	Twelve times per year

The base conversion rate is the first figure at the top of Column I for each compounding frequency.

The tables reproduced here are taken from:

Ellwood Tables for Real Estate Appraising and Financing, (Third Edition), compiled for the Amercian Institute of Real Estate Appraisers by L.W. Ellwood, MAI

and reprinted with the permission of Harper & Row Publishers, New York, NY.

5% MONTHLY COMPOUND INTEREST TABLE 5%

EFFECTIVE RATE = 5/12% BASE = 1.00416666+

MONTHS	1 AMOUNT OF 1 AT COMPOUND INTEREST $S^n = (1+i)^n$	2 ACCUMULATION OF 1 PER PERIOD $S_{\overline{n}\vert} = \frac{S^n - 1}{i}$	3 SINKING FUND FACTOR $1/S_{\overline{n}\vert} = \frac{i}{S^n - 1}$	4 PRES. VALUE REVERSION OF 1 $V^n = \frac{1}{S^n}$	5 PRESENT VALUE ORD. ANNUITY 1 PER PERIOD $a_{\overline{n}\vert} = \frac{1-V^n}{i}$	6 INSTALMENT TO AMORTIZE 1 $1/a_{\overline{n}\vert} = \frac{i}{1-V^n}$	n MONTHS
1	1.004167	1.000000	1.000000	.995851	.995851	1.004167	1
2	1.008351	2.004167	.498960	.991718	1.987569	.503127	2
3	1.012552	3.012517	.331948	.987603	2.975173	.336115	3
4	1.016771	4.025070	.248443	.983506	3.958678	.252610	4
5	1.021008	5.041841	.198340	.979425	4.938103	.202507	5
6	1.025262	6.062848	.164939	.975361	5.913463	.169106	6
7	1.029534	7.088110	.141081	.971313	6.884777	.145248	7
8	1.033824	8.117644	.123188	.967283	7.852060	.127355	8
9	1.038131	9.151467	.109272	.963269	8.815329	.113439	9
10	1.042457	10.189599	.098139	.959272	9.774602	.102306	10
11	1.046800	11.232055	.089031	.955292	10.729894	.093198	11
YEARS							
1	1.051162	12.278855	.081441	.951328	11.681222	.085608	12
2	1.104941	25.185921	.039705	.905025	22.793898	.043872	24
3	1.161472	38.753336	.025804	.860976	33.365701	.029971	36
4	1.220895	53.014885	.018863	.819071	43.422956	.023030	48
5	1.283359	68.006083	.014705	.779205	52.990706	.018872	60
6	1.349018	83.764259	.011938	.741280	62.092777	.016105	72
7	1.418036	100.328653	.009967	.705201	70.751835	.014134	84
8	1.490585	117.740513	.008493	.670877	78.989441	.012660	96
9	1.566847	136.043196	.007351	.638225	86.826108	.011518	108
10	1.647010	155.282280	.006440	.607161	94.281350	.010607	120
11	1.731274	175.505671	.005698	.577609	101.373733	.009865	132
12	1.819849	196.763730	.005082	.549496	108.120917	.009249	144
13	1.912956	219.109392	.004564	.522751	114.539704	.008731	156
14	2.010826	242.598300	.004122	.497308	120.646077	.008289	168
15	2.113704	267.288945	.003741	.473103	126.455243	.007908	180
16	2.221845	293.242810	.003410	.450076	131.981666	.007577	192
17	2.335519	320.524524	.003120	.428170	137.239108	.007287	204
18	2.455008	349.202023	.002864	.407331	142.240661	.007031	216
19	2.580611	379.346717	.002636	.387505	146.998780	.006803	228
20	2.712640	411.033670	.002433	.368645	151.525313	.006600	240
21	2.851424	444.341789	.002251	.350702	155.831531	.006418	252
22	2.997308	479.354014	.002086	.333633	159.928159	.006253	264
23	3.150656	516.157530	.001937	.317394	163.825396	.006104	276
24	3.311850	554.843985	.001802	.301946	167.532948	.005969	288
25	3.481290	595.509712	.001679	.287250	171.060047	.005846	300
26	3.659400	638.255975	.001567	.273269	174.415476	.005734	312
27	3.846622	683.189218	.001464	.259968	177.607590	.005631	324
28	4.043422	730.421330	.001369	.247315	180.644338	.005536	336
29	4.250291	780.069928	.001282	.235278	183.533282	.005449	348
30	4.467744	832.258641	.001202	.223827	186.281617	.005369	360
31	4.696323	887.117429	.001127	.212933	188.896185	.005294	372
32	4.936595	944.782896	.001058	.202569	191.383497	.005225	384
33	5.189161	1005.398638	.000995	.192709	193.749748	.005162	396
34	5.454648	1069.115596	.000935	.183330	196.000829	.005102	408
35	5.733719	1136.092435	.000880	.174407	198.142346	.005047	420
36	6.027066	1206.495936	.000829	.165918	200.179632	.004996	432
37	6.335423	1280.501414	.000781	.157843	202.117759	.004948	444
38	6.659555	1358.293153	.000736	.150160	203.961554	.004903	456
39	7.000270	1440.064865	.000694	.142852	205.715609	.004861	468
40	7.358417	1526.020172	.000655	.135899	207.384290	.004822	480
41	7.734888	1616.373117	.000619	.129284	208.971754	.004786	492
42	8.130620	1711.348689	.000584	.122992	210.481953	.004751	504
43	8.546598	1811.183392	.000552	.117006	211.918649	.004719	516
44	8.983858	1916.125828	.000522	.111311	213.285417	.004689	528
45	9.443489	2026.437318	.000493	.105893	214.585663	.004660	540
46	9.926636	2142.392554	.000467	.100739	215.822623	.004634	552
47	10.434501	2264.280279	.000442	.095836	216.999379	.004609	564
48	10.968350	2392.404012	.000418	.091171	218.118860	.004585	576
49	11.529512	2527.082798	.000396	.086734	219.183853	.004563	588
50	12.119383	2668.652007	.000375	.082512	220.197012	.004542	600

5% QUARTERLY COMPOUND INTEREST TABLE 5%

EFFECTIVE RATE = 1¼% BASE = 1.0125

QUARTERS	1 AMOUNT OF 1 AT COMPOUND INTEREST $S^n = (1+i)^n$	2 ACCUMULATION OF 1 PER PERIOD $S_{\overline{n}\vert} = \frac{S^n - 1}{i}$	3 SINKING FUND FACTOR $1/S_{\overline{n}\vert} = \frac{i}{S^n - 1}$	4 PRES. VALUE REVERSION OF 1 $V^n = \frac{1}{S^n}$	5 PRESENT VALUE ORD. ANNUITY 1 PER PERIOD $a_{\overline{n}\vert} = \frac{1 - V^n}{i}$	6 INSTALMENT TO AMORTIZE 1 $1/a_{\overline{n}\vert} = \frac{i}{1 - V^n}$	n QUARTERS
1	1.012500	1.000000	1.000000	.987654	.987654	1.012500	1
2	1.025156	2.012500	.496894	.975461	1.963115	.509394	2
3	1.037971	3.037656	.329201	.963418	2.926534	.341701	3
YEARS							
1	1.050945	4.075627	.245361	.951524	3.878058	.257861	4
2	1.104486	8.358888	.119633	.905398	7.568124	.132133	8
3	1.160755	12.860361	.077758	.861509	11.079312	.090258	12
4	1.219890	17.591164	.056847	.819746	14.420292	.069347	16
5	1.282037	22.562979	.044320	.780009	17.599316	.056820	20
6	1.347351	27.788084	.035987	.742197	20.624235	.048487	24
7	1.415992	33.279384	.030049	.706219	23.502518	.042549	28
8	1.488131	39.050441	.025608	.671984	26.241274	.038108	32
9	1.563944	45.115506	.022165	.639409	28.847267	.034665	36
10	1.643619	51.489557	.019421	.608413	31.326933	.031921	40
11	1.727354	58.188337	.017186	.578920	33.686395	.029686	44
12	1.815355	65.228388	.015331	.550856	35.931481	.027831	48
13	1.907839	72.627097	.013769	.524153	38.067734	.026269	52
14	2.005034	80.402736	.012437	.498745	40.100431	.024937	56
15	2.107181	88.574508	.011290	.474568	42.034592	.023790	60
16	2.214532	97.162593	.010292	.451563	43.874992	.022792	64
17	2.327353	106.188201	.009417	.429673	45.626178	.021917	68
18	2.445920	115.673621	.008645	.408844	47.292474	.021145	72
19	2.570529	125.642280	.007959	.389025	48.877995	.020459	76
20	2.701485	136.118795	.007347	.370167	50.386657	.019847	80
21	2.839113	147.129040	.006797	.352223	51.822185	.019297	84
22	2.983753	158.700206	.006301	.335148	53.188125	.018801	88
23	3.135761	170.860868	.005853	.318902	54.487850	.018353	92
24	3.295513	183.641059	.005445	.303443	55.724570	.017945	96
25	3.463404	197.072342	.005074	.288733	56.901339	.017574	100
26	3.639849	211.187886	.004735	.274737	58.021064	.017235	104
27	3.825282	226.022551	.004424	.261419	59.086509	.016924	108
28	4.020162	241.612973	.004139	.248746	60.100305	.016639	112
29	4.224971	257.997654	.003876	.236688	61.064957	.016376	116
30	4.440213	275.217058	.003633	.225214	61.982847	.016133	120
31	4.666421	293.313711	.003409	.214297	62.856242	.015909	124
32	4.904154	312.332304	.003202	.203909	63.687298	.015702	128
33	5.153998	332.319805	.003009	.194024	64.478068	.015509	132
34	5.416570	353.325577	.002830	.184619	65.230505	.015330	136
35	5.692519	375.401494	.002664	.175669	65.946467	.015164	140
36	5.982526	398.602077	.002509	.167153	66.627722	.015009	144
37	6.287308	422.984621	.002364	.159051	67.275953	.014864	148
38	6.607617	448.609342	.002229	.151340	67.892760	.014729	152
39	6.944244	475.539523	.002103	.144004	68.479668	.014603	156
40	7.298021	503.841671	.001985	.137023	69.038124	.014485	160
41	7.669821	533.585681	.001874	.130381	69.569509	.014374	164
42	8.060563	564.845011	.001770	.124061	70.075135	.014270	168
43	8.471211	597.696857	.001673	.118047	70.556250	.014173	172
44	8.902779	632.222352	.001582	.112324	71.014042	.014082	176
45	9.356334	668.506759	.001496	.106879	71.449643	.013996	180
46	9.832996	706.639689	.001415	.101698	71.864128	.013915	184
47	10.333941	746.715313	.001339	.096768	72.258520	.013839	188
48	10.860408	788.832603	.001268	.092078	72.633794	.013768	192
49	11.413695	833.095572	.001200	.087614	72.990876	.013700	196
50	11.995169	879.613534	.001137	.083367	73.330649	.013637	200
51	12.606267	928.501369	.001077	.079326	73.653950	.013577	204
52	13.248498	979.879811	.001021	.075480	73.961580	.013521	208
53	13.923447	1033.875745	.000967	.071821	74.254296	.013467	212
54	14.632781	1090.622520	.000917	.068340	74.532824	.013417	216
55	15.378253	1150.260278	.000869	.065027	74.797849	.013369	220
56	16.161704	1212.936303	.000824	.061875	75.050027	.013324	224
57	16.985067	1278.805378	.000782	.058875	75.289980	.013282	228
58	17.850377	1348.030176	.000742	.056021	75.518302	.013242	232
59	18.759771	1420.781655	.000704	.053306	75.735556	.013204	236
60	19.715494	1497.239482	.000668	.050722	75.942278	.013168	240

5% SEMI-ANNUAL COMPOUND INTEREST TABLE 5%

EFFECTIVE RATE = 2½% BASE = 1.025

HALF YEARS	1 AMOUNT OF 1 AT COMPOUND INTEREST $S^n = (1+i)^n$	2 ACCUMULATION OF 1 PER PERIOD $S_{\overline{n\rvert}} = \frac{S^n - 1}{i}$	3 SINKING FUND FACTOR $1/S_{\overline{n\rvert}} = \frac{i}{S^n - 1}$	4 PRES. VALUE REVERSION OF 1 $V^n = \frac{1}{S^n}$	5 PRESENT VALUE ORD. ANNUITY 1 PER PERIOD $a_{\overline{n\rvert}} = \frac{1 - V^n}{i}$	6 INSTALMENT TO AMORTIZE 1 $1/a_{\overline{n\rvert}} = \frac{i}{1 - V^n}$	n HALF YEARS
1	1.025000	1.000000	1.000000	.975610	.975610	1.025000	1
YEARS							
1	1.050625	2.025000	.493827	.951814	1.927424	.518827	2
2	1.103813	4.152516	.240818	.905951	3.761974	.265818	4
3	1.159693	6.387737	.156550	.862297	5.508125	.181550	6
4	1.218403	8.736116	.114467	.820747	7.170137	.139467	8
5	1.280085	11.203382	.089259	.781198	8.752064	.114259	10
6	1.344889	13.795553	.072487	.743556	10.257765	.097487	12
7	1.412974	16.518953	.060537	.707727	11.690912	.085537	14
8	1.484506	19.380225	.051599	.673625	13.055003	.076599	16
9	1.559659	22.386349	.044670	.641166	14.353364	.069670	18
10	1.638616	25.544658	.039147	.610271	15.589162	.064147	20
11	1.721571	28.862856	.034647	.580865	16.765413	.059647	22
12	1.808726	32.349038	.030913	.552875	17.884986	.055913	24
13	1.900293	36.011708	.027769	.526235	18.950611	.052769	26
14	1.996495	39.859801	.025088	.500878	19.964889	.050088	28
15	2.097568	43.902703	.022778	.476743	20.930293	.047778	30
16	2.203757	48.150278	.020768	.453771	21.849178	.045768	32
17	2.315322	52.612885	.019007	.431905	22.723786	.044007	34
18	2.432535	57.301413	.017452	.411094	23.556251	.042452	36
19	2.555682	62.227297	.016070	.391285	24.348603	.041070	38
20	2.685064	67.402554	.014836	.372431	25.102775	.039836	40
21	2.820995	72.839808	.013729	.354485	25.820607	.038729	42
22	2.963808	78.552323	.012730	.337404	26.503849	.037730	44
23	3.113851	84.554034	.011827	.321146	27.154170	.036827	46
24	3.271490	90.859582	.011006	.305671	27.773154	.036006	48
25	3.437109	97.484349	.010258	.290942	28.362312	.035258	50
26	3.611112	104.444494	.009574	.276923	28.923081	.034574	52
27	3.793925	111.756996	.008948	.263579	29.456829	.033948	54
28	3.985992	119.439694	.008372	.250879	29.964858	.033372	56
29	4.187783	127.511329	.007842	.238790	30.448407	.032842	58
30	4.399790	135.991590	.007353	.227284	30.908656	.032353	60
31	4.622529	144.901164	.006901	.216332	31.346728	.031901	62
32	4.856545	154.261786	.006482	.205908	31.763691	.031482	64
33	5.102407	164.096289	.006094	.195986	32.160563	.031094	66
34	5.360717	174.428663	.005733	.186542	32.538311	.030733	68
35	5.632103	185.284114	.005397	.177554	32.897857	.030397	70
36	5.917228	196.689122	.005084	.168998	33.240078	.030084	72
37	6.216788	208.671509	.004792	.160855	33.565809	.029792	74
38	6.531513	221.260504	.004520	.153104	33.875844	.029520	76
39	6.862170	234.486817	.004265	.145726	34.170940	.029265	78
40	7.209568	248.382713	.004026	.138705	34.451817	.029026	80
41	7.574552	262.982087	.003803	.132021	34.719160	.028803	82
42	7.958014	278.320556	.003593	.125659	34.973620	.028593	84
43	8.360888	294.435534	.003396	.119605	35.215819	.028396	86
44	8.784158	311.366333	.003212	.113841	35.446348	.028212	88
45	9.228856	329.154253	.003038	.108356	35.665768	.028038	90
46	9.696067	347.842687	.002875	.103135	35.874616	.027875	92
47	10.186931	367.477223	.002721	.098165	36.073400	.027721	94
48	10.702644	388.105758	.002577	.093435	36.262606	.027577	96
49	11.244465	409.778612	.002440	.088933	36.442694	.027440	98
50	11.813716	432.548654	.002312	.084647	36.614105	.027312	100
51	12.411786	456.471430	.002191	.080569	36.777257	.027191	102
52	13.040132	481.605296	.002076	.076686	36.932546	.027076	104
53	13.700289	508.011564	.001968	.072991	37.080354	.026968	106
54	14.393866	535.754649	.001867	.069474	37.221039	.026867	108
55	15.122556	564.902228	.001770	.066126	37.354944	.026770	110
56	15.888135	595.525404	.001679	.062940	37.482398	.026679	112
57	16.692472	627.698877	.001593	.059907	37.603710	.026593	114
58	17.537528	661.501133	.001512	.057021	37.719177	.026512	116
59	18.425366	697.014628	.001435	.054273	37.829080	.026435	118
60	19.358150	734.325993	.001362	.051658	37.933687	.026362	120

5% ANNUAL COMPOUND INTEREST TABLE 5%

EFFECTIVE RATE = 5% BASE = 1.05

YEARS	1 AMOUNT OF I AT COMPOUND INTEREST $S^n = (1+i)^n$	2 ACCUMULATION OF I PER PERIOD $S_{\overline{n}\mid} = \frac{S^n - 1}{i}$	3 SINKING FUND FACTOR $1/S_{\overline{n}\mid} = \frac{i}{S^n - 1}$	4 PRES. VALUE REVERSION OF I $V^n = \frac{1}{S^n}$	5 PRESENT VALUE ORD. ANNUITY 1 PER PERIOD $a_{\overline{n}\mid} = \frac{1 - V^n}{i}$	6 INSTALMENT TO AMORTIZE I $1/a_{\overline{n}\mid} = \frac{i}{1 - V^n}$	n YEARS
1	1.050000	1.000000	1.000000	.952381	.952381	1.050000	1
2	1.102500	2.050000	.487805	.907029	1.859410	.537805	2
3	1.157625	3.152500	.317209	.863838	2.723248	.367209	3
4	1.215506	4.310125	.232012	.822702	3.545951	.282012	4
5	1.276282	5.525631	.180975	.783526	4.329477	.230975	5
6	1.340096	6.801913	.147017	.746215	5.075692	.197017	6
7	1.407100	8.142008	.122820	.710681	5.786373	.172820	7
8	1.477455	9.549109	.104722	.676839	6.463213	.154722	8
9	1.551328	11.026564	.090690	.644609	7.107822	.140690	9
10	1.628895	12.577893	.079505	.613913	7.721735	.129505	10
11	1.710339	14.206787	.070389	.584679	8.306414	.120389	11
12	1.795856	15.917127	.062825	.556837	8.863252	.112825	12
13	1.885649	17.712983	.056456	.530321	9.393573	.106456	13
14	1.979932	19.598632	.051024	.505068	9.898641	.101024	14
15	2.078928	21.578564	.046342	.481017	10.379658	.096342	15
16	2.182875	23.657492	.042270	.458112	10.837770	.092270	16
17	2.292018	25.840366	.038699	.436297	11.274066	.088699	17
18	2.406619	28.132385	.035546	.415521	11.689587	.085546	18
19	2.526950	30.539004	.032745	.395734	12.085321	.082745	19
20	2.653298	33.065954	.030243	.376889	12.462210	.080243	20
21	2.785963	35.719252	.027996	.358942	12.821153	.077996	21
22	2.925261	38.505214	.025971	.341850	13.163003	.075971	22
23	3.071524	41.430475	.024137	.325571	13.488574	.074137	23
24	3.225100	44.501999	.022471	.310068	13.798642	.072471	24
25	3.386355	47.727099	.020952	.295303	14.093945	.070952	25
26	3.555673	51.113454	.019564	.281241	14.375185	.069564	26
27	3.733456	54.669126	.018292	.267848	14.643034	.068292	27
28	3.920129	58.402583	.017123	.255094	14.898127	.067123	28
29	4.116136	62.322712	.016046	.242946	15.141074	.066046	29
30	4.321942	66.438848	.015051	.231377	15.372451	.065051	30
31	4.538039	70.760790	.014132	.220359	15.592811	.064132	31
32	4.764941	75.298829	.013280	.209866	15.802677	.063280	32
33	5.003189	80.063771	.012490	.199873	16.002549	.062490	33
34	5.253348	85.066959	.011755	.190355	16.192904	.061755	34
35	5.516015	90.320307	.011072	.181290	16.374194	.061072	35
36	5.791816	95.836323	.010434	.172657	16.546852	.060434	36
37	6.081407	101.628139	.009840	.164436	16.711287	.059840	37
38	6.385477	107.709546	.009284	.156605	16.867893	.059284	38
39	6.704751	114.095023	.008765	.149148	17.017041	.058765	39
40	7.039989	120.799774	.008278	.142046	17.159086	.058278	40
41	7.391988	127.839763	.007822	.135282	17.294368	.057822	41
42	7.761588	135.231751	.007395	.128840	17.423208	.057395	42
43	8.149667	142.993339	.006993	.122704	17.545912	.056993	43
44	8.557150	151.143006	.006616	.116861	17.662773	.056616	44
45	8.985008	159.700156	.006262	.111297	17.774070	.056262	45
46	9.434258	168.685164	.005928	.105997	17.880067	.055928	46
47	9.905971	178.119422	.005614	.100949	17.981016	.055614	47
48	10.401270	188.025393	.005318	.096142	18.077158	.055318	48
49	10.921333	198.426663	.005040	.091564	18.168722	.055040	49
50	11.467400	209.347996	.004777	.087204	18.255925	.054777	50
51	12.040770	220.815395	.004529	.083051	18.338977	.054529	51
52	12.642808	232.856165	.004294	.079096	18.418073	.054294	52
53	13.274949	245.498974	.004073	.075330	18.493403	.054073	53
54	13.938696	258.773922	.003864	.071743	18.565146	.053864	54
55	14.635631	272.712618	.003667	.068326	18.633472	.053667	55
56	15.367412	287.348249	.003480	.065073	18.698545	.053480	56
57	16.135783	302.715662	.003303	.061974	18.760519	.053303	57
58	16.942572	318.851445	.003136	.059023	18.819542	.053136	58
59	17.789701	335.794017	.002978	.056212	18.875754	.052978	59
60	18.679186	353.583718	.002828	.053536	18.929290	.052828	60

6% MONTHLY COMPOUND INTEREST TABLE 6%

EFFECTIVE RATE = 1/2% BASE = 1.005

MONTHS	1 AMOUNT OF 1 AT COMPOUND INTEREST $S^n = (1+i)^n$	2 ACCUMULATION OF 1 PER PERIOD $S_{\overline{n}\|} = \frac{S^n - 1}{i}$	3 SINKING FUND FACTOR $1/S_{\overline{n}\|} = \frac{i}{S^n - 1}$	4 PRES. VALUE REVERSION OF 1 $V^n = \frac{1}{S^n}$	5 PRESENT VALUE ORD. ANNUITY 1 PER PERIOD $a_{\overline{n}\|} = \frac{1 - V^n}{i}$	6 INSTALMENT TO AMORTIZE 1 $1/a_{\overline{n}\|} = \frac{i}{1 - V^n}$	n MONTHS
1	1.005000	1.000000	1.000000	.995025	.995025	1.005000	1
2	1.010025	2.005000	.498753	.990075	1.985099	.503753	2
3	1.015075	3.015025	.331672	.985149	2.970248	.336672	3
4	1.020151	4.030100	.248133	.980248	3.950496	.253133	4
5	1.025251	5.050251	.198010	.975371	4.925866	.203010	5
6	1.030378	6.075502	.164595	.970518	5.896384	.169595	6
7	1.035529	7.105879	.140729	.965690	6.862074	.145729	7
8	1.040707	8.141409	.122829	.960885	7.822959	.127829	8
9	1.045911	9.182116	.108907	.956105	8.779064	.113907	9
10	1.051140	10.228026	.097771	.951348	9.730412	.102771	10
11	1.056396	11.279167	.088659	.946615	10.677027	.093659	11
YEARS							
1	1.061678	12.335562	.081066	.941905	11.618932	.086066	12
2	1.127160	25.431955	.039321	.887186	22.562866	.044321	24
3	1.196681	39.336105	.025422	.835645	32.871016	.030422	36
4	1.270489	54.097832	.018485	.787098	42.580318	.023485	48
5	1.348850	69.770031	.014333	.741372	51.725561	.019333	60
6	1.432044	86.408856	.011573	.698302	60.339514	.016573	72
7	1.520370	104.073927	.009609	.657735	68.453042	.014609	84
8	1.614143	122.828542	.008141	.619524	76.095218	.013141	96
9	1.713699	142.739900	.007006	.583533	83.293424	.012006	108
10	1.819397	163.879347	.006102	.549633	90.073453	.011102	120
11	1.931613	186.322629	.005367	.517702	96.459599	.010367	132
12	2.050751	210.150163	.004759	.487626	102.474743	.009759	144
13	2.177237	235.447328	.004247	.459298	108.140440	.009247	156
14	2.311524	262.304766	.003812	.432615	113.476990	.008812	168
15	2.454094	290.818713	.003439	.407482	118.503514	.008439	180
16	2.605457	321.091337	.003114	.383810	123.238025	.008114	192
17	2.766156	353.231110	.002831	.361513	127.697486	.007831	204
18	2.936766	387.353195	.002582	.340511	131.897876	.007582	216
19	3.117899	423.579854	.002361	.320729	135.854246	.007361	228
20	3.310204	462.040895	.002164	.302096	139.580771	.007164	240
21	3.514371	502.874129	.001989	.284546	143.090806	.006989	252
22	3.731129	546.225867	.001831	.268015	146.396926	.006831	264
23	3.961257	592.251446	.001688	.252445	149.510979	.006688	276
24	4.205579	641.115782	.001560	.237779	152.444121	.006560	288
25	4.464970	692.993963	.001443	.223966	155.206864	.006443	300
26	4.740359	748.071876	.001337	.210954	157.809106	.006337	312
27	5.032734	806.546875	.001240	.198699	160.260171	.006240	324
28	5.343142	868.628484	.001151	.187156	162.568843	.006151	336
29	5.672696	934.539150	.001070	.176283	164.743393	.006070	348
30	6.022575	1004.515043	.000996	.166042	166.791614	.005996	360
31	6.394034	1078.806895	.000927	.156396	168.720844	.005927	372
32	6.788405	1157.680906	.000864	.147310	170.537996	.005864	384
33	7.207098	1241.419694	.000806	.138752	172.249581	.005806	396
34	7.651617	1330.323306	.000752	.130691	173.861732	.005752	408
35	8.123551	1424.710299	.000702	.123099	175.380226	.005702	420
36	8.624594	1524.918875	.000656	.115947	176.810503	.005656	432
37	9.156540	1631.308097	.000613	.109212	178.157689	.005613	444
38	9.721296	1744.259174	.000573	.102867	179.426611	.005573	456
39	10.320884	1864.176825	.000536	.096891	180.621815	.005536	468
40	10.957454	1991.490735	.000502	.091262	181.747584	.005502	480
41	11.633285	2126.657088	.000470	.085960	182.807952	.005470	492
42	12.350801	2270.160207	.000440	.080966	183.806718	.005440	504
43	13.112571	2422.514283	.000413	.076263	184.747461	.005413	516
44	13.921326	2584.265226	.000387	.071832	185.633552	.005387	528
45	14.779963	2755.992612	.000363	.067659	186.468166	.005363	540
46	15.691559	2938.311769	.000340	.063729	187.254293	.005340	552
47	16.659380	3131.875972	.000319	.060026	187.994750	.005319	564
48	17.686894	3337.378791	.000300	.056539	188.692191	.005300	576
49	18.777783	3555.556574	.000281	.053254	189.349115	.005281	588
50	19.935955	3787.191086	.000264	.050161	189.967874	.005264	600

6% QUARTERLY COMPOUND INTEREST TABLE 6%

EFFECTIVE RATE = 1½% BASE = 1.015

QUARTERS	1 AMOUNT OF 1 AT COMPOUND INTEREST $S^n = (1+i)^n$	2 ACCUMULATION OF 1 PER PERIOD $S_{\overline{n}\mid} = \frac{S^n - 1}{i}$	3 SINKING FUND FACTOR $1/S_{\overline{n}\mid} = \frac{i}{S^n - 1}$	4 PRES. VALUE REVERSION OF 1 $V^n = \frac{1}{S^n}$	5 PRESENT VALUE ORD. ANNUITY 1 PER PERIOD $a_{\overline{n}\mid} = \frac{1-V^n}{i}$	6 INSTALMENT TO AMORTIZE 1 $1/a_{\overline{n}\mid} = \frac{i}{1-V^n}$	n QUARTERS
1	1.015000	1.000000	1.000000	.985222	.985222	1.015000	1
2	1.030225	2.015000	.496278	.970662	1.955883	.511278	2
3	1.045678	3.045225	.328383	.956317	2.912200	.343383	3
YEARS							
1	1.061364	4.090903	.244445	.942184	3.854385	.259445	4
2	1.126493	8.432839	.118584	.887711	7.485925	.133584	8
3	1.195618	13.041211	.076680	.836387	10.907505	.091680	12
4	1.268986	17.932370	.055765	.788031	14.131264	.070765	16
5	1.346855	23.123667	.043246	.742470	17.168639	.058246	20
6	1.429503	28.633521	.034924	.699544	20.030405	.049924	24
7	1.517222	34.481479	.029001	.659099	22.726717	.044001	28
8	1.610324	40.688288	.024577	.620993	25.267139	.039577	32
9	1.709140	47.275969	.021152	.585090	27.660684	.036152	36
10	1.814018	54.267894	.018427	.551262	29.915845	.033427	40
11	1.925333	61.688868	.016210	.519391	32.040622	.031210	44
12	2.043478	69.565219	.014375	.489362	34.042554	.029375	48
13	2.168873	77.924892	.012833	.461069	35.928742	.027833	52
14	2.301963	86.797543	.011521	.434412	37.705879	.026521	56
15	2.443220	96.214652	.010393	.409296	39.380269	.025393	60
16	2.593144	106.209628	.009415	.385632	40.957853	.024415	64
17	2.752269	116.817931	.008560	.363337	42.444228	.023560	68
18	2.921158	128.077197	.007808	.342330	43.844667	.022808	72
19	3.100411	140.027372	.007141	.322538	45.164138	.022141	76
20	3.290663	152.710852	.006548	.303890	46.407324	.021548	80
21	3.492590	166.172636	.006018	.286321	47.578633	.021018	84
22	3.706907	180.460482	.005541	.269767	48.682222	.020541	88
23	3.934376	195.625082	.005112	.254170	49.722007	.020112	92
24	4.175804	211.720235	.004723	.239475	50.701675	.019723	96
25	4.432046	228.803043	.004371	.225629	51.624704	.019371	100
26	4.704012	246.934114	.004050	.212585	52.494366	.019050	104
27	4.992667	266.177771	.003757	.200294	53.313749	.018757	108
28	5.299034	286.602288	.003489	.188714	54.085758	.018489	112
29	5.624202	308.280125	.003244	.177803	54.813133	.018244	116
30	5.969323	331.288192	.003019	.167523	55.498454	.018019	120
31	6.335622	355.708115	.002811	.157838	56.144153	.017811	124
32	6.724398	381.626531	.002620	.148712	56.752520	.017620	128
33	7.137031	409.135393	.002444	.140114	57.325714	.017444	132
34	7.574984	438.332297	.002281	.132013	57.865769	.017281	136
35	8.039812	469.320827	.002131	.124381	58.374599	.017131	140
36	8.533164	502.210922	.001991	.117190	58.854012	.016991	144
37	9.056789	537.119271	.001862	.110414	59.305706	.016862	148
38	9.612546	574.169720	.001742	.104031	59.731286	.016742	152
39	10.202406	613.493716	.001630	.098016	60.132260	.016630	156
40	10.828462	655.230772	.001526	.092349	60.510052	.016526	160
41	11.492934	699.528962	.001430	.087010	60.866001	.016430	164
42	12.198182	746.545446	.001340	.081979	61.201371	.016340	168
43	12.946705	796.447029	.001256	.077240	61.517352	.016256	172
44	13.741161	849.410750	.001177	.072774	61.815063	.016177	176
45	14.584368	905.624513	.001104	.068567	62.095562	.016104	180
46	15.479316	965.287752	.001036	.064602	62.359844	.016036	184
47	16.429182	1028.612139	.000972	.060867	62.608847	.015972	188
48	17.437335	1095.822336	.000913	.057348	62.843453	.015913	192
49	18.507352	1167.156788	.000857	.054033	63.064495	.015857	196
50	19.643029	1242.868576	.000805	.050909	63.272757	.015805	200
51	20.848395	1323.226308	.000756	.047965	63.468978	.015756	204
52	22.127726	1408.515076	.000710	.045192	63.653855	.015710	208
53	23.485562	1499.037466	.000667	.042579	63.828043	.015667	212
54	24.926719	1595.114631	.000627	.040118	63.992161	.015627	216
55	26.456311	1697.087432	.000589	.037798	64.146789	.015589	220
56	28.079765	1805.317645	.000554	.035613	64.292478	.015554	224
57	29.802839	1920.189250	.000521	.033554	64.429743	.015521	228
58	31.631647	2042.109783	.000490	.031614	64.559073	.015490	232
59	33.572677	2171.511794	.000461	.029786	64.680925	.015461	236
60	35.632816	2308.854371	.000433	.028064	64.795732	.015433	240

6% SEMI-ANNUAL COMPOUND INTEREST TABLE 6%

EFFECTIVE RATE = 3% BASE = 1.03

HALF YEARS	1 AMOUNT OF I AT COMPOUND INTEREST $S^n = (1+i)^n$	2 ACCUMULATION OF I PER PERIOD $S_{\overline{n}\vert} = \frac{S^n - 1}{i}$	3 SINKING FUND FACTOR $1/S_{\overline{n}\vert} = \frac{i}{S^n - 1}$	4 PRES. VALUE REVERSION OF I $V^n = \frac{1}{S^n}$	5 PRESENT VALUE ORD. ANNUITY 1 PER PERIOD $a_{\overline{n}\vert} = \frac{1 - V^n}{i}$	6 INSTALMENT TO AMORTIZE I $1/a_{\overline{n}\vert} = \frac{i}{1 - V^n}$	n HALF YEARS
1	1.030000	1.000000	1.000000	.970874	.970874	1.030000	1
YEARS							
1	1.060900	2.030000	.492611	.942596	1.913470	.522611	2
2	1.125509	4.183627	.239027	.888487	3.717098	.269027	4
3	1.194052	6.468410	.154598	.837484	5.417191	.184598	6
4	1.266770	8.892336	.112456	.789409	7.019692	.142456	8
5	1.343916	11.463879	.087231	.744094	8.530203	.117231	10
6	1.425761	14.192030	.070462	.701380	9.954004	.100462	12
7	1.512590	17.086324	.058526	.661118	11.296073	.088526	14
8	1.604706	20.156881	.049611	.623167	12.561102	.079611	16
9	1.702433	23.414435	.042709	.587395	13.753513	.072709	18
10	1.806111	26.870374	.037216	.553676	14.877475	.067216	20
11	1.916103	30.536780	.032747	.521893	15.936917	.062747	22
12	2.032794	34.426470	.029047	.491934	16.935542	.059047	24
13	2.156591	38.553042	.025938	.463695	17.876842	.055938	26
14	2.287928	42.930923	.023293	.437077	18.764108	.053293	28
15	2.427262	47.575416	.021019	.411987	19.600441	.051019	30
16	2.575083	52.502759	.019047	.388337	20.388766	.049047	32
17	2.731905	57.730177	.017322	.366045	21.131837	.047322	34
18	2.898278	63.275944	.015804	.345032	21.832252	.045804	36
19	3.074783	69.159449	.014459	.325226	22.492462	.044459	38
20	3.262038	75.401260	.013262	.306557	23.114772	.043262	40
21	3.460696	82.023196	.012192	.288959	23.701359	.042192	42
22	3.671452	89.048409	.011230	.272372	24.254274	.041230	44
23	3.895044	96.501457	.010363	.256737	24.775449	.040363	46
24	4.132252	104.408396	.009578	.241999	25.266707	.039578	48
25	4.383906	112.796867	.008865	.228107	25.729764	.038865	50
26	4.650886	121.696197	.008217	.215013	26.166240	.038217	52
27	4.934125	131.137495	.007626	.202670	26.577660	.037626	54
28	5.234613	141.153768	.007084	.191036	26.965464	.037084	56
29	5.553401	151.780033	.006588	.180070	27.331005	.036588	58
30	5.891603	163.053437	.006133	.169733	27.675564	.036133	60
31	6.250402	175.013391	.005714	.159990	28.000343	.035714	62
32	6.631051	187.701707	.005328	.150806	28.306478	.035328	64
33	7.034882	201.162741	.004971	.142149	28.595040	.034971	66
34	7.463307	215.443551	.004642	.133989	28.867038	.034642	68
35	7.917822	230.594064	.004337	.126297	29.123421	.034337	70
36	8.400017	246.667242	.004054	.119047	29.365088	.034054	72
37	8.911578	263.719277	.003792	.112214	29.592881	.033792	74
38	9.454293	281.809781	.003548	.105772	29.807598	.033548	76
39	10.030060	301.001997	.003322	.099700	30.009990	.033322	78
40	10.640891	321.363019	.003112	.093977	30.200763	.033112	80
41	11.288921	342.964026	.002916	.088582	30.380586	.032916	82
42	11.976416	365.880536	.002733	.083497	30.550086	.032733	84
43	12.705780	390.192660	.002563	.078704	30.709855	.032563	86
44	13.479562	415.985393	.002404	.074186	30.860454	.032404	88
45	14.300467	443.348904	.002256	.069928	31.002407	.032256	90
46	15.171366	472.378852	.002117	.065914	31.136212	.032117	92
47	16.095302	503.176724	.001987	.062130	31.262336	.031987	94
48	17.075506	535.850186	.001866	.058563	31.381219	.031866	96
49	18.115404	570.513463	.001753	.055202	31.493279	.031753	98
50	19.218632	607.287733	.001647	.052033	31.598905	.031647	100
51	20.389047	646.301556	.001547	.049046	31.698469	.031547	102
52	21.630740	687.691320	.001454	.046231	31.792317	.031454	104
53	22.948052	731.601722	.001367	.043577	31.880777	.031367	106
54	24.345588	778.186267	.001285	.041075	31.964160	.031285	108
55	25.828234	827.607810	.001208	.038717	32.042756	.031208	110
56	27.401174	880.039126	.001136	.036495	32.116840	.031136	112
57	29.069905	935.663509	.001069	.034400	32.186672	.031069	114
58	30.840262	994.675416	.001005	.032425	32.252495	.031005	116
59	32.718434	1057.281149	.000946	.030564	32.314540	.030946	118
60	34.710987	1123.699571	.000890	.028809	32.373023	.030890	120

6% ANNUAL COMPOUND INTEREST TABLE 6%

EFFECTIVE RATE = 6% BASE = 1.06

YEARS	1 AMOUNT OF 1 AT COMPOUND INTEREST $S^n = (1+i)^n$	2 ACCUMULATION OF 1 PER PERIOD $S_{\overline{n}\vert} = \frac{S^n - 1}{i}$	3 SINKING FUND FACTOR $1/S_{\overline{n}\vert} = \frac{i}{S^n - 1}$	4 PRES. VALUE REVERSION OF 1 $V^n = \frac{1}{S^n}$	5 PRESENT VALUE ORD. ANNUITY 1 PER PERIOD $a_{\overline{n}\vert} = \frac{1-V^n}{i}$	6 INSTALMENT TO AMORTIZE 1 $1/a_{\overline{n}\vert} = \frac{i}{1-V^n}$	n YEARS
1	1.060000	1.000000	1.000000	.943396	.943396	1.060000	1
2	1.123600	2.060000	.485437	.889996	1.833393	.545437	2
3	1.191016	3.183600	.314110	.839619	2.673012	.374110	3
4	1.262477	4.374616	.228591	.792094	3.465106	.288591	4
5	1.338226	5.637093	.177396	.747258	4.212364	.237396	5
6	1.418519	6.975319	.143363	.704961	4.917324	.203363	6
7	1.503630	8.393838	.119135	.665057	5.582381	.179135	7
8	1.593848	9.897468	.101036	.627412	6.209794	.161036	8
9	1.689479	11.491316	.087022	.591898	6.801692	.147022	9
10	1.790848	13.180795	.075868	.558395	7.360087	.135868	10
11	1.898299	14.971643	.066793	.526788	7.886875	.126793	11
12	2.012196	16.869941	.059277	.496969	8.383844	.119277	12
13	2.132928	18.882138	.052960	.468839	8.852683	.112960	13
14	2.260904	21.015066	.047585	.442301	9.294984	.107585	14
15	2.396558	23.275970	.042963	.417265	9.712249	.102963	15
16	2.540352	25.672528	.038952	.393646	10.105895	.098952	16
17	2.692773	28.212880	.035445	.371364	10.477260	.095445	17
18	2.854339	30.905653	.032357	.350344	10.827603	.092357	18
19	3.025600	33.759992	.029621	.330513	11.158116	.089621	19
20	3.207135	36.785591	.027185	.311805	11.469921	.087185	20
21	3.399564	39.992727	.025005	.294155	11.764077	.085005	21
22	3.603537	43.392290	.023046	.277505	12.041582	.083046	22
23	3.819750	46.995828	.021278	.261797	12.303379	.081278	23
24	4.048935	50.815577	.019679	.246979	12.550358	.079679	24
25	4.291871	54.864512	.018227	.232999	12.783356	.078227	25
26	4.549383	59.156383	.016904	.219810	13.003166	.076904	26
27	4.822346	63.705766	.015697	.207368	13.210534	.075697	27
28	5.111687	68.528112	.014593	.195630	13.406164	.074593	28
29	5.418388	73.639798	.013580	.184557	13.590721	.073580	29
30	5.743491	79.058186	.012649	.174110	13.764831	.072649	30
31	6.088101	84.801677	.011792	.164255	13.929086	.071792	31
32	6.453387	90.889778	.011002	.154957	14.084043	.071002	32
33	6.840590	97.343165	.010273	.146186	14.230230	.070273	33
34	7.251025	104.183755	.009598	.137912	14.368141	.069598	34
35	7.686087	111.434780	.008974	.130105	14.498246	.068974	35
36	8.147252	119.120867	.008395	.122741	14.620987	.068395	36
37	8.636087	127.268119	.007857	.115793	14.736780	.067857	37
38	9.154252	135.904206	.007358	.109239	14.846019	.067358	38
39	9.703507	145.058458	.006894	.103056	14.949075	.066894	39
40	10.285718	154.761966	.006462	.097222	15.046297	.066462	40
41	10.902861	165.047684	.006059	.091719	15.138016	.066059	41
42	11.557033	175.950545	.005683	.086527	15.224543	.065683	42
43	12.250455	187.507577	.005333	.081630	15.306173	.065333	43
44	12.985482	199.758032	.005006	.077009	15.383182	.065006	44
45	13.764611	212.743514	.004700	.072650	15.455832	.064700	45
46	14.590487	226.508125	.004415	.068538	15.524370	.064415	46
47	15.465917	241.098612	.004148	.064658	15.589028	.064148	47
48	16.393872	256.564529	.003898	.060998	15.650027	.063898	48
49	17.377504	272.958401	.003664	.057546	15.707572	.063664	49
50	18.420154	290.335905	.003444	.054288	15.761861	.063444	50
51	19.525364	308.756059	.003239	.051215	15.813076	.063239	51
52	20.696885	328.281422	.003046	.048316	15.861393	.063046	52
53	21.938698	348.978308	.002866	.045582	15.906974	.062866	53
54	23.255020	370.917006	.002696	.043001	15.949976	.062696	54
55	24.650322	394.172027	.002537	.040567	15.990543	.062537	55
56	26.129341	418.822348	.002388	.038271	16.028814	.062388	56
57	27.697101	444.951689	.002247	.036105	16.064919	.062247	57
58	29.358927	472.648790	.002116	.034061	16.098980	.062116	58
59	31.120463	502.007718	.001992	.032133	16.131113	.061992	59
60	32.987691	533.128181	.001876	.030314	16.161428	.061876	60

7½% MONTHLY COMPOUND INTEREST TABLE 7½%

EFFECTIVE RATE = 5/8% BASE = 1.00625

MONTHS	1 AMOUNT OF 1 AT COMPOUND INTEREST $S^n = (1+i)^n$	2 ACCUMULATION OF 1 PER PERIOD $S_{\overline{n}\vert} = \frac{S^n - 1}{i}$	3 SINKING FUND FACTOR $1/S_{\overline{n}\vert} = \frac{i}{S^n - 1}$	4 PRES. VALUE REVERSION OF 1 $V^n = \frac{1}{S^n}$	5 PRESENT VALUE ORD. ANNUITY 1 PER PERIOD $a_{\overline{n}\vert} = \frac{1 - V^n}{i}$	6 INSTALMENT TO AMORTIZE 1 $1/a_{\overline{n}\vert} = \frac{i}{1 - V^n}$	n MONTHS
1	1.006250	1.000000	1.000000	.993789	.993789	1.006250	1
2	1.012539	2.006250	.498442	.987616	1.981405	.504692	2
3	1.018867	3.018789	.331259	.981482	2.962887	.337509	3
4	1.025235	4.037656	.247668	.975386	3.938273	.253918	4
5	1.031643	5.062892	.197516	.969327	4.907600	.203766	5
6	1.038091	6.094535	.164081	.963307	5.870907	.170331	6
7	1.044579	7.132626	.140201	.957324	6.828231	.146451	7
8	1.051108	8.177205	.122291	.951377	7.779608	.128541	8
9	1.057677	9.228312	.108362	.945468	8.725076	.114612	9
10	1.064287	10.285989	.097220	.939596	9.664672	.103470	10
11	1.070939	11.350277	.088104	.933760	10.598432	.094354	11
YEARS							
1	1.077633	12.421216	.080507	.927960	11.526392	.086757	12
2	1.161292	25.806723	.038750	.861110	22.222423	.045000	24
3	1.251446	40.231382	.024856	.799076	32.147913	.031106	36
4	1.348599	55.775864	.017929	.741510	41.358371	.024179	48
5	1.453294	72.527105	.013788	.688092	49.905308	.020038	60
6	1.566117	90.578789	.011040	.638522	57.836524	.017290	72
7	1.687699	110.031871	.009088	.592523	65.196376	.015338	84
8	1.818720	130.995147	.007634	.549837	72.026024	.013884	96
9	1.959912	153.585857	.006511	.510227	78.363665	.012761	108
10	2.112065	177.930342	.005620	.473470	84.244743	.011870	120
11	2.276030	204.164753	.004898	.439362	89.702148	.011148	132
12	2.452724	232.435809	.004302	.407710	94.766402	.010552	144
13	2.643135	262.901621	.003804	.378339	99.465827	.010054	156
14	2.848329	295.732572	.003381	.351083	103.826706	.009631	168
15	3.069452	331.112276	.003020	.325791	107.873427	.009270	180
16	3.307741	369.238599	.002708	.302321	111.628623	.008958	192
17	3.564530	410.324767	.002437	.280542	115.113294	.008687	204
18	3.841254	454.600560	.002200	.260332	118.346930	.008450	216
19	4.139460	502.313599	.001991	.241577	121.347616	.008241	228
20	4.460817	553.730725	.001806	.224174	124.132131	.008056	240
21	4.807122	609.139496	.001642	.208025	126.716051	.007892	252
22	5.180311	668.849794	.001495	.193039	129.113825	.007745	264
23	5.582472	733.195558	.001364	.179132	131.338864	.007614	276
24	6.015854	802.536650	.001246	.166227	133.403610	.007496	288
25	6.482880	877.260872	.001140	.154252	135.319613	.007390	300
26	6.986163	957.786129	.001044	.143140	137.097587	.007294	312
27	7.528517	1044.562771	.000957	.132828	138.747476	.007207	324
28	8.112976	1138.076110	.000879	.123259	140.278507	.007129	336
29	8.742807	1238.849131	.000807	.114380	141.699242	.007057	348
30	9.421534	1347.445425	.000742	.106140	143.017628	.006992	360
31	10.152952	1464.472331	.000683	.098494	144.241037	.006933	372
32	10.941152	1590.584340	.000629	.091398	145.376312	.006879	384
33	11.790542	1726.486752	.000579	.084814	146.429802	.006829	396
34	12.705873	1872.939621	.000534	.078704	147.407398	.006784	408
35	13.692263	2030.762007	.000492	.073034	148.314569	.006742	420
36	14.755228	2200.836555	.000454	.067773	149.156387	.006704	432
37	15.900715	2384.114432	.000419	.062890	149.937560	.006669	444
38	17.135129	2581.620647	.000387	.058360	150.662458	.006637	456
39	18.465374	2794.459783	.000358	.054155	151.335134	.006608	468
40	19.898889	3023.822175	.000331	.050254	151.959350	.006581	480
41	21.443691	3270.990564	.000306	.046634	152.538598	.006556	492
42	23.108420	3537.347278	.000283	.043274	153.076118	.006533	504
43	24.902387	3824.381956	.000261	.040157	153.574914	.006511	516
44	26.835624	4133.699883	.000242	.037264	154.037777	.006492	528
45	28.918944	4467.030963	.000224	.034579	154.467295	.006474	540
46	31.163996	4826.239402	.000207	.032088	154.865871	.006457	552
47	33.583338	5213.334125	.000192	.029777	155.235733	.006442	564
48	36.190500	5630.480018	.000178	.027632	155.578951	.006428	576
49	39.000063	6080.010030	.000164	.025641	155.897443	.006414	588
50	42.027739	6564.438226	.000152	.023794	156.192991	.006402	600

7 ½% QUARTERLY COMPOUND INTEREST TABLE 7 ½%

EFFECTIVE RATE = 1-7/8% BASE = 1.01875

QUARTERS	1 AMOUNT OF 1 AT COMPOUND INTEREST $s^n = (1+i)^n$	2 ACCUMULATION OF 1 PER PERIOD $s_{\overline{n}\vert} = \frac{s^n - 1}{i}$	3 SINKING FUND FACTOR $1/s_{\overline{n}\vert} = \frac{i}{s^n - 1}$	4 PRES. VALUE REVERSION OF 1 $v^n = \frac{1}{s^n}$	5 PRESENT VALUE ORD. ANNUITY 1 PER PERIOD $a_{\overline{n}\vert} = \frac{1 - v^n}{i}$	6 INSTALMENT TO AMORTIZE 1 $1/a_{\overline{n}\vert} = \frac{i}{1 - v^n}$	n QUARTERS
1	1.018750	1.000000	1.000000	.981595	.981595	1.018750	1
2	1.037852	2.018750	.495356	.963529	1.945124	.514106	2
3	1.057311	3.056602	.327161	.945795	2.890919	.345911	3
YEARS							
1	1.077136	4.113913	.243078	.928388	3.819307	.261828	4
2	1.160222	8.545156	.117025	.861904	7.365106	.135775	8
3	1.249716	13.318207	.075085	.800182	10.656983	.093835	12
4	1.346114	18.459431	.054173	.742879	13.713123	.072923	16
5	1.449948	23.997228	.041671	.689680	16.550406	.060421	20
6	1.561791	29.962188	.033375	.640291	19.184505	.052125	24
7	1.682261	36.387260	.027482	.594438	21.629971	.046232	28
8	1.812024	43.307936	.023090	.551869	23.900313	.041840	32
9	1.951796	50.762444	.019700	.512349	26.008071	.038450	36
10	2.102349	58.791961	.017009	.475658	27.964888	.035759	40
11	2.264516	67.440843	.014828	.441596	29.781573	.033578	44
12	2.439191	76.756864	.013028	.409972	31.468162	.031778	48
13	2.627340	86.791484	.011522	.380613	33.033971	.030272	52
14	2.830002	97.600133	.010246	.353357	34.487649	.028996	56
15	3.048297	109.242516	.009154	.328052	35.837226	.027904	60
16	3.283430	121.782945	.008211	.304560	37.090158	.026961	64
17	3.536700	135.290691	.007391	.282749	38.253364	.026141	68
18	3.809507	149.840369	.006674	.262501	39.333271	.025424	72
19	4.103357	165.512348	.006042	.243703	40.335844	.024792	76
20	4.419872	182.393199	.005483	.226251	41.266620	.024233	80
21	4.760803	200.576169	.004986	.210049	42.130742	.023736	84
22	5.128032	220.161699	.004542	.195007	42.932982	.023292	88
23	5.523587	241.257975	.004145	.181042	43.677772	.022895	92
24	5.949654	263.981530	.003788	.168077	44.369226	.022538	96
25	6.408585	288.457887	.003467	.156041	45.011164	.022217	100
26	6.902917	314.822249	.003176	.144866	45.607131	.021926	104
27	7.435380	343.220248	.002914	.134492	46.160420	.021664	108
28	8.008914	373.808752	.002675	.124861	46.674087	.021425	112
29	8.626689	406.756727	.002458	.115919	47.150969	.021208	116
30	9.292116	442.246172	.002261	.107618	47.593700	.021011	120
31	10.008871	480.473126	.002081	.099911	48.004727	.020831	124
32	10.780914	521.648749	.001917	.092757	48.386319	.020667	128
33	11.612509	566.000490	.001767	.086114	48.740585	.020517	132
34	12.508250	613.773341	.001629	.079947	49.069481	.020379	136
35	13.473085	665.231192	.001503	.074222	49.374824	.020253	140
36	14.512343	720.658289	.001388	.068907	49.658301	.020138	144
37	15.631765	780.360802	.001281	.063972	49.921477	.020031	148
38	16.837535	844.668535	.001184	.059391	50.165807	.019934	152
39	18.136313	913.936672	.001094	.055138	50.392640	.019844	156
40	19.535273	988.547881	.001012	.051189	50.603229	.019762	160
41	21.042143	1068.914291	.000936	.047524	50.798737	.019686	164
42	22.665247	1155.479833	.000865	.044120	50.980245	.019615	168
43	24.413550	1248.722683	.000801	.040961	51.148754	.019551	172
44	26.296711	1349.157901	.000741	.038028	51.305196	.019491	176
45	28.325130	1457.340277	.000686	.035304	51.450435	.019436	180
46	30.510014	1573.867394	.000635	.032776	51.585273	.019385	184
47	32.863430	1699.382931	.000588	.030429	51.710455	.019338	188
48	35.398379	1834.580217	.000545	.028250	51.826673	.019295	192
49	38.128864	1980.206063	.000505	.026227	51.934568	.019255	196
50	41.069967	2137.064885	.000468	.024349	52.034736	.019218	200
51	44.237934	2306.023148	.000434	.022605	52.127731	.019184	204
52	47.650265	2488.014153	.000402	.020986	52.214067	.019152	208
53	51.325810	2684.043192	.000373	.019483	52.294220	.019123	212
54	55.284871	2895.193100	.000345	.018088	52.368633	.019095	216
55	59.549317	3122.630239	.000320	.016793	52.437717	.019070	220
56	64.142705	3367.610939	.000297	.015590	52.501854	.019047	224
57	69.090408	3631.488437	.000275	.014474	52.561398	.019025	228
58	74.419757	3915.720355	.000255	.013437	52.616678	.019005	232
59	80.160189	4221.876748	.000237	.012475	52.667999	.018987	236
60	86.343415	4551.648779	.000220	.011582	52.715645	.018970	240

7 ½% SEMI-ANNUAL COMPOUND INTEREST TABLE 7 ½%

EFFECTIVE RATE = 3¾% BASE = 1.0375

HALF YEARS	1 AMOUNT OF I AT COMPOUND INTEREST $S^n = (1+i)^n$	2 ACCUMULATION OF I PER PERIOD $S_{\overline{n}\|} = \frac{S^n - 1}{i}$	3 SINKING FUND FACTOR $1/S_{\overline{n}\|} = \frac{i}{S^n - 1}$	4 PRES. VALUE REVERSION OF I $V^n = \frac{1}{S^n}$	5 PRESENT VALUE ORD. ANNUITY 1 PER PERIOD $a_{\overline{n}\|} = \frac{1 - V^n}{i}$	6 INSTALMENT TO AMORTIZE I $1/a_{\overline{n}\|} = \frac{i}{1 - V^n}$	n HALF YEARS
1	1.037500	1.000000	1.000000	.963855	.963855	1.037500	1
YEARS							
1	1.076406	2.037500	.490798	.929017	1.892873	.528298	2
2	1.158650	4.230678	.236369	.863073	3.651384	.273869	4
3	1.247179	6.591428	.151712	.801810	5.285072	.189212	6
4	1.342471	9.132554	.109498	.744895	6.802796	.146998	8
5	1.445044	11.867838	.084261	.692020	8.212787	.121761	10
6	1.555454	14.812116	.067512	.642899	9.522694	.105012	12
7	1.674301	17.981354	.055613	.597264	10.739620	.093113	14
8	1.802228	21.392742	.046745	.554869	11.870165	.084245	16
9	1.939929	25.064781	.039897	.515483	12.920461	.077397	18
10	2.088152	29.017387	.034462	.478892	13.896204	.071962	20
11	2.247700	33.271996	.030055	.444899	14.802686	.067555	22
12	2.419438	37.851685	.026419	.413319	15.644824	.063919	24
13	2.604298	42.781290	.023375	.383981	16.427185	.060875	26
14	2.803283	48.087548	.020795	.356725	17.154011	.058295	28
15	3.017471	53.799237	.018588	.331403	17.829245	.056088	30
16	3.248025	59.947335	.016681	.307879	18.456549	.054181	32
17	3.496194	66.565186	.015023	.286025	19.039326	.052523	34
18	3.763326	73.688682	.013571	.265722	19.580735	.051071	36
19	4.050867	81.356458	.012292	.246861	20.083714	.049792	38
20	4.360379	89.610100	.011159	.229338	20.550990	.048659	40
21	4.693539	98.494372	.010153	.213059	20.985097	.047653	42
22	5.052155	108.057458	.009254	.197935	21.388391	.046754	44
23	5.438171	118.351223	.008449	.183885	21.763057	.045949	46
24	5.853681	129.431496	.007726	.170833	22.111129	.045226	48
25	6.300939	141.358371	.007074	.158707	22.434493	.044574	50
26	6.782370	154.196534	.006485	.147441	22.734904	.043985	52
27	7.300585	168.015613	.005952	.136975	23.013992	.043452	54
28	7.858396	182.890556	.005468	.127252	23.273268	.042968	56
29	8.458826	198.902037	.005028	.118220	23.514141	.042528	58
30	9.105134	216.136896	.004627	.109828	23.737916	.042127	60
31	9.800823	234.688606	.004261	.102032	23.945807	.041761	62
32	10.549667	254.657782	.003927	.094790	24.138941	.041427	64
33	11.355727	276.152729	.003621	.088061	24.318366	.041121	66
34	12.223376	299.290023	.003341	.081810	24.485054	.040841	68
35	13.157318	324.195151	.003085	.076003	24.639911	.040585	70
36	14.162620	351.003187	.002849	.070608	24.783776	.040349	72
37	15.244732	379.859524	.002633	.065596	24.917429	.040133	74
38	16.409525	410.920666	.002434	.060940	25.041594	.039934	76
39	17.663315	444.355073	.002250	.056615	25.156946	.039750	78
40	19.012903	480.344078	.002082	.052596	25.264110	.039582	80
41	20.465608	519.082868	.001926	.048862	25.363668	.039426	82
42	22.029308	560.781543	.001783	.045394	25.456158	.039283	84
43	23.712485	605.666258	.001651	.042172	25.542083	.039151	86
44	25.524267	653.980445	.001529	.039178	25.621909	.039029	88
45	27.474480	705.986139	.001416	.036397	25.696069	.038916	90
46	29.573702	761.965392	.001312	.033814	25.764965	.038812	92
47	31.833318	822.221810	.001216	.031414	25.828970	.038716	94
48	34.265582	887.082196	.001127	.029184	25.888432	.038627	96
49	36.883687	956.898320	.001045	.027112	25.943673	.038545	98
50	39.701831	1032.048832	.000969	.025188	25.994993	.038469	100
51	42.735299	1112.941313	.000899	.023400	26.042670	.038399	102
52	46.000543	1200.014485	.000833	.021739	26.086963	.038333	104
53	49.515272	1293.740592	.000773	.020196	26.128112	.038273	106
54	53.298548	1394.627959	.000717	.018762	26.166340	.038217	108
55	57.370891	1503.223751	.000665	.017430	26.201855	.038165	110
56	61.754385	1620.116941	.000617	.016193	26.234848	.038117	112
57	66.472806	1745.941501	.000573	.015044	26.265500	.038073	114
58	71.551744	1881.379844	.000532	.013976	26.293976	.038032	116
59	77.018745	2027.166523	.000493	.012984	26.320431	.037993	118
60	82.903458	2184.092215	.000458	.012062	26,345007	.037958	120

7½% ANNUAL COMPOUND INTEREST TABLE 7½%

EFFECTIVE RATE = 7½% BASE = 1.075

YEARS	1 AMOUNT OF 1 AT COMPOUND INTEREST $s^n = (1+i)^n$	2 ACCUMULATION OF 1 PER PERIOD $s_{\overline{n}\|} = \frac{s^n - 1}{i}$	3 SINKING FUND FACTOR $1/s_{\overline{n}\|} = \frac{i}{s^n - 1}$	4 PRES. VALUE REVERSION OF 1 $v^n = \frac{1}{s^n}$	5 PRESENT VALUE ORD. ANNUITY 1 PER PERIOD $a_{\overline{n}\|} = \frac{1 - v^n}{i}$	6 INSTALMENT TO AMORTIZE 1 $1/a_{\overline{n}\|} = \frac{i}{1 - v^n}$	n YEARS
1	1.075000	1.000000	1.000000	.930233	.930233	1.075000	1
2	1.155625	2.075000	.481928	.865333	1.795565	.556928	2
3	1.242297	3.230625	.309538	.804961	2.600526	.384538	3
4	1.335469	4.472922	.223568	.748801	3.349326	.298568	4
5	1.435629	5.808391	.172165	.696559	4.045885	.247165	5
6	1.543302	7.244020	.138045	.647962	4.693846	.213045	6
7	1.659049	8.787322	.113800	.602755	5.296601	.188800	7
8	1.783478	10.446371	.095727	.560702	5.857304	.170727	8
9	1.917239	12.229849	.081767	.521583	6.378887	.156767	9
10	2.061032	14.147087	.070686	.485194	6.864081	.145686	10
11	2.215609	16.208119	.061697	.451343	7.315424	.136697	11
12	2.381780	18.423728	.054278	.419854	7.735278	.129278	12
13	2.560413	20.805508	.048064	.390562	8.125840	.123064	13
14	2.752444	23.365921	.042797	.363313	8.489154	.117797	14
15	2.958877	26.118365	.038287	.337966	8.827120	.113287	15
16	3.180793	29.077242	.034391	.314387	9.141507	.109391	16
17	3.419353	32.258035	.031000	.292453	9.433960	.106000	17
18	3.675804	35.677388	.028029	.272049	9.706009	.103029	18
19	3.951489	39.353192	.025411	.253069	9.959078	.100411	19
20	4.247851	43.304681	.023092	.235413	10.194491	.098092	20
21	4.566440	47.552532	.021029	.218989	10.413480	.096029	21
22	4.908923	52.118972	.019187	.203711	10.617191	.094187	22
23	5.277092	57.027895	.017535	.189498	10.806689	.092535	23
24	5.672874	62.304987	.016050	.176277	10.982967	.091050	24
25	6.098340	67.977862	.014711	.163979	11.146946	.089711	25
26	6.555715	74.076201	.013500	.152539	11.299485	.088500	26
27	7.047394	80.631916	.012402	.141896	11.441381	.087402	27
28	7.575948	87.679310	.011405	.131997	11.573378	.086405	28
29	8.144144	95.255258	.010498	.122788	11.696165	.085498	29
30	8.754955	103.399403	.009671	.114221	11.810386	.084671	30
31	9.411577	112.154358	.008916	.106252	11.916638	.083916	31
32	10.117445	121.565935	.008226	.098839	12.015478	.083226	32
33	10.876253	131.683380	.007594	.091943	12.107421	.082594	33
34	11.691972	142.559633	.007015	.085529	12.192950	.082015	34
35	12.568870	154.251606	.006483	.079562	12.272511	.081483	35
36	13.511536	166.820476	.005994	.074011	12.346522	.080994	36
37	14.524901	180.332012	.005545	.068847	12.415370	.080545	37
38	15.614268	194.856913	.005132	.064044	12.479414	.080132	38
39	16.785339	210.471181	.004751	.059576	12.538989	.079751	39
40	18.044239	227.256520	.004400	.055419	12.594409	.079400	40
41	19.397557	245.300759	.004077	.051553	12.645962	.079077	41
42	20.852374	264.698315	.003778	.047956	12.693918	.078778	42
43	22.416302	285.550689	.003502	.044610	12.738528	.078502	43
44	24.097524	307.966991	.003247	.041498	12.780026	.078247	44
45	25.904839	332.064515	.003011	.038603	12.818629	.078011	45
46	27.847702	357.969354	.002794	.035910	12.854539	.077794	46
47	29.936279	385.817055	.002592	.033404	12.887943	.077592	47
48	32.181500	415.753334	.002405	.031074	12.919017	.077405	48
49	34.595113	447.934835	.002232	.028906	12.947922	.077232	49
50	37.189746	482.529947	.002072	.026889	12.974812	.077072	50
51	39.978977	519.719693	.001924	.025013	12.999825	.076924	51
52	42.977400	559.698670	.001787	.023268	13.023093	.076787	52
53	46.200705	602.676070	.001659	.021645	13.044737	.076659	53
54	49.665758	648.876776	.001541	.020135	13.064872	.076541	54
55	53.390690	698.542534	.001432	.018730	13.083602	.076432	55
56	57.394992	751.933224	.001330	.017423	13.101025	.076330	56
57	61.699616	809.328216	.001236	.016208	13.117233	.076236	57
58	66.327087	871.027832	.001148	.015077	13.132309	.076148	58
59	71.301619	937.354919	.001067	.014025	13.146334	.076067	59
60	76.649240	1008.656538	.000991	.013046	13.159381	.075991	60

9% MONTHLY COMPOUND INTEREST TABLE 9%

EFFECTIVE RATE = 3/4% BASE = 1.0075

MONTHS	1 AMOUNT OF I AT COMPOUND INTEREST $S^n = (1+i)^n$	2 ACCUMULATION OF I PER PERIOD $S_{\overline{n}\|} = \frac{S^n - 1}{i}$	3 SINKING FUND FACTOR $1/S_{\overline{n}\|} = \frac{i}{S^n - 1}$	4 PRES. VALUE REVERSION OF I $V^n = \frac{1}{S^n}$	5 PRESENT VALUE ORD. ANNUITY 1 PER PERIOD $a_{\overline{n}\|} = \frac{1 - V^n}{i}$	6 INSTALMENT TO AMORTIZE I $1/a_{\overline{n}\|} = \frac{i}{1 - V^n}$	n MONTHS
1	1.007500	1.000000	1.000000	.992555	.992555	1.007500	1
2	1.015056	2.007500	.498132	.985167	1.977722	.505632	2
3	1.022669	3.022556	.330845	.977833	2.955556	.338345	3
4	1.030339	4.045225	.247205	.970554	3.926110	.254705	4
5	1.038066	5.075564	.197022	.963329	4.889439	.204522	5
6	1.045852	6.113631	.163568	.956158	5.845597	.171068	6
7	1.053696	7.159483	.139674	.949040	6.794637	.147174	7
8	1.061598	8.213179	.121755	.941975	7.736613	.129255	8
9	1.069560	9.274778	.107819	.934963	8.671576	.115319	9
10	1.077582	10.344339	.096671	.928003	9.599579	.104171	10
11	1.085664	11.421921	.087550	.921094	10.520674	.095050	11
YEARS							
1	1.093806	12.507586	.079951	.914238	11.434912	.087451	12
2	1.196413	26.188470	.038184	.835831	21.889146	.045684	24
3	1.308645	41.152716	.024299	.764148	31.446805	.031799	36
4	1.431405	57.520711	.017385	.698614	40.184781	.024885	48
5	1.565681	75.424136	.013258	.638699	48.173373	.020758	60
6	1.712552	95.007027	.010525	.583923	55.476848	.018025	72
7	1.873201	116.426928	.008589	.533845	62.153964	.016089	84
8	2.048921	139.856163	.007150	.488061	68.258438	.014650	96
9	2.241124	165.483222	.006042	.446204	73.839381	.013542	108
10	2.451357	193.514276	.005167	.407937	78.941692	.012667	120
11	2.681311	224.174837	.004460	.372951	83.606419	.011960	132
12	2.932836	257.711569	.003880	.340966	87.871091	.011380	144
13	3.207957	294.394278	.003396	.311724	91.770017	.010896	156
14	3.508885	334.518079	.002989	.284990	95.334563	.010489	168
15	3.838043	378.405768	.002642	.260549	98.593409	.010142	180
16	4.198078	426.410426	.002345	.238204	101.572769	.009845	192
17	4.591886	478.918251	.002088	.217775	104.296613	.009588	204
18	5.022637	536.351673	.001864	.199098	106.786855	.009364	216
19	5.493795	599.172746	.001668	.182023	109.063530	.009168	228
20	6.009151	667.886868	.001497	.166412	111.144953	.008997	240
21	6.572851	743.046850	.001345	.152140	113.047869	.008845	252
22	7.189430	825.257356	.001211	.139093	114.787589	.008711	264
23	7.863848	915.179775	.001092	.127164	116.378106	.008592	276
24	8.601531	1013.537537	.000986	.116258	117.832217	.008486	288
25	9.408414	1121.121935	.000891	.106287	119.161622	.008391	300
26	10.290988	1238.798492	.000807	.097172	120.377014	.008307	312
27	11.256354	1367.513922	.000731	.088838	121.488171	.008231	324
28	12.312278	1508.303747	.000662	.081219	122.504035	.008162	336
29	13.467254	1662.300628	.000601	.074254	123.432775	.008101	348
30	14.730576	1830.743479	.000546	.067886	124.281865	.008046	360
31	16.112405	2014.987432	.000496	.062063	125.058136	.007996	372
32	17.623860	2216.514738	.000451	.056741	125.767833	.007951	384
33	19.277100	2436.946695	.000410	.051875	126.416663	.007910	396
34	21.085425	2678.056691	.000373	.047426	127.009849	.007873	408
35	23.063383	2941.784467	.000339	.043358	127.552164	.007839	420
36	25.226887	3230.251727	.000309	.039640	128.047967	.007809	432
37	27.593344	3545.779207	.000282	.036240	128.501249	.007782	444
38	30.181790	3890.905340	.000257	.033132	128.915658	.007757	456
39	33.013050	4268.406685	.000234	.030291	129.294525	.007734	468
40	36.109901	4681.320260	.000213	.027693	129.640901	.007713	480
41	39.497259	5132.967977	.000194	.025318	129.957571	.007694	492
42	43.202375	5626.983364	.000177	.023146	130.247083	.007677	504
43	47.255056	6167.340803	.000162	.021161	130.511766	.007662	516
44	51.687906	6758.387497	.000147	.019346	130.753748	.007647	528
45	56.536588	7404.878447	.000135	.017687	130.974978	.007635	540
46	61.840110	8112.014707	.000123	.016170	131.177236	.007623	552
47	67.641139	8885.485227	.000112	.014783	131.362146	.007612	564
48	73.986344	9731.512616	.000102	.013516	131.531199	.007602	576
49	80.926774	10656.903210	.000093	.012356	131.685753	.007593	588
50	88.518263	11669.101820	.000085	.011297	131.827052	.007585	600

9% QUARTERLY COMPOUND INTEREST TABLE 9%

EFFECTIVE RATE = 2¼% BASE = 1.0225

QUARTERS	1 AMOUNT OF I AT COMPOUND INTEREST $S^n = (1+i)^n$	2 ACCUMULATION OF I PER PERIOD $S_{\overline{n}\rceil} = \frac{S^n - 1}{i}$	3 SINKING FUND FACTOR $1/S_{\overline{n}\rceil} = \frac{i}{S^n - 1}$	4 PRES. VALUE REVERSION OF I $V^n = \frac{1}{S^n}$	5 PRESENT VALUE ORD. ANNUITY 1 PER PERIOD $a_{\overline{n}\rceil} = \frac{1 - V^n}{i}$	6 INSTALMENT TO AMORTIZE I $1/a_{\overline{n}\rceil} = \frac{i}{1 - V^n}$	n QUARTERS
1	1.022500	1.000000	1.000000	.977995	.977995	1.022500	1
2	1.045506	2.022500	.494438	.956474	1.934470	.516938	2
3	1.069030	3.068006	.325945	.935427	2.869897	.348445	3
YEARS							
1	1.093083	4.137036	.241719	.914843	3.784740	.264219	4
2	1.194831	8.659162	.115485	.836938	7.247185	.137985	8
3	1.306050	13.602222	.073517	.765667	10.414779	.096017	12
4	1.427621	19.005398	.052617	.700466	13.312631	.075117	16
5	1.560509	24.911520	.040142	.640816	15.963712	.062642	20
6	1.705767	31.367403	.031880	.586247	18.389036	.054380	24
7	1.864545	38.424222	.026025	.536324	20.607828	.048525	28
8	2.038103	46.137912	.021674	.490652	22.637674	.044174	32
9	2.227816	54.569619	.018325	.448870	24.494666	.040825	36
10	2.435189	63.786176	.015677	.410646	26.193522	.038177	40
11	2.661864	73.860642	.013539	.375677	27.747710	.036039	44
12	2.909640	84.872872	.011782	.343685	29.169548	.034282	48
13	3.180479	96.910157	.010319	.314418	30.470307	.032819	52
14	3.476528	110.067912	.009085	.287643	31.660298	.031585	56
15	3.800135	124.450435	.008035	.263149	32.748953	.030535	60
16	4.153864	140.171731	.007134	.240740	33.744902	.029634	64
17	4.540519	157.356417	.006355	.220239	34.656039	.028855	68
18	4.963166	176.140711	.005677	.201484	35.489587	.028177	72
19	5.425154	196.673510	.005085	.184327	36.252153	.027585	76
20	5.930145	219.117569	.004564	.168630	36.949781	.027064	80
21	6.482143	243.650796	.004104	.154270	37.588001	.026604	84
22	7.085522	270.467657	.003697	.141133	38.171873	.026197	88
23	7.745066	299.780721	.003336	.129114	38.706024	.025836	92
24	8.466003	331.822342	.003014	.118119	39.194689	.025514	96
25	9.254046	366.846503	.002726	.108061	39.641741	.025226	100
26	10.115444	405.130829	.002468	.098859	40.050723	.024968	104
27	11.057023	446.978788	.002237	.090440	40.424877	.024737	108
28	12.086247	492.722093	.002030	.082739	40.767170	.024530	112
29	13.211275	542.723337	.001843	.075693	41.080315	.024343	116
30	14.441024	597.378863	.001674	.069247	41.366793	.024174	120
31	15.785243	657.121907	.001522	.063350	41.628875	.024022	124
32	17.254586	722.426031	.001384	.057956	41.868640	.023884	128
33	18.860700	793.808880	.001260	.053020	42.087987	.023760	132
34	20.616316	871.836281	.001147	.048505	42.288655	.023647	136
35	22.535351	957.126733	.001045	.044375	42.472234	.023545	140
36	24.633017	1050.356302	.000952	.040596	42.640181	.023452	144
37	26.925940	1152.263989	.000868	.037139	42.793826	.023368	148
38	29.432296	1263.657582	.000791	.033976	42.934387	.023291	152
39	32.171951	1385.420060	.000722	.031083	43.062979	.023222	156
40	35.166623	1518.516594	.000659	.028436	43.180620	.023159	160
41	38.440049	1664.002195	.000601	.026015	43.288243	.023101	164
42	42.018177	1823.030078	.000549	.023799	43.386701	.023049	168
43	45.929368	1996.860804	.000501	.021773	43.476775	.023001	172
44	50.204626	2186.872272	.000457	.019918	43.559179	.022957	176
45	54.877839	2394.570637	.000418	.018222	43.634565	.022918	180
46	59.986051	2621.602256	.000381	.016671	43.703531	.022881	184
47	65.569751	2869.766731	.000348	.015251	43.766625	.022848	188
48	71.673202	3141.031179	.000318	.013952	43.824346	.022818	192
49	78.344781	3437.545822	.000291	.012764	43.877151	.022791	196
50	85.637373	3761.661032	.000266	.011677	43.925460	.022766	200
51	93.608784	4115.945962	.000243	.010683	43.969655	.022743	204
52	102.322200	4503.208907	.000222	.009773	44.010087	.022722	208
53	111.846690	4926.519573	.000203	.008941	44.047075	.022703	212
54	122.257752	5389.233400	.000186	.008179	44.080914	.022686	216
55	133.637909	5895.018169	.000170	.007483	44.111871	.022670	220
56	146.077369	6447.883062	.000155	.006846	44.140192	.022655	224
57	159.674735	7052.210453	.000142	.006263	44.166101	.022642	228
58	174.537790	7712.790645	.000130	.005729	44.189804	.022630	232
59	190.784346	8434.859831	.000119	.005242	44.211488	.022619	236
60	208.543186	9224.141613	.000108	.004795	44.231326	.022608	240

9% SEMI-ANNUAL COMPOUND INTEREST TABLE 9%

EFFECTIVE RATE = 4½% BASE = 1.045

HALF YEARS	1 AMOUNT OF I AT COMPOUND INTEREST $S^n = (1+i)^n$	2 ACCUMULATION OF I PER PERIOD $S_{\overline{n}\vert} = \frac{S^n - 1}{i}$	3 SINKING FUND FACTOR $1/S_{\overline{n}\vert} = \frac{i}{S^n - 1}$	4 PRES. VALUE REVERSION OF I $V^n = \frac{1}{S^n}$	5 PRESENT VALUE ORD. ANNUITY 1 PER PERIOD $a_{\overline{n}\vert} = \frac{1 - V^n}{i}$	6 INSTALMENT TO AMORTIZE I $1/a_{\overline{n}\vert} = \frac{i}{1 - V^n}$	n HALF YEARS
1	1.045000	1.000000	1.000000	.956938	.956938	1.045000	1
YEARS							
1	1.092025	2.045000	.488998	.915730	1.872668	.533998	2
2	1.192519	4.278191	.233744	.838561	3.587526	.278744	4
3	1.302260	6.716892	.148878	.767896	5.157872	.193878	6
4	1.422101	9.380014	.106610	.703185	6.595886	.151610	8
5	1.552969	12.288209	.081379	.643928	7.912718	.126379	10
6	1.695881	15.464032	.064666	.589664	9.118581	.109666	12
7	1.851945	18.932109	.052820	.539973	10.222825	.097820	14
8	2.022370	22.719337	.044015	.494469	11.234015	.089015	16
9	2.208479	26.855084	.037237	.452800	12.159992	.082237	18
10	2.411714	31.371423	.031876	.414643	13.007936	.076876	20
11	2.633652	36.303378	.027546	.379701	13.784425	.072546	22
12	2.876014	41.689196	.023987	.347703	14.495478	.068987	24
13	3.140679	47.570645	.021021	.318402	15.146611	.066021	26
14	3.429700	53.993333	.018521	.291571	15.742874	.063521	28
15	3.745318	61.007070	.016392	.267000	16.288889	.061392	30
16	4.089981	68.666245	.014563	.244500	16.788891	.059563	32
17	4.466362	77.030256	.012982	.223896	17.246758	.057982	34
18	4.877378	86.163966	.011606	.205028	17.666041	.056606	36
19	5.326219	96.138205	.010402	.187750	18.049990	.055402	38
20	5.816365	107.030323	.009343	.171929	18.401584	.054343	40
21	6.351615	118.924789	.008409	.157440	18.723550	.053409	42
22	6.936123	131.913842	.007581	.144173	19.018383	.052581	44
23	7.574420	146.098214	.006845	.132023	19.288371	.051845	46
24	8.271456	161.587902	.006189	.120898	19.535607	.051189	48
25	9.032636	178.503028	.005602	.110710	19.762008	.050602	50
26	9.863865	196.974769	.005077	.101380	19.969330	.050077	52
27	10.771587	217.146372	.004605	.092837	20.159181	.049605	54
28	11.762842	239.174267	.004181	.085013	20.333034	.049181	56
29	12.845318	263.229279	.003799	.077849	20.492236	.048799	58
30	14.027408	289.497954	.003454	.071289	20.638022	.048454	60
31	15.318280	318.184003	.003143	.065281	20.771523	.048143	62
32	16.727945	349.509886	.002861	.059780	20.893773	.047861	64
33	18.267334	383.718533	.002606	.054743	21.005722	.047606	66
34	19.948385	421.075231	.002375	.050129	21.108236	.047375	68
35	21.784136	461.869679	.002165	.045905	21.202112	.047165	70
36	23.788821	506.418237	.001975	.042037	21.288077	.046975	72
37	25.977987	555.066375	.001802	.038494	21.366797	.046802	74
38	28.368611	608.191358	.001644	.035250	21.438884	.046644	76
39	30.979233	666.205168	.001501	.032280	21.504896	.046501	78
40	33.830096	729.557698	.001371	.029559	21.565345	.046371	80
41	36.943311	798.740245	.001252	.027068	21.620700	.046252	82
42	40.343019	874.289317	.001144	.024787	21.671390	.046144	84
43	44.055586	956.790791	.001045	.022699	21.717809	.046045	86
44	48.109801	1046.884463	.000955	.020786	21.760316	.045955	88
45	52.537105	1145.269006	.000873	.019034	21.799241	.045873	90
46	57.371832	1252.707386	.000798	.017430	21.834885	.045798	92
47	62.651475	1370.032783	.000730	.015961	21.867526	.045730	94
48	68.416977	1498.155050	.000667	.014616	21.897417	.045667	96
49	74.713050	1638.067768	.000610	.013385	21.924788	.045610	98
50	81.588518	1790.855955	.000558	.012257	21.949853	.045558	100
51	89.096701	1957.704474	.000511	.011224	21.972805	.045511	102
52	97.295825	2139.907228	.000467	.010278	21.993824	.045467	104
53	106.249474	2338.877191	.000428	.009412	22.013071	.045428	106
54	116.027081	2556.157364	.000391	.008619	22.030696	.045391	108
55	126.704474	2793.432747	.000358	.007892	22.046836	.045358	110
56	138.364453	3052.543396	.000328	.007227	22.061616	.045328	112
57	151.097442	3335.498702	.000300	.006618	22.075150	.045300	114
58	165.002184	3644.492971	.000274	.006061	22.087544	.045274	116
59	180.186510	3981.922436	.000251	.005550	22.098893	.045251	118
60	196.768173	4350.403847	.000230	.005082	22.109286	.045230	120

9% ANNUAL COMPOUND INTEREST TABLE 9%

EFFECTIVE RATE = 9% BASE = 1.09

YEARS	1 AMOUNT OF I AT COMPOUND INTEREST $S^n = (1+i)^n$	2 ACCUMULATION OF I PER PERIOD $S_{\overline{n}\vert} = \frac{S^n - 1}{i}$	3 SINKING FUND FACTOR $1/S_{\overline{n}\vert} = \frac{i}{S^n - 1}$	4 PRES. VALUE REVERSION OF I $V^n = \frac{1}{S^n}$	5 PRESENT VALUE ORD. ANNUITY 1 PER PERIOD $a_{\overline{n}\vert} = \frac{1 - V^n}{i}$	6 INSTALMENT TO AMORTIZE I $1/a_{\overline{n}\vert} = \frac{i}{1 - V^n}$	n YEARS
1	1.090000	1.000000	1.000000	.917431	.917431	1.090000	1
2	1.188100	2.090000	.478469	.841680	1.759111	.568469	2
3	1.295029	3.278100	.305055	.772183	2.531295	.395055	3
4	1.411582	4.573129	.218669	.708425	3.239720	.308669	4
5	1.538624	5.984711	.167092	.649931	3.889651	.257092	5
6	1.667100	7.523335	.132920	.596267	4.485919	.222920	6
7	1.828039	9.200435	.108691	.547034	5.032953	.198691	7
8	1.992563	11.028474	.090674	.501866	5.534819	.180674	8
9	2.171893	13.021036	.076799	.460428	5.995247	.166799	9
10	2.367364	15.192930	.065820	.422411	6.417658	.155820	10
11	2.580426	17.560293	.056947	.387533	6.805191	.146947	11
12	2.812665	20.140720	.049651	.355535	7.160725	.139651	12
13	3.065805	22.953385	.043567	.326179	7.486904	.133567	13
14	3.341727	26.019189	.038433	.299246	7.786150	.128433	14
15	3.642482	29.360916	.034059	.274538	8.060688	.124059	15
16	3.970306	33.003399	.030300	.251870	8.312558	.120300	16
17	4.327633	36.973705	.027046	.231073	8.543631	.117046	17
18	4.717120	41.301338	.024212	.211994	8.755625	.114212	18
19	5.141661	46.018458	.021730	.194490	8.950115	.111730	19
20	5.604411	51.160120	.019546	.178431	9.128546	.109546	20
21	6.108808	56.764530	.017617	.163698	9.292244	.107617	21
22	6.658600	62.873338	.015905	.150182	9.442425	.105905	22
23	7.257874	69.531939	.014382	.137781	9.580207	.104382	23
24	7.911083	76.789813	.013023	.126405	9.706612	.103023	24
25	8.623081	84.700896	.011806	.115968	9.822580	.101806	25
26	9.399158	93.323977	.010715	.106393	9.928972	.100715	26
27	10.245082	102.723135	.009735	.097608	10.026580	.099735	27
28	11.167140	112.968217	.008852	.089548	10.116128	.098852	28
29	12.172182	124.135356	.008056	.082155	10.198283	.098056	29
30	13.267678	136.307539	.007336	.075371	10.273654	.097336	30
31	14.461770	149.575217	.006686	.069148	10.342802	.096686	31
32	15.763329	164.036987	.006096	.063438	10.406240	.096096	32
33	17.182028	179.800315	.005562	.058200	10.464441	.095562	33
34	18.728411	196.982344	.005077	.053395	10.517835	.095077	34
35	20.413968	215.710755	.004636	.048986	10.566821	.094636	35
36	22.251225	236.124723	.004235	.044941	10.611763	.094235	36
37	24.253835	258.375948	.003870	.041231	10.652993	.093870	37
38	26.436680	282.629783	.003538	.037826	10.690820	.093538	38
39	28.815982	309.066463	.003236	.034703	10.725523	.093236	39
40	31.409420	337.882445	.002960	.031838	10.757360	.092960	40
41	34.236268	369.291865	.002708	.029209	10.786569	.092708	41
42	37.317532	403.528133	.002478	.026797	10.813366	.092478	42
43	40.676110	440.845665	.002268	.024584	10.837951	.092268	43
44	44.336960	481.521775	.002077	.022555	10.860505	.092077	44
45	48.327286	525.858735	.001902	.020692	10.881197	.091902	45
46	52.676742	574.186021	.001742	.018984	10.900181	.091742	46
47	57.417649	626.862762	.001595	.017416	10.917597	.091595	47
48	62.585237	684.280411	.001461	.015978	10.933575	.091461	48
49	68.217908	746.865648	.001339	.014659	10.948234	.091339	49
50	74.357520	815.083556	.001227	.013449	10.961683	.091227	50
51	81.049697	889.441077	.001124	.012338	10.974021	.091124	51
52	88.344170	970.490773	.001030	.011319	10.985340	.091030	52
53	96.295145	1058.834943	.000944	.010385	10.995725	.090944	53
54	104.961708	1155.130088	.000866	.009527	11.005252	.090866	54
55	114.408262	1260.091796	.000794	.008741	11.013993	.090794	55
56	124.705005	1374.500057	.000728	.008019	11.022012	.090728	56
57	135.928456	1499.205063	.000667	.007357	11.029369	.090667	57
58	148.162017	1635.133518	.000612	.006749	11.036118	.090612	58
59	161.496598	1783.295535	.000561	.006192	11.042310	.090561	59
60	176.031292	1944.792133	.000514	.005681	11.047991	.090514	60

10% MONTHLY COMPOUND INTEREST TABLE 10%

EFFECTIVE RATE = 5/6% BASE = 1.00833333

MONTHS	1 AMOUNT OF I AT COMPOUND INTEREST $S^n = (1 + i)^n$	2 ACCUMULATION OF I PER PERIOD $S_{\overline{n}\rceil} = \frac{S^n - 1}{i}$	3 SINKING FUND FACTOR $1/S_{\overline{n}\rceil} = \frac{i}{S^n - 1}$	4 PRES. VALUE REVERSION OF I $V^n = \frac{1}{S^n}$	5 PRESENT VALUE ORD. ANNUITY 1 PER PERIOD $a_{\overline{n}\rceil} = \frac{1 - V^n}{i}$	6 INSTALMENT TO AMORTIZE I $1/a_{\overline{n}\rceil} = \frac{i}{1 - V^n}$	n MONTHS
1	1.008333	1.000000	1.000000	.991735	.991735	1.008333	1
2	1.016736	2.008333	.497925	.983539	1.975274	.506258	2
3	1.025208	3.025069	.330570	.975410	2.950685	.338904	3
4	1.033752	4.050278	.246896	.967349	3.918035	.255229	4
5	1.042366	5.084030	.196694	.959355	4.877390	.205027	5
6	1.051053	6.126397	.163228	.951426	5.828817	.171561	6
7	1.059812	7.177450	.139325	.943563	6.772380	.147658	7
8	1.068643	8.237262	.121399	.935765	7.708146	.129732	8
9	1.077549	9.305906	.107458	.928031	8.636177	.115791	9
10	1.086528	10.383456	.096307	.920362	9.556540	.104640	10
11	1.095583	11.469984	.087184	.912755	10.469295	.095517	11
YEARS							
1	1.104713	12.565568	.079582	.905212	11.374508	.087915	12
2	1.220390	26.446915	.037811	.819409	21.670854	.046144	24
3	1.348181	41.781821	.023933	.741739	30.991235	.032267	36
4	1.489354	58.722491	.017029	.671432	39.428160	.025362	48
5	1.645308	77.437072	.012913	.607788	47.065369	.021247	60
6	1.817594	98.111313	.010192	.550177	53.978665	.018525	72
7	2.007920	120.950418	.008267	.498027	60.236667	.016601	84
8	2.218175	146.181075	.006840	.450820	65.901488	.015174	96
9	2.450447	174.053712	.005745	.408088	71.029355	.014078	108
10	2.707041	204.844978	.004881	.369406	75.671163	.013215	120
11	2.990504	238.860492	.004186	.334391	79.872985	.012519	132
12	3.303648	276.437875	.003617	.302695	83.676528	.011950	144
13	3.649584	317.950100	.003145	.274003	87.119542	.011478	156
14	4.031743	363.809198	.002748	.248031	90.236200	.011082	168
15	4.453919	414.470344	.002412	.224521	93.057438	.010746	180
16	4.920303	470.436373	.002125	.203239	95.611258	.010459	192
17	5.435523	532.262776	.001878	.183974	97.923008	.010212	204
18	6.004693	600.563212	.001665	.166536	100.015632	.009998	216
19	6.633463	676.015596	.001479	.150750	101.909902	.009812	228
20	7.328073	759.368830	.001316	.136461	103.624619	.009650	240
21	8.095418	851.450237	.001174	.123526	105.176801	.009507	252
22	8.943114	953.173772	.001049	.111817	106.581857	.009382	264
23	9.879575	1065.549089	.000938	.101218	107.853729	.009271	276
24	10.914096	1189.691570	.000840	.091624	109.005045	.009173	288
25	12.056944	1326.833392	.000753	.082939	110.047230	.009087	300
26	13.319464	1478.335753	.000676	.075078	110.990629	.009009	312
27	14.714186	1645.702391	.000607	.067961	111.844605	.008940	324
28	16.254954	1830.594505	.000546	.061519	112.617636	.008879	336
29	17.957060	2034.847238	.000491	.055688	113.317391	.008824	348
30	19.837399	2260.487900	.000442	.050409	113.950820	.008775	360
31	21.914633	2509.756088	.000398	.045631	114.524207	.008731	372
32	24.209382	2785.125915	.000359	.041306	115.043244	.008692	384
33	26.744421	3089.330559	.000323	.037390	115.513083	.008657	396
34	29.544911	3425.389403	.000291	.033846	115.938387	.008625	408
35	32.638649	3796.638004	.000263	.030638	116.323378	.008596	420
36	36.056343	4206.761180	.000237	.027734	116.671875	.008571	432
37	39.831913	4659.829611	.000214	.025105	116.987341	.008547	444
38	44.002835	5160.340233	.000193	.022725	117.272903	.008527	456
39	48.610506	5713.260852	.000175	.020571	117.531398	.008508	468
40	53.700662	6324.079483	.000158	.018621	117.765390	.008491	480
41	59.323823	6998.858807	.000142	.016856	117.977204	.008476	492
42	65.535802	7744.296352	.000129	.015258	118.168940	.008462	504
43	72.398257	8567.790939	.000116	.013812	118.342502	.008450	516
44	79.979301	9477.516170	.000105	.012503	118.499611	.008438	528
45	88.354179	10482.501530	.000095	.011318	118.641830	.008428	540
46	97.606016	11592.721980	.000086	.010245	118.770568	.008419	552
47	107.826641	12819.197020	.000078	.009274	118.887103	.008411	564
48	119.117499	14174.100030	.000070	.008395	118.992592	.008403	576
49	131.590658	15670.879080	.000063	.007599	119.088082	.008397	588
50	145.369919	17324.390450	.000057	.006879	119.174520	.008391	600

10% QUARTERLY COMPOUND INTEREST TABLE 10%

EFFECTIVE RATE = 2½%   BASE = 1.025

	1 AMOUNT OF I AT COMPOUND INTEREST $S^n = (1+i)^n$	2 ACCUMULATION OF I PER PERIOD $s_{\overline{n}\rvert} = \frac{S^n - 1}{i}$	3 SINKING FUND FACTOR $1/s_{\overline{n}\rvert} = \frac{i}{S^n - 1}$	4 PRES. VALUE REVERSION OF I $V^n = \frac{1}{S^n}$	5 PRESENT VALUE ORD. ANNUITY 1 PER PERIOD $a_{\overline{n}\rvert} = \frac{1 - V^n}{i}$	6 INSTALMENT TO AMORTIZE I $1/a_{\overline{n}\rvert} = \frac{i}{1 - V^n}$	n
QUARTERS							QUARTERS
1	1.025000	1.000000	1.000000	.975610	.975610	1.025000	1
2	1.050625	2.025000	.493827	.951814	1.927424	.518827	2
3	1.076891	3.075625	.325137	.928599	2.856024	.350137	3
YEARS							
1	1.103813	4.152516	.240818	.905951	3.761974	.265818	4
2	1.218403	8.736116	.114467	.820747	7.170137	.139467	8
3	1.344889	13.795553	.072487	.743556	10.257765	.097487	12
4	1.484506	19.380225	.051599	.673625	13.055003	.076599	16
5	1.638616	25.544658	.039147	.610271	15.589162	.064147	20
6	1.808726	32.349038	.030913	.552875	17.884986	.055913	24
7	1.996495	39.859801	.025088	.500878	19.964889	.050088	28
8	2.203757	48.150278	.020768	.453771	21.849178	.045768	32
9	2.432535	57.301413	.017452	.411094	23.556251	.042452	36
10	2.685064	67.402554	.014836	.372431	25.102775	.039836	40
11	2.963808	78.552323	.012730	.337404	26.503849	.037730	44
12	3.271490	90.859583	.011006	.305671	27.773154	.036006	48
13	3.611112	104.444494	.009574	.276923	28.923081	.034574	52
14	3.985992	119.439695	.008372	.250879	29.964858	.033372	56
15	4.399790	135.991590	.007353	.227284	30.908657	.032353	60
16	4.856545	154.261786	.006482	.205908	31.763692	.031482	64
17	5.360717	174.428664	.005733	.186542	32.538311	.030733	68
18	5.917228	196.689123	.005084	.168998	33.240078	.030084	72
19	6.531513	221.260505	.004520	.153104	33.875844	.029520	76
20	7.209568	248.382713	.004026	.138705	34.451817	.029026	80
21	7.958014	278.320556	.003593	.125659	34.973620	.028593	84
22	8.784158	311.366333	.003212	.113841	35.446348	.028212	88
23	9.696067	347.842688	.002875	.103135	35.874616	.027875	92
24	10.702644	388.105759	.002577	.093435	36.262606	.027577	96
25	11.813716	432.548655	.002312	.084647	36.614105	.027312	100
26	13.040132	481.605297	.002076	.076686	36.932546	.027076	104
27	14.393866	535.754651	.001867	.069474	37.221039	.026867	108
28	15.888135	595.525406	.001679	.062940	37.482398	.026679	112
29	17.537528	661.501135	.001512	.057021	37.719177	.026512	116
30	19.358150	734.325996	.001362	.051658	37.933687	.026362	120
31	21.367775	814.711016	.001227	.046799	38.128022	.026227	124
32	23.586026	903.441037	.001107	.042398	38.304081	.026107	128
33	26.034559	1001.382378	.000999	.038410	38.463581	.025999	132
34	28.737282	1109.491294	.000901	.034798	38.608080	.025901	136
35	31.720583	1228.823308	.000814	.031525	38.738989	.025814	140
36	35.013588	1360.543523	.000735	.028560	38.857586	.025735	144
37	38.648450	1505.937994	.000664	.025874	38.965030	.025664	148
38	42.660657	1666.426286	.000600	.023441	39.062368	.025600	152
39	47.089383	1843.575332	.000542	.021236	39.150552	.025542	156
40	51.977868	2039.114732	.000490	.019239	39.230442	.025490	160
41	57.373841	2254.953642	.000443	.017430	39.302818	.025443	164
42	63.329985	2493.199414	.000401	.015790	39.368388	.025401	168
43	69.904454	2756.178168	.000363	.014305	39.427790	.025363	172
44	77.161438	3046.457506	.000328	.012960	39.481606	.025328	176
45	85.171790	3366.871582	.000297	.011741	39.530361	.025297	180
46	94.013719	3720.548769	.000269	.010637	39.574530	.025269	184
47	103.773555	4110.942208	.000243	.009636	39.614545	.025243	188
48	114.546588	4541.863516	.000220	.008730	39.650797	.025220	192
49	126.438000	5017.520012	.000199	.007909	39.683639	.025199	196
50	139.563895	5542.555784	.000180	.007165	39.713393	.025180	200
51	154.052426	6122.097036	.000163	.006491	39.740348	.025163	204
52	170.045054	6761.802144	.000148	.005881	39.764768	.025148	208
53	187.697922	7467.916888	.000134	.005328	39.786892	.025134	212
54	207.183386	8247.335444	.000121	.004827	39.806934	.025121	216
55	228.691692	9107.667692	.000110	.004373	39.825092	.025110	220
56	252.432838	10057.313520	.000099	.003961	39.841542	.025099	224
57	278.638621	11105.544820	.000090	.003589	39.856445	.025090	228
58	307.564901	12262.596050	.000082	.003251	39.869946	.025082	232
59	339.494103	13539.764110	.000074	.002946	39.882178	.025074	236
60	374.737967	14949.518680	.000067	.002669	39.893259	.025067	240

10% SEMI-ANNUAL COMPOUND INTEREST TABLE 10%

EFFECTIVE RATE = 5% BASE = 1.05

HALF YEARS	1 AMOUNT OF I AT COMPOUND INTEREST $S^n = (1+i)^n$	2 ACCUMULATION OF I PER PERIOD $s_{\overline{n}\vert} = \frac{S^n - 1}{i}$	3 SINKING FUND FACTOR $1/s_{\overline{n}\vert} = \frac{i}{S^n - 1}$	4 PRES. VALUE REVERSION OF I $V^n = \frac{1}{S^n}$	5 PRESENT VALUE ORD. ANNUITY 1 PER PERIOD $a_{\overline{n}\vert} = \frac{1 - V^n}{i}$	6 INSTALMENT TO AMORTIZE I $1/a_{\overline{n}\vert} = \frac{i}{1 - V^n}$	n HALF YEARS
1	1.050000	1.000000	1.000000	.952381	.952381	1.050000	1
YEARS							
1	1.102500	2.050000	.487805	.907029	1.859410	.537805	2
2	1.215506	4.310125	.232012	.822702	3.545951	.282012	4
3	1.340096	6.801913	.147017	.746215	5.075692	.197017	6
4	1.477455	9.549109	.104722	.676839	6.463213	.154722	8
5	1.628895	12.577893	.079505	.613913	7.721735	.129505	10
6	1.795856	15.917127	.062825	.556837	8.863252	.112825	12
7	1.979932	19.598632	.051024	.505068	9.898641	.101024	14
8	2.182875	23.657492	.042270	.458112	10.837770	.092270	16
9	2.406619	28.132385	.035546	.415521	11.689587	.085546	18
10	2.653298	33.065954	.030243	.376889	12.462210	.080243	20
11	2.925261	38.505214	.025971	.341850	13.163003	.075971	22
12	3.225100	44.501999	.022471	.310068	13.798642	.072471	24
13	3.555673	51.113454	.019564	.281241	14.375185	.069564	26
14	3.920129	58.402583	.017123	.255094	14.898127	.067123	28
15	4.321942	66.438847	.015051	.231377	15.372451	.065051	30
16	4.764941	75.298829	.013280	.209866	15.802677	.063280	32
17	5.253348	85.066959	.011755	.190355	16.192904	.061755	34
18	5.791816	95.836323	.010434	.172657	16.546852	.060434	36
19	6.385477	107.709546	.009284	.156605	16.867893	.059284	38
20	7.039989	120.799774	.008278	.142046	17.159086	.058278	40
21	7.761588	135.231751	.007395	.128840	17.423208	.057395	42
22	8.557150	151.143005	.006616	.116861	17.662773	.056616	44
23	9.434258	168.685164	.005928	.105997	17.880066	.055928	46
24	10.401270	188.025393	.005318	.096142	18.077158	.055318	48
25	11.467400	209.347996	.004777	.087204	18.255925	.054777	50
26	12.642808	232.856165	.004294	.079096	18.418073	.054294	52
27	13.938696	258.773922	.003864	.071743	18.565146	.053864	54
28	15.367412	287.348249	.003480	.065073	18.698545	.053480	56
29	16.942572	318.851445	.003136	.059023	18.819542	.053136	58
30	18.679186	353.583718	.002828	.053536	18.929290	.052828	60
31	20.593802	391.876049	.002552	.048558	19.028834	.052552	62
32	22.704667	434.093344	.002304	.044044	19.119124	.052304	64
33	25.031896	480.637912	.002081	.039949	19.201019	.052081	66
34	27.597665	531.953298	.001880	.036235	19.275301	.051880	68
35	30.426426	588.528511	.001699	.032866	19.342677	.051699	70
36	33.545134	650.902683	.001536	.029811	19.403788	.051536	72
37	36.983510	719.670208	.001390	.027039	19.459218	.051390	74
38	40.774320	795.486404	.001257	.024525	19.509495	.051257	76
39	44.953688	879.073761	.001138	.022245	19.555098	.051138	78
40	49.561441	971.228821	.001030	.020177	19.596460	.051030	80
41	54.641489	1072.829775	.000932	.018301	19.633978	.050932	82
42	60.242241	1184.844827	.000844	.016600	19.668007	.050844	84
43	66.417071	1308.341422	.000764	.015056	19.698873	.050764	86
44	73.224821	1444.496418	.000692	.013657	19.726869	.050692	88
45	80.730365	1594.607301	.000627	.012387	19.752262	.050627	90
46	89.005227	1760.104549	.000568	.011235	19.775294	.050568	92
47	98.128263	1942.565265	.000515	.010191	19.796185	.050515	94
48	108.186410	2143.728204	.000466	.009243	19.815134	.050466	96
49	119.275517	2365.510344	.000423	.008384	19.832321	.050423	98
50	131.501258	2610.025154	.000383	.007604	19.847910	.050383	100
51	144.980137	2879.602732	.000347	.006897	19.862050	.050347	102
52	159.840601	3176.812012	.000315	.006256	19.874875	.050315	104
53	176.224262	3504.485244	.000285	.005675	19.886508	.050285	106
54	194.287249	3865.744982	.000259	.005147	19.897060	.050259	108
55	214.201692	4264.033842	.000235	.004668	19.906630	.050235	110
56	236.157366	4703.147310	.000213	.004234	19.915311	.050213	112
57	260.363496	5187.269910	.000193	.003841	19.923184	.050193	114
58	287.050754	5721.015076	.000175	.003484	19.930326	.050175	116
59	316.473456	6309.469122	.000158	.003160	19.936804	.050158	118
60	348.911985	6958.239706	.000144	.002866	19.942679	.050144	120

10% ANNUAL COMPOUND INTEREST TABLE 10%

EFFECTIVE RATE = 10% BASE = 1.10

YEARS	1 AMOUNT OF 1 AT COMPOUND INTEREST $S^n = (1+i)^n$	2 ACCUMULATION OF 1 PER PERIOD $S_{\overline{n}\|} = \frac{S^n - 1}{i}$	3 SINKING FUND FACTOR $1/S_{\overline{n}\|} = \frac{i}{S^n - 1}$	4 PRES. VALUE REVERSION OF 1 $V^n = \frac{1}{S^n}$	5 PRESENT VALUE ORD. ANNUITY 1 PER PERIOD $a_{\overline{n}\|} = \frac{1-V^n}{i}$	6 INSTALMENT TO AMORTIZE 1 $1/a_{\overline{n}\|} = \frac{i}{1-V^n}$	n YEARS
1	1.100000	1.000000	1.000000	.909091	.909091	1.100000	1
2	1.210000	2.100000	.476190	.826446	1.735537	.576190	2
3	1.331000	3.310000	.302115	.751315	2.486852	.402115	3
4	1.464100	4.641000	.215471	.683013	3.169865	.315471	4
5	1.610510	6.105100	.163797	.620921	3.790787	.263797	5
6	1.771561	7.715610	.129607	.564474	4.355261	.229607	6
7	1.948717	9.487171	.105405	.513158	4.868419	.205405	7
8	2.143589	11.435888	.087444	.466507	5.334926	.187444	8
9	2.357948	13.579477	.073641	.424098	5.759024	.173641	9
10	2.593742	15.937425	.062745	.385543	6.144567	.162745	10
11	2.853117	18.531167	.053963	.350494	6.495061	.153963	11
12	3.138428	21.384284	.046763	.318631	6.813692	.146763	12
13	3.452271	24.522712	.040779	.289664	7.103356	.140779	13
14	3.797498	27.974983	.035746	.263331	7.366687	.135746	14
15	4.177248	31.772482	.031474	.239392	7.606080	.131474	15
16	4.594973	35.949730	.027817	.217629	7.823709	.127817	16
17	5.054470	40.544703	.024664	.197845	8.021553	.124664	17
18	5.559917	45.599173	.021930	.179859	8.201412	.121930	18
19	6.115909	51.159090	.019547	.163508	8.364920	.119547	19
20	6.727500	57.274999	.017460	.148644	8.513564	.117460	20
21	7.400250	64.002499	.015624	.135131	8.648694	.115624	21
22	8.140275	71.402749	.014005	.122846	8.771540	.114005	22
23	8.954302	79.543024	.012572	.111678	8.883218	.112572	23
24	9.849733	88.497327	.011300	.101526	8.984744	.111300	24
25	10.834706	98.347059	.010168	.092296	9.077040	.110168	25
26	11.918177	109.181765	.009159	.083905	9.160945	.109159	26
27	13.109994	121.099942	.008258	.076278	9.237223	.108258	27
28	14.420994	134.209936	.007451	.069343	9.306567	.107451	28
29	15.863093	148.630930	.006728	.063039	9.369606	.106728	29
30	17.449402	164.494023	.006079	.057309	9.426914	.106079	30
31	19.194342	181.943425	.005496	.052099	9.479013	.105496	31
32	21.113777	201.137767	.004972	.047362	9.526376	.104972	32
33	23.225154	222.251544	.004499	.043057	9.569432	.104499	33
34	25.547670	245.476699	.004074	.039143	9.608575	.104074	34
35	28.102437	271.024368	.003690	.035584	9.644159	.103690	35
36	30.912681	299.126805	.003343	.032349	9.676508	.103343	36
37	34.003949	330.039486	.003030	.029408	9.705917	.103030	37
38	37.404343	364.043434	.002747	.026735	9.732651	.102747	38
39	41.144778	401.447778	.002491	.024304	9.756956	.102491	39
40	45.259256	442.592556	.002259	.022095	9.779051	.102259	40
41	49.785181	487.851811	.002050	.020086	9.799137	.102050	41
42	54.763699	537.636992	.001860	.018260	9.817397	.101860	42
43	60.240069	592.400692	.001688	.016600	9.833998	.101688	43
44	66.264076	652.640761	.001532	.015091	9.849089	.101532	44
45	72.890484	718.904837	.001391	.013719	9.862808	.101391	45
46	80.179532	791.795321	.001263	.012472	9.875280	.101263	46
47	88.197485	871.974853	.001147	.011338	9.886618	.101147	47
48	97.017234	960.172338	.001041	.010307	9.896926	.101041	48
49	106.718957	1057.189572	.000946	.009370	9.906296	.100946	49
50	117.390853	1163.908529	.000859	.008519	9.914814	.100859	50
51	129.129938	1281.299382	.000780	.007744	9.922559	.100780	51
52	142.042932	1410.429320	.000709	.007040	9.929599	.100709	52
53	156.247225	1552.472252	.000644	.006400	9.935999	.100644	53
54	171.871948	1708.719477	.000585	.005818	9.941817	.100585	54
55	189.059142	1880.591425	.000532	.005289	9.947106	.100532	55
56	207.965057	2069.650567	.000483	.004809	9.951915	.100483	56
57	228.761562	2277.615624	.000439	.004371	9.956286	.100439	57
58	251.637719	2506.377186	.000399	.003974	9.960260	.100399	58
59	276.801490	2758.014905	.000363	.003613	9.963873	.100363	59
60	304.481640	3034.816395	.000330	.003284	9.967157	.100330	60

10 ¼ % MONTHLY COMPOUND INTEREST TABLE 10 ¼ %

EFFECTIVE RATE = 41/48% BASE = 1.00854167

	1 AMOUNT OF I AT COMPOUND INTEREST $S^n = (1+i)^n$	2 ACCUMULATION OF I PER PERIOD $S_{\overline{n}\rvert} = \frac{S^n - 1}{i}$	3 SINKING FUND FACTOR $1/S_{\overline{n}\rvert} = \frac{i}{S^n - 1}$	4 PRES. VALUE REVERSION OF I $V^n = \frac{1}{S^n}$	5 PRESENT VALUE ORD. ANNUITY 1 PER PERIOD $a_{\overline{n}\rvert} = \frac{1 - V^n}{i}$	6 INSTALMENT TO AMORTIZE I $1/a_{\overline{n}\rvert} = \frac{i}{1 - V^n}$	n MONTHS
MONTHS							
1	1.008541	1.000000	1.000000	.991530	.991530	1.008541	1
2	1.017156	2.008541	.497873	.983133	1.974663	.506415	2
3	1.025844	3.025697	.330502	.974806	2.949470	.339043	3
4	1.034606	4.051542	.246819	.966550	3.916021	.255361	4
5	1.043444	5.086149	.196612	.958364	4.874385	.205154	5
6	1.052356	6.129593	.163142	.950247	5.824633	.171684	6
7	1.061345	7.181950	.139237	.942199	6.766833	.147779	7
8	1.070411	8.243296	.121310	.934220	7.701053	.129852	8
9	1.079554	9.313707	.107368	.926307	8.627361	.115910	9
10	1.088775	10.393262	.096216	.918462	9.545824	.104757	10
11	1.098075	11.482038	.087092	.910683	10.456508	.095634	11
YEARS							
1	1.107455	12.580113	.079490	.902971	11.359479	.088032	12
2	1.226456	26.512025	.037718	.815356	21.616761	.046260	24
3	1.358245	41.940993	.023843	.736243	30.878790	.032384	36
4	1.504196	59.027882	.016941	.664806	39.242135	.025482	48
5	1.665830	77.950845	.012828	.600301	46.793993	.021370	60
6	1.844832	98.907178	.010110	.542054	53.613104	.018652	72
7	2.043068	122.115377	.008188	.489459	59.770564	.016730	84
8	2.262607	147.817416	.006765	.441968	65.330571	.015306	96
9	2.505735	176.281272	.005672	.399084	70.351099	.014214	108
10	2.774990	207.803714	.004812	.360361	74.884489	.013353	120
11	3.073177	242.713406	.004120	.325396	78.978010	.012661	132
12	3.403405	281.374323	.003553	.293823	82.674340	.012095	144
13	3.769119	324.189554	.003084	.265313	86.012021	.011626	156
14	4.174130	371.605502	.002691	.239570	89.025850	.011232	168
15	4.622662	424.116538	.002357	.216325	91.747250	.010899	180
16	5.119390	482.270154	.002073	.195335	94.204596	.010615	192
17	5.669495	546.672675	.001829	.176382	96.423508	.010370	204
18	6.278712	617.995578	.001618	.159268	98.427121	.010159	216
19	6.953392	696.982494	.001434	.143814	100.236327	.009976	228
20	7.700569	784.456959	.001274	.129860	101.869987	.009816	240
21	8.528035	881.331006	.001134	.117260	103.345135	.009676	252
22	9.444416	988.614667	.001011	.105882	104.677151	.009553	264
23	10.459268	1107.426510	.000902	.095608	105.879922	.009444	276
24	11.583170	1239.005295	.000807	.086332	106.965991	.009348	288
25	12.827841	1384.722897	.000722	.077955	107.946680	.009263	300
26	14.206258	1546.098605	.000646	.070391	108.832212	.009188	312
27	15.732794	1724.814960	.000579	.063561	109.631824	.009121	324
28	17.423364	1922.735308	.000520	.057394	110.353849	.009061	336
29	19.295594	2141.923215	.000466	.051825	111.005818	.009008	348
30	21.369004	2384.663989	.000419	.046796	111.594526	.008961	360
31	23.665214	2653.488507	.000376	.042256	112.126112	.008918	372
32	26.208163	2951.199602	.000338	.038156	112.606120	.008880	384
33	29.024365	3280.901284	.000304	.034453	113.039553	.008846	396
34	32.143182	3646.031107	.000274	.031110	113.430931	.008815	408
35	35.597132	4050.396006	.000246	.028092	113.784333	.008788	420
36	39.422227	4498.211992	.000222	.025366	114.103444	.008763	432
37	43.658348	4994.148108	.000200	.022905	114.391595	.008741	444
38	48.349662	5543.375103	.000180	.020682	114.651785	.008722	456
39	53.545082	6151.619368	.000162	.018675	114.886729	.008704	468
40	59.298776	6825.222606	.000146	.016863	115.098876	.008688	480
41	65.670735	7571.207975	.000132	.015227	115.290440	.008673	492
42	72.727393	8397.353306	.000119	.013749	115.463417	.008660	504
43	80.542325	9312.272200	.000107	.012415	115.619609	.008649	516
44	89.197012	10325.503830	.000096	.011211	115.760646	.008638	528
45	98.781689	11447.612410	.000087	.010123	115.887999	.008629	540
46	109.396290	12690.297330	.000078	.009141	116.002994	.008620	552
47	121.151483	14066.515120	.000071	.008254	116.106833	.008612	564
48	134.169833	15590.614580	.000064	.007453	116.200595	.008605	576
49	148.587071	17278.486380	.000057	.006730	116.285261	.008599	588
50	164.553516	19147.728680	.000052	.006077	116.361710	.008593	600

10¼% QUARTERLY COMPOUND INTEREST TABLE 10¼%

EFFECTIVE RATE = 2-9/16% BASE = 1.025625

QUARTERS	1 AMOUNT OF I AT COMPOUND INTEREST $s^n = (1+i)^n$	2 ACCUMULATION OF I PER PERIOD $s_{\overline{n}\mid} = \frac{s^n - 1}{i}$	3 SINKING FUND FACTOR $1/s_{\overline{n}\mid} = \frac{i}{s^n - 1}$	4 PRES. VALUE REVERSION OF I $v^n = \frac{1}{s^n}$	5 PRESENT VALUE ORD. ANNUITY 1 PER PERIOD $a_{\overline{n}\mid} = \frac{1 - v^n}{i}$	6 INSTALMENT TO AMORTIZE I $1/a_{\overline{n}\mid} = \frac{i}{1 - v^n}$	n QUARTERS
1	1.025625	1.000000	1.000000	.975015	.975015	1.025625	1
2	1.051907	2.025625	.493675	.950655	1.925670	.519300	2
3	1.078862	3.077532	.324936	.926903	2.852573	.350561	3
YEARS							
1	1.106508	4.156393	.240593	.903744	3.756317	.266218	4
2	1.224359	8.755474	.114214	.816754	7.151068	.139839	8
3	1.354763	13.844392	.072231	.738137	10.219054	.097856	12
4	1.499055	19.475318	.051347	.667087	12.991730	.076972	16
5	1.658716	25.705980	.038901	.602876	15.497520	.064526	20
6	1.835382	32.600256	.030675	.544846	17.762114	.056300	24
7	2.030864	40.228823	.024858	.492401	19.808727	.050483	28
8	2.247166	48.669891	.020547	.445005	21.658343	.046172	32
9	2.486506	58.009997	.017238	.402171	23.329923	.042863	36
10	2.751338	68.344895	.014632	.363460	24.840604	.040257	40
11	3.044376	79.780538	.012534	.328475	26.205873	.038159	44
12	3.368625	92.434163	.010819	.296857	27.439727	.036444	48
13	3.727410	106.435496	.009395	.268283	28.554816	.035020	52
14	4.124407	121.928076	.008202	.242459	29.562572	.033827	56
15	4.563688	139.070734	.007191	.219121	30.473325	.032816	60
16	5.049755	158.039215	.006328	.198029	31.296413	.031953	64
17	5.587592	179.027983	.005586	.178968	32.040274	.031211	68
18	6.182713	202.252213	.004944	.161741	32.712535	.030569	72
19	6.841219	227.950001	.004387	.146173	33.320086	.030012	76
20	7.569860	256.384797	.003900	.132103	33.869158	.029525	80
21	8.376108	287.848115	.003474	.119387	34.365378	.029099	84
22	9.268227	322.662515	.003099	.107896	34.813834	.028724	88
23	10.255363	361.184912	.002769	.097510	35.219124	.028394	92
24	11.347637	403.810236	.002476	.088124	35.585402	.028101	96
25	12.556247	450.975481	.002217	.079642	35.916424	.027842	100
26	13.893582	503.164182	.001987	.071976	36.215583	.027612	104
27	15.373354	560.911374	.001783	.065048	36.485947	.027408	108
28	17.010733	624.809081	.001600	.058786	36.730286	.027225	112
29	18.822505	695.512378	.001438	.053128	36.951107	.027063	116
30	20.827244	773.746112	.001292	.048014	37.150672	.026917	120
31	23.045504	860.312332	.001162	.043392	37.331028	.026787	124
32	25.500024	956.098510	.001046	.039216	37.494023	.026671	128
33	28.215970	1062.086642	.000942	.035441	37.641330	.026567	132
34	31.221185	1179.363314	.000848	.032030	37.774457	.026473	136
35	34.546478	1309.130841	.000764	.028947	37.894770	.026389	140
36	38.225940	1452.719593	.000688	.026160	38.003503	.026313	144
37	42.297292	1611.601636	.000621	.023642	38.101769	.026246	148
38	46.802274	1787.405820	.000559	.021366	38.190576	.026184	152
39	51.787071	1981.934482	.000505	.019310	38.270836	.026130	156
40	57.302787	2197.181922	.000455	.017451	38.343369	.026080	160
41	63.405968	2435.354846	.000411	.015771	38.408922	.026036	164
42	70.159184	2698.894992	.000371	.014253	38.468164	.025996	168
43	77.631669	2990.504162	.000334	.012881	38.521704	.025959	172
44	85.900030	3313.171918	.000302	.011641	38.570090	.025927	176
45	95.049035	3670.206236	.000272	.010521	38.613819	.025897	180
46	105.172478	4065.267415	.000246	.009508	38.653339	.025871	184
47	116.374144	4502.405604	.000222	.008593	38.689055	.025847	188
48	128.768872	4986.102326	.000201	.007766	38.721333	.025826	192
49	142.483733	5521.316414	.000181	.007018	38.750504	.025806	196
50	157.659331	6113.534861	.000164	.006343	38.776867	.025789	200
51	174.451245	6768.829061	.000148	.005732	38.800692	.025773	204
52	193.031625	7493.917061	.000133	.005180	38.822224	.025758	208
53	213.590956	8296.232429	.000121	.004682	38.841684	.025746	212
54	236.340012	9184.000468	.000109	.004231	38.859271	.025734	216
55	261.512015	10166.322530	.000098	.003824	38.875164	.025723	220
56	289.365027	11253.269340	.000089	.003456	38.889528	.025714	224
57	320.184596	12455.984230	.000080	.003123	38.902509	.025705	228
58	354.286682	13786.797360	.000073	.002823	38.914241	.025698	232
59	392.020900	15259.352190	.000066	.002551	38.924844	.025691	236
60	433.774097	16888.745260	.000059	.002305	38.934425	.025684	240

10 ¼ % SEMI-ANNUAL COMPOUND INTEREST TABLE 10 ¼ %

EFFECTIVE RATE = 5-1/8% BASE = 1.05125

HALF YEARS	1 AMOUNT OF I AT COMPOUND INTEREST $S^n = (1+i)^n$	2 ACCUMULATION OF I PER PERIOD $S_{\overline{n\rvert}} = \frac{S^n - 1}{i}$	3 SINKING FUND FACTOR $1/S_{\overline{n\rvert}} = \frac{i}{S^n - 1}$	4 PRES. VALUE REVERSION OF I $V^n = \frac{1}{S^n}$	5 PRESENT VALUE ORD. ANNUITY 1 PER PERIOD $a_{\overline{n\rvert}} = \frac{1 - V^n}{i}$	6 INSTALMENT TO AMORTIZE I $1/a_{\overline{n\rvert}} = \frac{i}{1 - V^n}$	n HALF YEARS
1	1.051250	1.000000	1.000000	.951249	.951249	1.051250	1
YEARS							
1	1.105127	2.051250	.487508	.904874	1.856122	.538758	2
2	1.221305	4.318141	.231581	.818796	3.535679	.282831	4
3	1.349696	6.823342	.146556	.740907	5.055465	.197806	6
4	1.491585	9.591907	.104255	.670428	6.430680	.155505	8
5	1.648390	12.651521	.079042	.606652	7.675075	.130292	10
6	1.821680	16.032782	.062372	.548944	8.801096	.113622	12
7	2.013187	19.769503	.050583	.496725	9.820003	.101833	14
8	2.224826	23.899053	.041843	.449473	10.741985	.093093	16
9	2.458715	28.462728	.035134	.406717	11.576263	.086384	18
10	2.717191	33.506167	.029845	.368027	12.331178	.081095	20
11	3.002840	39.079805	.025589	.333018	13.014281	.076839	22
12	3.318518	45.239381	.022105	.301339	13.632404	.073355	24
13	3.667383	52.046491	.019214	.272674	14.191726	.070464	26
14	4.052922	59.569210	.016787	.246736	14.697843	.068037	28
15	4.478992	67.882766	.014731	.223265	15.155814	.065981	30
16	4.949853	77.070298	.012975	.202026	15.570220	.064225	32
17	5.470214	87.223684	.011465	.182808	15.945206	.062715	34
18	6.045279	98.444460	.010158	.165418	16.284520	.061408	36
19	6.680798	110.844837	.009022	.149683	16.591557	.060272	38
20	7.383127	124.548824	.008029	.135444	16.869386	.059279	40
21	8.159290	139.693464	.007159	.122560	17.120787	.058409	42
22	9.017048	156.430207	.006393	.110901	17.348272	.057643	44
23	9.964979	174.926427	.005717	.100351	17.554118	.056967	46
24	11.012563	195.367091	.005119	.090805	17.740383	.056369	48
25	12.170276	217.956612	.004588	.082167	17.908929	.055838	50
26	13.449696	242.920892	.004117	.074351	18.061441	.055367	52
27	14.863616	270.509580	.003697	.067278	18.199446	.054947	54
28	16.426177	300.998572	.003322	.060878	18.324323	.054572	56
29	18.153004	334.692767	.002988	.055087	18.437321	.054238	58
30	20.061367	371.929117	.002689	.049847	18.539570	.053939	60
31	22.170350	413.079997	.002421	.045105	18.632092	.053671	62
32	24.501043	458.556927	.002181	.040815	18.715813	.053431	64
33	27.076753	508.814690	.001965	.036932	18.791570	.053215	66
34	29.923239	564.355880	.001772	.033419	18.860120	.053022	68
35	33.068966	625.735923	.001598	.030240	18.922150	.052848	70
36	36.545393	693.568640	.001442	.027363	18.978278	.052692	72
37	40.387284	768.532377	.001301	.024760	19.029068	.052551	74
38	44.633061	851.376794	.001175	.022405	19.075026	.052425	76
39	49.325181	942.930360	.001061	.020274	19.116612	.052311	78
40	54.510568	1044.108637	.000958	.018345	19.154243	.052208	80
41	60.241076	1155.923439	.000865	.016600	19.188293	.052115	82
42	66.574014	1279.492947	.000782	.015021	19.219105	.052032	84
43	73.572711	1416.052892	.000706	.013592	19.246985	.051956	86
44	81.307157	1566.968915	.000638	.012299	19.272214	.051888	88
45	89.854699	1733.750220	.000577	.011129	19.295042	.051827	90
46	99.300814	1918.064671	.000521	.010070	19.315699	.051771	92
47	109.739968	2121.755467	.000471	.009112	19.334391	.051721	94
48	121.276553	2346.859577	.000426	.008246	19.351305	.051676	96
49	134.025941	2595.628107	.000385	.007461	19.366610	.051635	98
50	148.115627	2870.548818	.000348	.006751	19.380459	.051598	100
51	163.686514	3174.370997	.000315	.006109	19.392990	.051565	102
52	180.894314	3510.132958	.000285	.005528	19.404330	.051535	104
53	199.911112	3881.192420	.000258	.005002	19.414591	.051508	106
54	220.927080	4291.260088	.000233	.004526	19.423876	.051483	108
55	244.152384	4744.436759	.000211	.004096	19.432277	.051461	110
56	269.819285	5245.254336	.000191	.003706	19.439879	.051441	112
57	298.184459	5798.721143	.000172	.003354	19.446758	.051422	114
58	329.531566	6410.372014	.000156	.003035	19.452983	.051406	116
59	364.174086	7086.323637	.000141	.002746	19.458616	.051391	118
60	402.458456	7833.335733	.000128	.002485	19.463713	.051378	120

10¼% ANNUAL COMPOUND INTEREST TABLE 10¼%

EFFECTIVE RATE = 10¼% BASE = 1.1025

YEARS	1 AMOUNT OF I AT COMPOUND INTEREST $S^n = (1+i)^n$	2 ACCUMULATION OF I PER PERIOD $s_{\overline{n}\vert} = \frac{S^n - 1}{i}$	3 SINKING FUND FACTOR $1/s_{\overline{n}\vert} = \frac{i}{S^n - 1}$	4 PRES. VALUE REVERSION OF I $V^n = \frac{1}{S^n}$	5 PRESENT VALUE ORD. ANNUITY 1 PER PERIOD $a_{\overline{n}\vert} = \frac{1 - V^n}{i}$	6 INSTALMENT TO AMORTIZE I $1/a_{\overline{n}\vert} = \frac{i}{1 - V^n}$	n YEARS
1	1.102500	1.000000	1.000000	.907029	.907029	1.102500	1
2	1.215506	2.102500	.475624	.822702	1.729732	.578124	2
3	1.340096	3.318006	.301386	.746215	2.475947	.403886	3
4	1.477455	4.658102	.214680	.676839	3.152787	.317180	4
5	1.628895	6.135557	.162984	.613913	3.766700	.265484	5
6	1.795856	7.764452	.128792	.556837	4.323537	.231292	6
7	1.979932	9.560308	.104599	.505068	4.828605	.207099	7
8	2.182875	11.540240	.086653	.458112	5.286717	.189153	8
9	2.406619	13.723114	.072870	.415521	5.702238	.175370	9
10	2.653298	16.129734	.061997	.376889	6.079127	.164497	10
11	2.925261	18.783031	.053240	.341850	6.420977	.155740	11
12	3.225100	21.708292	.046565	.310068	6.731045	.148565	12
13	3.555673	24.933392	.040107	.281241	7.012286	.142607	13
14	3.920129	28.489065	.035101	.255094	7.267379	.137601	14
15	4.321942	32.409194	.030855	.231377	7.498757	.133355	15
16	4.764941	36.731136	.027225	.209866	7.708623	.129725	16
17	5.253348	41.496078	.024099	.190355	7.898978	.126599	17
18	5.791816	46.749426	.021391	.172657	8.071635	.123891	18
19	6.385477	52.541242	.019033	.156605	8.228240	.121533	19
20	7.039989	58.926719	.016970	.142046	8.370286	.119470	20
21	7.761588	65.966708	.015159	.128840	8.499126	.117659	21
22	8.557150	73.728295	.013563	.116861	8.615987	.116063	22
23	9.434258	82.285446	.012153	.105997	8.721984	.114653	23
24	10.401270	91.719704	.010903	.096142	8.818126	.113403	24
25	11.467400	102.120974	.009792	.087204	8.905329	.112292	25
26	12.642808	113.588373	.008804	.079096	8.984426	.111304	26
27	13.938696	126.231182	.007922	.071743	9.056169	.110422	27
28	15.367412	140.169878	.007134	.065073	9.121241	.109634	28
29	16.942572	155.537290	.006429	.059023	9.180264	.108929	29
30	18.679186	172.479862	.005798	.053536	9.233800	.108298	30
31	20.593802	191.159048	.005231	.048558	9.282358	.107731	31
32	22.704667	211.752851	.004722	.044044	9.326402	.107222	32
33	25.031896	234.457518	.004265	.039949	9.366351	.106765	33
34	27.597665	259.489414	.003854	.036235	9.402586	.106354	34
35	30.426426	287.087078	.003483	.032866	9.435452	.105983	35
36	33.545134	317.513504	.003149	.029811	9.465263	.105649	36
37	36.983510	351.058638	.002849	.027039	9.492302	.105349	37
38	40.774320	388.042148	.002577	.024525	9.516827	.105077	38
39	44.953688	428.816469	.002332	.022245	9.539072	.104832	39
40	49.561441	473.770157	.002111	.020177	9.559249	.104611	40
41	54.641489	523.331598	.001911	.018301	9.577550	.104411	41
42	60.242241	577.973086	.001730	.016600	9.594150	.104230	42
43	66.417071	638.215328	.001567	.015056	9.609206	.104067	43
44	73.224821	704.632399	.001419	.013657	9.622863	.103919	44
45	80.730365	777.857220	.001286	.012387	9.635250	.103786	45
46	89.005227	858.587585	.001165	.011235	9.646485	.103665	46
47	98.128263	947.592812	.001055	.010191	9.656676	.103555	47
48	108.186410	1045.721075	.000956	.009243	9.665919	.103456	48
49	119.275517	1153.907485	.000867	.008384	9.674303	.103367	49
50	131.501258	1273.183002	.000785	.007604	9.681907	.103285	50
51	144.980137	1404.684260	.000712	.006897	9.688805	.103212	51
52	159.840601	1549.664396	.000645	.006256	9.695061	.103145	52
53	176.224262	1709.504997	.000585	.005675	9.700736	.103085	53
54	194.287249	1885.729260	.000530	.005147	9.705883	.103030	54
55	214.201692	2080.016508	.000481	.004668	9.710551	.102981	55
56	236.157366	2294.218200	.000436	.004234	9.714786	.102936	56
57	260.363496	2530.375566	.000395	.003841	9.718626	.102895	57
58	287.050754	2790.739061	.000358	.003484	9.722110	.102858	58
59	316.473456	3077.789816	.000325	.003160	9.725270	.102825	59
60	348.911985	3394.263271	.000295	.002866	9.728136	.102795	60

10½% MONTHLY COMPOUND INTEREST TABLE 10½%

EFFECTIVE RATE = 7/8% BASE = 1.00875

MONTHS	1 AMOUNT OF I AT COMPOUND INTEREST $S^n = (1+i)^n$	2 ACCUMULATION OF I PER PERIOD $s_{\overline{n}\vert} = \frac{S^n - 1}{i}$	3 SINKING FUND FACTOR $1/s_{\overline{n}\vert} = \frac{i}{S^n - 1}$	4 PRES. VALUE REVERSION OF I $V^n = \frac{1}{S^n}$	5 PRESENT VALUE ORD. ANNUITY 1 PER PERIOD $a_{\overline{n}\vert} = \frac{1 - V^n}{i}$	6 INSTALMENT TO AMORTIZE I $1/a_{\overline{n}\vert} = \frac{i}{1 - V^n}$	n MONTHS
1	1.008750	1.000000	1.000000	.991325	.991325	1.008750	1
2	1.017576	2.008750	.497822	.982727	1.974052	.506572	2
3	1.026480	3.026326	.330433	.974202	2.948255	.339183	3
4	1.035462	4.052806	.246742	.965752	3.914008	.255492	4
5	1.044522	5.088268	.196530	.957375	4.871383	.205280	5
6	1.053661	6.132791	.163057	.949071	5.820454	.171807	6
7	1.062881	7.186453	.139150	.940838	6.761293	.147900	7
8	1.072181	8.249334	.121221	.932677	7.693970	.129971	8
9	1.081563	9.321516	.107278	.924587	8.618558	.116028	9
10	1.091026	10.403079	.096125	.916567	9.535126	.104875	10
11	1.100573	11.494106	.087001	.908617	10.443743	.095751	11
YEARS							
1	1.110203	12.594680	.079398	.900735	11.344479	.088148	12
2	1.232551	26.577337	.037626	.811324	21.562858	.046376	24
3	1.368383	42.100931	.023752	.730789	30.766917	.032502	36
4	1.519183	59.335279	.016853	.658248	39.057343	.025603	48
5	1.686602	78.468912	.012743	.592907	46.524827	.021493	60
6	1.872472	99.711137	.010028	.534053	53.251056	.018778	72
7	2.078825	123.294328	.008110	.481040	59.309612	.016860	84
8	2.307919	149.476469	.006690	.433290	64.766771	.015440	96
9	2.562259	178.543971	.005600	.390280	69.682229	.014350	108
10	2.844629	210.814813	.004743	.351539	74.109758	.013493	120
11	3.158117	246.642013	.004054	.316644	78.097792	.012804	132
12	3.506153	286.417494	.003491	.285212	81.689957	.012241	144
13	3.892543	330.576370	.003025	.256901	84.925548	.011775	156
14	4.321514	379.601707	.002634	.231400	87.839961	.011384	168
15	4.797760	434.029805	.002303	.208430	90.465078	.011053	180
16	5.326490	494.456067	.002022	.187740	92.829614	.010772	192
17	5.913488	561.541511	.001780	.169104	94.959437	.010530	204
18	6.565175	636.020004	.001572	.152318	96.877844	.010322	216
19	7.288679	718.706283	.001391	.137199	98.605822	.010141	228
20	8.091917	810.504875	.001233	.123580	100.162273	.009983	240
21	8.983674	912.419989	.001095	.111313	101.564226	.009845	252
22	9.973706	1025.566500	.000975	.100263	102.827013	.009725	264
23	11.072843	1151.182148	.000868	.090311	103.964452	.009618	276
24	12.293109	1290.641073	.000774	.081346	104.988984	.009524	288
25	13.647852	1445.468852	.000691	.073271	105.911816	.009441	300
26	15.151892	1617.359187	.000618	.065998	106.743045	.009368	312
27	16.821683	1808.192429	.000553	.059447	107.491762	.009303	324
28	18.675491	2020.056156	.000495	.053546	108.166158	.009245	336
29	20.733594	2255.267994	.000443	.048230	108.773610	.009193	348
30	23.018508	2516.400988	.000397	.043443	109.320766	.009147	360
31	25.555227	2806.311739	.000356	.039130	109.813607	.009106	372
32	28.371501	3128.171655	.000319	.035246	110.257526	.009069	384
33	31.498139	3485.501648	.000286	.031747	110.657382	.009036	396
34	34.969343	3882.210635	.000257	.028596	111.017545	.009007	408
35	38.823085	4322.638321	.000231	.025757	111.341957	.008981	420
36	43.101523	4811.602659	.000207	.023201	111.634166	.008957	432
37	47.851459	5354.452558	.000186	.020898	111.897370	.008936	444
38	53.124855	5957.126384	.000167	.018823	112.134447	.008917	456
39	58.979398	6626.216945	.000150	.016955	112.347991	.008900	468
40	65.479131	7369.043594	.000135	.015272	112.540338	.008885	480
41	72.695157	8193.732303	.000122	.013756	112.713591	.008872	492
42	80.706414	9109.304562	.000109	.012390	112.869646	.008859	504
43	89.600540	10125.776030	.000098	.011160	113.010211	.008848	516
44	99.474828	11254.266170	.000088	.010052	113.136823	.008838	528
45	110.437298	12507.119810	.000079	.009054	113.250866	.008829	540
46	122.607869	13898.042240	.000071	.008156	113.353590	.008821	552
47	136.119680	15442.249150	.000064	.007346	113.446117	.008814	564
48	151.120538	17156.632960	.000058	.006617	113.529458	.008808	576
49	167.774543	19059.947790	.000052	.005960	113.604528	.008802	588
50	186.263876	21173.014470	.000047	.005368	113.672145	.008797	600

10¼% QUARTERLY COMPOUND INTEREST TABLE 10¼%

EFFECTIVE RATE = 2-5/8% BASE = 1.02625

QUARTERS	1 AMOUNT OF I AT COMPOUND INTEREST $S^n = (1+i)^n$	2 ACCUMULATION OF I PER PERIOD $S_{\overline{n}\rceil} = \frac{S^n - 1}{i}$	3 SINKING FUND FACTOR $1/S_{\overline{n}\rceil} = \frac{i}{S^n - 1}$	4 PRES. VALUE REVERSION OF I $V^n = \frac{1}{S^n}$	5 PRESENT VALUE ORD. ANNUITY 1 PER PERIOD $a_{\overline{n}\rceil} = \frac{1 - V^n}{i}$	6 INSTALMENT TO AMORTIZE I $1/a_{\overline{n}\rceil} = \frac{i}{1 - V^n}$	n QUARTERS
1	1.026250	1.000000	1.000000	.974421	.974421	1.026250	1
2	1.053189	2.026250	.493523	.949497	1.923919	.519773	2
3	1.080835	3.079439	.324734	.925210	2.849129	.350984	3
YEARS							
1	1.109207	4.160274	.240369	.901545	3.750674	.266619	4
2	1.230341	8.774881	.113962	.812783	7.132074	.140212	8
3	1.364703	13.893435	.071976	.732760	10.180558	.098226	12
4	1.513738	19.570973	.051096	.660616	12.928903	.077346	16
5	1.679049	25.868538	.038657	.595575	15.406659	.064907	20
6	1.862413	32.853843	.030438	.536938	17.640468	.056688	24
7	2.065802	40.601994	.024629	.484073	19.654346	.050879	28
8	2.291403	49.196298	.020327	.436414	21.469947	.046577	32
9	2.541641	58.729162	.017027	.393447	23.106793	.043277	36
10	2.819206	69.303084	.014429	.354710	24.582484	.040679	40
11	3.127084	81.031754	.012341	.319787	25.912884	.038591	44
12	3.468584	94.041280	.010634	.288302	27.112300	.036884	48
13	3.847378	108.471539	.009219	.259917	28.193627	.035469	52
14	4.267539	124.477687	.008034	.234327	29.168492	.034284	56
15	4.733585	142.231821	.007031	.211256	30.047377	.033281	60
16	5.250527	161.924834	.006176	.190457	30.839730	.032426	64
17	5.823922	183.768467	.005442	.171706	31.554073	.031692	68
18	6.459936	207.997581	.004808	.154800	32.198084	.031058	72
19	7.165408	234.872689	.004258	.139559	32.778690	.030508	76
20	7.947922	264.682752	.003778	.125819	33.302132	.030028	80
21	8.815893	297.748289	.003359	.113432	33.774038	.029609	84
22	9.778652	334.424821	.002990	.102264	34.199482	.029240	88
23	10.846551	375.106694	.002666	.092195	34.583040	.028916	92
24	12.031072	420.231321	.002380	.083118	34.928834	.028630	96
25	13.344952	470.283882	.002126	.074935	35.240583	.028376	100
26	14.802317	525.802543	.001902	.067557	35.521638	.028152	104
27	16.418836	587.384241	.001702	.060906	35.775023	.027952	108
28	18.211891	655.691104	.001525	.054909	36.003460	.027775	112
29	20.200761	731.457569	.001367	.049503	36.209406	.027617	116
30	22.406830	815.498277	.001226	.044629	36.395076	.027476	120
31	24.853817	908.716836	.001100	.040235	36.562466	.027350	124
32	27.568033	1012.115533	.000988	.036274	36.713375	.027238	128
33	30.578660	1126.806112	.000887	.032703	36.849427	.027137	132
34	33.918070	1254.021728	.000797	.029483	36.972083	.027047	136
35	37.622168	1395.130206	.000717	.026580	37.082664	.026967	140
36	41.730780	1551.648745	.000644	.023963	37.182357	.026894	144
37	46.288081	1725.260237	.000580	.021604	37.272235	.026830	148
38	51.343073	1917.831353	.000521	.019477	37.353264	.026771	152
39	56.950106	2131.432622	.000469	.017559	37.426315	.026719	156
40	63.169468	2368.360688	.000422	.015830	37.492174	.026672	160
41	70.068029	2631.163005	.000380	.014272	37.551549	.026630	164
42	77.719962	2922.665227	.000342	.012867	37.605078	.026592	168
43	86.207542	3246.001591	.000308	.011600	37.653337	.026558	172
44	95.622026	3604.648615	.000277	.010458	37.696844	.026527	176
45	106.064640	4002.462476	.000250	.009428	37.736068	.026500	180
46	117.647663	4443.720476	.000225	.008500	37.771430	.026475	184
47	130.495635	4933.167029	.000203	.007663	37.803311	.026453	188
48	144.746698	5476.064667	.000183	.006909	37.832053	.026433	192
49	160.554079	6078.250636	.000165	.006228	37.857965	.026415	196
50	178.087741	6746.199653	.000148	.005615	37.881325	.026398	200
51	197.536205	7487.093512	.000134	.005062	37.902386	.026384	204
52	219.108581	8308.898316	.000120	.004564	37.921373	.026370	208
53	243.036816	9220.450122	.000108	.004115	37.938491	.026358	212
54	269.578186	10231.549950	.000098	.003709	37.953924	.026348	216
55	299.018066	11353.069160	.000088	.003344	37.967837	.026338	220
56	331.672992	12597.066350	.000079	.003015	37.980380	.026329	224
57	367.894071	13976.916980	.000072	.002718	37.991689	.026322	228
58	408.070753	15507.457250	.000064	.002451	38.001884	.026314	232
59	452.635018	17205.143520	.000058	.002209	38.011075	.026308	236
60	502.066021	19088.229370	.000052	.001992	38.019361	.026302	240

10 ½ % SEMI-ANNUAL COMPOUND INTEREST TABLE 10 ½ %

EFFECTIVE RATE = 5¼% BASE = 1.0525

HALF YEARS	1 AMOUNT OF I AT COMPOUND INTEREST $S^n = (1+i)^n$	2 ACCUMULATION OF I PER PERIOD $S_{\overline{n}\vert} = \frac{S^n - 1}{i}$	3 SINKING FUND FACTOR $1/S_{\overline{n}\vert} = \frac{i}{S^n - 1}$	4 PRES. VALUE REVERSION OF I $V^n = \frac{1}{S^n}$	5 PRESENT VALUE ORD. ANNUITY 1 PER PERIOD $a_{\overline{n}\vert} = \frac{1 - V^n}{i}$	6 INSTALMENT TO AMORTIZE I $1/a_{\overline{n}\vert} = \frac{i}{1 - V^n}$	n HALF YEARS
1	1.052500	1.000000	1.000000	.950119	.950119	1.052500	1
YEARS							
1	1.107756	2.052500	.487211	.902726	1.852844	.539711	2
2	1.227124	4.326170	.231151	.814914	3.525455	.283651	4
3	1.359354	6.844842	.146095	.735643	5.035363	.198595	6
4	1.505833	9.634916	.103789	.664084	6.398396	.156289	8
5	1.668096	12.725638	.078582	.599486	7.628840	.131082	10
6	1.847844	16.149405	.061922	.541171	8.739595	.114422	12
7	2.046961	19.942105	.050145	.488529	9.742301	.102645	14
8	2.267533	24.143491	.041419	.441008	10.647469	.093919	16
9	2.511874	28.797603	.034725	.398109	11.464588	.087225	18
10	2.782544	33.953225	.029452	.359383	12.202223	.081952	20
11	3.082381	39.664397	.025212	.324425	12.868104	.077712	22
12	3.414527	45.990984	.021743	.292866	13.469212	.074243	24
13	3.782463	52.999300	.018868	.264378	14.011848	.071368	26
14	4.190047	60.762806	.016457	.238661	14.501699	.068957	28
15	4.641551	69.362878	.014417	.215445	14.943901	.066917	30
16	5.141707	78.889662	.012676	.194488	15.343087	.065176	32
17	5.695758	89.443016	.011180	.175569	15.703443	.063680	34
18	6.309512	101.133560	.009888	.158491	16.028745	.062388	36
19	6.989401	114.083833	.008765	.143074	16.322404	.061265	38
20	7.742553	128.429579	.007786	.129156	16.587498	.060286	40
21	8.576861	144.321169	.006929	.116593	16.826804	.059429	42
22	9.501072	161.925177	.006176	.105251	17.042833	.058676	44
23	10.524872	181.426126	.005512	.095013	17.237847	.058012	46
24	11.658992	203.028425	.004925	.085771	17.413891	.057425	48
25	12.915322	226.958507	.004406	.077427	17.572811	.056906	50
26	14.307028	253.467205	.003945	.069896	17.716272	.056445	52
27	15.848700	282.832380	.003536	.063097	17.845778	.056036	54
28	17.556496	315.361837	.003171	.056959	17.962686	.055671	56
29	19.448319	351.396546	.002846	.051418	18.068222	.055346	58
30	21.543997	391.314220	.002555	.046417	18.163493	.055055	60
31	23.865497	435.533273	.002296	.041901	18.249495	.054796	62
32	26.437153	484.517205	.002064	.037826	18.327132	.054564	64
33	29.285922	538.779462	.001856	.034146	18.397217	.054356	66
34	32.441663	598.888817	.001670	.030825	18.460485	.054170	68
35	35.937455	665.475330	.001503	.027826	18.517598	.054003	70
36	39.809940	739.236956	.001353	.025119	18.569155	.053853	72
37	44.099710	820.946858	.001218	.022676	18.615697	.053718	74
38	48.851729	911.461513	.001097	.020470	18.657712	.053597	76
39	54.115809	1011.729688	.000988	.018479	18.695640	.053488	78
40	59.947125	1122.802385	.000891	.016681	18.729879	.053391	80
41	66.406803	1245.843859	.000803	.015059	18.760787	.053303	82
42	73.562551	1382.143822	.000724	.013594	18.788688	.053224	84
43	81.489375	1533.130957	.000652	.012272	18.813875	.053152	86
44	90.270365	1700.387900	.000588	.011078	18.836613	.053088	88
45	99.997561	1885.667824	.000530	.010000	18.857138	.053030	90
46	110.772923	2090.912817	.000478	.009027	18.875667	.052978	92
47	122.709398	2318.274242	.000431	.008149	18.892394	.052931	94
48	135.932102	2570.135280	.000389	.007357	18.907493	.052889	96
49	150.579636	2849.135920	.000351	.006641	18.921124	.052851	98
50	166.805533	3158.200623	.000317	.005995	18.933428	.052817	100
51	184.779871	3500.568979	.000286	.005412	18.944536	.052786	102
52	204.691057	3879.829665	.000258	.004885	18.954564	.052758	104
53	226.747798	4299.958061	.000233	.004410	18.963616	.052733	106
54	251.181291	4765.357916	.000210	.003981	18.971787	.052710	108
55	278.247645	5280.907516	.000189	.003594	18.979163	.052689	110
56	308.230567	5852.010808	.000171	.003244	18.985822	.052671	112
57	341.444338	6484.654048	.000154	.002929	18.991834	.052654	114
58	378.237099	7185.468551	.000139	.002644	18.997260	.052639	116
59	418.994510	7961.800196	.000126	.002387	19.002159	.052626	118
60	464.143788	8821.786429	.000113	.002155	19.006581	.052613	120

10½% ANNUAL COMPOUND INTEREST TABLE 10½%

EFFECTIVE RATE = 10½% BASE = 1.1050

YEARS	1 AMOUNT OF I AT COMPOUND INTEREST $S^n = (1+i)^n$	2 ACCUMULATION OF I PER PERIOD $S_{\overline{n}\rvert} = \frac{S^n - 1}{i}$	3 SINKING FUND FACTOR $1/S_{\overline{n}\rvert} = \frac{i}{S^n - 1}$	4 PRES. VALUE REVERSION OF I $V^n = \frac{1}{S^n}$	5 PRESENT VALUE ORD. ANNUITY 1 PER PERIOD $a_{\overline{n}\rvert} = \frac{1 - V^n}{i}$	6 INSTALMENT TO AMORTIZE I $1/a_{\overline{n}\rvert} = \frac{i}{1 - V^n}$	n YEARS
1	1.105000	1.000000	1.000000	.904977	.904977	1.105000	1
2	1.221025	2.105000	.475059	.818984	1.723961	.580059	2
3	1.349233	3.326025	.300659	.741162	2.465123	.405659	3
4	1.490902	4.675258	.213892	.670735	3.135858	.318892	4
5	1.647447	6.166160	.162175	.607000	3.742858	.267175	5
6	1.820429	7.813606	.127982	.549321	4.292179	.232982	6
7	2.011574	9.634035	.103799	.497123	4.789303	.208799	7
8	2.222789	11.645609	.085869	.449885	5.239188	.190869	8
9	2.456182	13.868398	.072106	.407136	5.646324	.177106	9
10	2.714081	16.324580	.061257	.368449	6.014773	.166257	10
11	2.999059	19.038660	.052525	.333438	6.348211	.157525	11
12	3.313961	22.037720	.045377	.301754	6.649964	.150377	12
13	3.661926	25.351680	.039445	.273080	6.923045	.144445	13
14	4.046429	29.013607	.034467	.247132	7.170176	.139467	14
15	4.471304	33.060035	.030248	.223648	7.393825	.135248	15
16	4.940791	37.531339	.026644	.202397	7.596221	.131644	16
17	5.459574	42.472130	.023545	.183164	7.779386	.128545	17
18	6.032829	47.931703	.020863	.165760	7.945146	.125863	18
19	6.666276	53.964532	.018531	.150009	8.095154	.123531	19
20	7.366235	60.630808	.016493	.135755	8.230909	.121493	20
21	8.139690	67.997043	.014707	.122855	8.353764	.119707	21
22	8.994357	76.136732	.013134	.111181	8.464945	.118134	22
23	9.938764	85.131089	.011747	.100616	8.565561	.116747	23
24	10.982335	95.069854	.010519	.091055	8.656616	.115519	24
25	12.135480	106.052188	.009429	.082403	8.739019	.114429	25
26	13.409705	118.187668	.008461	.074573	8.813592	.113461	26
27	14.817724	131.597373	.007599	.067487	8.881079	.112599	27
28	16.373585	146.415098	.006830	.061074	8.942153	.111830	28
29	18.092812	162.788683	.006143	.055271	8.997423	.111143	29
30	19.992557	180.881495	.005528	.050019	9.047442	.110528	30
31	22.091775	200.874051	.004978	.045266	9.092707	.109978	31
32	24.411412	222.965827	.004485	.040964	9.133672	.109485	32
33	26.974610	247.377239	.004042	.037072	9.170744	.109042	33
34	29.806944	274.351849	.003645	.033549	9.204293	.108645	34
35	32.936673	304.158793	.003288	.030361	9.234654	.108288	35
36	36.395024	337.095466	.002967	.027476	9.262131	.107967	36
37	40.216501	373.490490	.002677	.024865	9.286996	.107677	37
38	44.439234	413.706992	.002417	.022503	9.309499	.107417	38
39	49.105354	458.146226	.002183	.020364	9.329863	.107183	39
40	54.261416	507.251579	.001971	.018429	9.348292	.106971	40
41	59.958865	561.512995	.001781	.016678	9.364970	.106781	41
42	66.254545	621.471860	.001609	.015093	9.380064	.106609	42
43	73.211273	687.726405	.001454	.013659	9.393723	.106454	43
44	80.898456	760.937678	.001314	.012361	9.406084	.106314	44
45	89.392794	841.836134	.001188	.011187	9.417271	.106188	45
46	98.779037	931.228928	.001074	.010124	9.427394	.106074	46
47	109.150836	1030.007966	.000971	.009162	9.436556	.105971	47
48	120.611674	1139.158802	.000878	.008291	9.444847	.105878	48
49	133.275900	1259.770476	.000794	.007503	9.452350	.105794	49
50	147.269870	1393.046376	.000718	.006790	9.459140	.105718	50
51	162.733206	1540.316246	.000649	.006145	9.465285	.105649	51
52	179.820192	1703.049451	.000587	.005561	9.470847	.105587	52
53	198.701313	1882.869644	.000531	.005033	9.475879	.105531	53
54	219.564950	2081.570956	.000480	.004554	9.480434	.105480	54
55	242.619270	2301.135907	.000435	.004122	9.484555	.105435	55
56	268.094294	2543.755177	.000393	.003730	9.488285	.105393	56
57	296.244194	2811.849471	.000356	.003376	9.491661	.105356	57
58	327.349835	3108.093665	.000322	.003055	9.494716	.105322	58
59	361.721568	3435.443500	.000291	.002765	9.497480	.105291	59
60	399.702332	3797.165068	.000263	.002502	9.499982	.105263	60

10 ¾ % MONTHLY COMPOUND INTEREST TABLE 10 ¾ %

EFFECTIVE RATE = 43/48% BASE = 1.00895833

MONTHS	1 AMOUNT OF I AT COMPOUND INTEREST $S^n = (1+i)^n$	2 ACCUMULATION OF I PER PERIOD $S_{\overline{n}\rvert} = \frac{S^n - 1}{i}$	3 SINKING FUND FACTOR $1/S_{\overline{n}\rvert} = \frac{i}{S^n - 1}$	4 PRES. VALUE REVERSION OF I $V^n = \frac{1}{S^n}$	5 PRESENT VALUE ORD. ANNUITY 1 PER PERIOD $a_{\overline{n}\rvert} = \frac{1 - V^n}{i}$	6 INSTALMENT TO AMORTIZE I $1/a_{\overline{n}\rvert} = \frac{i}{1 - V^n}$	n MONTHS
1	1.008958	1.000000	1.000000	.991121	.991121	1.008958	1
2	1.017996	2.008958	.497770	.982321	1.973442	.506728	2
3	1.027116	3.026955	.330364	.973599	2.947041	.339323	3
4	1.036317	4.054071	.246665	.964955	3.911996	.255623	4
5	1.045601	5.090389	.196448	.956387	4.868384	.205406	5
6	1.054968	6.135990	.162972	.947895	5.816280	.171931	6
7	1.064419	7.190959	.139063	.939479	6.755759	.148021	7
8	1.073954	8.255378	.121133	.931138	7.686897	.130091	8
9	1.083575	9.329332	.107188	.922870	8.609768	.116147	9
10	1.093282	10.412907	.096034	.914676	9.524445	.104992	10
11	1.103076	11.506190	.086909	.906555	10.431001	.095868	11
YEARS							
1	1.112958	12.609266	.079306	.898506	11.329507	.088265	12
2	1.238675	26.642850	.037533	.807313	21.509144	.046491	24
3	1.378593	42.261640	.023662	.725376	30.655613	.032620	36
4	1.534317	59.644697	.016765	.651755	38.873775	.025724	48
5	1.707630	78.991310	.012659	.585606	46.257847	.021617	60
6	1.900521	100.523277	.009947	.526171	52.892483	.018906	72
7	2.115200	124.487453	.008032	.472768	58.853748	.016991	84
8	2.354128	151.158575	.006615	.424785	64.209982	.015573	96
9	2.620046	180.842413	.005529	.381672	69.022594	.014488	108
10	2.916001	213.879279	.004675	.342935	73.346756	.013633	120
11	3.245387	250.647924	.003989	.308129	77.232044	.012947	132
12	3.611980	291.569881	.003429	.276856	80.723001	.012388	144
13	4.019982	337.114301	.002966	.248757	83.859649	.011924	156
14	4.474071	387.803328	.002578	.223510	86.677946	.011536	168
15	4.979453	444.218087	.002251	.200825	89.210205	.011209	180
16	5.541922	507.005346	.001972	.180442	91.485456	.010930	192
17	6.167927	576.884927	.001733	.162129	93.529784	.010691	204
18	6.864644	654.657968	.001527	.145673	95.366626	.010485	216
19	7.640060	741.216096	.001349	.130889	97.017041	.010307	228
20	8.503066	837.551658	.001193	.117604	98.499949	.010152	240
21	9.463556	944.769095	.001058	.105668	99.832351	.010016	252
22	10.532540	1064.097599	.000939	.094943	101.029524	.009898	264
23	11.722275	1196.905214	.000835	.085307	102.105191	.009793	276
24	13.046400	1344.714512	.000743	.076649	103.071684	.009701	288
25	14.520096	1509.220055	.000662	.068870	103.940085	.009620	300
26	16.160257	1692.307818	.000590	.061880	104.720350	.009549	312
27	17.985688	1896.076808	.000527	.055599	105.421422	.009485	324
28	20.017315	2122.863140	.000471	.049956	106.051340	.009429	336
29	22.278431	2375.266803	.000421	.044886	106.617325	.009379	348
30	24.794959	2656.181484	.000376	.040330	107.125867	.009334	360
31	27.595748	2968.827729	.000336	.036237	107.582794	.009295	372
32	30.712909	3316.789869	.000301	.032559	107.993348	.009259	384
33	34.182178	3704.057123	.000269	.029255	108.362232	.009228	396
34	38.043329	4135.069312	.000241	.026285	108.693676	.009200	408
35	42.340627	4614.767785	.000216	.023617	108.991482	.009175	420
36	47.123341	5148.652038	.000194	.021220	109.259062	.009152	432
37	52.446299	5742.842801	.000174	.019067	109.499484	.009132	444
38	58.370529	6404.152170	.000156	.017131	109.715505	.009114	456
39	64.963948	7140.161723	.000140	.015393	109.909601	.009098	468
40	72.302146	7959.309459	.000125	.013830	110.083999	.009083	480
41	80.469253	8870.986494	.000112	.012427	110.240695	.009071	492
42	89.558900	9885.644744	.000101	.011165	110.381488	.009059	504
43	99.675295	11014.916780	.000090	.010032	110.507991	.009049	516
44	110.934418	12271.749130	.000081	.009014	110.621655	.009039	528
45	123.465350	13670.550780	.000073	.008099	110.723784	.009031	540
46	137.411750	15227.358270	.000065	.007277	110.815546	.009024	552
47	152.933508	16960.019630	.000058	.006538	110.897996	.009017	564
48	170.208573	18888.398990	.000052	.005875	110.972077	.009011	576
49	189.434995	21034.604230	.000047	.005278	111.038639	.009005	588
50	210.833195	23423.2[illegible]0560	.000042	.004743	111.098447	.009001	600

10¾% QUARTERLY COMPOUND INTEREST TABLE 10¾%

EFFECTIVE RATE = 2-11/16% BASE = 1.026875

QUARTERS	1 AMOUNT OF I AT COMPOUND INTEREST $S^n = (1+i)^n$	2 ACCUMULATION OF I PER PERIOD $S_{\overline{n}\rceil} = \frac{S^n - 1}{i}$	3 SINKING FUND FACTOR $1/S_{\overline{n}\rceil} = \frac{i}{S^n - 1}$	4 PRES. VALUE REVERSION OF I $V^n = \frac{1}{S^n}$	5 PRESENT VALUE ORD. ANNUITY 1 PER PERIOD $a_{\overline{n}\rceil} = \frac{1 - V^n}{i}$	6 INSTALMENT TO AMORTIZE I $1/a_{\overline{n}\rceil} = \frac{i}{1 - V^n}$	n QUARTERS
1	1.026875	1.000000	1.000000	.973828	.973828	1.026875	1
2	1.054472	2.026875	.493370	.948342	1.922170	.520245	2
3	1.082811	3.081347	.324533	.923522	2.845692	.351408	3
YEARS							
1	1.111912	4.164158	.240145	.899352	3.745044	.267020	4
2	1.236348	8.794335	.113710	.808834	7.113157	.140585	8
3	1.374710	13.942683	.071722	.727426	10.142275	.098597	12
4	1.528556	19.667192	.050846	.654212	12.866519	.077721	16
5	1.699619	26.032340	.038414	.588367	15.316573	.065289	20
6	1.889827	33.109824	.030203	.529149	17.520034	.057078	24
7	2.101320	40.979361	.024403	.475891	19.501720	.051278	28
8	2.336483	49.729592	.020109	.427994	21.283954	.046984	32
9	2.597963	59.459076	.016818	.384917	22.886809	.043693	36
10	2.888705	70.277405	.014229	.346176	24.328340	.041104	40
11	3.211985	82.306431	.012150	.311334	25.624784	.039025	44
12	3.571444	95.681647	.010451	.279999	26.790743	.037326	48
13	3.971131	110.553707	.009045	.251817	27.839351	.035920	52
14	4.415547	127.090125	.007868	.226473	28.782419	.034743	56
15	4.909699	145.477163	.006874	.203678	29.630568	.033749	60
16	5.459152	165.921927	.006027	.183179	30.393353	.032902	64
17	6.070095	188.654700	.005301	.164742	31.079365	.032176	68
18	6.749410	213.931538	.004674	.148161	31.696331	.031549	72
19	7.504748	242.037151	.004132	.133249	32.251201	.031007	76
20	8.344618	273.288113	.003659	.119838	32.750224	.030534	80
21	9.278479	308.036425	.003246	.107776	33.199022	.030121	84
22	10.316850	346.673481	.002885	.096929	33.602649	.029760	88
23	11.471427	389.634479	.002567	.087173	33.965652	.029442	92
24	12.755214	437.403317	.002286	.078399	34.292119	.029161	96
25	14.182673	490.518050	.002039	.070509	34.585728	.028914	100
26	15.769880	549.576947	.001820	.063412	34.849785	.028695	104
27	17.534716	615.245228	.001625	.057030	35.087266	.028500	108
28	19.497056	688.262562	.001453	.051290	35.300845	.028328	112
29	21.679006	769.451394	.001300	.046128	35.492927	.028175	116
30	24.105142	859.726212	.001163	.041485	35.665677	.028038	120
31	26.802791	960.103843	.001042	.037310	35.821040	.027917	124
32	29.802338	1071.714911	.000933	.033554	35.960766	.027808	128
33	33.137570	1195.816570	.000836	.030177	36.086429	.027711	132
34	36.846054	1333.806664	.000750	.027140	36.199444	.027625	136
35	40.969561	1487.239472	.000672	.024408	36.301084	.027547	140
36	45.554536	1657.843216	.000603	.021952	36.392494	.027478	144
37	50.652625	1847.539525	.000541	.019742	36.474705	.527416	148
38	56.321249	2058.465081	.000486	.017755	36.548640	.027361	152
39	62.624259	2292.995688	.000436	.015968	36.615135	.027311	156
40	69.632650	2553.773027	.000392	.014361	36.674937	.027267	160
41	77.425362	2843.734417	.000352	.012916	36.728719	.027227	164
42	86.090171	3166.145896	.000316	.011616	36.777089	.027191	168
43	95.724673	3524.639011	.000284	.010447	36.820591	.027159	172
44	106.437390	3923.251721	.000255	.009395	36.859714	.027130	176
45	118.348986	4366.473879	.000229	.008450	36.894899	.027104	180
46	131.593629	4859.297808	.000206	.007599	36.926543	.027081	184
47	146.320503	5407.274530	.000185	.006834	36.955002	.027060	188
48	162.695488	6016.576294	.000166	.006146	36.980597	.027041	192
49	180.903026	6694.066087	.000149	.005528	37.003616	.027024	196
50	201.148202	7447.374954	.000134	.004971	37.024318	.027009	200
51	223.659051	8284.987944	.000121	.004471	37.042936	.026996	204
52	248.689129	9216.339676	.000109	.004021	37.059681	.026984	208
53	276.520367	10251.920620	.000098	.003616	37.074740	.026973	212
54	307.466247	11403.395240	.000088	.003252	37.088283	.026963	216
55	341.875336	12683.733420	.000079	.002925	37.100464	.026954	220
56	380.135206	14107.356500	.000071	.002631	37.111418	.026946	224
57	422.676805	15690.299740	.000064	.002366	37.121270	.026939	228
58	469.979310	17450.392940	.000057	.002128	37.130130	.026932	232
59	522.575522	19407.461270	.000052	.001914	37.138099	.026927	236
60	581.057867	21583.548550	.000046	.001721	37.145265	.026921	240

10 ¾ % SEMI-ANNUAL COMPOUND INTEREST TABLE 10 ¾ %

EFFECTIVE RATE = 5-3/8% BASE = 1.05375

HALF YEARS	1 AMOUNT OF I AT COMPOUND INTEREST $S^n = (1+i)^n$	2 ACCUMULATION OF I PER PERIOD $S_{\overline{n}\rceil} = \frac{S^n - 1}{i}$	3 SINKING FUND FACTOR $1/S_{\overline{n}\rceil} = \frac{i}{S^n - 1}$	4 PRES. VALUE REVERSION OF I $V^n = \frac{1}{S^n}$	5 PRESENT VALUE ORD. ANNUITY 1 PER PERIOD $a_{\overline{n}\rceil} = \frac{1 - V^n}{i}$	6 INSTALMENT TO AMORTIZE I $1/a_{\overline{n}\rceil} = \frac{i}{1 - V^n}$	n HALF YEARS
1	1.053750	1.000000	1.000000	.948992	.948992	1.053750	1
YEARS							
1	1.110389	2.053750	.486914	.900585	1.849577	.540664	2
2	1.232964	4.334212	.230722	.811054	3.515279	.284472	4
3	1.369070	6.866411	.145636	.730423	5.015385	.199386	6
4	1.520200	9.678138	.103326	.657808	6.366359	.157076	8
5	1.688013	12.800248	.078123	.592412	7.583026	.131873	10
6	1.874352	16.267006	.061474	.533518	8.678738	.115224	12
7	2.081259	20.116455	.049711	.480478	9.665520	.103461	14
8	2.311008	24.390842	.040999	.432712	10.554202	.094749	16
9	2.566118	29.137074	.034321	.389694	11.354535	.088071	18
10	2.849389	34.407238	.029064	.350952	12.075304	.082814	20
11	3.163930	40.259171	.024839	.316063	12.724417	.078589	22
12	3.513194	46.757093	.021387	.284641	13.308999	.075137	24
13	3.901012	53.972315	.018528	.256344	13.835465	.072278	26
14	4.331641	61.984018	.016133	.230859	14.309593	.069883	28
15	4.809807	70.880126	.014108	.207909	14.736585	.067858	30
16	5.340757	80.758267	.012383	.187239	15.121128	.066133	32
17	5.930318	91.726846	.010902	.168625	15.467441	.064652	34
18	6.584960	103.906236	.009624	.151861	15.779326	.063374	36
19	7.311868	117.430099	.008516	.136764	16.060205	.062266	38
20	8.119018	132.446847	.007550	.123168	16.313161	.061300	40
21	9.015269	149.121280	.006706	.110923	16.540969	.060456	42
22	10.010456	167.636389	.005965	.099896	16.746129	.059715	44
23	11.115501	188.195362	.005314	.089964	16.930894	.059064	46
24	12.342530	211.023822	.004739	.081021	17.097290	.058489	48
25	13.705011	236.372294	.004231	.072966	17.247144	.057981	50
26	15.217894	264.518959	.003780	.065712	17.382100	.057530	52
27	16.897783	295.772709	.003381	.059179	17.503640	.057131	54
28	18.763114	330.476532	.003026	.053296	17.613097	.056776	56
29	20.834356	369.011276	.002710	.047998	17.711672	.056460	58
30	23.134241	411.799835	.002428	.043226	17.800447	.056178	60
31	25.688008	459.311783	.002177	.038929	17.880397	.055927	62
32	28.523683	512.068530	.001953	.035059	17.952398	.055703	64
33	31.672386	570.649045	.001752	.031573	18.017242	.055502	66
34	35.168671	635.696208	.001573	.028434	18.075639	.055323	68
35	39.050908	707.923866	.001413	.025608	18.128231	.055163	70
36	43.361701	788.124669	.001269	.023062	18.175594	.055019	72
37	48.148358	877.178762	.001140	.020769	18.218249	.054890	74
38	53.463411	976.063453	.001025	.018704	18.256663	.054775	76
39	59.365186	1085.863933	.000921	.016845	18.291258	.054671	78
40	65.918454	1207.785184	.000828	.015170	18.322414	.054578	80
41	73.195130	1343.165208	.000745	.013662	18.350472	.054495	82
42	81.275072	1493.489707	.000670	.012304	18.375741	.054420	84
43	90.246951	1660.408385	.000602	.011081	18.398498	.054352	86
44	100.209227	1845.753060	.000542	.009979	18.418993	.054292	88
45	111.271230	2051.557760	.000487	.008987	18.437450	.054237	90
46	123.554356	2280.081047	.000439	.008094	18.454072	.054189	92
47	137.193406	2533.830807	.000395	.007289	18.469042	.054145	94
48	152.338057	2815.591766	.000355	.006564	18.482524	.054105	96
49	169.154513	3128.456050	.000320	.005912	18.494665	.054070	98
50	187.827321	3475.857131	.000288	.005324	18.505599	.054038	100
51	208.561403	3861.607492	.000259	.004795	18.515446	.054009	102
52	231.584300	4289.940473	.000233	.004318	18.524315	.053983	104
53	257.148674	4765.556729	.000210	.003889	18.532301	.053960	106
54	285.535075	5293.675820	.000189	.003502	18.539494	.053939	108
55	317.055025	5880.093481	.000170	.003154	18.545972	.053920	110
56	352.054432	6531.245237	.000153	.002840	18.551805	.053903	112
57	390.917390	7254.277027	.000138	.002558	18.557059	.053888	114
58	434.070394	8057.123617	.000124	.002304	18.561790	.053874	116
59	481.987018	8948.595689	.000112	.002075	18.566051	.053862	118
60	535.193113	9938.476528	.000101	.001868	18.569889	.053851	120

10 ¾ % ANNUAL COMPOUND INTEREST TABLE 10 ¾ %

EFFECTIVE RATE = 29/48% BASE = 1.00604167

YEARS	1 AMOUNT OF I AT COMPOUND INTEREST $S^n = (1+i)^n$	2 ACCUMULATION OF I PER PERIOD $S_{\overline{n}\rceil} = \frac{S^n - 1}{i}$	3 SINKING FUND FACTOR $1/S_{\overline{n}\rceil} = \frac{i}{S^n - 1}$	4 PRES. VALUE REVERSION OF I $V^n = \frac{1}{S^n}$	5 PRESENT VALUE ORD. ANNUITY 1 PER PERIOD $a_{\overline{n}\rceil} = \frac{1 - V^n}{i}$	6 INSTALMENT TO AMORTIZE I $1/a_{\overline{n}\rceil} = \frac{i}{1 - V^n}$	n YEARS
1	1.107500	1.000000	1.000000	.902935	.902935	1.107500	1
2	1.226556	2.107500	.474496	.815291	1.718225	.581996	2
3	1.358411	3.334056	.299935	.736154	2.454380	.407435	3
4	1.504440	4.692467	.213108	.664699	3.119079	.320608	4
5	1.666168	6.196908	.161371	.600180	3.719258	.268871	5
6	1.845281	7.863075	.127177	.541923	4.261181	.234677	6
7	2.043648	9.708356	.103004	.489321	4.750502	.210504	7
8	2.263340	11.752004	.085092	.441825	5.192327	.192592	8
9	2.506650	14.015344	.071350	.398939	5.591266	.178850	9
10	2.776114	16.521994	.060525	.360216	5.951482	.168025	10
11	3.074547	19.298108	.051819	.325251	6.276733	.159319	11
12	3.405060	22.372655	.044697	.293681	6.570414	.152197	12
13	3.771104	25.777715	.038793	.265174	6.835588	.146293	13
14	4.176498	29.548820	.033842	.239435	7.075023	.141342	14
15	4.625472	33.725318	.029651	.216194	7.291217	.137151	15
16	5.122710	38.350789	.026075	.195209	7.486426	.133575	16
17	5.673401	43.473499	.023003	.176261	7.662687	.130503	17
18	6.283292	49.146900	.020347	.159152	7.821840	.127847	18
19	6.958746	55.430192	.018041	.143704	7.965544	.125541	19
20	7.706811	62.388938	.016028	.129755	8.095299	.123528	20
21	8.535293	70.095749	.014266	.117161	8.212460	.121766	21
22	9.452837	78.631042	.012718	.105788	8.318248	.120218	22
23	10.469017	88.083879	.011353	.095520	8.413768	.118853	23
24	11.594436	98.552895	.010147	.086248	8.500016	.117647	24
25	12.840838	110.147332	.009079	.077877	8.577893	.116579	25
26	14.221228	122.988170	.008131	.070317	8.648210	.115631	26
27	15.750010	137.209398	.007288	.063492	8.711702	.114788	27
28	17.443136	152.959409	.006538	.057329	8.769031	.114038	28
29	19.318274	170.402545	.005868	.051764	8.820796	.113368	29
30	21.394988	189.720818	.005271	.046740	8.867536	.112771	30
31	23.694949	211.115806	.004737	.042203	8.909739	.112237	31
32	26.242156	234.810756	.004259	.038107	8.947845	.111759	32
33	29.063188	261.052912	.003831	.034408	8.982253	.111331	33
34	32.187481	290.116100	.003447	.031068	9.013321	.110947	34
35	35.647635	322.303581	.003103	.028052	9.041373	.110603	35
36	39.479756	357.951215	.002794	.025329	9.066703	.110294	36
37	43.723829	397.430971	.002516	.022871	9.089574	.110016	37
38	48.424141	441.154801	.002267	.020651	9.110225	.109767	38
39	53.629736	489.578942	.002043	.018646	9.128871	.109543	39
40	59.394933	543.208678	.001841	.016836	9.145707	.109341	40
41	65.779888	602.603611	.001659	.015202	9.160910	.109159	41
42	72.851226	668.383499	.001496	.013727	9.174636	.108996	42
43	80.682733	741.234725	.001349	.012394	9.187030	.108849	43
44	89.356127	821.917458	.001217	.011191	9.198222	.108717	44
45	98.961910	911.273584	.001097	.010105	9.208327	.108597	45
46	109.600316	1010.235495	.000990	.009124	9.217451	.108490	46
47	121.382350	1119.835810	.000893	.008238	9.225689	.108393	47
48	134.430952	1241.218160	.000806	.007439	9.233128	.108306	48
49	148.882280	1375.649113	.000727	.006717	9.239845	.108227	49
50	164.887125	1524.531393	.000656	.006065	9.245909	.108156	50
51	182.612491	1689.418517	.000592	.005476	9.251385	.108092	51
52	202.243333	1872.031007	.000534	.004945	9.256330	.108034	52
53	223.984492	2074.274340	.000482	.004465	9.260794	.107982	53
54	248.062824	2298.258832	.000435	.004031	9.264826	.107935	54
55	274.729578	2546.321656	.000393	.003640	9.268466	.107893	55
56	304.263008	2821.051233	.000354	.003287	9.271752	.107854	56
57	336.971281	3125.314241	.000320	.002968	9.274720	.107820	57
58	373.195694	3462.285522	.000289	.002680	9.277399	.107789	58
59	413.314231	3835.481216	.000261	.002419	9.279819	.107761	59
60	457.745511	4248.795446	.000235	.002185	9.282004	.107735	60

11% MONTHLY COMPOUND INTEREST TABLE 11%

EFFECTIVE RATE = 11/12% BASE = 1.00916667

MONTHS	1 AMOUNT OF I AT COMPOUND INTEREST $S^n = (1+i)^n$	2 ACCUMULATION OF I PER PERIOD $s_{\overline{n}\rvert} = \frac{S^n - 1}{i}$	3 SINKING FUND FACTOR $1/s_{\overline{n}\rvert} = \frac{i}{S^n - 1}$	4 PRES. VALUE REVERSION OF I $V^n = \frac{1}{S^n}$	5 PRESENT VALUE ORD. ANNUITY 1 PER PERIOD $a_{\overline{n}\rvert} = \frac{1 - V^n}{i}$	6 INSTALMENT TO AMORTIZE I $1/a_{\overline{n}\rvert} = \frac{i}{1 - V^n}$	n MONTHS
1	1.009166	1.000000	1.000000	.990916	.990916	1.009166	1
2	1.018417	2.009166	.497718	.981915	1.972832	.506885	2
3	1.027752	3.027584	.330296	.972996	2.945828	.339463	3
4	1.037173	4.055336	.246588	.964158	3.909987	.255755	4
5	1.046681	5.092510	.196366	.955400	4.865387	.205533	5
6	1.056275	6.139192	.162887	.946722	5.812110	.172054	6
7	1.065958	7.195468	.138976	.938122	6.750233	.148143	7
8	1.075729	8.261426	.121044	.929601	7.679834	.130211	8
9	1.085590	9.337156	.107098	.921157	8.600992	.116265	9
10	1.095541	10.422746	.095943	.912790	9.513782	.105110	10
11	1.105584	11.518288	.086818	.904499	10.418281	.095985	11
YEARS							
1	1.115718	12.623873	.079214	.896283	11.314564	.088381	12
2	1.244828	26.708565	.037441	.803323	21.455618	.046607	24
3	1.388878	42.423123	.023572	.720005	30.544874	.032738	36
4	1.549598	59.956150	.016678	.645328	38.691421	.025845	48
5	1.728915	79.518079	.012575	.578397	45.993033	.021742	60
6	1.928983	101.343692	.009867	.518407	52.537346	.019034	72
7	2.152203	125.694939	.007955	.464640	58.402903	.017122	84
8	2.401254	152.864084	.006541	.416449	63.660103	.015708	96
9	2.679124	183.177212	.005459	.373256	68.372043	.014625	108
10	2.989149	216.998138	.004608	.334543	72.595274	.013775	120
11	3.335050	254.732784	.003925	.299845	76.380486	.013092	132
12	3.720978	296.834038	.003368	.268746	79.773108	.012535	144
13	4.151566	343.807201	.002908	.240872	82.813858	.012075	156
14	4.631980	396.216043	.002523	.215890	85.539231	.011690	168
15	5.167987	454.689576	.002199	.193498	87.981936	.011365	180
16	5.766021	519.929598	.001923	.173429	90.171292	.011090	192
17	6.433258	592.719119	.001687	.155442	92.133575	.010853	204
18	7.177707	673.931759	.001483	.139320	93.892336	.010650	216
19	8.008303	764.542231	.001307	.124870	95.468684	.010474	228
20	8.935015	865.638042	.001155	.111919	96.881538	.010321	240
21	9.968965	978.432542	.001022	.100311	98.147855	.010188	252
22	11.122562	1104.279491	.000905	.089907	99.282835	.010072	264
23	12.409651	1244.689302	.000803	.080582	100.300097	.009970	276
24	13.845682	1401.347173	.000713	.072224	101.211853	.009880	288
25	15.447888	1576.133312	.000634	.064733	102.029043	.009801	300
26	17.235500	1771.145496	.000564	.058019	102.761477	.009731	312
27	19.229972	1988.724266	.000502	.052002	103.417946	.009669	324
28	21.455242	2231.480999	.000448	.046608	104.006327	.009614	336
29	23.938018	2502.329255	.000399	.041774	104.533684	.009566	348
30	26.708097	2804.519759	.000356	.037441	105.006345	.009523	360
31	29.798727	3141.679397	.000318	.033558	105.429983	.009484	372
32	33.247002	3517.854756	.000284	.030077	105.809682	.009450	384
33	37.094306	3937.560686	.000253	.026958	106.150002	.009420	396
34	41.386816	4405.834502	.000226	.024162	106.455022	.009393	408
35	46.176050	4928.296419	.000202	.021656	106.728408	.009369	420
36	51.519489	5511.217017	.000181	.019410	106.973440	.009348	432
37	57.481264	6161.592513	.000162	.017396	107.193057	.009328	444
38	64.132930	6887.228705	.000145	.015592	107.389896	.009311	456
39	71.554318	7696.834666	.000129	.013975	107.566320	.009296	468
40	79.834500	8600.127295	.000116	.012525	107.724446	.009282	480
41	89.072856	9607.947896	.000104	.011226	107.866170	.009270	492
42	99.380263	10732.392330	.000093	.010062	107.993196	.009259	504
43	110.880431	11986.956140	.000083	.009018	108.107048	.009250	516
44	123.711386	13386.696640	.000074	.008083	108.209091	.009241	528
45	138.027124	14948.413480	.000066	.007244	108.300550	.009233	540
46	153.999462	16690.850360	.000059	.006493	108.382523	.009226	552
47	171.820100	18634.920020	.000053	.005820	108.455995	.009220	564
48	191.702923	20803.955170	.000048	.005216	108.521846	.009214	576
49	213.886562	23223.988540	.000043	.004675	108.580868	.009209	588
50	238.637266	25924.065330	.000038	.004190	108.633767	.009205	600

11% QUARTERLY COMPOUND INTEREST TABLE 11%

EFFECTIVE RATE = 2¾% BASE = 1.0275

QUARTERS	1 AMOUNT OF I AT COMPOUND INTEREST $S^n = (1+i)^n$	2 ACCUMULATION OF I PER PERIOD $s_{\overline{n}\rvert} = \frac{S^n - 1}{i}$	3 SINKING FUND FACTOR $1/s_{\overline{n}\rvert} = \frac{i}{S^n - 1}$	4 PRES. VALUE REVERSION OF I $V^n = \frac{1}{S^n}$	5 PRESENT VALUE ORD. ANNUITY 1 PER PERIOD $a_{\overline{n}\rvert} = \frac{1 - V^n}{i}$	6 INSTALMENT TO AMORTIZE I $1/a_{\overline{n}\rvert} = \frac{i}{1 - V^n}$	n QUARTERS
1	1.027500	1.000000	1.000000	.973236	.973236	1.027500	1
2	1.055756	2.027500	.493218	.947188	1.920424	.520718	2
3	1.084790	3.083256	.324332	.921838	2.842262	.351832	3
YEARS							
1	1.114621	4.168046	.239921	.897166	3.739428	.267421	4
2	1.242381	8.813838	.113458	.804906	7.094314	.140958	8
3	1.384784	13.992137	.071469	.722134	10.104204	.098969	12
4	1.543509	19.763980	.050597	.647874	12.804573	.078097	16
5	1.720428	26.197398	.038172	.581251	15.227252	.065672	20
6	1.917626	33.368222	.029969	.521478	17.400797	.057469	24
7	2.137427	41.360975	.024177	.467852	19.350826	.051677	28
8	2.382421	50.269868	.019893	.419741	21.100326	.047393	32
9	2.655498	60.199910	.016611	.376577	22.669918	.044111	36
10	2.959874	71.268145	.014032	.337852	24.078101	.041532	40
11	3.299138	83.605035	.011961	.303109	25.341475	.039461	44
12	3.677290	97.355996	.010272	.271939	26.474931	.037772	48
13	4.098785	112.683108	.008874	.243975	27.491829	.036374	52
14	4.568593	129.767034	.007706	.218886	28.404155	.035206	56
15	5.092251	148.809141	.006720	.196377	29.222662	.034220	60
16	5.675932	170.033877	.005881	.176183	29.956999	.033381	64
17	6.326514	193.691420	.005163	.158065	30.615821	.032663	68
18	7.051667	220.060621	.004544	.141810	31.206893	.032044	72
19	7.859938	249.452292	.004009	.127227	31.737183	.031509	76
20	8.760854	282.212874	.003543	.114144	32.212941	.031043	80
21	9.765034	318.728514	.003137	.102406	32.639775	.030637	84
22	10.884315	359.429624	.002782	.091875	33.022715	.030282	88
23	12.131889	404.795946	.002470	.082427	33.366276	.029970	92
24	13.522461	455.362213	.002196	.073951	33.674508	.029696	96
25	15.072422	511.724449	.001954	.066346	33.951042	.029454	100
26	16.800042	574.546995	.001741	.059524	34.199140	.029241	104
27	18.725684	644.570341	.001551	.053403	34.421724	.029051	108
28	20.872046	722.619851	.001384	.047911	34.621419	.028884	112
29	23.264426	809.615495	.001235	.042984	34.800579	.028735	116
30	25.931024	906.582688	.001103	.038564	34.961315	.028603	120
31	28.903271	1014.664383	.000986	.034598	35.105521	.028486	124
32	32.216200	1135.134539	.000881	.031040	35.234899	.028381	128
33	35.908861	1269.413135	.000788	.027848	35.350972	.028288	132
34	40.024780	1419.082912	.000705	.024985	35.455108	.028205	136
35	44.612471	1585.908029	.000631	.022415	35.548536	.028131	140
36	49.726008	1771.854850	.000564	.020110	35.632356	.028064	144
37	55.425666	1979.115130	.000505	.018042	35.707557	.028005	148
38	61.778626	2210.131845	.000452	.016187	35.775024	.027952	152
39	68.859770	2467.627986	.000405	.014522	35.835554	.027905	156
40	76.752563	2754.638659	.000363	.013029	35.889859	.027863	160
41	85.550039	3074.546857	.000325	.011689	35.938579	.027825	164
42	95.355892	3431.123335	.000291	.010487	35.982290	.027791	168
43	106.285704	3828.571058	.000261	.009409	36.021505	.027761	172
44	118.468305	4271.574742	.000234	.008441	36.056688	.027734	176
45	132.047292	4765.356065	.000210	.007573	36.088253	.027710	180
46	147.182719	5315.735225	.000188	.006794	36.116572	.027688	184
47	164.052987	5929.199538	.000169	.006096	36.141978	.027669	188
48	182.856947	6612.979902	.000151	.005469	36.164773	.027651	192
49	203.816241	7375.136033	.000136	.004906	36.185223	.027636	196
50	227.177915	8224.651458	.000122	.004402	36.203570	.027622	200
51	253.217334	9171.539411	.000109	.003949	36.220030	.027609	204
52	282.241424	10226.960850	.000098	.003543	36.234798	.027598	208
53	314.592291	11403.356030	.000088	.003179	36.248047	.027588	212
54	350.651256	12714.591110	.000079	.002852	36.259933	.027579	216
55	390.843344	14176.121600	.000071	.002559	36.270597	.027571	220
56	435.642300	15805.174560	.000063	.002295	36.280165	.027563	224
57	485.576169	17620.951610	.000057	.002059	36.288749	.027557	228
58	541.233522	19644.855330	.000051	.001848	36.296450	.027551	232
59	603.270389	21900.741430	.000046	.001658	36.303359	.027546	236
60	672.418001	24415.200040	.000041	.001487	36.309557	.027541	240

11% SEMI-ANNUAL COMPOUND INTEREST TABLE 11%

EFFECTIVE RATE = 5½% BASE = 1.00977

HALF YEARS	1 AMOUNT OF I AT COMPOUND INTEREST $S^n = (1+i)^n$	2 ACCUMULATION OF I PER PERIOD $S_{\overline{n}\vert} = \frac{S^n - 1}{i}$	3 SINKING FUND FACTOR $1/S_{\overline{n}\vert} = \frac{i}{S^n - 1}$	4 PRES. VALUE REVERSION OF I $V^n = \frac{1}{S^n}$	5 PRESENT VALUE ORD. ANNUITY 1 PER PERIOD $a_{\overline{n}\vert} = \frac{1 - V^n}{i}$	6 INSTALMENT TO AMORTIZE I $1/a_{\overline{n}\vert} = \frac{i}{1 - V^n}$	n HALF YEARS
1	1.055000	1.000000	1.000000	.947867	.947867	1.055000	1
YEARS							
1	1.113025	2.055000	.486618	.898452	1.846320	.541618	2
2	1.238825	4.342266	.230294	.807217	3.505150	.285294	4
3	1.378843	6.888051	.145179	.725246	4.995530	.200179	6
4	1.534687	9.721573	.102864	.651599	6.334566	.157864	8
5	1.708144	12.875354	.077668	.585431	7.537626	.132668	10
6	1.901207	16.385591	.061029	.525982	8.618518	.116029	12
7	2.116091	20.292572	.049279	.472569	9.589648	.104279	14
8	2.355263	24.641140	.040583	.424581	10.462162	.095583	16
9	2.621466	29.481205	.033920	.381466	11.246074	.088920	18
10	2.917757	34.868318	.028679	.342729	11.950382	.083679	20
11	3.247537	40.864310	.024471	.307926	12.583170	.079471	22
12	3.614590	47.537998	.021036	.276657	13.151699	.076036	24
13	4.023129	54.965980	.018193	.248563	13.662495	.073193	26
14	4.477843	63.233510	.015814	.223322	14.121422	.070814	28
15	4.983951	72.435478	.013805	.200644	14.533745	.068805	30
16	5.547262	82.677498	.012095	.180269	14.904198	.067095	32
17	6.174242	94.077122	.010630	.161963	15.237033	.065630	34
18	6.872085	106.765189	.009366	.145516	15.536068	.064366	36
19	7.648803	120.887324	.008272	.130739	15.804738	.063272	38
20	8.513309	136.605614	.007320	.117463	16.046125	.062320	40
21	9.475526	154.100464	.006489	.105535	16.262999	.061489	42
22	10.546497	173.572669	.005761	.094818	16.457851	.060761	44
23	11.738515	195.245720	.005122	.085190	16.632915	.060122	46
24	13.065260	219.368367	.004559	.076539	16.790203	.059559	48
25	14.541961	246.217477	.004061	.068767	16.931518	.059061	50
26	16.185566	276.101207	.003622	.061783	17.058483	.058622	52
27	18.014940	309.362546	.003232	.055509	17.172555	.058232	54
28	20.051079	346.383248	.002887	.049873	17.275043	.057887	56
29	22.317352	387.588214	.002580	.044808	17.367124	.057580	58
30	24.839770	433.450372	.002307	.040258	17.449854	.057307	60
31	27.647286	484.496101	.002064	.036170	17.524183	.057064	62
32	30.772120	541.311272	.001847	.032497	17.590965	.056847	64
33	34.250139	604.547979	.001654	.029197	17.650964	.056654	66
34	38.121261	674.932014	.001482	.026232	17.704871	.056482	68
35	42.429916	753.271205	.001328	.023568	17.753304	.056328	70
36	47.225558	840.464683	.001190	.021175	17.796819	.056190	72
37	52.563226	937.513204	.001067	.019025	17.835914	.056067	74
38	58.504185	1045.530634	.000956	.017093	17.871040	.055956	76
39	65.116620	1165.756734	.000858	.015357	17.902599	.055858	78
40	72.476426	1299.571389	.000769	.013798	17.930953	.055769	80
41	80.668074	1448.510445	.000690	.012396	17.956428	.055690	82
42	89.785584	1614.283338	.000619	.011138	17.979316	.055619	84
43	99.933599	1798.792713	.000556	.010007	17.999879	.055556	86
44	111.228594	2004.156260	.000499	.008990	18.018355	.055499	88
45	123.800206	2232.731022	.000448	.008078	18.034954	.055448	90
46	137.792725	2487.140445	.000402	.007257	18.049868	.055402	92
47	153.366747	2770.304495	.000361	.006520	18.063267	.055361	94
48	170.701024	3085.473160	.000324	.005858	18.075306	.055324	96
49	189.994507	3436.263764	.000291	.005263	18.086122	.055291	98
50	211.468636	3826.702476	.000261	.004729	18.095839	.055261	100
51	235.369879	4261.270524	.000235	.004249	18.104570	.055235	102
52	261.972559	4744.955625	.000211	.003817	18.112415	.055211	104
53	291.582008	5283.309235	.000189	.003430	18.119462	.055189	106
54	324.538064	5882.510262	.000170	.003081	18.125795	.055170	108
55	361.218979	6549.435984	.000153	.002768	18.131484	.055153	110
56	402.045754	7291.740985	.000137	.002487	18.136595	.055137	112
57	447.486976	8117.945011	.000123	.002235	18.141187	.055123	114
58	498.064191	9037.530746	.000111	.002008	18.145313	.055111	116
59	554.357896	10061.052660	.000099	.001804	18.149020	.055099	118
60	617.014197	11200.258130	.000089	.001621	18.152351	.055089	120

11% ANNUAL COMPOUND INTEREST TABLE 11%

EFFECTIVE RATE = 11% BASE = 1.11

YEARS	1 AMOUNT OF I AT COMPOUND INTEREST $S^n = (1+i)^n$	2 ACCUMULATION OF I PER PERIOD $s_{\overline{n}\rvert} = \frac{S^n - 1}{i}$	3 SINKING FUND FACTOR $1/s_{\overline{n}\rvert} = \frac{i}{S^n - 1}$	4 PRES. VALUE REVERSION OF I $V^n = \frac{1}{S^n}$	5 PRESENT VALUE ORD. ANNUITY 1 PER PERIOD $a_{\overline{n}\rvert} = \frac{1 - V^n}{i}$	6 INSTALMENT TO AMORTIZE I $1/a_{\overline{n}\rvert} = \frac{i}{1 - V^n}$	n YEARS
1	1.110000	1.000000	1.000000	.900901	.900901	1.110000	1
2	1.232100	2.110000	.473934	.811622	1.712523	.583934	2
3	1.367631	3.342100	.299213	.731191	2.443715	.409213	3
4	1.518070	4.709731	.212326	.658731	3.102446	.322326	4
5	1.685058	6.227801	.160570	.593451	3.695897	.270570	5
6	1.870415	7.912860	.126377	.534641	4.230538	.236377	6
7	2.076160	9.783274	.102215	.481658	4.712196	.212215	7
8	2.304538	11.859434	.084321	.433926	5.146123	.194321	8
9	2.558037	14.163972	.070602	.390925	5.537048	.180602	9
10	2.839421	16.722009	.059801	.352184	5.889232	.169801	10
11	3.151757	19.561430	.051121	.317283	6.206515	.161121	11
12	3.498451	22.713187	.044027	.285841	6.492356	.154027	12
13	3.883280	26.211638	.038151	.257514	6.749870	.148151	13
14	4.310441	30.094918	.033228	.231995	6.981865	.143228	14
15	4.784589	34.405359	.029065	.209004	7.190870	.139065	15
16	5.310894	39.189948	.025517	.188292	7.379162	.135517	16
17	5.895093	44.500843	.022471	.169633	7.548794	.132471	17
18	6.543553	50.395936	.019843	.152822	7.701617	.129843	18
19	7.263344	56.939488	.017563	.137678	7.839294	.127563	19
20	8.062312	64.202832	.015576	.124034	7.963328	.125576	20
21	8.949166	72.265144	.013838	.111742	8.075070	.123838	21
22	9.933574	81.214310	.012313	.100669	8.175739	.122313	22
23	11.026267	91.147884	.010971	.090693	8.266432	.120971	23
24	12.239157	102.174151	.009787	.081705	8.348137	.119787	24
25	13.585464	114.413307	.008740	.073608	8.421745	.118740	25
26	15.079865	127.998771	.007813	.066314	8.488058	.117813	26
27	16.738650	143.078636	.006989	.059742	8.547800	.116989	27
28	18.579901	159.817286	.006257	.053822	8.601622	.116257	28
29	20.623691	178.397187	.005605	.048488	8.650110	.115605	29
30	22.892297	199.020878	.005025	.043683	8.693793	.115025	30
31	25.410449	221.913175	.004506	.039354	8.733146	.114506	31
32	28.205599	247.323624	.004043	.035454	8.768600	.114043	32
33	31.308214	275.529222	.003629	.031940	8.800541	.113629	33
34	34.752118	306.837437	.003259	.028775	8.829316	.113259	34
35	38.574851	341.589555	.002927	.025924	8.855240	.112927	35
36	42.818085	380.164406	.002630	.023355	8.878594	.112630	36
37	47.528074	422.982490	.002364	.021040	8.899635	.112364	37
38	52.756162	470.510564	.002125	.018955	8.918590	.112125	38
39	58.559340	523.266726	.001911	.017077	8.935666	.111911	39
40	65.000867	581.826066	.001719	.015384	8.951051	.111719	40
41	72.150963	646.826934	.001546	.013860	8.964911	.111546	41
42	80.087569	718.977896	.001391	.012486	8.977397	.111391	42
43	88.897201	799.065465	.001251	.011249	8.988646	.111251	43
44	98.675893	887.962666	.001126	.010134	8.998780	.111126	44
45	109.530242	986.638559	.001014	.009130	9.007910	.111014	45
46	121.578568	1096.168801	.000912	.008225	9.016135	.110912	46
47	134.952211	1217.747369	.000821	.007410	9.023545	.110821	47
48	149.796954	1352.699580	.000739	.006676	9.030221	.110739	48
49	166.274619	1502.496534	.000666	.006014	9.036235	.110666	49
50	184.564827	1668.771153	.000599	.005418	9.041653	.110599	50
51	204.866958	1853.335979	.000540	.004881	9.046534	.110540	51
52	227.402323	2058.202936	.000486	.004397	9.050932	.110486	52
53	252.416579	2285.605259	.000438	.003962	9.054894	.110438	53
54	280.182402	2538.021837	.000394	.003569	9.058463	.110394	54
55	311.002466	2818.204239	.000355	.003215	9.061678	.110355	55
56	345.212738	3129.206705	.000320	.002897	9.064575	.110320	56
57	383.186139	3474.419443	.000288	.002610	9.067185	.110288	57
58	425.336614	3857.605581	.000259	.002351	9.069536	.110259	58
59	472.123641	4282.942195	.000233	.002118	9.071654	.110233	59
60	524.057242	4755.065835	.000210	.001908	9.073562	.110210	60

11¼% MONTHLY COMPOUND INTEREST TABLE 11¼%

EFFECTIVE RATE = 15/16% BASE = 1.009375

MONTHS	1 AMOUNT OF I AT COMPOUND INTEREST $S^n = (1+i)^n$	2 ACCUMULATION OF I PER PERIOD $S_{\overline{n}\vert} = \frac{S^n - 1}{i}$	3 SINKING FUND FACTOR $1/S_{\overline{n}\vert} = \frac{i}{S^n - 1}$	4 PRES. VALUE REVERSION OF I $V^n = \frac{1}{S^n}$	5 PRESENT VALUE ORD. ANNUITY 1 PER PERIOD $a_{\overline{n}\vert} = \frac{1 - V^n}{i}$	6 INSTALMENT TO AMORTIZE I $1/a_{\overline{n}\vert} = \frac{i}{1 - V^n}$	n MONTHS
1	1.009375	1.000000	1.000000	.990712	.990712	1.009375	1
2	1.018837	2.009375	.497667	.981510	1.972222	.507042	2
3	1.028389	3.028212	.330227	.972394	2.944616	.339602	3
4	11038030	4.056602	.246511	.963362	3.907979	.255886	4
5	1.047762	5.094633	.196284	.954415	4.862394	.205659	5
6	1.057584	6.142395	.162802	.945550	5.807944	.172177	6
7	1.067499	7.199980	.138889	.936768	6.744713	.148264	7
8	1.077507	8.267479	.120955	.928067	7.672780	.130330	8
9	1.087609	9.344987	.107009	.919447	8.592228	.116384	9
10	1.097805	10.432596	.095853	.910908	9.503136	.105228	10
11	1.108097	11.530402	.086727	.902447	10.405584	.096102	11
YEARS							
1	1.118485	12.638499	.079123	.894065	11.299650	.088498	12
2	1.251010	26.774484	.037348	.799353	21.402281	.046723	24
3	1.399237	42.585384	.023482	.714674	30.434697	.032857	36
4	1.565028	60.269653	.016592	.638966	38.510271	.025967	48
5	1.750461	80.049259	.012492	.571277	45.730366	.021867	60
6	1.957866	102.172471	.009787	.510759	52.185605	.019162	72
7	2.189846	126.916972	.007879	.456652	57.957014	.017254	84
8	2.449312	154.593349	.006468	.408277	63.117033	.015843	96
9	2.739521	185.548986	.005389	.365027	67.730430	.014764	108
10	3.064116	220.172432	.004541	.326358	71.855110	.013916	120
11	3.427171	258.898269	.003862	.291785	75.542845	.013237	132
12	3.833242	302.212573	.003308	.260875	78.839922	.012683	144
13	4.287428	350.659013	.002851	.233240	81.787727	.012226	156
14	4.795428	404.845675	.002470	.208531	84.423258	.011845	168
15	5.363619	465.452695	.002148	.186441	86.779597	.011523	180
16	5.999132	533.240794	.001875	.166690	88.886317	.011250	192
17	6.709945	609.060829	.001641	.149032	90.769865	.011016	204
18	7.504979	693.864472	.001441	.133244	92.453880	.010816	216
19	8.394213	788.716154	.001267	.119129	93.959501	.010642	228
20	9.388810	894.806427	.001117	.106509	95.305625	.010492	240
21	10.501252	1013.466906	.000986	.095226	96.509148	.010361	252
22	11.745502	1146.186982	.000872	.085138	971585176	.010247	264
23	13.137179	1294.632521	.000772	.076119	98.547216	.010147	276
24	14.693750	1460.666770	.000684	.068056	99.407345	.010059	288
25	16.434753	1646.373741	.000607	.060846	100.176355	.009982	300
26	18.382041	1854.084377	.000539	.054400	100.863901	.009914	312
27	20.560054	2086.405802	.000479	.048638	101.478613	.009854	324
28	22.996131	2346.254048	.000426	.043485	102.028205	.009801	336
29	25.720849	2636.890658	.000379	.038878	102.519577	.009754	348
30	28.768408	2961.963619	.000337	.034760	102.958895	.009712	360
31	32.177060	3325.553155	.000300	.031078	103.351675	.009675	372
32	35.989590	3732.222937	.000267	.027785	103.702847	.009642	384
33	40.253850	4187.077370	.000238	.024842	104.016816	.009613	396
34	45.023365	4695.825661	.000212	.022210	104.297526	.009587	408
35	50.358001	5264.853466	.000189	.019857	104.548499	.009564	420
36	56.324716	5901.303063	.000169	.017754	104.772885	.009544	432
37	62.998403	6613.162988	.000151	.015873	104.973501	.009526	444
38	70.462827	7409.368302	.000134	.014191	105.152865	.009509	456
39	78.811682	8299.912750	.000120	.012688	105.313229	.009495	468
40	88.149758	9295.974191	.000107	.011344	105.456605	.009482	480
41	98.594264	10410.054910	.000096	.010142	105.584791	.009471	492
42	110.276298	11656.138520	.000085	.009068	105.699399	.009460	504
43	123.342489	13049.865530	.000076	.008107	105.801866	.009451	516
44	137.956839	14608.729580	.000068	.007248	105.893478	.009443	528
45	154.302785	16352.297090	.000061	.006480	105.975385	.009436	540
46	172.585495	18302.452840	.000054	.005794	106.048615	.009429	552
47	193.034449	20483.674620	.000048	.005180	106.114087	.009423	564
48	215.906317	22923.340500	.000043	.004631	106.172624	.009418	576
49	241.488179	25652.072490	.000038	.004140	106.224961	.009413	588
50	270.101132	28704.120840	.000034	.003702	106.271752	.009409	600

11¼ % QUARTERLY COMPOUND INTEREST TABLE 11¼ %

EFFECTIVE RATE = 2-13/16% BASE = 1.028125

QUARTERS	1 AMOUNT OF I AT COMPOUND INTEREST $S^n = (1+i)^n$	2 ACCUMULATION OF I PER PERIOD $S_{\overline{n}\rvert} = \frac{S^n - 1}{i}$	3 SINKING FUND FACTOR $1/S_{\overline{n}\rvert} = \frac{i}{S^n - 1}$	4 PRES. VALUE REVERSION OF I $V^n = \frac{1}{S^n}$	5 PRESENT VALUE ORD. ANNUITY 1 PER PERIOD $a_{\overline{n}\rvert} = \frac{1 - V^n}{i}$	6 INSTALMENT TO AMORTIZE I $1/a_{\overline{n}\rvert} = \frac{i}{1 - V^n}$	n QUARTERS
1	1.028125	1.000000	1.000000	.972644	.972644	1.028125	1
2	1.057041	2.028125	.493066	.946037	1.918681	.521191	2
3	1.086770	3.085166	.324132	.920158	2.838839	.352257	3
YEARS							
1	1.117336	4.171936	.239697	.894986	3.733825	.267822	4
2	1.248439	8.833390	.113207	.801000	7.075547	.141332	8
3	1.394926	14.041798	.071216	.716884	10.066342	.099341	12
4	1.558600	19.861339	.050349	.641601	12.743062	.078474	16
5	1.741480	26.363719	.037931	.574224	15.138690	.066056	20
6	1.945817	33.629061	.029736	.513923	17.282743	.057861	24
7	2.174131	41.746887	.023954	.459954	19.201641	.052079	28
8	2.429234	50.817224	.019678	.411652	20.919028	.047803	32
9	2.714270	60.951836	.016406	.368423	22.456066	.044531	36
10	3.032751	72.275599	.013836	.329734	23.831694	.041961	40
11	3.388601	84.928044	.011775	.295107	25.062862	.039900	44
12	3.786205	99.065072	.010094	.264117	26.164740	.038219	48
13	4.230462	114.860879	.008706	.236381	27.150905	.036831	52
14	4.726847	132.510098	.007547	.211558	28.033510	.035672	56
15	5.281474	152.230201	.006569	.189341	28.823429	.034694	60
16	5.901180	174.264175	.005738	.169458	29.530395	.033863	64
17	6.593599	198.883522	.005028	.151662	30.163120	.033153	68
18	7.367264	226.391598	.004417	.135736	30.729401	.032542	72
19	8.231707	257.127353	.003889	.121481	31.236214	.032014	76
20	9.197580	291.469509	.003431	.108724	31.689804	.031556	80
21	10.276785	329.841227	.003032	.097307	32.095762	.031157	84
22	11.482618	372.715317	.002683	.087088	32.459088	.030808	88
23	12.829939	420.620069	.002377	.077943	32.784260	.030502	92
24	14.335349	474.145760	.002109	.069758	33.075284	.030234	96
25	16.017398	533.951925	.001873	.062432	33.335747	.029998	100
26	17.896811	600.775488	.001665	.055876	33.568858	.029790	104
27	19.996746	675.439843	.001481	.050008	33.777488	.029606	108
28	22.343078	758.864991	.001318	.044757	33.964210	.029443	112
29	24.964719	852.078889	.001174	.040057	34.131323	.029299	116
30	27.893972	956.230106	.001046	.035850	34.280887	.029171	120
31	31.166931	1072.601979	.000932	.032085	34.414745	.029057	124
32	34.823925	1202.628429	.000832	.028716	34.534546	.028957	128
33	38.910014	1347.911625	.000742	.025700	34.641766	.028867	132
34	43.475549	1510.241727	.000662	.023001	34.737727	.028787	136
35	48.576783	1691.618946	.000591	.020586	34.823610	.028716	140
36	54.276574	1894.278191	.000528	.018424	34.900475	.028653	144
37	60.645154	2120.716601	.000472	.016489	34.969267	.028597	148
38	67.760997	2373.724322	.000421	.014758	35.030835	.028546	152
39	75.711781	2656.418885	.000376	.013208	35.085938	.028501	156
40	84.595477	2972.283614	.000336	.011821	35.135255	.028461	160
41	94.521547	3325.210554	.000301	.010580	35.179392	.028426	164
42	105.612300	3719.548427	.000269	.009469	35.218894	.028394	168
43	118.004394	4160.156213	.000240	.008474	35.254249	.028365	172
44	131.850523	4652.463026	.000215	.007584	35.285890	.028340	176
45	147.321297	5202.535008	.000192	.006788	35.314209	.028317	180
46	164.607346	5817.150076	.000172	.006075	35.339553	.028297	184
47	183.921666	6503.881440	.000154	.005437	35.362237	.028279	188
48	205.502245	7271.190916	.000138	.004866	35.382538	.028263	192
49	229.614996	8128.533191	.000123	.004355	35.400707	.028248	196
50	256.557034	9086.472331	.000110	.003898	35.416968	.028235	200
51	286.660336	10156.811940	.000098	.003488	35.431522	.028223	204
52	320.295830	11352.740600	.000088	.003122	35.444547	.028213	208
53	357.877968	12688.994410	.000079	.002794	35.456204	.028204	212
54	399.869833	14182.038500	.000071	.002501	35.466638	.028196	216
55	446.788843	15850.269970	.000063	.002238	35.475975	.028188	220
56	499.213128	17714.244570	.000056	.002003	35.484332	.028181	224
57	557.788655	19796.929940	.000051	.001793	35.491812	.028176	228
58	623.237182	22123.988680	.000045	.001605	35.498506	.028170	232
59	696.365158	24724.094510	.000040	.001436	35.504497	.028165	236
60	778.073658	27629.285600	.000036	.001285	35.509859	.028161	240

11¼ % SEMI-ANNUAL COMPOUND INTEREST TABLE 11¼ %

EFFECTIVE RATE = 5-5/8% BASE = 1.05625

	1 AMOUNT OF I AT COMPOUND INTEREST $S^n = (1+i)^n$	2 ACCUMULATION OF I PER PERIOD $S_{\overline{n}|} = \frac{S^n - 1}{i}$	3 SINKING FUND FACTOR $1/S_{\overline{n}|} = \frac{i}{S^n - 1}$	4 PRES. VALUE REVERSION OF I $V^n = \frac{1}{S^n}$	5 PRESENT VALUE ORD. ANNUITY 1 PER PERIOD $a_{\overline{n}|} = \frac{1 - V^n}{i}$	6 INSTALMENT TO AMORTIZE I $1/a_{\overline{n}|} = \frac{i}{1 - V^n}$	n
HALF YEARS							HALF YEARS
1	1.056250	1.000000	1.000000	.946746	.946746	1.056250	1
YEARS							
1	1.115664	2.056250	.486322	.896327	1.843073	.542572	2
2	1.244706	4.350334	.229867	.803402	3.495069	.286117	4
3	1.388674	6.909762	.144723	.720111	4.975798	.200973	6
4	1.549294	9.765223	.102404	.645455	6.303015	.158654	8
5	1.728491	12.950958	.077214	.578539	7.492637	.133464	10
6	1.928416	16.505168	.060587	.518560	8.558926	.116837	12
7	2.151464	20.470473	.048851	.464800	9.514671	.105101	14
8	2.400311	24.894421	.040170	.416613	10.371331	.096420	16
9	2.677941	29.830061	.033523	.373421	11.139178	.089773	18
10	2.987682	35.336577	.028299	.334708	11.827421	.084549	20
11	3.333250	41.479999	.024108	.300008	12.444311	.080358	22
12	3.718787	48.333995	.020689	.268905	12.997247	.076939	24
13	4.148917	55.980751	.017863	.241027	13.492858	.074113	26
14	4.628798	64.511962	.015501	.216039	13.937088	.071751	28
15	5.164183	74.029928	.013508	.193641	14.335263	.069758	30
16	5.761494	84.648780	.011814	.173566	14.692158	.068064	32
17	6.427892	96.495851	.010363	.155572	15.012053	.066613	34
18	7.171368	109.713204	.009115	.139443	15.298784	.065365	36
19	8.000837	124.459329	.008035	.124987	15.555788	.064285	38
20	8.926247	140.911050	.007097	.112029	15.786148	.063347	40
21	9.958693	159.265645	.006279	.100415	15.992626	.062529	42
22	11.110555	179.743206	.005563	.090005	16.177698	.061813	44
23	12.395647	202.589286	.004936	.080673	16.343583	.061186	46
24	13.829378	228.077835	.004384	.072310	16.492270	.060634	48
25	15.428940	256.514494	.003898	.064813	16.625542	.060148	50
26	17.213514	288.240253	.003469	.058094	16.744998	.059719	52
27	19.204499	323.635542	.003090	.052071	16.852069	.059340	54
28	21.425770	363.124793	.002754	.046673	16.948040	.059004	56
29	23.903961	407.181532	.002456	.041834	17.034061	.058706	58
30	26.668790	456.334052	.002191	.037497	17.111164	.058441	60
31	29.753411	511.171753	.001956	.033610	17.180274	.058206	62
32	33.194811	572.352204	.001747	.030125	17.242219	.057997	64
33	37.034258	640.609035	.001561	.027002	17.297742	.057811	66
34	41.317791	716.760729	.001395	.024203	17.347508	.057645	68
35	46.096775	801.720437	.001247	.021693	17.392116	.057497	70
36	51.428515	896.506929	.001115	.019444	17.432098	.057365	72
37	57.376946	1002.256813	.000998	.017429	17.467936	.057248	74
38	64.013396	1120.238158	.000893	.015622	17.500058	.057143	76
39	71.417446	1251.865704	.000799	.014002	17.528850	.057049	78
40	79.677878	1398.717827	.000715	.012551	17.554657	.056965	80
41	88.893745	1562.555463	.000640	.011249	17.577789	.056890	82
42	99.175556	1745.343226	.000573	.010083	17.598522	.056823	84
43	110.646604	1949.272964	.000513	.009038	17.617106	.056763	86
44	123.444440	2176.790043	.000459	.008101	17.633763	.056709	88
45	137.722525	2430.622672	.000411	.007261	17.648694	.056661	90
46	153.652072	2713.814615	.000368	.006508	17.662076	.056618	92
47	171.424095	3029.761689	.000330	.005833	17.674071	.056580	94
48	191.251702	3382.252484	.000296	.005229	17.684823	.056546	96
49	213.372651	3775.513796	.000265	.004687	17.694460	.056515	98
50	238.052199	4214.261308	.000237	.004201	17.703098	.056487	100
51	265.586283	4703.756142	.000213	.003765	17.710840	.056463	102
52	296.305071	5249.867936	.000190	.003375	17.717780	.056440	104
53	330.576920	5859.145239	.000171	.003025	17.724000	.056421	106
54	368.812789	6538.894030	.000153	.002711	17.729575	.056403	108
55	411.471175	7297.265328	.000137	.002430	17.734572	.056387	110
56	459.063602	8143.352932	.000123	.002178	17.739052	.056373	112
57	512.160764	9087.302464	.000110	.001953	17.743066	.056360	114
58	571.399358	10140.433030	.000099	.001750	17.746665	.056349	116
59	637.489729	11315.372970	.000088	.001569	17.749891	.056338	118
60	711.224381	12626.211220	.000079	.001406	17.752782	.056329	120

11¼ % ANNUAL COMPOUND INTEREST TABLE 11¼ %

EFFECTIVE RATE = 11¼% BASE = 1.1125

YEARS	1 AMOUNT OF I AT COMPOUND INTEREST $S^n = (1+i)^n$	2 ACCUMULATION OF I PER PERIOD $s_{\overline{n}\rceil} = \frac{S^n - 1}{i}$	3 SINKING FUND FACTOR $1/s_{\overline{n}\rceil} = \frac{i}{S^n - 1}$	4 PRES. VALUE REVERSION OF I $V^n = \frac{1}{S^n}$	5 PRESENT VALUE ORD. ANNUITY 1 PER PERIOD $a_{\overline{n}\rceil} = \frac{1 - V^n}{i}$	6 INSTALMENT TO AMORTIZE I $1/a_{\overline{n}\rceil} = \frac{i}{1 - V^n}$	n YEARS
1	1.112500	1.000000	1.000000	.898876	.898876	1.112500	1
2	1.237656	2.112500	.473373	.807979	1.706855	.585873	2
3	1.376893	3.350156	.298494	.726273	2.433128	.410994	3
4	1.531793	4.727049	.211548	.652830	3.085958	.324048	4
5	1.704120	6.258842	.159774	.586813	3.672771	.272274	5
6	1.895833	7.962962	.125581	.527473	4.200244	.238081	6
7	2.109114	9.858795	.101432	.474133	4.674376	.213932	7
8	2.346390	11.967909	.083557	.426187	5.100563	.196057	8
9	2.610359	14.314299	.069860	.383089	5.483652	.182360	9
10	2.904024	16.924658	.059085	.344350	5.828002	.171585	10
11	3.230727	19.828681	.050432	.309528	6.137530	.162932	11
12	3.594183	23.059408	.043366	.278227	6.415757	.155866	12
13	3.998529	26.653592	.037516	.250092	6.665849	.150018	13
14	4.448364	30.652121	.032624	.224802	6.890651	.145124	14
15	4.948804	35.100484	.028490	.202069	7.092720	.140990	15
16	5.505545	40.049289	.024969	.181635	7.274355	.137469	16
17	6.124919	45.554834	.021952	.163267	7.437622	.134452	17
18	6.813972	51.679752	.019350	.146757	7.584380	.131850	18
19	7.580544	58.493725	.017096	.131917	7.716296	.129596	19
20	8.433355	66.074269	.015134	.118577	7.834873	.127634	20
21	9.382108	74.507624	.013421	.106586	7.941459	.125921	21
22	10.437595	83.889732	.011920	.095808	8.037267	.124420	22
23	11.611824	94.327326	.010601	.086119	8.123386	.123101	23
24	12.918154	105.939151	.009439	.077410	8.200796	.121939	24
25	14.371447	118.857305	.008413	.069582	8.270379	.120913	25
26	15.988235	133.228752	.007506	.062546	8.332925	.120006	26
27	17.786911	149.216987	.006702	.056221	8.389146	.119202	27
28	19.787938	167.003898	.005988	.050536	8.439681	.118488	28
29	22.014082	186.791836	.005354	.045425	8.485107	.117854	29
30	24.490666	208.805918	.004789	.040832	8.525939	.117289	30
31	27.245866	233.296584	.004286	.036703	8.562642	.116786	31
32	30.311026	260.542449	.003838	.032991	8.595633	.116338	32
33	33.721016	290.853475	.003438	.029655	8.625288	.115938	33
34	37.514630	324.574491	.003081	.026656	8.651944	.115581	34
35	41.735026	362.089121	.002762	.023961	8.675905	.115262	35
36	46.430217	403.824147	.002476	.021538	8.697443	.114976	36
37	51.653616	450.254364	.002221	.019360	8.716802	.114721	37
38	57.464648	501.907979	.001992	.017402	8.734204	.114492	38
39	63.929421	559.372627	.001788	.015642	8.749847	.114288	39
40	71.121480	623.302048	.001604	.014060	8.763907	.114104	40
41	79.122647	694.423528	.001440	.012639	8.776546	.113940	41
42	88.023945	773.546175	.001293	.011361	8.787906	.113793	42
43	97.926638	861.570120	.001161	.010212	8.798118	.113661	43
44	108.943385	959.496758	.001042	.009179	8.807297	.113542	44
45	121.199516	1068.440144	.000936	.008251	8.815548	.113436	45
46	134.834462	1189.639660	.000841	.007417	8.822964	.113341	46
47	150.003339	1324.474123	.000755	.006667	8.829631	.113255	47
48	166.878714	1474.477461	.000678	.005992	8.835623	.113178	48
49	185.652570	1641.356176	.000609	.005386	8.841010	.113109	49
50	206.538484	1827.008746	.000547	.004842	8.845851	.113047	50
51	229.774063	2033.547230	.000492	.004352	8.850204	.112992	51
52	255.623646	2263.321293	.000442	.003912	8.854116	.112942	52
53	284.381306	2518.944939	.000397	.003516	8.857632	.112897	53
54	316.374203	2803.326244	.000357	.003161	8.860793	.112857	54
55	351.966300	3119.700447	.000321	.002841	8.863634	.112821	55
56	391.562509	3471.666748	.000288	.002554	8.866188	.112788	56
57	435.613291	3863.229257	.000259	.002296	8.868483	.112759	57
58	484.619787	4298.842548	.000233	.002063	8.870547	.112733	58
59	539.139513	4783.462335	.000209	.001855	8.872402	.112709	59
60	599.792708	5322.601848	.000188	.001667	8.874069	.112688	60

11½ % MONTHLY COMPOUND INTEREST TABLE 11½ %

EFFECTIVE RATE = 23/24% BASE = 1.00958333

MONTHS	1 AMOUNT OF I AT COMPOUND INTEREST $S^n = (1+i)^n$	2 ACCUMULATION OF I PER PERIOD $S_{\overline{n\|}} = \frac{S^n - 1}{i}$	3 SINKING FUND FACTOR $1/S_{\overline{n\|}} = \frac{i}{S^n - 1}$	4 PRES. VALUE REVERSION OF I $V^n = \frac{1}{S^n}$	5 PRESENT VALUE ORD. ANNUITY 1 PER PERIOD $a_{\overline{n\|}} = \frac{1 - V^n}{i}$	6 INSTALMENT TO AMORTIZE I $1/a_{\overline{n\|}} = \frac{i}{1 - V^n}$	n MONTHS
1	1.009583	1.000000	1.000000	.990507	.990507	1.009583	1
2	1.019258	2.009583	.497615	.981105	1.971613	.507198	2
3	1.029026	3.028841	.330159	.971792	2.943405	.339742	3
4	1.038887	4.057868	.246434	.962567	3.905973	.256018	4
5	1.048843	5.096756	.196203	.953430	4.859403	.205786	5
6	1.058895	6.145600	.162718	.944380	5.803784	.172301	6
7	1.069043	7.204495	.138802	.935415	6.739200	.148385	7
8	1.079288	8.273538	.120867	.926536	7.665736	.130450	8
9	1.089631	9.352826	.106919	.917741	8.583478	.116502	9
10	1.100073	10.442457	.095762	.909030	9.492508	.105346	10
11	1.110615	11.542531	.086636	.900401	10.392910	.096219	11
YEARS							
1	1.121259	12.653147	.079031	.891854	11.284764	.088615	12
2	1.257222	26.840606	.037256	.795404	21.349130	.046840	24
3	1.409672	42.748427	.023392	.709384	30.325079	.032976	36
4	1.580608	60.585220	.016505	.632667	38.330317	.026089	48
5	1.772271	80.584891	.012409	.564247	45.469824	.021992	60
6	1.987176	103.009708	.009707	.503226	51.837225	.019291	72
7	2.228140	128.153743	.007803	.448804	57.516018	.017386	84
8	2.498322	156.346727	.006396	.400268	62.580675	.015979	96
9	2.801267	187.958374	.005320	.356981	67.097611	.014903	108
10	3.140947	223.403227	.004476	.318375	71.126060	.014059	120
11	3.521816	263.146099	.003800	.283944	74.718850	.013383	132
12	3.948869	307.708166	.003249	.253237	77.923095	.012833	144
13	4.427707	357.673798	.002795	.225850	80.780815	.012379	156
14	4.964608	413.698230	.002417	.201425	83.329484	.012000	168
15	5.566613	476.516147	.002098	.179642	85.602527	.011681	180
16	6.241616	546.951321	.001828	.160214	87.629749	.011411	192
17	6.998471	625.927419	.001597	.142888	89.437737	.011180	204
18	7.847100	714.480104	.001399	.127435	91.050198	.010982	216
19	8.798635	813.770629	.001228	.113653	92.488279	.010812	228
20	9.865551	925.101055	.001080	.101362	93.770837	.010664	240
21	11.061841	1049.931334	.000952	.090400	94.914693	.010535	252
22	12.403193	1189.898450	.000840	.080624	95.934845	.010423	264
23	13.907196	1346.837883	.000742	.071905	96.844672	.010325	276
24	15.593573	1522.807687	.000656	.064128	97.656106	.010240	288
25	17.484439	1720.115470	.000581	.057193	98.379787	.010164	300
26	19.604591	1941.348663	.000515	.051008	99.025204	.010098	312
27	21.981830	2189.408445	.000456	.045492	99.600822	.010040	324
28	24.647332	2467.547787	.000405	.040572	100.114191	.009988	336
29	27.636051	2779.414122	.000359	.036184	100.572039	.009943	348
30	30.987180	3129.097156	.000319	.032271	100.980375	.009902	360
31	34.744665	3521.182519	.000283	.028781	101.344550	.009867	372
32	38.957780	3960.811894	.000252	.025668	101.669341	.009835	384
33	43.681774	4453.750427	.000224	.022892	101.959007	.009807	396
34	48.978597	5006.462360	.000199	.020417	102.217348	.009783	408
35	54.917709	5626.195765	.000177	.018209	102.447750	.009761	420
36	61.576993	6321.077626	.000158	.016239	102.653235	.009741	432
37	69.043778	7100.220401	.000140	.014483	102.836498	.009724	444
38	77.415980	7973.841498	.000125	.012917	102.999941	.009708	456
39	86.803390	8953.397310	.000111	.011520	103.145710	.009695	468
40	97.329111	10051.733390	.000099	.010274	103.275713	.009682	480
41	109.131174	11283.252980	.000088	.009163	103.391657	.009671	492
42	122.364346	12664.105790	.000078	.008172	103.495063	.009662	504
43	137.202165	14212.399890	.000070	.007288	103.587285	.009653	516
44	153.839207	15948.439100	.000062	.006500	103.669534	.009646	528
45	172.493646	17894.989250	.000055	.005797	103.742888	.009639	540
46	193.410110	20077.576770	.000049	.005170	103.808310	.009633	552
47	216.862889	22524.823370	.000044	.004611	103.866656	.009627	564
48	243.159538	25268.821450	.000039	.004112	103.918692	.009622	576
49	272.644900	28345.554910	.000035	.003667	103.965102	.009618	588
50	305.705637	31795.370980	.000031	.003271	104.006492	.009614	600

11½ % QUARTERLY COMPOUND INTEREST TABLE 11½ %

EFFECTIVE RATE = 2-7/8% BASE = 1.02875

	1 AMOUNT OF I AT COMPOUND INTEREST $S^n = (1+i)^n$	2 ACCUMULATION OF I PER PERIOD $s_{\overline{n}\vert} = \frac{S^n - 1}{i}$	3 SINKING FUND FACTOR $1/s_{\overline{n}\vert} = \frac{i}{S^n - 1}$	4 PRES. VALUE REVERSION OF I $V^n = \frac{1}{S^n}$	5 PRESENT VALUE ORD. ANNUITY 1 PER PERIOD $a_{\overline{n}\vert} = \frac{1 - V^n}{i}$	6 INSTALMENT TO AMORTIZE I $1/a_{\overline{n}\vert} = \frac{i}{1 - V^n}$	n QUARTERS
QUARTERS							
1	1.028750	1.000000	1.000000	.972053	.972053	1.028750	1
2	1.058327	2.028750	.492914	.944888	1.916941	.521664	2
3	1.088753	3.087077	.323931	.918482	2.835423	.352681	3
YEARS							
1	1.120055	4.175830	.239473	.892813	3.728236	.268223	4
2	1.254523	8.852990	.112956	.797115	7.056855	.141706	8
3	1.405135	14.091666	.070964	.711675	10.028689	.099714	12
4	1.573829	19.959273	.050102	.635393	12.681982	.078852	16
5	1.762775	26.531316	.037691	.567287	15.050878	.066441	20
6	1.974406	33.892366	.029505	.506482	17.165859	.058255	24
7	2.211443	42.137148	.023732	.452193	19.054141	.052482	28
8	2.476938	51.371758	.019466	.403724	20.740025	.048216	32
9	2.774307	61.715030	.016204	.360450	22.245205	.044954	36
10	3.107377	73.300065	.013643	.321815	23.589049	.042393	40
11	3.480433	86.275943	.011591	.287321	24.788851	.040341	44
12	3.898277	100.809641	.009920	.256524	25.860050	.038670	48
13	4.366285	117.088183	.008541	.229028	26.816430	.037291	52
14	4.890480	135.321049	.007390	.204479	27.670299	.036140	56
15	5.477607	155.742862	.006421	.182561	28.432645	.035171	60
16	6.135222	178.616419	.005599	.162993	29.113277	.034349	64
17	6.871787	204.236064	.004896	.145523	29.720954	.033646	68
18	7.696780	232.931477	.004293	.129924	30.263497	.033043	72
19	8.620818	265.071922	.003773	.115998	30.747886	.032523	76
20	9.655791	301.070992	.003321	.103565	31.180355	.032071	80
21	10.815018	341.391934	.002929	.092464	31.566469	.031679	84
22	12.113416	386.553611	.002587	.082553	31.911197	.031337	88
23	13.567694	437.137178	.002288	.073704	32.218974	.031038	92
24	15.196565	493.793561	.002025	.065804	32.493762	.030775	96
25	17.020990	557.251833	.001795	.058751	32.739096	.030545	100
26	19.064447	628.328595	.001592	.052454	32.958134	.030342	104
27	21.353231	707.938485	.001413	.046831	33.153693	.030163	108
28	23.916796	797.105950	.001255	.041812	33.328291	.030005	112
29	26.788130	896.978425	.001115	.037330	33.484175	.029865	116
30	30.004182	1008.841101	.000991	.033329	33.623350	.029741	120
31	33.606337	1134.133463	.000882	.029756	33.747607	.029632	124
32	37.640950	1274.467814	.000785	.026567	33.858546	.029535	128
33	42.159938	1431.650021	.000698	.023719	33.957593	.029448	132
34	47.221454	1607.702756	.000622	.021177	34.046024	.029372	136
35	52.890631	1804.891522	.000554	.018907	34.124976	.029304	140
36	59.240422	2025.753807	.000494	.016880	34.195466	.029244	144
37	66.352538	2273.131739	.000440	.015071	34.258400	.029190	148
38	74.318499	2550.208657	.000392	.013456	34.314588	.029142	152
39	83.240815	2860.550075	.000350	.012013	34.364753	.029100	156
40	93.234300	3208.149567	.000312	.010726	34.409542	.029062	160
41	104.427555	3597.480157	.000278	.009576	34.449530	.029028	164
42	116.964616	4033.551871	.000248	.008550	34.485232	.028998	168
43	131.006817	4521.976226	.000221	.007633	34.517106	.028971	172
44	146.734855	5069.038421	.000197	.006815	34.545565	.028947	176
45	164.351124	5681.778230	.000176	.006085	34.570973	.028926	180
46	184.082317	6368.080588	.000157	.005432	34.593657	.028907	184
47	206.182340	7136.777050	.000140	.004850	34.613910	.028890	188
48	230.935584	7997.759454	.000125	.004330	34.631993	.028875	192
49	258.660582	8962.107196	.000112	.003866	34.648137	.028862	196
50	289.714107	10042.229820	.000100	.003452	34.662550	.028850	200
51	324.495767	11252.026680	.000089	.003082	34.675419	.028839	204
52	363.453143	12607.065840	.000079	.002751	34.686908	.028829	208
53	407.087551	14124.784390	.000071	.002456	34.697166	.028821	212
54	455.960493	15824.712800	.000063	.002193	34.706324	.028813	216
55	510.700881	17728.726310	.000056	.001958	34.714501	.028806	220
56	572.013133	19861.326380	.000050	.001748	34.721801	.028800	224
57	640.686235	22249.955990	.000045	.001561	34.728319	.028795	228
58	717.603893	24925.352800	.000040	.001394	34.734138	.028790	232
59	803.755909	27921.944670	.000036	.001244	34.739334	.028786	236
60	900.250916	31278.292720	.000032	.001111	34.743972	.028782	240

11½ % SEMI-ANNUAL COMPOUND INTEREST TABLE 11½ %

EFFECTIVE RATE = 5¾% BASE = 1.0575

HALF YEARS	1 AMOUNT OF I AT COMPOUND INTEREST $S^n = (1+i)^n$	2 ACCUMULATION OF I PER PERIOD $S_{\overline{n}\rvert} = \frac{S^n - 1}{i}$	3 SINKING FUND FACTOR $1/S_{\overline{n}\rvert} = \frac{i}{S^n - 1}$	4 PRES. VALUE REVERSION OF I $V^n = \frac{1}{S^n}$	5 PRESENT VALUE ORD. ANNUITY 1 PER PERIOD $a_{\overline{n}\rvert} = \frac{1 - V^n}{i}$	6 INSTALMENT TO AMORTIZE I $1/a_{\overline{n}\rvert} = \frac{i}{1 - V^n}$	n HALF YEARS
1	1.057500	1.000000	1.000000	.945626	.945626	1.057500	1
YEARS							
1	1.118306	2.057500	.486027	.894209	1.839836	.543527	2
2	1.250609	4.358415	.229441	.799611	3.485035	.286941	4
3	1.398564	6.931543	.144268	.715019	4.956187	.201768	6
4	1.564023	9.809088	.101946	.639377	6.271705	.159446	8
5	1.749056	13.027064	.076763	.571737	7.448054	.134263	10
6	1.955980	16.625747	.060148	.511253	8.499956	.117648	12
7	2.187385	20.650177	.048426	.457167	9.440576	.105926	14
8	2.446167	25.150722	.039760	.408803	10.281688	.097260	16
9	2.735563	30.183710	.033130	.365555	11.033819	.090630	18
10	3.059198	35.812131	.027923	.326883	11.706381	.085423	20
11	3.421120	42.106430	.023749	.292302	12.307792	.081249	22
12	3.825860	49.145384	.020348	.261379	12.845580	.077848	24
13	4.278483	57.017090	.017539	.233728	13.326474	.075039	26
14	4.784654	65.820068	.015193	.209002	13.756495	.072693	28
15	5.350708	75.664494	.013216	.186891	14.141024	.070716	30
16	5.983731	86.673576	.011538	.167120	14.484873	.069038	32
17	6.691643	98.985102	.010103	.149440	14.792346	.067603	34
18	7.483307	112.753158	.008869	.133631	15.067291	.066369	36
19	8.368629	128.150061	.007803	.119494	15.313150	.065303	38
20	9.358690	145.368514	.006879	.106853	15.532999	.064379	40
21	10.465881	164.624018	.006074	.095549	15.729590	.063574	42
22	11.704060	186.157569	.005372	.085440	15.905384	.062872	44
23	13.088724	210.238672	.004756	.076402	16.062580	.062256	46
24	14.637201	237.168721	.004216	.068319	16.203147	.061716	48
25	16.368874	267.284763	.003741	.061092	16.328842	.061241	50
26	18.305414	300.963721	.003323	.054629	16.441241	.060823	52
27	20.471059	338.627111	.002953	.048849	16.541749	.060453	54
28	22.892913	380.746314	.002626	.043682	16.631624	.060126	56
29	25.601288	427.848483	.002337	.039061	16.711991	.059837	58
30	28.630080	480.523133	.002081	.034928	16.783856	.059581	60
31	32.017198	539.429522	.001854	.031233	16.848118	.059354	62
32	35.805032	605.304906	.001652	.027929	16.905582	.059152	64
33	40.040991	678.973760	.001473	.024974	16.956967	.058973	66
34	44.778091	761.358100	.001313	.022332	17.002916	.058813	68
35	50.075619	853.489021	.001172	.019970	17.044004	.058672	70
36	55.999877	956.519607	.001045	.017857	17.080745	.058545	72
37	62.625013	1071.739355	.000933	.015968	17.113599	.058433	74
38	70.033943	1200.590319	.000833	.014279	17.142978	.058333	76
39	78.319397	1344.685157	.000744	.012768	17.169248	.058244	78
40	87.585071	1505.827315	.000664	.011417	17.192740	.058164	80
41	97.946932	1686.033598	.000593	.010210	17.213746	.058093	82
42	109.534666	1887.559410	.000530	.009130	17.232530	.058030	84
43	122.493302	2112.926986	.000473	.008164	17.249327	.057973	86
44	136.985025	2364.956955	.000423	.007300	17.264347	.057923	88
45	153.191210	2646.803643	.000378	.006528	17.277778	.057878	90
46	171.314687	2961.994557	.000338	.005837	17.289788	.057838	92
47	191.582285	3314.474525	.000302	.005220	17.300527	.057802	94
48	214.247667	3708.655077	.000270	.004667	17.310131	.057770	96
49	239.594505	4149.469652	.000241	.004174	17.318718	.057741	98
50	267.940032	4642.435346	.000215	.003732	17.326397	.057715	100
51	299.639013	5193.721963	.000193	.003337	17.333263	.057693	102
52	335.088181	5810.229233	.000172	.002984	17.339404	.057672	104
53	374.731207	6499.673165	.000154	.002669	17.344894	.057654	106
54	419.064251	7270.682624	.000138	.002386	17.349804	.057638	108
55	468.642171	8132.907320	.000123	.002134	17.354194	.057623	110
56	524.085469	9097.138586	.000110	.001908	17.358120	.057610	112
57	586.088055	10175.444440	.000098	.001706	17.361631	.057598	114
58	655.425935	11381.320610	.000088	.001526	17.364770	.057588	116
59	732.966920	12729.859470	.000079	.001364	17.367577	.057579	118
60	819.681488	14237.938910	.000070	.001220	17.370087	.057570	120

11½ % ANNUAL COMPOUND INTEREST TABLE 11½ %

EFFECTIVE RATE = 11½% BASE = 1.1150

YEARS	1 AMOUNT OF I AT COMPOUND INTEREST $S^n = (1+i)^n$	2 ACCUMULATION OF I PER PERIOD $S_{\overline{n}\vert} = \frac{S^n - 1}{i}$	3 SINKING FUND FACTOR $1/S_{\overline{n}\vert} = \frac{i}{S^n - 1}$	4 PRES. VALUE REVERSION OF I $V^n = \frac{1}{S^n}$	5 PRESENT VALUE ORD. ANNUITY 1 PER PERIOD $a_{\overline{n}\vert} = \frac{1 - V^n}{i}$	6 INSTALMENT TO AMORTIZE I $1/a_{\overline{n}\vert} = \frac{i}{1 - V^n}$	n YEARS
1	1.115000	1.000000	1.000000	.896861	.896861	1.115000	1
2	1.243225	2.115000	.472813	.804360	1.701221	.587813	2
3	1.386196	3.358225	.297776	.721399	2.422619	.412776	3
4	1.545608	4.744421	.210774	.646994	3.069614	.325774	4
5	1.723353	6.290029	.158982	.580264	3.649878	.273982	5
6	1.921539	8.013383	.124791	.520416	4.170294	.239791	6
7	2.142516	9.934922	.100655	.466741	4.637035	.215655	7
8	2.388905	12.077438	.082799	.418602	5.055637	.197799	8
9	2.663629	14.466343	.069126	.375428	5.431064	.184126	9
10	2.969947	17.129972	.058377	.336706	5.767771	.173377	10
11	3.311491	20.099919	.049751	.301979	6.069750	.164751	11
12	3.692312	23.411410	.042714	.270833	6.340583	.157714	12
13	4.116928	27.103722	.036895	.242900	6.583482	.151895	13
14	4.590375	31.220650	.032030	.217847	6.801329	.147030	14
15	5.118268	35.811025	.027924	.195379	6.996708	.142924	15
16	5.706869	40.929293	.024432	.175227	7.171935	.139432	16
17	6.363159	46.636161	.021443	.157155	7.329090	.136443	17
18	7.094922	52.999320	.018868	.140946	7.470036	.133868	18
19	7.910838	60.094242	.016641	.126409	7.596445	.131641	19
20	8.820584	68.005080	.014705	.113371	7.709816	.129705	20
21	9.834951	76.825664	.013016	.101678	7.811494	.128016	21
22	10.965971	86.660615	.011539	.091191	7.902685	.126539	22
23	12.227057	97.626586	.010243	.081786	7.984471	.125243	23
24	13.633169	109.853643	.009103	.073351	8.057822	.124103	24
25	15.200983	123.486812	.008098	.065785	8.123607	.123098	25
26	16.949097	138.687796	.007210	.059000	8.182607	.122210	26
27	18.898243	155.636892	.006425	.052915	8.235522	.121425	27
28	21.071541	174.535135	.005730	.047457	8.282979	.120730	28
29	23.494768	195.606675	.005112	.042563	8.325542	.120112	29
30	26.196666	219.101443	.004564	.038173	8.363715	.119564	30
31	29.209283	245.298109	.004077	.034236	8.397951	.119077	31
32	32.568350	274.507391	.003643	.030705	8.428655	.118643	32
33	36.313710	307.075741	.003257	.027538	8.456193	.118257	33
34	40.489787	343.389452	.002912	.024698	8.480891	.117912	34
35	45.146112	383.879239	.002605	.022150	8.503041	.117605	35
36	50.337915	429.025351	.002331	.019866	8.522907	.117331	36
37	56.126776	479.363266	.002086	.017817	8.540723	.117086	37
38	62.581355	535.490042	.001867	.015979	8.556703	.116867	38
39	69.778211	598.071397	.001672	.014331	8.571034	.116672	39
40	77.802705	667.849608	.001497	.012853	8.583887	.116497	40
41	86.750016	745.652312	.001341	.011527	8.595414	.116341	41
42	96.726268	832.402328	.001201	.010338	8.605753	.116201	42
43	107.849789	929.128597	.001076	.009272	8.615025	.116076	43
44	120.252514	1036.978385	.000964	.008316	8.623341	.115964	44
45	134.081553	1157.230899	.000864	.007458	8.630799	.115864	45
46	149.500932	1291.312452	.000774	.006689	8.637488	.115774	46
47	166.693539	1440.813384	.000694	.005999	8.643487	.115694	47
48	185.863296	1607.506923	.000622	.005380	8.648867	.115622	48
49	207.237575	1793.370220	.000558	.004825	8.653692	.115558	49
50	231.069897	2000.607796	.000500	.004328	8.658020	.115500	50
51	257.642935	2231.677692	.000448	.003881	8.661901	.115448	51
52	287.271872	2489.320627	.000402	.003481	8.665382	.115402	52
53	320.308137	2776.592499	.000360	.003122	8.668504	.115360	53
54	357.143573	3096.900637	.000323	.002800	8.671304	.115323	54
55	398.215084	3454.044210	.000290	.002511	8.673816	.115290	55
56	444.009819	3852.259294	.000260	.002252	8.676068	.115260	56
57	495.070948	4296.269113	.000233	.002020	8.678088	.115233	57
58	552.004107	4791.340061	.000209	.001812	8.679899	.115209	58
59	615.484579	5343.344168	.000187	.001625	8.681524	.115187	59
60	686.265306	5958.828747	.000168	.001457	8.682981	.115168	60

11 ¾ % MONTHLY COMPOUND INTEREST TABLE 11 ¾ %

EFFECTIVE RATE = 47/48% BASE = 1.00979167

MONTHS	1 AMOUNT OF I AT COMPOUND INTEREST $S^n = (1+i)^n$	2 ACCUMULATION OF I PER PERIOD $S_{\overline{n}\rvert} = \frac{S^n - 1}{i}$	3 SINKING FUND FACTOR $1/S_{\overline{n}\rvert} = \frac{i}{S^n - 1}$	4 PRES. VALUE REVERSION OF I $V^n = \frac{1}{S^n}$	5 PRESENT VALUE ORD. ANNUITY 1 PER PERIOD $a_{\overline{n}\rvert} = \frac{1 - V^n}{i}$	6 INSTALMENT TO AMORTIZE I $1/a_{\overline{n}\rvert} = \frac{i}{1 - V^n}$	n MONTHS
1	1.009791	1.000000	1.000000	.990303	.990303	1.009791	1
2	1.019679	2.009791	.497564	.980700	1.971003	.507355	2
3	1.029663	3.029470	.330090	.971191	2.942194	.339882	3
4	1.039745	4.059134	.246357	.961773	3.903968	.256149	4
5	1.049926	5.098880	.196121	.952447	4.856416	.205913	5
6	1.060207	6.148806	.162633	.943211	5.799628	.172424	6
7	1.070588	7.209013	.138715	.934065	6.733694	.148506	7
8	1.081071	8.279601	.120778	.925008	7.658702	.130570	8
9	1.091656	9.360673	.106829	.916038	8.574741	.116621	9
10	1.102345	10.452329	.095672	.907156	9.481897	.105464	10
11	1.113139	11.554675	.086545	.898359	10.380257	.096336	11
YEARS							
1	1.124039	12.667814	.078940	.889648	11.269906	.088731	12
2	1.263463	26.906933	.037165	.791475	21.296166	.046956	24
3	1.420182	42.912257	.023303	.704134	30.216015	.033095	36
4	1.596340	60.902867	.016419	.626432	38.151549	.026211	48
5	1.794349	81.125014	.012326	.557305	45.211388	.022118	60
6	2.016918	103.855496	.009628	.495805	51.492165	.019420	72
7	2.267094	129.405446	.007727	.441093	57.079851	.017519	84
8	2.548303	158.124585	.006324	.392417	62.050930	.016115	96
9	2.864392	190.406019	.005251	.349114	66.473443	.015043	108
10	3.219688	226.691611	.004411	.310589	70.407928	.014202	120
11	3.619055	267.478031	.003738	.276315	73.908237	.013530	132
12	4.067959	313.323560	.003191	.245823	77.022283	.012983	144
13	4.572545	364.855722	.002740	.218696	79.792691	.012532	156
14	5.139719	422.779885	.002365	.194563	82.257381	.012156	168
15	5.777245	487.888903	.002049	.173092	84.450090	.011841	180
16	6.493849	561.073980	.001782	.153991	86.400829	.011573	192
17	7.299340	643.336863	.001554	.136998	88.136304	.011346	204
18	8.204743	735.803553	.001359	.121880	89.680266	.011150	216
19	9.222451	839.739721	.001190	.108431	91.053850	.010982	228
20	10.366395	956.568030	.001045	.096465	92.275858	.010837	240
21	11.652232	1087.887608	.000919	.085820	93.363016	.010710	252
22	13.097564	1235.495938	.000809	.076350	94.330204	.010601	264
23	14.722173	1401.413461	.000713	.067924	95.190663	.010505	276
24	16.548297	1587.911230	.000629	.060429	95.956169	.010421	288
25	18.600932	1797.542001	.000556	.053760	96.637200	.010347	300
26	20.908173	2033.175167	.000491	.047828	97.243078	.010283	312
27	23.501602	2298.036042	.000435	.042550	97.782097	.010226	324
28	26.416718	2595.750000	.000385	.037854	98.261635	.010176	336
29	29.693422	2930.392104	.000341	.033677	98.688255	.010132	348
30	33.376565	3306.542889	.000302	.029961	99.067797	.010094	360
31	37.516562	3729.351051	.000268	.026654	99.405456	.010059	372
32	42.170080	4204.603923	.000237	.023713	99.705855	.010029	384
33	47.400815	4738.806697	.000211	.021096	99.973104	.010002	396
34	53.280366	5339.271454	.000187	.018768	100.210861	.009978	408
35	59.889211	6014.217279	.000166	.016697	100.422382	.009957	420
36	67.317810	6772.882724	.000147	.014854	100.610562	.009939	432
37	75.667845	7625.652288	.000131	.013215	100.777975	.009922	444
38	85.053611	8584.198556	.000116	.011757	100.926914	.009908	456
39	95.603577	9661.641955	.000103	.010459	101.059418	.009895	468
40	107.462152	10872.730390	.000091	.009305	101.177300	.009883	480
41	120.791652	12234.041050	.000081	.008278	101.282173	.009873	492
42	135.774530	13764.207350	.000072	.007365	101.375473	.009864	504
43	152.615870	15484.173990	.000064	.006552	101.458477	.009856	516
44	171.546193	17417.483580	.000057	.005829	101.532322	.009849	528
45	192.824616	19590.599030	.000051	.005186	101.598019	.009842	540
46	216.742392	22033.265590	.000045	.004613	101.656465	.009837	552
47	243.626907	24778.918120	.000040	004104	101.708462	.009832	564
48	273.846150	27865.138700	.000035	.003651	101.754721	.009827	576
49	307.813759	31334.171040	.000031	.003248	101.795875	.009823	588
50	345.994676	35233.498790	.000028	.002890	101.832487	.009820	600

11¾% QUARTERLY COMPOUND INTEREST TABLE 11¾%

EFFECTIVE RATE = 2-15/16% BASE = 1.029375

QUARTERS	1 AMOUNT OF I AT COMPOUND INTEREST $S^n = (1+i)^n$	2 ACCUMULATION OF I PER PERIOD $S_{\overline{n}\vert} = \frac{S^n - 1}{i}$	3 SINKING FUND FACTOR $1/S_{\overline{n}\vert} = \frac{i}{S^n - 1}$	4 PRES. VALUE REVERSION OF I $V^n = \frac{1}{S^n}$	5 PRESENT VALUE ORD. ANNUITY 1 PER PERIOD $a_{\overline{n}\vert} = \frac{1-V^n}{i}$	6 INSTALMENT TO AMORTIZE I $1/a_{\overline{n}\vert} = \frac{i}{1-V^n}$	n QUARTERS
1	1.029375	1.000000	1.000000	.971463	.971463	1.029375	1
2	1.059613	2.029375	.492763	.943741	1.915204	.522138	2
3	1.090739	3.088988	.323731	.916810	2.832014	.353106	3
YEARS							
1	1.122779	4.179727	.239250	.890647	3.722661	.268625	4
2	1.260634	8.872639	.112706	.793252	7.038237	.142081	8
3	1.415414	14.141743	.070713	.706507	9.991244	.100088	12
4	1.589197	20.057786	.049856	.629248	12.621330	.079231	16
5	1.784318	26.700198	.037453	.560438	14.963809	.066828	20
6	2.003396	34.158161	.029276	.499152	17.050130	.058651	24
7	2.249372	42.531809	.023512	.444569	18.908305	.052887	28
8	2.525549	51.933569	.019255	.395954	20.563282	.048630	32
9	2.835634	62.489673	.016003	.352655	22.037283	.045378	36
10	3.183792	74.341849	.013451	.314091	23.350097	.042826	40
11	3.574696	87.649229	.011409	.279744	24.519351	.040784	44
12	4.013595	102.590483	.009747	.249153	25.560743	.039122	48
13	4.506383	119.366215	.008378	.221907	26.488256	.037753	52
14	5.059674	138.201664	.007236	.197641	27.314342	.036611	56
15	5.680898	159.349719	.006276	.176029	28.050093	.035651	60
16	6.378396	183.094321	.005462	.156779	28.705388	.034837	64
17	7.161532	209.754273	.004767	.139635	29.289024	.034142	68
18	8.040821	239.687521	.004172	.124365	29.808837	.033547	72
19	9.028069	273.295956	.003659	.110766	30.271807	.033034	76
20	10.136530	311.030818	.003215	.098653	30.684150	.032590	80
21	11.381088	353.398746	.002830	.087865	31.051402	.032205	84
22	12.778452	400.968587	.002494	.078257	31.378494	.031869	88
23	14.347384	454.379027	.002201	.069699	31.669817	.031576	92
24	16.108948	514.347174	.001944	.062077	31.929283	.031319	96
25	18.086796	581.678178	.001719	.055289	32.160376	.031094	100
26	20.307484	657.276048	.001521	.049243	32.366198	.030896	104
27	22.800826	742.155785	.001347	.043858	32.549513	.030722	108
28	25.600300	837.457012	.001194	.039062	32.712782	.030569	112
29	28.743491	944.459274	.001059	.034790	32.858196	.030434	116
30	32.272602	1064.599217	.000939	.030986	32.987709	.030314	120
31	36.235015	1199.489880	.000834	.027598	33.103060	.030209	124
32	40.683931	1350.942348	.000740	.024580	33.205796	.030115	128
33	45.679083	1520.990071	.000657	.021892	33.297298	.030032	132
34	51.287537	1711.916165	.000584	.019498	33.378794	.029959	136
35	57.584594	1926.284065	.000519	.017366	33.451379	.029894	140
36	64.654801	2166.971944	.000461	.015467	33.516025	.029836	144
37	72.593084	2437.211355	.000410	.013775	33.573603	.029785	148
38	81.506024	2740.630620	.000365	.012269	33.624884	.029740	152
39	91.513292	3081.303544	.000325	.010927	33.670557	.029700	156
40	102.749246	3463.804112	.000289	.009732	33.711236	.029664	160
41	115.364745	3893.267901	.000257	.008668	33.747467	.029632	164
42	129.529168	4375.461028	.000229	.007720	33.779736	.029604	168
43	145.432691	4916.857576	.000203	.006876	33.808475	.029578	172
44	163.288841	5524.726509	.000181	.006124	33.834073	.029556	176
45	183.337360	6207.229273	.000161	.005454	33.856871	.029536	180
46	205.847425	6973.529369	.000143	.004858	33.877176	.029518	184
47	231.121265	7833.915391	.000128	.004327	33.895260	.029503	188
48	259.498213	8799.939159	.000114	.003854	33.911367	.029489	192
49	291.359268	9884.570822	.000101	.003432	33.925713	.029476	196
50	327.132207	11102.372990	.000090	.003057	33.938490	.029465	200
51	367.297328	12469.696280	.000080	.002723	33.949869	.029455	204
52	412.393903	14004.898810	.000071	.002425	33.960005	.029446	208
53	463.027411	15728.592700	.000064	.002160	33.969032	.029439	212
54	519.877674	17663.920830	.000057	.001924	33.977071	.029432	216
55	583.707984	19836.867540	.000050	.001713	33.984232	.029425	220
56	655.375346	22276.607510	.000045	.001526	33.990610	.029420	224
57	735.841988	25015.897470	.000040	.001359	33.996290	.029415	228
58	826.188284	28091.516030	.000036	.001210	34.001349	.029411	232
59	927.627250	31544.757440	.000032	.001078	34.005855	.029407	236
60	1041.520839	35421.986010	.000028	.000960	34.009868	.029403	240

11¾% SEMI-ANNUAL COMPOUND INTEREST TABLE 11¾%

EFFECTIVE RATE = 5-7/8%   BASE = 1.05875

	1 AMOUNT OF I AT COMPOUND INTEREST $S^n = (1+i)^n$	2 ACCUMULATION OF I PER PERIOD $S_{\overline{n}\vert} = \frac{S^n - 1}{i}$	3 SINKING FUND FACTOR $1/S_{\overline{n}\vert} = \frac{i}{S^n - 1}$	4 PRES. VALUE REVERSION OF I $V^n = \frac{1}{S^n}$	5 PRESENT VALUE ORD. ANNUITY 1 PER PERIOD $a_{\overline{n}\vert} = \frac{1 - V^n}{i}$	6 INSTALMENT TO AMORTIZE I $1/a_{\overline{n}\vert} = \frac{i}{1 - V^n}$	n HALF YEARS
HALF YEARS 1	1.058750	1.000000	1.000000	.944510	.944510	1.058750	1
YEARS							
1	1.120952	2.058750	.485732	.892099	1.836609	.544482	2
2	1.256532	4.366509	.229016	.795841	3.475047	.287766	4
3	1.408512	6.953395	.143815	.709969	4.936696	.202565	6
4	1.578874	9.853169	.101490	.633363	6.240632	.160240	8
5	1.769841	13.103675	.076314	.565023	7.403872	.135064	10
6	1.983906	16.747335	.059711	.504056	8.441597	.118461	12
7	2.223862	20.831702	.048004	.449668	9.367352	.106754	14
8	2.492842	25.410079	.039354	.401149	10.193216	.098104	16
9	2.794355	30.542217	.032742	.357864	10.929969	.091492	18
10	3.132337	36.295096	.027552	.319250	11.587226	.086302	20
11	3.511198	42.743795	.023395	.284803	12.173565	.082145	22
12	3.935883	49.972474	.020011	.254073	12.696637	.078761	24
13	4.411934	58.075472	.017219	.226658	13.163269	.075969	26
14	4.945564	67.158542	.014890	.202201	13.579551	.073640	28
15	5.543738	77.340222	.012930	.180384	13.950916	.071680	30
16	6.214262	88.753393	.011267	.160920	14.282210	.070017	32
17	6.965887	101.547004	.009848	.143557	14.577758	.068598	34
18	7.808421	115.888023	.008629	.128067	14.841415	.067379	36
19	8.752862	131.963611	.007578	.114248	15.076624	.066328	38
20	9.811534	149.983566	.006667	.101921	15.286454	.065417	40
21	10.998255	170.183062	.005876	.090924	15.473642	.064626	42
22	12.328511	192.825720	.005186	.081113	15.640633	.063936	44
23	13.819664	218.207042	.004583	.072361	15.789606	.063333	46
24	15.491174	246.658274	.004054	.064553	15.922504	.062804	48
25	17.364855	278.550728	.003590	.057588	16.041062	.062340	50
26	19.465162	314.300624	.003182	.051374	16.146828	.061932	52
27	21.819503	354.374525	.002822	.045831	16.241182	.061572	54
28	24.458606	399.295428	.002504	.040885	16.325355	.061254	56
29	27.416913	449.649584	.002224	.036474	16.400445	.060974	58
30	30.733032	506.094154	.001976	.032538	16.467434	.060726	60
31	34.450240	569.365783	.001756	.029027	16.527194	.060506	62
32	38.617050	640.290213	.001562	.025895	16.580506	.060312	64
33	43.287843	719.793065	.001389	.023101	16.628065	.060139	66
34	48.523575	808.911911	.001236	.020609	16.670493	.059986	68
35	54.392577	908.809821	.001100	.018385	16.708343	.059850	70
36	60.971444	1020.790539	.000980	.016401	16.742109	.059730	72
37	68.346036	1146.315499	.000872	.014631	16.772231	.059622	74
38	76.612595	1287.022900	.000777	.013053	16.799103	.059527	76
39	85.879009	1444.749081	.000692	.011644	16.823076	.059442	78
40	96.266209	1621.552490	.000617	.010388	16.844462	.059367	80
41	107.909757	1819.740548	.000550	.009267	16.863540	.059300	82
42	120.961611	2041.899760	.000490	.008267	16.880560	.059240	84
43	135.592107	2290.929476	.000437	.007375	16.895744	.059187	86
44	151.992184	2570.079726	.000389	.006579	16.909289	.059139	88
45	170.375876	2882.993634	.000347	.005869	16.921372	.059097	90
46	190.983104	3233.754969	.000309	.005236	16.932152	.059059	92
47	214.082809	3626.941435	.000276	.004671	16.941769	.059026	94
48	239.976460	4067.684419	.000246	.004167	16.950348	.058996	96
49	269.001987	4561.735956	.000219	.003717	16.958001	.058969	98
50	301.538198	5115.543797	.000195	.003316	16.964828	.058945	100
51	338.009714	5736.335563	.000174	.002958	16.970919	.058924	102
52	378.892517	6432.213062	.000155	.002639	16.976353	.058905	104
53	424.720159	7212.258032	.000139	.002354	16.981200	.058889	106
54	476.090726	8086.650660	.000124	.002100	16.985524	.058874	108
55	533.674644	9066.802444	.000110	.001874	16.989382	.058860	110
56	598.223426	10165.505120	.000098	.001672	16.992824	.058848	112
57	670.579484	11397.097590	.000088	.001491	16.995894	.058838	114
58	751.687120	12777.653110	.000078	.001330	16.998633	.058828	116
59	842.604852	14325.188970	.000070	.001187	17.001076	.058820	118
60	944.519225	16059.901710	.000062	.001059	17.003255	.058812	120

11¾% ANNUAL COMPOUND INTEREST TABLE 11¾%

EFFECTIVE RATE = 11¾% BASE = 1.1175

YEARS	1 AMOUNT OF I AT COMPOUND INTEREST $S^n = (1+i)^n$	2 ACCUMULATION OF I PER PERIOD $S_{\overline{n}\vert} = \frac{S^n - 1}{i}$	3 SINKING FUND FACTOR $1/S_{\overline{n}\vert} = \frac{i}{S^n - 1}$	4 PRES. VALUE REVERSION OF I $V^n = \frac{1}{S^n}$	5 PRESENT VALUE ORD. ANNUITY 1 PER PERIOD $a_{\overline{n}\vert} = \frac{1 - V^n}{i}$	6 INSTALMENT TO AMORTIZE I $1/a_{\overline{n}\vert} = \frac{i}{1 - V^n}$	n YEARS
1	1.117500	1.000000	1.000000	.894855	.894855	1.117500	1
2	1.248806	2.117500	.472255	.800765	1.695619	.589755	2
3	1.395541	3.366306	.297062	.716568	2.412187	.414562	3
4	1.559517	4.761847	.210003	.641224	3.053411	.327503	4
5	1.742760	6.321364	.158194	.573802	3.627214	.275694	5
6	1.947535	8.064125	.124006	.513470	4.140684	.241506	6
7	2.176370	10.011659	.099884	.459481	4.600164	.217384	7
8	2.432093	12.188029	.082048	.411168	5.011333	.199548	8
9	2.717864	14.620123	.068399	.367936	5.379269	.185899	9
10	3.037213	17.337987	.057677	.329249	5.708518	.175177	10
11	3.394086	20.375200	.049079	.294630	6.003148	.166579	11
12	3.792891	23.769287	.042071	.263651	6.266799	.159571	12
13	4.238556	27.562178	.036282	.235929	6.502728	.153782	13
14	4.736586	31.800734	.031446	.211123	6.713851	.148946	14
15	5.293135	36.537320	.027369	.188924	6.902775	.144869	15
16	5.915078	41.830455	.023906	.169059	7.071834	.141406	16
17	6.610100	47.745533	.020944	.151284	7.223118	.138444	17
18	7.386787	54.355633	.018397	.135377	7.358495	.135897	18
19	8.254734	61.742420	.016196	.121143	7.479637	.133696	19
20	9.224666	69.997155	.014286	.108405	7.588042	.131786	20
21	10.308564	79.221821	.012623	.097007	7.685049	.130123	21
22	11.519820	89.530384	.011169	.086807	7.771856	.128669	22
23	12.873399	101.050205	.009896	.077680	7.849536	.127396	23
24	14.386023	113.923604	.008778	.069512	7.919048	.126278	24
25	16.076381	128.309627	.007794	.062203	7.981251	.125294	25
26	17.965356	144.386008	.006926	.055663	8.036913	.124426	26
27	20.076285	162.351364	.006159	.049810	8.086723	.123659	27
28	22.435249	182.427650	.005482	.044573	8.131296	.122982	28
29	25.071391	204.862898	.004881	.039886	8.171182	.122381	29
30	28.517279	229.934289	.004349	.035692	8.206874	.121849	30
31	31.309309	257.951568	.003877	.031939	8.238814	.121377	31
32	34.988153	289.260877	.003457	.028581	8.267395	.120957	32
33	39.099261	324.249030	.003084	.025576	8.292971	.120584	33
34	43.693424	363.348291	.002752	.022887	8.315858	.120252	34
35	48.827402	407.041715	.002457	.020480	8.336338	.119957	35
36	54.564621	455.869117	.002194	.018327	8.354665	.119694	36
37	60.975964	510.433738	.001959	.016400	8.371065	.119459	37
38	68.140640	571.409703	.001750	.014676	8.385740	.119250	38
39	76.147165	639.550343	.001564	.013132	8.398873	.119064	39
40	85.094457	715.697508	.001397	.011752	8.410624	.118897	40
41	95.093056	800.791965	.001249	.010516	8.421140	.118749	41
42	106.266490	895.885020	.001116	.009410	8.430551	.118616	42
43	118.752803	1002.151511	.000998	.008421	8.438971	.118498	43
44	132.706257	1120.904313	.000892	.007535	8.446507	.118392	44
45	148.299242	1253.610570	.000798	.006743	8.453250	.118298	45
46	165.724403	1401.909812	.000713	.006034	8.459284	.118213	46
47	185.197020	1567.634214	.000638	.005400	8.464684	.118138	47
48	206.957670	1752.831235	.000571	.004832	8.469516	.118071	48
49	231.275196	1959.788905	.000510	.004324	8.473840	.118010	49
50	258.450032	2191.064101	.000456	.003869	8.477709	.117956	50
51	288.817911	2449.514134	.000408	.003462	8.481171	.117908	51
52	322.754015	2738.332044	.000365	.003098	8.484269	.117865	52
53	360.677612	3061.086060	.000327	.002773	8.487042	.117827	53
54	403.057231	3421.763672	.000292	.002481	8.489523	.117792	54
55	450.416456	3824.820903	.000261	.002220	8.491743	.117761	55
56	503.340390	4275.237359	.000234	.001987	8.493730	.117734	56
57	562.482886	4778.577749	.000209	.001778	8.495508	.117709	57
58	628.574625	5341.060634	.000187	.001591	8.497099	.117687	58
59	702.432143	5969.635259	.000168	.001424	8.498522	.117668	59
60	784.967920	6672.067402	.000150	.001274	8.499796	.117650	60

12% MONTHLY COMPOUND INTEREST TABLE 12%

EFFECTIVE RATE = 1% BASE = 1.0100

	1 AMOUNT OF 1 AT COMPOUND INTEREST $S^n = (1+i)^n$	2 ACCUMULATION OF 1 PER PERIOD $S_{\overline{n}\rceil} = \frac{S^n - 1}{i}$	3 SINKING FUND FACTOR $1/S_{\overline{n}\rceil} = \frac{i}{S^n - 1}$	4 PRES. VALUE REVERSION OF 1 $V^n = \frac{1}{S^n}$	5 PRESENT VALUE ORD. ANNUITY 1 PER PERIOD $a_{\overline{n}\rceil} = \frac{1 - V^n}{i}$	6 INSTALMENT TO AMORTIZE 1 $1/a_{\overline{n}\rceil} = \frac{i}{1 - V^n}$	n MONTHS
MONTHS							
1	1.010000	1.000000	1.000000	.990099	.990099	1.010000	1
2	1.020099	2.009999	.497512	.980296	1.970395	.507512	2
3	1.030300	3.030099	.330022	.970590	2.940985	.340022	3
4	1.040604	4.060400	.246281	.960980	3.901965	.256281	4
5	1.051010	5.101005	.196039	.951465	4.853431	.206039	5
6	1.061520	6.152015	.162548	.942045	5.795476	.172548	6
7	1.072135	7.213535	.138628	.932718	6.728194	.148628	7
8	1.082856	8.285670	.120690	.923483	7.651677	.130690	8
9	1.093685	9.368527	.106740	.914339	8.566017	.116740	9
10	1.104622	10.462212	.095582	.905286	9.471304	.105582	10
11	1.115668	11.566834	.086454	.896323	10.367628	.096454	11
YEARS							
1	1.126825	12.682503	.078848	.887449	11.255077	.088848	12
2	1.269734	26.973464	.037073	.787566	21.243387	.047073	24
3	1.430768	43.076878	.023214	.698924	30.107505	.033214	36
4	1.612226	61.222607	.016333	.620260	37.973959	.026333	48
5	1.816696	81.669669	.012244	.550449	44.955038	.022244	60
6	2.047099	104.709931	.009550	.488496	51.150391	.019550	72
7	2.306722	130.672274	.007652	.433515	56.648452	.017652	84
8	2.599272	159.927292	.006252	.384722	61.527703	.016252	96
9	2.928925	192.892579	.005184	.341422	65.857789	.015184	108
10	3.300386	230.038689	.004347	.302994	69.700522	.014347	120
11	3.718958	271.895856	.003677	.268892	73.110751	.013677	132
12	4.190615	319.061559	.003134	.238628	76.137157	.013134	144
13	4.722090	372.209054	.002686	.211770	78.822938	.012686	156
14	5.320969	432.096981	.002314	.187935	81.206433	.012314	168
15	5.995801	499.580197	.002001	.166783	83.321664	.012001	180
16	6.756219	575.621973	.001737	.148011	85.198823	.011787	192
17	7.613077	661.307750	.001512	.131352	86.864707	.011512	204
18	8.578606	757.860629	.001319	.116569	88.343095	.011319	216
19	9.666588	866.658829	.001153	.103449	89.655088	.011153	228
20	10.892553	989.255364	.001010	.091805	90.819416	.011010	240
21	12.274002	1127.400209	.000886	.081473	91.852697	.010886	252
22	13.830652	1283.065277	.000779	.072303	92.769683	.010779	264
23	15.584725	1458.472573	.000685	.064165	93.583461	.010685	276
24	17.561259	1656.125904	.000603	.056943	94.305647	.010603	288
25	19.788466	1878.846624	.000532	.050534	94.946551	.010532	300
26	22.298139	2129.813907	.000469	.044846	95.515320	.010469	312
27	25.126101	2412.610122	.000414	.039799	96.020074	.010414	324
28	28.312719	2731.271978	.000366	.035319	96.468018	.010366	336
29	31.903481	3090.348132	.000323	.031344	96.865546	.010323	348
30	35.949641	3494.964129	.000286	.027816	97.218330	.010286	360
31	40.508955	3950.895562	.000253	.024685	97.531409	.010253	372
32	45.646505	4464.650512	.000223	.021907	97.809251	.010223	384
33	51.435624	5043.562455	.000198	.019441	98.055821	.010198	396
34	57.958949	5695.894917	.000175	.017253	98.274641	.010175	408
35	65.309594	6430.959463	.000155	.015311	98.468831	.010155	420
36	73.592485	7259.248592	.000137	.013588	98.641165	.010137	432
37	82.925855	8192.585514	.000122	.012058	98.794103	.010122	444
38	93.442929	9244.292929	.000108	.010701	98.929827	.010108	456
39	105.293831	10429.383160	.000095	.009497	99.050277	.010095	468
40	118.647724	11764.772490	.000084	.008428	99.157169	.010084	480
41	133.695226	13269.522620	.000075	.007479	99.252029	.010075	492
42	150.651127	14965.112740	.000066	.006637	99.336214	.010066	504
43	169.757461	16875.746110	.000059	.005890	99.410924	.010059	516
44	191.286956	19028.695620	.000052	.005227	99.477225	.010052	528
45	215.546930	21454.693010	.000046	.004639	99.536064	.010046	540
46	242.883675	24188.367600	.000041	.004117	99.588280	.010041	552
47	273.687405	27268.740570	.000036	.003653	99.634619	.010036	564
48	308.397819	30739.781910	.000032	.003242	99.675743	.010032	576
49	347.510381	34651.038170	.000028	.002877	99.712238	.010028	588
50	391.583396	39058.339630	.000025	.002553	99.744626	.010025	600

12% QUARTERLY COMPOUND INTEREST TABLE 12%

EFFECTIVE RATE = 3% BASE = 1.0300

QUARTERS	1 AMOUNT OF I AT COMPOUND INTEREST $S^n = (1+i)^n$	2 ACCUMULATION OF I PER PERIOD $s_{\overline{n}\vert} = \frac{S^n - 1}{i}$	3 SINKING FUND FACTOR $1/s_{\overline{n}\vert} = \frac{i}{S^n - 1}$	4 PRES. VALUE REVERSION OF I $V^n = \frac{1}{S^n}$	5 PRESENT VALUE ORD. ANNUITY 1 PER PERIOD $a_{\overline{n}\vert} = \frac{1 - V^n}{i}$	6 INSTALMENT TO AMORTIZE I $1/a_{\overline{n}\vert} = \frac{i}{1 - V^n}$	n QUARTERS
1	1.030000	1.000000	1.000000	.970874	.970874	1.030000	1
2	1.060900	2.030000	.492611	.942596	1.913470	.522611	2
3	1.092727	3.090900	.323530	.915142	2.828611	.353530	3
YEARS							
1	1.125509	4.183627	.239027	.888487	3.717098	.269027	4
2	1.266770	8.892336	.112456	.789409	7.019692	.142456	8
3	1.425761	14.192030	.070462	.701380	9.954004	.100462	12
4	1.604706	20.156881	.049611	.623167	12.561102	.079611	16
5	1.806111	26.870374	.037216	.553676	14.877475	.067216	20
6	2.032794	34.426470	.029047	.491934	16.935542	.059047	24
7	2.287928	42.930923	.023293	.437077	18.764108	.053293	28
8	2.575083	52.502759	.019047	.388337	20.388766	.049047	32
9	2.898278	63.275944	.015804	.345032	21.832252	.045804	36
10	3.262038	75.401260	.013262	.306557	23.114772	.043262	40
11	3.671452	89.048409	.011230	.272372	24.254274	.041230	44
12	4.132252	104.408396	.009578	.241999	25.266707	.039578	48
13	4.650886	121.696197	.008217	.215013	26.166240	.038217	52
14	5.234613	141.153768	.007084	.191036	26.965464	.037084	56
15	5.891603	163.053437	.006133	.169733	27.675564	.036133	60
16	6.631051	187.701707	.005328	.150806	28.306478	.035328	64
17	7.463307	215.443551	.004642	.133989	28.867038	.034642	68
18	8.400017	246.667242	.004054	.119047	29.365088	.034054	72
19	9.454293	281.809781	.003548	.105772	29.807598	.033548	76
20	10.640891	321.363019	.003112	.093977	30.200763	.033112	80
21	11.976416	365.880536	.002733	.083497	30.550086	.032733	84
22	13.479562	415.985393	.002404	.074186	30.860454	.032404	88
23	15.171366	472.378852	.002117	.065914	31.136212	.032117	92
24	17.075506	535.850187	.001866	.058563	31.381219	.031866	96
25	19.218632	607.287733	.001647	.052033	31.598905	.031647	100
26	21.630740	687.691321	.001454	.046231	31.792317	.031454	104
27	24.345588	778.186267	.001285	.041075	31.964160	.031285	108
28	27.401174	880.039126	.001136	.036495	32.116840	.031136	112
29	30.840263	994.675417	.001005	.032425	32.252495	.031005	116
30	34.710987	1123.699572	.000890	.028809	32.373023	.030890	120
31	39.067522	1268.917395	.000788	.025597	32.480110	.030788	124
32	43.970840	1432.361334	.000698	.022742	32.575255	.030698	128
33	49.489568	1616.318928	.000619	.020206	32.659791	.030619	132
34	55.700945	1823.364820	.000548	.017953	32.734899	.030548	136
35	62.691904	2056.396796	.000486	.015951	32.801633	.030486	140
36	70.560290	2318.676338	.000431	.014172	32.860924	.030431	144
37	79.416228	2613.874273	.000383	.012592	32.913604	.030383	148
38	89.383665	2946.122150	.000339	.011188	32.960409	.030339	152
39	100.602102	3320.070063	.000301	.009940	33.001995	.030301	156
40	113.228552	3740.951733	.000267	.008832	33.038944	.030267	160
41	127.439733	4214.657760	.000237	.007847	33.071772	.030237	164
42	143.434542	4747.818067	.000211	.006972	33.100939	.030211	168
43	161.436841	5347.894690	.000187	.006194	33.126854	.030187	172
44	181.698587	6023.286217	.000166	.005504	33.149879	.030166	176
45	204.503360	6783.445330	.000147	.004890	33.170337	.030147	180
46	230.170333	7639.011110	.000131	.004345	33.188513	.030131	184
47	259.058738	8601.957930	.000116	.003860	33.204662	.030116	188
48	291.572892	9685.763060	.000103	.003430	33.219011	.030103	192
49	328.167859	10905.595280	.000092	.003047	33.231759	.030092	196
50	369.355816	12278.527200	.000081	.002707	33.243086	.030081	200
51	415.713225	13823.774160	.000072	.002406	33.253150	.030072	204
52	467.888897	15562.963230	.000064	.002137	33.262091	.030064	208
53	526.613076	17520.435860	.000057	.001899	33.270036	.030057	212
54	592.707656	19723.588540	.000051	.001687	33.277094	.030051	216
55	667.097689	22203.256290	.000045	.001499	33.283366	.030045	220
56	750.824326	24994.144200	.000040	.001332	33.288938	.030040	224
57	845.059394	28135.313120	.000036	.001183	33.293888	.030036	228
58	951.121793	31670.726420	.000032	.001051	33.298287	.030032	232
59	1070.495957	35649.865230	.000028	.000934	33.302195	.030028	236
60	1204.852631	40128.421030	.000025	.000830	33.305667	.030025	240

12% SEMI-ANNUAL COMPOUND INTEREST TABLE 12%

EFFECTIVE RATE = 6% BASE = 1.0600

HALF YEARS	1 AMOUNT OF I AT COMPOUND INTEREST $S^n = (1+i)^n$	2 ACCUMULATION OF I PER PERIOD $S_{\overline{n}\vert} = \frac{S^n - 1}{i}$	3 SINKING FUND FACTOR $1/S_{\overline{n}\vert} = \frac{i}{S^n - 1}$	4 PRES. VALUE REVERSION OF I $V^n = \frac{1}{S^n}$	5 PRESENT VALUE ORD. ANNUITY 1 PER PERIOD $a_{\overline{n}\vert} = \frac{1 - V^n}{i}$	6 INSTALMENT TO AMORTIZE I $1/a_{\overline{n}\vert} = \frac{i}{1 - V^n}$	n HALF YEARS
1	1.060000	1.000000	1.000000	.943396	.943396	1.060000	1
YEARS							
1	1.123600	2.060000	.485437	.889996	1.833393	.545437	2
2	1.262477	4.374616	.228591	.792094	3.465106	.288591	4
3	1.418519	6.975319	.143363	.704961	4.917324	.203363	6
4	1.593848	9.897468	.101036	.627412	6.209794	.161036	8
5	1.790848	13.180795	.075868	.558395	7.360087	.135868	10
6	2.012196	16.869941	.059277	.496969	8.383844	.119277	12
7	2.260904	21.015066	.047585	.442301	9.294984	.107585	14
8	2.540352	25.672528	.038952	.393646	10.105895	.098952	16
9	2.854339	30.905653	.032357	.350344	10.827603	.092357	18
10	3.207135	36.785591	.027185	.311805	11.469921	.087185	20
11	3.603537	43.392290	.023046	.277505	12.041582	.083046	22
12	4.048935	50.815577	.019679	.246979	12.550358	.079679	24
13	4.549383	59.156383	.016904	.219810	13.003166	.076904	26
14	5.111687	68.528112	.014593	.195630	13.406164	.074593	28
15	5.743491	79.058186	.012649	.174110	13.764831	.072649	30
16	6.453387	90.889778	.011002	.154957	14.084043	.071002	32
17	7.251025	104.183755	.009598	.137912	14.368141	.069598	34
18	8.147252	119.120867	.008395	.122741	14.620987	.068395	36
19	9.154252	135.904206	.007358	.109239	14.846019	.067358	38
20	10.285718	154.761966	.006462	.097222	15.046297	.066462	40
21	11.557033	175.950545	.005683	.086527	15.224543	.065683	42
22	12.985482	199.758032	.005006	.077009	15.383182	.065006	44
23	14.590487	226.508125	.004415	.068538	15.524370	.064415	46
24	16.393872	256.564529	.003898	.060998	15.650027	.063898	48
25	18.420154	290.335904	.003444	.054288	15.761861	.063444	50
26	20.696885	328.281422	.003046	.048316	15.861393	.063046	52
27	23.255020	370.917006	.002696	.043001	15.949976	.062696	54
28	26.129341	418.822348	.002388	.038271	16.028814	.062388	56
29	29.358927	472.648790	.002116	.034061	16.098980	.062116	58
30	32.987691	533.128181	.001876	.030314	16.161428	.061876	60
31	37.064969	601.082824	.001664	.026980	16.217006	.061664	62
32	41.646200	677.436661	.001476	.024012	16.266470	.061476	64
33	46.793670	763.227832	.001310	.021370	16.310493	.061310	66
34	52.577368	859.622792	.001163	.019020	16.349673	.061163	68
35	59.075930	967.932169	.001033	.016927	16.384544	.061033	70
36	66.377715	1089.628585	.000918	.015065	16.415578	.060918	72
37	74.582001	1226.366678	.000815	.013408	16.443199	.060815	74
38	83.800336	1380.005599	.000725	.011933	16.467781	.060725	76
39	94.158057	1552.634291	.000644	.010620	16.489659	.060644	78
40	105.795993	1746.599890	.000573	.009452	16.509131	.060573	80
41	118.872378	1964.539637	.000509	.008412	16.526460	.060509	82
42	133.565004	2209.416735	.000453	.007487	16.541883	.060453	84
43	150.073639	2484.560643	.000402	.006663	16.555610	.060402	86
44	168.622740	2793.712338	.000358	.005930	16.567827	.060358	88
45	189.464511	3141.075183	.000318	.005278	16.578699	.060318	90
46	212.882325	3531.372077	.000283	.004697	16.588376	.060283	92
47	239.194580	3969.909665	.000252	.004181	16.596988	.060252	94
48	268.759030	4462.650500	.000224	.003721	16.604653	.060224	96
49	301.977646	5016.294102	.000199	.003312	16.611475	.060199	98
50	339.302083	5638.368052	.000177	.002947	16.617546	.060177	100
51	381.239821	6337.330343	.000158	.002623	16.622950	.060158	102
52	428.361062	7122.684373	.000140	.002334	16.627759	.060140	104
53	481.306490	8005.108162	.000125	.002078	16.632039	.060125	106
54	540.795972	8996.599530	.000111	.001849	16.635848	.060111	108
55	607.638354	10110.639230	.000099	.001646	16.639238	.060099	110
56	682.742454	11362.374240	.000088	.001465	16.642255	.060088	112
57	767.129422	12768.823700	.000078	.001304	16.644941	.060078	114
58	861.946618	14349.110300	.000070	.001160	16.647331	.060070	116
59	968.483220	16124.720340	.000062	.001033	16.649458	.060062	118
60	1088.187746	18119.795770	.000055	.000919	16.651351	.060055	120

12% ANNUAL COMPOUND INTEREST TABLE 12%

EFFECTIVE RATE = 12% BASE = 1.1200

YEARS	1 AMOUNT OF I AT COMPOUND INTEREST $S^n = (1+i)^n$	2 ACCUMULATION OF I PER PERIOD $s_{\overline{n}\mid} = \frac{S^n - 1}{i}$	3 SINKING FUND FACTOR $1/s_{\overline{n}\mid} = \frac{i}{S^n - 1}$	4 PRES. VALUE REVERSION OF I $V^n = \frac{1}{S^n}$	5 PRESENT VALUE ORD. ANNUITY 1 PER PERIOD $a_{\overline{n}\mid} = \frac{1 - V^n}{i}$	6 INSTALMENT TO AMORTIZE I $1/a_{\overline{n}\mid} = \frac{i}{1 - V^n}$	n YEARS
1	1.120000	1.000000	1.000000	.892857	.892857	1.120000	1
2	1.254400	2.120000	.471698	.797194	1.690051	.591698	2
3	1.404928	3.374400	.296349	.711780	2.401831	.416349	3
4	1.573519	4.779328	.209234	.635518	3.037349	.329234	4
5	1.762342	6.352847	.157410	.567427	3.604776	.277410	5
6	1.973823	8.115189	.123226	.506631	4.111407	.243226	6
7	2.210681	10.089012	.099118	.452349	4.563757	.219118	7
8	2.475963	12.299693	.081303	.403883	4.967640	.201303	8
9	2.773079	14.775656	.067679	.360610	5.328250	.187679	9
10	3.105848	17.548735	.056984	.321973	5.650223	.176984	10
11	3.478550	20.654583	.048415	.287476	5.937699	.168415	11
12	3.895976	24.133133	.041437	.256675	6.194374	.161437	12
13	4.363493	28.029109	.035677	.229174	6.423548	.155677	13
14	4.887112	32.392602	.030871	.204620	6.628168	.150871	14
15	5.473566	37.279715	.026824	.182696	6.810864	.146824	15
16	6.130394	42.753280	.023390	.163122	6.973986	.143390	16
17	6.866041	48.883674	.020457	.145644	7.119630	.140457	17
18	7.689966	55.749715	.017937	.130040	7.249670	.137937	18
19	8.612762	63.439681	.015763	.116107	7.365777	.135763	19
20	9.646293	72.052442	.013879	.103667	7.469444	.133879	20
21	10.803848	81.698736	.012240	.092560	7.562003	.132240	21
22	12.100310	92.502584	.010811	.082643	7.644646	.130811	22
23	13.552347	104.602894	.009560	.073788	7.718434	.129560	23
24	15.178629	118.155241	.008463	.065882	7.784316	.128463	24
25	17.000064	133.333870	.007500	.058823	7.843139	.127500	25
26	19.040072	150.333934	.006652	.052521	7.895660	.126652	26
27	21.324881	169.374007	.005904	.046894	7.942554	.125904	27
28	23.883866	190.698887	.005244	.041869	7.984423	.125244	28
29	26.749930	214.582754	.004660	.037383	8.021806	.124660	29
30	29.959922	241.332684	.004144	.033378	8.055184	.124144	30
31	33.555113	271.292606	.003686	.029802	8.084986	.123686	31
32	37.581726	304.847719	.003280	.026609	8.111594	.123280	32
33	42.091533	342.429445	.002920	.023758	8.135352	.122920	33
34	47.142517	384.520979	.002601	.021212	8.156564	.122601	34
35	52.799620	431.663496	.002317	.018940	8.175504	.122317	35
36	59.135574	484.463116	.002064	.016910	8.192414	.122064	36
37	66.231843	543.598690	.001840	.015098	8.207513	.121840	37
38	74.179664	609.830532	.001640	.013481	8.220993	.121640	38
39	83.081224	684.010196	.001462	.012036	8.233030	.121462	39
40	93.050970	767.091420	.001304	.010747	8.243777	.121304	40
41	104.217087	860.142390	.001163	.009595	8.253372	.121163	41
42	116.723137	964.359477	.001037	.008567	8.261939	.121037	42
43	130.729914	1081.082614	.000925	.007649	8.269589	.120925	43
44	146.417503	1211.812527	.000825	.006830	8.276418	.120825	44
45	163.987604	1358.230031	.000736	.006098	8.282516	.120736	45
46	183.666116	1522.217634	.000657	.005445	8.287961	.120657	46
47	205.706050	1705.883750	.000586	.004861	8.292822	.120586	47
48	230.390776	1911.589800	.000523	.004340	8.297163	.120523	48
49	258.037669	2141.980576	.000467	.003875	8.301038	.120467	49
50	289.002189	2400.018245	.000417	.003460	8.304498	.120417	50
51	323.682452	2689.020434	.000372	.003089	8.307588	.120372	51
52	362.524346	3012.702886	.000332	.002758	8.310346	.120332	52
53	406.027268	3375.227233	.000296	.002463	8.312809	.120296	53
54	454.750540	3781.254500	.000264	.002199	8.315008	.120264	54
55	509.320605	4236.005040	.000236	.001963	8.316972	.120236	55
56	570.439077	4745.325645	.000211	.001753	8.318725	.120211	56
57	638.891767	5315.764723	.000188	.001565	8.320290	.120188	57
58	715.558779	5954.656489	.000168	.001398	8.321687	.120168	58
59	801.425832	6670.215267	.000150	.001248	8.322935	.120150	59
60	897.596932	7471.641099	.000134	.001114	8.324049	.120134	60

13% ANNUAL COMPOUND INTEREST TABLE 13%

EFFECTIVE RATE = 13% BASE = 1.13

YEARS	1 AMOUNT OF 1 AT COMPOUND INTEREST $S^n = (1+i)^n$	2 ACCUMULATION OF 1 PER PERIOD $s_{\overline{n}\vert} = \frac{S^n - 1}{i}$	3 SINKING FUND FACTOR $1/s_{\overline{n}\vert} = \frac{i}{S^n - 1}$	4 PRES. VALUE REVERSION OF 1 $V^n = \frac{1}{S^n}$	5 PRESENT VALUE ORD. ANNUITY 1 PER PERIOD $a_{\overline{n}\vert} = \frac{1-V^n}{i}$	6 INSTALMENT TO AMORTIZE 1 $1/a_{\overline{n}\vert} = \frac{i}{1-V^n}$	n YEARS
1	1.130000	1.0000	1.000000	.884956	.884956	1.130000	1
2	1.276900	2.1300	.469483	.783147	1.668103	.599483	2
3	1.442897	3.4069	.293522	.693050	2.361153	.423522	3
4	1.630474	4.8498	.206194	.613319	2.974472	.336194	4
5	1.842436	6.4803	.154314	.542760	3.517232	.284314	5
6	2.081952	8.3227	.120153	.480318	3.997550	.250153	6
7	2.352607	10.4047	.096111	.425060	4.422610	.226111	7
8	2.658446	12.7573	.078387	.376160	4.798770	.208387	8
9	3.004044	15.4157	.064869	.332885	5.131655	.194869	9
10	3.394570	18.4198	.054290	.294588	5.426243	.184290	10
11	3.835864	21.8143	.045841	.260697	5.686940	.175841	11
12	4.334526	25.6502	.038986	.230706	5.917646	.168986	12
13	4.898014	29.9847	.033350	.204164	6.121810	.163350	13
14	5.534756	34.8827	.028668	.180676	6.302486	.158668	14
15	6.254274	40.4175	.024742	.159891	6.462377	.154742	15
16	7.067330	46.6718	.021426	.141496	6.603873	.151426	16
17	7.986083	53.7391	.018608	.125218	6.729091	.148608	17
18	9.024274	61.7252	.016201	.110812	6.839903	.146201	18
19	10.197430	70.7494	.014134	.098064	6.937967	.144134	19
20	11.523096	80.9469	.012354	.086782	7.024749	.142354	20
21	13.021098	92.4700	.010814	.076798	7.101547	.140814	21
22	14.713841	105.4911	.009480	.067963	7.169510	.139480	22
23	16.626640	120.2049	.008319	.060144	7.229654	.138319	23
24	18.788103	136.8316	.007308	.053225	7.282879	.137308	24
25	21.230556	155.6197	.006426	.047102	7.329984	.136426	25
26	23.990528	176.8502	.005655	.041683	7.371664	.135655	26
27	27.109297	200.8407	.004979	.036888	7.408552	.134979	27
28	30.633506	227.9500	.004387	.032644	7.441196	.134387	28
29	34.615862	258.5835	.003867	.028888	7.470084	.133867	29
30	39.115924	293.1994	.003411	.025565	7.495653	.133411	30

14% ANNUAL COMPOUND INTEREST TABLE 14%

EFFECTIVE RATE = 14% BASE = 1.14

YEARS	1 AMOUNT OF 1 AT COMPOUND INTEREST $S^n = (1+i)^n$	2 ACCUMULATION OF 1 PER PERIOD $S_{\overline{n}\vert} = \frac{S^n - 1}{i}$	3 SINKING FUND FACTOR $1/S_{\overline{n}\vert} = \frac{i}{S^n - 1}$	4 PRES. VALUE REVERSION OF 1 $V^n = \frac{1}{S^n}$	5 PRESENT VALUE ORD. ANNUITY 1 PER PERIOD $a_{\overline{n}\vert} = \frac{1-V^n}{i}$	6 INSTALMENT TO AMORTIZE 1 $1/a_{\overline{n}\vert} = \frac{i}{1-V^n}$	n YEARS
1	1.140000	1.0000	1.000000	.877193	.877193	1.140000	1
2	1.299600	2.1400	.467290	.769468	1.646661	.607290	2
3	1.481544	3.4396	.290731	.674971	2.321623	.430731	3
4	1.688960	4.9211	.203205	.592080	2.913712	.343205	4
5	1.925415	6.6101	.151284	.519368	3.433080	.291284	5
6	2.194973	8.5355	.117158	.455587	3.888667	.257158	6
7	2.502269	10.7305	.093192	.399637	4.288304	.233192	7
8	2.852586	13.2328	.075570	.350559	4.638863	.215570	8
9	3.251949	16.0853	.062168	.307508	4.946371	.202168	9
10	3.707221	19.3373	.051714	.269744	5.216115	.191714	10
11	4.226232	23.0445	.043394	.236617	5.452732	.183394	11
12	4.817905	27.2707	.036669	.207559	5.660291	.176669	12
13	5.492411	32.0887	.031164	.182069	5.842360	.171164	13
14	6.261349	37.5811	.026609	.159710	6.002070	.166609	14
15	7.137938	43.8424	.022809	.140096	6.142166	.162809	15
16	8.137249	50.9804	.019615	.122892	6.265058	.159615	16
17	9.276464	59.1176	.016915	.107800	6.372858	.156915	17
18	10.575169	68.3941	.014621	.094561	6.467419	.154621	18
19	12.055693	78.9692	.012663	.082948	6.550367	.152663	19
20	13.743490	91.0249	.010986	.072762	6.623129	.150986	20
21	15.667578	104.7684	.009545	.063826	6.686955	.149545	21
22	17.861039	120.4360	.008303	.055988	6.742943	.148303	22
23	20.361585	138.2970	.007231	.049112	6.792055	.147231	23
24	23.212207	158.6586	.006303	.043081	6.835136	.146303	24
25	26.461916	181.8708	.005498	.037790	6.872926	.145498	25
26	30.166584	208.3327	.004800	.033149	6.906075	.144800	26
27	34.389906	238.4993	.004193	.029078	6.935153	.144193	27
28	39.204492	272.8892	.003665	.025507	6.960660	.143665	28
29	44.693121	312.0937	.003204	.022375	6.983035	.143204	29
30	50.950158	356.7868	.002803	.019627	7.002662	.142803	30

15% ANNUAL COMPOUND INTEREST TABLE 15%

EFFECTIVE RATE = 15% BASE = 1.15

YEARS	1 AMOUNT OF 1 AT COMPOUND INTEREST $S^n = (1+i)^n$	2 ACCUMULATION OF 1 PER PERIOD $S_{\overline{n}\rvert} = \frac{S^n - 1}{i}$	3 SINKING FUND FACTOR $1/S_{\overline{n}\rvert} = \frac{i}{S^n - 1}$	4 PRES. VALUE REVERSION OF 1 $V^n = \frac{1}{S^n}$	5 PRESENT VALUE ORD. ANNUITY 1 PER PERIOD $a_{\overline{n}\rvert} = \frac{1 - V^n}{i}$	6 INSTALMENT TO AMORTIZE 1 $1/a_{\overline{n}\rvert} = \frac{i}{1 - V^n}$	n YEARS
1	1.150000	1.0000	1.000000	.869565	.869565	1.150000	1
2	1.322500	2.1500	.465116	.756144	1.625709	.615116	2
3	1.520875	3.4725	.287976	.657516	2.283225	.437976	3
4	1.749006	4.9934	.200265	.571753	2.854978	.350265	4
5	2.011357	6.7424	.148315	.497177	3.352155	.298315	5
6	2.313061	8.7537	.114236	.432328	3.784483	.264236	6
7	2.660020	11.0668	.090360	.375937	4.160420	.240360	7
8	3.059023	13.7268	.072850	.326902	4.487322	.222850	8
9	3.517876	16.7858	.059574	.284262	4.771584	.209574	9
10	4.045558	20.3037	.049252	.247185	5.018769	.199252	10
11	4.652391	24.3493	.041068	.214943	5.233712	.191068	11
12	5.350250	29.0017	.034480	.186907	5.420619	.184480	12
13	6.152788	34.3519	.029110	.162528	5.583147	.179110	13
14	7.075706	40.5047	.024688	.141329	5.724476	.174688	14
15	8.137062	47.5804	.021017	.122894	5.847370	.171017	15
16	9.357621	55.7175	.017947	.106865	5.954235	.167947	16
17	10.761264	65.0751	.015366	.092926	6.047161	.165366	17
18	12.375454	75.8364	.013186	.080805	6.127966	.163186	18
19	14.231772	88.2118	.011336	.070265	6.198231	.161336	19
20	16.366537	102.4436	.009761	.061100	6.259331	.159761	20
21	18.821518	118.8101	.008416	.053131	6.312462	.158416	21
22	21.644746	137.6316	.007265	.046201	6.358663	.157265	22
23	24.891458	159.2764	.006278	.040174	6.398837	.156278	23
24	28.625176	184.1678	.005429	.034934	6.433771	.155429	24
25	32.918953	212.7930	.004699	.030378	6.464149	.154699	25
26	37.856796	245.7120	.004069	.026415	6.490564	.154069	26
27	43.535315	283.5688	.003526	.022970	6.513534	.153526	27
28	50.065612	327.1041	.003010	.019974	6.535508	153010	28
29	57.575454	377.1697	.002651	.017369	6.550877	.152651	29
30	66.211772	434.7451	.002300	.015103	6.565980	.152300	30

16% ANNUAL COMPOUND INTEREST TABLE 16%

EFFECTIVE RATE = 16% BASE = 1.16

YEARS	1 AMOUNT OF I AT COMPOUND INTEREST $S^n = (1+i)^n$	2 ACCUMULATION OF I PER PERIOD $S_{\overline{n}\vert} = \frac{S^n - 1}{i}$	3 SINKING FUND FACTOR $1/S_{\overline{n}\vert} = \frac{i}{S^n - 1}$	4 PRES. VALUE REVERSION OF I $V^n = \frac{1}{S^n}$	5 PRESENT VALUE ORD. ANNUITY I PER PERIOD $a_{\overline{n}\vert} = \frac{1-V^n}{i}$	6 INSTALMENT TO AMORTIZE I $1/a_{\overline{n}\vert} = \frac{i}{1-V^n}$	n YEARS
1	1.160000	1.0000	1.000000	.862068	.862068	1.160000	1
2	1.345600	2.1600	.462963	.743163	1.605231	.622963	2
3	1.560896	3.5056	.285257	.640658	2.245889	.445257	3
4	1.810639	5.0665	.197375	.552291	2.798180	.357375	4
5	2.100342	6.8771	.145409	.476113	3.274293	.305409	5
6	2.436396	8.9775	.111390	.410442	3.684735	.271390	6
7	2.826220	11.4139	.087613	.353829	4.038564	.247613	7
8	3.278415	14.2401	.070224	.305025	4.343589	.230224	8
9	3.802961	17.5185	.057083	.262953	4.606542	.217083	9
10	4.411435	21.3215	.046901	.226684	4.833226	.206901	10
11	5.117265	25.7329	.038861	.195417	5.028643	.198861	11
12	5.936027	30.8502	.032415	.168463	5.197106	.192415	12
13	6.885792	36.7862	.027184	.145227	5.342333	.187184	13
14	7.987518	43.6720	.022898	.125195	5.467528	.182898	14
15	9.265521	51.6595	.019358	.107927	5.575455	.179358	15
16	10.748005	60.9250	.016414	.093041	5.668496	.176414	16
17	12.467685	71.6730	.013952	.080207	5.748703	.173952	17
18	14.462515	84.1407	.011885	.069144	5.817847	.171885	18
19	16.776517	98.6032	.010142	.059607	5.877454	.170142	19
20	19.460760	115.3797	.008667	.051385	5.928839	.168667	20
21	22.574482	134.8405	.007416	.044298	5.973137	.167416	21
22	26.186399	157.4150	.006353	.038188	6.011325	.166353	22
23	30.376223	183.6014	.005447	.032920	6.044245	.165447	23
24	35 236418	213.9776	.004673	.028380	6.072625	.164673	24
25	40.874245	249.2140	.004013	.024465	6.097090	.164013	25
26	47.414124	290.0883	.003447	.021091	6.118181	.163447	26
27	55.000384	337.5024	.002963	.018182	6.136363	.162963	27
28	63.800446	392.5028	.002548	.015674	6.152037	.162548	28
29	74.008517	456.3032	.002192	.013512	6.165549	.162192	29
30	85.849880	530.3117	.001886	.011648	6.177197	.161886	30

B.

Loan Amortization Tables

Monthly Payments

Table of Constant Annual Percent needed to amortize a principal amount, calculated on a monthly basis. Divide by 12 to determine monthly payment.

Interest Rate	2 YEARS	3 YEARS	4 YEARS	5 YEARS	6 YEARS	7 YEARS	8 YEARS
7	53.73	37.06	28.74	23.77	20.46	18.12	16.37
1/4	53.87	37.19	28.88	23.91	20.61	18.26	16.52
1/2	54.00	37.33	29.02	24.05	20.75	18.41	16.67
3/4	54.14	37.47	29.16	24.19	20.90	18.56	16.82
8	54.28	37.61	29.30	24.34	21.04	18.71	16.97
1/8	54.35	37.68	29.37	24.41	21.12	18.78	17.05
1/4	54.41	37.75	29.44	24.48	21.19	18.86	17.12
3/8	54.48	37.82	29.51	24.55	21.27	18.93	17.20
1/2	54.55	37.89	29.58	24.62	21.34	19.01	17.28
5/8	54.62	37.96	29.65	24.70	21.41	19.08	17.35
3/4	54.69	38.03	29.72	24.77	21.49	19.16	17.43
7/8	54.76	38.09	29.80	24.84	21.56	19.24	17.51
9	54.83	38.16	29.87	24.92	21.64	19.31	17.59
1/8	54.90	38.23	29.94	24.99	21.71	19.39	17.66
1/4	54.96	38.30	30.01	25.06	21.78	19.46	17.74
3/8	55.03	38.37	30.08	25.13	21.86	19.54	17.82
1/2	55.10	38.44	30.15	25.21	21.93	19.62	17.90
5/8	55.17	38.51	30.22	25.28	22.01	19.69	17.98
3/4	55.24	38.58	30.30	25.35	22.09	19.77	18.06
7/8	55.31	38.66	30.37	25.43	22.16	19.85	18.13
10	55.38	38.73	30.44	25.50	22.24	19.93	18.21
1/8	55.45	38.80	30.51	25.58	22.31	20.00	18.29
1/4	55.52	38.87	30.58	25.65	22.39	20.08	18.37
3/8	55.59	38.94	30.66	25.72	22.46	20.16	18.45
1/2	55.66	39.01	30.73	25.80	22.54	20.24	18.53
5/8	55.73	39.08	30.80	25.87	22.62	20.32	18.61
3/4	55.80	39.15	30.87	25.95	22.69	20.39	18.69
7/8	55.86	39.22	30.95	26.02	22.77	20.47	18.77
11	55.93	39.29	31.02	26.10	22.85	20.55	18.86
1/8	56.00	39.36	31.09	26.17	22.92	20.63	18.94
1/4	56.07	39.43	31.17	26.25	23.00	20.71	19.02
3/8	56.14	39.50	31.24	26.32	23.08	20.79	19.10
1/2	56.21	39.58	31.31	26.40	23.15	20.87	19.18
5/8	56.28	39.65	31.39	26.47	23.23	20.95	19.26
3/4	56.35	39.72	31.46	26.55	23.31	21.03	19.34
7/8	56.42	39.79	31.53	26.62	23.39	21.11	19.43
12	56.49	39.86	31.61	26.70	23.47	21.19	19.51
1/4	56.63	40.01	31.75	26.85	23.62	21.35	19.67
1/2	56.77	40.15	31.90	27.00	23.78	21.51	19.84
3/4	56.91	40.29	32.05	27.16	23.94	21.67	20.01
13	57.06	40.44	32.20	27.31	24.09	21.84	20.17
1/4	57.20	40.58	32.35	27.46	24.25	22.00	20.34
1/2	57.34	40.73	32.50	27.62	24.41	22.16	20.51
3/4	57.48	40.87	32.65	27.77	24.57	22.33	20.68
14	57.62	41.02	32.80	27.93	24.73	22.49	20.85
1/4	57.76	41.16	32.95	28.08	24.89	22.66	21.02
1/2	57.90	41.31	33.10	28.24	25.05	22.83	21.19
3/4	58.05	41.46	33.25	28.40	25.22	22.99	21.37
15	58.19	41.60	33.40	28.55	25.38	23.16	21.54

*Reprinted from *Financial Constant Percent Amortizations Tables,* Publication No. 287. With permission of Financial Publishing Company, 82 Brookline Avenue, Boston, MA 02215.

Monthly Payments

Table of Constant Annual Percent needed to amortize a principal amount, calculated on a monthly basis. Divide by 12 to determine monthly payment.

Interest Rate	9 YEARS	10 YEARS	11 YEARS	12 YEARS	13 YEARS	14 YEARS	15 YEARS
7	15.01	13.94	13.07	12.35	11.74	11.23	10.79
1/4	15.16	14.09	13.22	12.51	11.91	11.40	10.96
1/2	15.32	14.25	13.38	12.67	12.07	11.56	11.13
3/4	15.47	14.41	13.54	12.83	12.24	11.73	11.30
8	15.63	14.56	13.70	12.99	12.40	11.90	11.47
1/8	15.71	14.64	13.78	13.08	12.49	11.99	11.56
1/4	15.78	14.72	13.87	13.16	12.57	12.07	11.65
3/8	15.86	14.80	13.95	13.24	12.65	12.16	11.73
1/2	15.94	14.88	14.03	13.33	12.74	12.24	11.82
5/8	16.02	14.96	14.11	13.41	12.82	12.33	11.91
3/4	16.10	15.04	14.19	13.49	12.91	12.42	12.00
7/8	16.18	15.13	14.28	13.58	13.00	12.50	12.09
9	16.26	15.21	14.36	13.66	13.08	12.59	12.18
1/8	16.34	15.29	14.44	13.75	13.17	12.68	12.27
1/4	16.42	15.37	14.52	13.83	13.25	12.77	12.36
3/8	16.50	15.45	14.61	13.92	13.34	12.86	12.45
1/2	16.58	15.53	14.69	14.00	13.43	12.95	12.54
5/8	16.66	15.61	14.78	14.09	13.52	13.03	12.63
3/4	16.74	15.70	14.86	14.17	13.60	13.12	12.72
7/8	16.82	15.78	14.94	14.26	13.69	13.21	12.81
10	16.90	15.86	15.03	14.35	13.78	13.30	12.90
1/8	16.98	15.95	15.11	14.43	13.87	13.39	12.99
1/4	17.06	16.03	15.20	14.52	13.96	13.48	13.08
3/8	17.14	16.11	15.28	14.61	14.05	13.58	13.18
1/2	17.23	16.20	15.37	14.69	14.14	13.67	13.27
5/8	17.31	16.28	15.46	14.78	14.22	13.76	13.36
3/4	17.39	16.37	15.54	14.87	14.31	13.85	13.46
7/8	17.47	16.45	15.63	14.96	14.40	13.94	13.55
11	17.56	16.54	15.72	15.05	14.50	14.03	13.64
1/8	17.64	16.62	15.80	15.14	14.59	14.13	13.74
1/4	17.72	16.71	15.89	15.23	14.68	14.22	13.83
3/8	17.81	16.79	15.98	15.32	14.77	14.31	13.93
1/2	17.89	16.88	16.07	15.40	14.86	14.41	14.02
5/8	17.97	16.96	16.15	15.49	14.95	14.50	14.12
3/4	18.06	17.05	16.24	15.58	15.04	14.59	14.21
7/8	18.14	17.13	16.33	15.68	15.14	14.69	14.31
12	18.23	17.22	16.42	15.77	15.23	14.78	14.41
1/4	18.40	17.40	16.60	15.95	15.42	14.97	14.60
1/2	18.57	17.57	16.78	16.13	15.60	15.16	14.80
3/4	18.74	17.75	16.96	16.32	15.79	15.36	14.99
13	18.91	17.92	17.14	16.50	15.98	15.55	15.19
1/4	19.08	18.10	17.32	16.69	16.17	15.74	15.39
1/2	19.26	18.28	17.50	16.87	16.36	15.94	15.58
3/4	19.43	18.46	17.68	17.06	16.55	16.13	15.78
14	19.61	18.64	17.87	17.25	16.75	16.33	15.99
1/4	19.78	18.82	18.05	17.44	16.94	16.53	16.19
1/2	19.96	19.00	18.24	17.63	17.14	16.73	16.39
3/4	20.14	19.18	18.43	17.82	17.33	16.93	16.60
15	20.31	19.37	18.62	18.02	17.53	17.13	16.80

Monthly Payments

Table of Constant Annual Percent needed to amortize a principal amount, calculated on a monthly basis. Divide by 12 to determine monthly payment.

Interest Rate	16 YEARS	17 YEARS	18 YEARS	19 YEARS	20 YEARS	21 YEARS	22 YEARS
7	10.41	10.08	9.79	9.54	9.31	9.11	8.93
1/4	10.58	10.25	9.97	9.71	9.49	9.29	9.11
1/2	10.75	10.43	10.14	9.89	9.67	9.47	9.30
3/4	10.93	10.61	10.32	10.08	9.86	9.66	9.49
8	11.10	10.78	10.50	10.26	10.04	9.85	9.68
1/8	11.19	10.87	10.60	10.35	10.14	9.94	9.78
1/4	11.28	10.96	10.69	10.44	10.23	10.04	9.87
3/8	11.37	11.05	10.78	10.54	10.32	10.14	9.97
1/2	11.46	11.14	10.87	10.63	10.42	10.23	10.07
5/8	11.55	11.24	10.96	10.72	10.51	10.33	10.16
3/4	11.64	11.33	11.06	10.82	10.61	10.43	10.26
7/8	11.73	11.42	11.15	10.91	10.71	10.52	10.36
9	11.82	11.51	11.24	11.01	10.80	10.62	10.46
1/8	11.91	11.60	11.34	11.10	10.90	10.72	10.56
1/4	12.00	11.70	11.43	11.20	11.00	10.82	10.66
3/8	12.09	11.79	11.53	11.29	11.09	10.92	10.76
1/2	12.18	11.88	11.62	11.39	11.19	11.01	10.86
5/8	12.28	11.98	11.72	11.49	11.29	11.11	10.96
3/4	12.37	12.07	11.81	11.58	11.39	11.21	11.06
7/8	12.46	12.16	11.91	11.68	11.49	11.31	11.16
10	12.56	12.26	12.00	11.78	11.59	11.41	11.26
1/8	12.65	12.35	12.10	11.88	11.68	11.52	11.37
1/4	12.74	12.45	12.20	11.98	11.78	11.62	11.47
3/8	12.84	12.55	12.29	12.08	11.88	11.72	11.57
1/2	12.93	12.64	12.39	12.17	11.99	11.82	11.68
5/8	13.03	12.74	12.49	12.27	12.09	11.92	11.78
3/4	13.12	12.84	12.59	12.37	12.19	12.03	11.88
7/8	13.22	12.93	12.69	12.47	12.29	12.13	11.99
11	13.31	13.03	12.79	12.57	12.39	12.23	12.09
1/8	13.41	13.13	12.88	12.68	12.49	12.34	12.20
1/4	13.51	13.23	12.98	12.78	12.60	12.44	12.30
3/8	13.60	13.32	13.08	12.88	12.70	12.54	12.41
1/2	13.70	13.42	13.18	12.98	12.80	12.65	12.51
5/8	13.80	13.52	13.29	13.08	12.91	12.75	12.62
3/4	13.89	13.62	13.39	13.18	13.01	12.86	12.73
7/8	13.99	13.72	13.49	13.29	13.11	12.96	12.83
12	14.09	13.82	13.59	13.39	13.22	13.07	12.94
1/4	14.29	14.02	13.79	13.60	13.43	13.28	13.16
1/2	14.49	14.22	14.00	13.80	13.64	13.50	13.37
3/4	14.68	14.42	14.20	14.01	13.85	13.71	13.59
13	14.88	14.63	14.41	14.22	14.06	13.93	13.81
1/4	15.09	14.83	14.62	14.44	14.28	14.14	14.03
1/2	15.29	15.04	14.83	14.65	14.49	14.36	14.25
3/4	15.49	15.25	15.04	14.86	14.71	14.58	14.47
14	15.70	15.45	15.25	15.08	14.93	14.80	14.69
1/4	15.90	15.66	15.46	15.29	15.15	15.02	14.92
1/2	16.11	15.87	15.68	15.51	15.36	15.24	15.14
3/4	16.32	16.09	15.89	15.72	15.59	15.47	15.37
15	16.53	16.30	16.11	15.94	15.81	15.69	15.59

Monthly Payments

Table of Constant Annual Percent needed to amortize a principal amount, calculated on a monthly basis. Divide by 12 to determine monthly payment.

Interest Rate	23 YEARS	24 YEARS	25 YEARS	26 YEARS	27 YEARS	28 YEARS	29 YEARS
7	8.76	8.62	8.49	8.37	8.26	8.16	8.07
1/4	8.95	8.81	8.68	8.56	8.46	8.36	8.27
1/2	9.14	9.00	8.87	8.76	8.65	8.56	8.47
3/4	9.33	9.19	9.07	8.96	8.85	8.76	8.68
8	9.53	9.39	9.27	9.16	9.06	8.97	8.88
1/8	9.62	9.49	9.37	9.26	9.16	9.07	8.99
1/4	9.72	9.59	9.47	9.36	9.26	9.17	9.09
3/8	9.82	9.69	9.57	9.46	9.36	9.28	9.20
1/2	9.92	9.79	9.67	9.56	9.47	9.38	9.30
5/8	10.02	9.89	9.77	9.66	9.57	9.48	9.41
3/4	10.12	9.99	9.87	9.77	9.67	9.59	9.51
7/8	10.22	10.09	9.97	9.87	9.78	9.69	9.62
9	10.32	10.19	10.08	9.97	9.88	9.80	9.73
1/8	10.42	10.29	10.18	10.08	9.99	9.91	9.83
1/4	10.52	10.39	10.28	10.18	10.09	10.01	9.94
3/8	10.62	10.50	10.39	10.29	10.20	10.12	10.05
1/2	10.72	10.60	10.49	10.39	10.31	10.23	10.16
5/8	10.82	10.70	10.59	10.50	10.41	10.34	10.27
3/4	10.93	10.81	10.70	10.60	10.52	10.44	10.38
7/8	11.03	10.91	10.80	10.71	10.63	10.55	10.48
10	11.13	11.01	10.91	10.82	10.73	10.66	10.59
1/8	11.23	11.12	11.02	10.92	10.84	10.77	10.70
1/4	11.34	11.22	11.12	11.03	10.95	10.88	10.82
3/8	11.44	11.33	11.23	11.14	11.06	10.99	10.93
1/2	11.55	11.43	11.34	11.25	11.17	11.10	11.04
5/8	11.65	11.54	11.44	11.36	11.28	11.21	11.15
3/4	11.76	11.65	11.55	11.46	11.39	11.32	11.26
7/8	11.86	11.75	11.66	11.57	11.50	11.43	11.37
11	11.97	11.86	11.77	11.68	11.61	11.54	11.48
1/8	12.08	11.97	11.87	11.79	11.72	11.65	11.60
1/4	12.18	12.08	11.98	11.90	11.83	11.77	11.71
3/8	12.29	12.18	12.09	12.01	11.94	11.88	11.82
1/2	12.40	12.29	12.20	12.12	12.05	11.99	11.94
5/8	12.50	12.40	12.31	12.23	12.16	12.10	12.05
3/4	12.61	12.51	12.42	12.35	12.28	12.22	12.16
7/8	12.72	12.62	12.53	12.46	12.39	12.33	12.28
12	12.83	12.73	12.64	12.57	12.50	12.44	12.39
1/4	13.05	12.95	12.87	12.79	12.73	12.67	12.62
1/2	13.26	13.17	13.09	13.02	12.96	12.90	12.85
3/4	13.48	13.39	13.31	13.24	13.18	13.13	13.09
13	13.71	13.62	13.54	13.47	13.41	13.36	13.32
1/4	13.93	13.84	13.77	13.70	13.64	13.59	13.55
1/2	14.15	14.07	13.99	13.93	13.87	13.83	13.79
3/4	14.37	14.29	14.22	14.16	14.11	14.06	14.02
14	14.60	14.52	14.45	14.39	14.34	14.30	14.26
1/4	14.82	14.75	14.68	14.62	14.57	14.53	14.49
1/2	15.05	14.98	14.91	14.86	14.81	14.77	14.73
3/4	15.28	15.21	15.14	15.09	15.04	15.00	14.97
15	15.51	15.44	15.37	15.32	15.28	15.24	15.21

Monthly Payments

Table of Constant Annual Percent needed to amortize a principal amount, calculated on a monthly basis. Divide by 12 to determine monthly payment.

Interest Rate	30 YEARS	31 YEARS	32 YEARS	33 YEARS	34 YEARS	35 YEARS	36 YEARS
7	7.99	7.91	7.85	7.78	7.72	7.67	7.62
1/4	8.19	8.12	8.05	7.99	7.93	7.88	7.84
1/2	8.40	8.32	8.26	8.20	8.15	8.10	8.05
3/4	8.60	8.53	8.47	8.41	8.36	8.31	8.27
8	8.81	8.74	8.68	8.63	8.57	8.53	8.49
1/8	8.91	8.85	8.79	8.73	8.68	8.64	8.60
1/4	9.02	8.95	8.90	8.84	8.79	8.75	8.71
3/8	9.13	9.06	9.00	8.95	8.90	8.86	8.82
1/2	9.23	9.17	9.11	9.06	9.01	8.97	8.93
5/8	9.34	9.28	9.22	9.17	9.12	9.08	9.04
3/4	9.45	9.38	9.33	9.28	9.23	9.19	9.15
7/8	9.55	9.49	9.44	9.39	9.34	9.30	9.26
9	9.66	9.60	9.55	9.50	9.45	9.41	9.38
1/8	9.77	9.71	9.66	9.61	9.56	9.53	9.49
1/4	9.88	9.82	9.77	9.72	9.68	9.64	9.60
3/8	9.99	9.93	9.88	9.83	9.79	9.75	9.72
1/2	10.10	10.04	9.99	9.94	9.90	9.86	9.83
5/8	10.20	10.15	10.10	10.05	10.01	9.98	9.95
3/4	10.31	10.26	10.21	10.17	10.13	10.09	10.06
7/8	10.43	10.37	10.32	10.28	10.24	10.21	10.17
10	10.54	10.48	10.44	10.39	10.36	10.32	10.29
1/8	10.65	10.60	10.55	10.51	10.47	10.44	10.41
1/4	10.76	10.71	10.66	10.62	10.58	10.55	10.52
3/8	10.87	10.82	10.77	10.73	10.70	10.67	10.64
1/2	10.98	10.93	10.89	10.85	10.81	10.78	10.75
5/8	11.09	11.05	11.00	10.96	10.93	10.90	10.87
3/4	11.21	11.16	11.12	11.08	11.05	11.02	10.99
7/8	11.32	11.27	11.23	11.19	11.16	11.13	11.11
11	11.43	11.39	11.35	11.31	11.28	11.25	11.22
1/8	11.55	11.50	11.46	11.43	11.39	11.37	11.34
1/4	11.66	11.62	11.58	11.54	11.51	11.48	11.46
3/8	11.77	11.73	11.69	11.66	11.63	11.60	11.58
1/2	11.89	11.85	11.81	11.77	11.74	11.72	11.69
5/8	12.00	11.96	11.92	11.89	11.86	11.84	11.81
3/4	12.12	12.08	12.04	12.01	11.98	11.95	11.93
7/8	12.23	12.19	12.16	12.13	12.10	12.07	12.05
12	12.35	12.31	12.27	12.24	12.22	12.19	12.17
1/4	12.58	12.54	12.51	12.48	12.45	12.43	12.41
1/2	12.81	12.78	12.74	12.71	12.69	12.67	12.65
3/4	13.05	13.01	12.98	12.95	12.93	12.91	12.89
13	13.28	13.25	13.22	13.19	13.17	13.15	13.13
1/4	13.51	13.48	13.45	13.43	13.41	13.39	13.37
1/2	13.75	13.72	13.69	13.67	13.65	13.63	13.61
3/4	13.99	13.96	13.93	13.91	13.89	13.87	13.86
14	14.22	14.19	14.17	14.15	14.13	14.11	14.10
1/4	14.46	14.43	14.41	14.39	14.37	14.36	14.34
1/2	14.70	14.67	14.65	14.63	14.61	14.60	14.59
3/4	14.94	14.91	14.89	14.87	14.86	14.84	14.83
15	15.18	15.15	15.13	15.12	15.10	15.09	15.08

Monthly Payments

Table of Constant Annual Percent needed to amortize a principal amount, calculated on a monthly basis. Divide by 12 to determine monthly payment.

Interest Rate	37 YEARS	38 YEARS	39 YEARS	40 YEARS	41 YEARS	45 YEARS	50 YEARS
7	7.58	7.54	7.50	7.46	7.43	7.32	7.23
1/4	7.79	7.75	7.72	7.68	7.65	7.55	7.46
1/2	8.01	7.97	7.93	7.90	7.87	7.77	7.69
3/4	8.23	8.19	8.16	8.12	8.10	8.00	7.92
8	8.45	8.41	8.38	8.35	8.32	8.23	8.16
1/8	8.56	8.52	8.49	8.46	8.43	8.35	8.27
1/4	8.67	8.63	8.60	8.57	8.55	8.46	8.39
3/8	8.78	8.75	8.72	8.69	8.66	8.58	8.51
1/2	8.89	8.86	8.83	8.80	8.78	8.70	8.63
5/8	9.00	8.97	8.94	8.92	8.89	8.81	8.75
3/4	9.12	9.09	9.06	9.03	9.01	8.93	8.87
7/8	9.23	9.20	9.17	9.15	9.12	9.05	8.99
9	9.34	9.31	9.29	9.26	9.24	9.17	9.11
1/8	9.46	9.43	9.40	9.38	9.35	9.29	9.23
1/4	9.57	9.54	9.52	9.49	9.47	9.40	9.35
3/8	9.69	9.66	9.63	9.61	9.59	9.52	9.47
1/2	9.80	9.77	9.75	9.73	9.71	9.64	9.59
5/8	9.92	9.89	9.86	9.84	9.82	9.76	9.71
3/4	10.03	10.00	9.98	9.96	9.94	9.88	9.83
7/8	10.15	10.12	10.10	10.08	10.06	10.00	9.95
10	10.26	10.24	10.22	10.19	10.18	10.12	10.07
1/8	10.38	10.35	10.33	10.31	10.29	10.24	10.20
1/4	10.50	10.47	10.45	10.43	10.41	10.36	10.32
3/8	10.61	10.59	10.57	10.55	10.53	10.48	10.44
1/2	10.73	10.71	10.69	10.67	10.65	10.60	10.56
5/8	10.85	10.82	10.80	10.79	10.77	10.72	10.68
3/4	10.96	10.94	10.92	10.91	10.89	10.84	10.81
7/8	11.08	11.06	11.04	11.03	11.01	10.96	10.93
11	11.20	11.18	11.16	11.14	11.13	11.09	11.05
1/8	11.32	11.30	11.28	11.26	11.25	11.21	11.17
1/4	11.44	11.42	11.40	11.38	11.37	11.33	11.30
3/8	11.56	11.54	11.52	11.50	11.49	11.45	11.42
1/2	11.67	11.66	11.64	11.62	11.61	11.57	11.54
5/8	11.79	11.78	11.76	11.74	11.73	11.69	11.67
3/4	11.91	11.89	11.88	11.87	11.85	11.82	11.79
7/8	12.03	12.01	12.00	11.99	11.97	11.94	11.91
12	12.15	12.13	12.12	12.11	12.10	12.06	12.04
1/4	12.39	12.38	12.36	12.35	12.34	12.31	12.28
1/2	12.63	12.62	12.60	12.59	12.58	12.55	12.53
3/4	12.87	12.86	12.85	12.84	12.83	12.80	12.78
13	13.11	13.10	13.09	13.08	13.07	13.04	13.03
1/4	13.36	13.34	13.33	13.32	13.31	13.29	13.27
1/2	13.60	13.59	13.58	13.57	13.56	13.54	13.52
3/4	13.84	13.83	13.82	13.81	13.81	13.78	13.77
14	14.09	14.08	14.07	14.06	14.05	14.03	14.02
1/4	14.33	14.32	14.31	14.30	14.30	14.28	14.27
1/2	14.58	14.57	14.56	14.55	14.54	14.53	14.52
3/4	14.82	14.81	14.80	14.80	14.79	14.78	14.76
15	15.07	15.06	15.05	15.04	15.04	15.02	15.01

C.

Bibliography

Ellwood, L.W. *Ellwood Tables for Real Estate Appraising and Financing,* Third Edition. Harper & Row Publishers, New York NY.

Johnson, Irvin E. *Mini-Math for Appraisers.* International Association of Assessing Officers, 1313 E. 60th St., Chicago IL 60637.

Johnson, Irvin E. *Selling Real Estate by Mortgage-Equity Analysis.* Heath Lexington Books, D.C. Heath & Co., Lexington MA.

Kinnard, William N. Jr. *Income Property Valuation.* Heath Lexington Books, D. C. Heath & Co., Lexington MA.

Weston, Fred J. and Eugene F. Bingham, *Managerial Finance.* The Dryden Press, Hinsdale IL.

D.

Abbreviations Used in This Text

AGM	annual gross multiplier
AILC	all-inclusive land contract
AIM	all-inclusive mortgage
AISD	all-inclusive security device
ANPV	annualized net present value
ATCF	after-tax cash flow
ATROE	after-tax return on equity
ATY	after-tax yield
ATYOE	after-tax yield on equity
BOMA	Building Owners and Managers Association
BOY	beginning of year
Cap	capitalization
CAM	common area maintenance
CPI	Consumer Price Index
DC	debt coverage
DSC	debt service coverage
EOY	end of year
FMRR	financial management rate of return
GLA	gross leaseable area
I	income (cash flow)
IRR	internal rate of return
K	constant
K%	constant rate (percentage)
K$	constant dollar payment
M-E	mortgage-equity
MEP	mechanical, engineering, plumbing

N	net
NCF	net cash flow
NN	double net
NNN	triple net
NOI	net operating income
NPV	net present value
PV	present value
R	rate of yield
REA	reciprocal easement agreement
ROE	return on equity
ROI	return on investment
TD	trust deed
TIM	taxes, insurance, maintenance
V	value
W/A	wrap-around
YOE	yield on equity

Index